# The Philosophy of Legal Change

AF901316

Democratic legal systems have recently been subject to rapid and multi-directional processes of change. There are numerous sociological, technological, ideological, or purely political processes which result in law's amendment and transformation. This book argues that this legal change is best understood from a political philosophy perspective. This can be used as an interpretative device to understand the ongoing processes of change as well as their outcomes such as new laws, judicial interpretations, or constitutional amendments.

The work has three main objectives: to provide deeper understanding of the problems of legal change within the diversity of Western political and legal thought; to examine the development of the processes of change in terms of their normative and prudential acceptability; to interpret actual processes of change with a view to the general theoretical and normative background. The book is divided into three parts: Part I sets the scene and is focused on the general issues important for understanding and evaluating legal change from the perspective of political philosophy; Part II focuses on the spectrum of politico-philosophical justifications present in the political culture of democratic states; Part III offers selected case studies to specify and apply the philosophical ideas in the previous parts.

The book will be a valuable resource for students and scholars of law and jurisprudence, including comparative legal studies and human rights law, political theory, and philosophy.

**Maciej Chmieliński** is Professor of Law, member of the Department of Political and Legal Doctrines and the Alexis de Tocqueville Center for Political and Legal Thought within the Faculty of Law and Administration at the University of Łódź.

**Michał Rupniewski** is Assistant Professor of Law and Philosophy at the University of Łódź, Branch in Tomaszów Mazowiecki, Poland.

# The Philosophy of Legal Change

## Theoretical Perspectives and Practical Processes

**Edited by Maciej Chmieliński and Michał Rupniewski**

Routledge
Taylor & Francis Group
LONDON AND NEW YORK

First published 2020 by Routledge

2 Park Square, Milton Park, Abingdon, Oxon, OX14 4RN
605 Third Avenue, New York, NY 10017

*Routledge is an imprint of the Taylor & Francis Group, an informa business*

First issued in paperback 2020



*British Library Cataloguing-in-Publication Data*
A catalogue record for this book is available from the British Library

*Library of Congress Cataloging-in-Publication Data*
Names: Chmieliński, Maciej, editor. | Rupniewski, Michał, editor.
Title: The philosophy of legal change : theoretical perspectives and practical processes / Maciej Chmielinski and Michal Rupniewski.
Description: Abingdon, Oxon ; New York, NY : Routledge, 2020.
Identifiers: LCCN 2019009238| ISBN 9781138586284 (hardback) | ISBN 9780429504709 (ebook)
Subjects: LCSH: Sociological jurisprudence. | Law—Philosophy. | Social change.
Classification: LCC K376 .P48 2019 | DDC 340/.115—dc23
LC record available at https://lccn.loc.gov/2019009238

ISBN: 978-1-138-58628-4 (hbk)
ISBN: 978-0-367-72704-8 (pbk)

Typeset in Galliard
by Swales & Willis Ltd, Exeter, Devon, UK

# Contents

# Preface

Undoubtedly, democratic legal systems are currently subjected to rapid and multi-directional processes of change. The reasons for this may vary, and one could point toward numerous socio-economic, technological, ideological, or purely political processes which result not only in changing particular laws, but also change the ways in which law is being understood and applied. This affects all crucial spheres of law, such as human rights, constitutional law, ordinary legislation (covering i.a. private and penal law), as well as judicial interpretation and practice. In our view, to understand these dynamics, scholars can and should re-engage with political philosophy to better understand the justification and legitimacy of legal change. Various traditions of political thought, we assume, are explicitly or implicitly present in the practical processes of change and shape the way we deal with day-to-day demands for legislative or judicial action. A heuristic background developed from political philosophy should complement other methods of researching law.

Taking this for granted, the purpose of this volume is threefold: first, to present a general theoretical framework in which legal change may be conceptualized in the contemporary world (Part I); second, to enhance the politico-philosophical understanding of legal change by paradigmatic philosophical-normative accounts about the law's justification and legitimacy (Part II); and finally, to provide examples of how philosophical heuristic tools work in examining socio-legal reality (Part III). Such a framework enables us to reveal and explore the specific, ***explanatory*** way in which political philosophy may be applied to jurisprudence. In other words, this volume does not conceive of political philosophy as primarily a tool of legal critique, but of legal interpretation. The structure of this book is determined by two basic commitments. The first is the dynamic conceptual relation between public reason and background culture: we take this Rawlsian distinction as providing an ample device to sort out the manifold justifying reasons supporting change within law. The second commitment is the fundamental opposition between individualism and holism as a point of reference for competing political philosophies. This opposition yields a twofold approach to legal change: on the one hand, following individualism, law is perceived as a generally free creation of the democratic sovereign; on the other hand, following social holism, law can be perceived as determined by various communitarian, extra-legal factors.

As this book shows, the practical processes always constitute a mix of these two positions, always remaining in some (possibly fragile) equilibrium.

This book gathers contributors with different scholarly and national backgrounds, which ensures that the presented picture is wide and pluralistic. We do hope this will contribute to productive exchange between legal scholars, philosophers, legal theorists, and sociologists interested in justification, legitimacy, and factual dynamics of legal institutions. The philosophy of legal change as conceived here constitutes a bridge between disciplines, providing an explanatory, interpretative scheme.

# Acknowledgements[1]

This volume is based on, although not exclusively composed of, papers presented at MANCEPT Workshops at the University of Manchester, September 2017. Within the panel we discussed the issue of legal change in a democratic state. The friendly and focused atmosphere of the conference enabled a productive exchange of ideas, and encouraged us to assemble the papers in one volume. We want to express our gratitude toward the whole MANCEPT 2017 team, particularly to Nicola Mulkeen and Sara Van Goozen.

We also thank all the contributors to this book, who, despite pursuing their own research on their own terms, decided to connect in the pluralistic dialogue that this volume provides. We hope that the way we structured the chapters forms a cohesive whole informed by our own approach to the titular issue, but, at the same time, respects the scientific autonomy of each contributor.

Our own research on the topic was conducted at the University of Łódź, Faculty of Law and Administration. A particularly important environment was the Alexis de Tocqueville Center for Political and Legal Thought. We want to thank all our colleagues in the Center, particularly Professor Zbigniew Rau, our director, for the ongoing inspiration and support, and J. Patrick Higgins, for his helpful comments and indispensable assistance in linguistic matters.

Maciej Chmieliński and Michał Rupniewski

1 The research conducted by Maciej Chmieliński and Michał Rupniewski, presented in this book, was financially supported by the National Science Centre, Poland, as part of the project No. 2015/19/B/HS5/02522.

# Contributors

**Kamil Aksiuto** is an Assistant Professor at the Faculty of Political Science of the Maria Curie-Skłodowska University in Lublin. He completed his PhD studies at the Graduate School for Social Research in Warsaw and obtained his doctoral degree from the Institute of Political Studies of the Polish Academy of Science. In his academic work he specializes in history of political ideas and political philosophy. Email: kamaks@poczta.umcs.lublin.pl

**Tadeusz Biernat** is Professor of Politics and Law at the Andrzej Frycz Modrzewski Krakow University. His scholarship focuses on political philosophy, philosophy of law, and theory of legislation. His most noted works are: *Political Myth* (1989), *The Legitimacy of Political Power* (1999), *The Community of Law: On Particularities of the European System* (2000), *Policy of Law and Legal Policy: Between Modern and Post-modern Jurisprudence* (co-author) (2008), and *Legislation: Analysis of the Process* (2016). He is former Dean of the Faculty of Law and Administration Andrzej Frycz Modrzewski Krakow University. Email: tadeuszbiernat@gmail.com

**Eduardo Charpenel** is Associate Professor of the Faculty of Philosophy at the Universidad Panamericana in Mexico City. He is the author of *Ethos und Praxis: Der Charakterbegriff bei Aristoteles* (2017), and has published several articles. He specializes in Ancient Philosophy and German Idealism, with particular focus on ethics, political philosophy, and philosophy of religion. Email: echarpen@up.edu.mx

**Maciej Chmieliński** is Professor of Law, member of the Department of Political and Legal Doctrines and the Alexis de Tocqueville Center for Political and Legal Thought within the Faculty of Law and Administration at the University of Łódź. He has published in, among others, *Polish Sociological Review*, *Res Publica, Revista de Historia de las Ideas Politicas* (Res Publica. Review of the History of Political Ideas), *Politeja. Pismo Studiów Międzynarodowych i Politycznych Uniwersytetu Jagiellońskiego* (Politeja. Magazine of the International and Political Studies of Jagiellonian University) and *Studia Prawno-Ekonomiczne* (Legal-Economic Studies). His scientific interests are focused on the legal and political theory of the current democratic society and on the history of ideas, especially anarchism, libertarianism, liberalism, and communitarianism. Email: chmieliński@o2.pl

**Marc Goetzmann** is a PhD candidate in Philosophy from the University of Nice Sophia Antipolis (Université Côte d'Azur). After teaching to undergraduates in Nice for several years, he now teaches at the Sorbonne (Université Paris 1) until the end of his PhD (2019). He is also the Editor-in-Chief of *Implications Philosophiques*. His main interests are political philosophy and the philosophy of law, as well as the philosophy of the social sciences. His thesis deals with the way 19th century British thinkers reconceptualized customary law on the basis of anthropological observations of property rights in colonial India. Email: marcgtz11@gmail.com

**Melissa Hamilton** is a Senior Lecturer of Law & Criminal Justice at the University of Surrey School of Law. She holds a JD in law and a PhD in criminology/criminal justice from the University of Texas at Austin. Dr Hamilton's main areas of research interest are in conducting interdisciplinary research on issues related to domestic and sexual violence, trauma responses in victims of assault, risk assessment practices, policing, sentencing, and corrections. Email: melissa.hamilton@surrey.ac.uk

**J. Patrick Higgins** is a doctoral candidate at the Faculty of Law and Administration, the University of Łódź, Łódź, Poland, where he is associated with the Alexander de Tocqueville Center for Political and Legal Thought. Patrick's research interests are in constitutional political economy, history of economic thought, new economic sociology, new institutional economics, the Austrian school, and classical political economy. He is currently is applying these lenses to interpret contemporary and ancient Polish history to search for deep institutional roots of contemporary Polish social, economic, legal, and political institutions. Email: pat.higgins2014@gmail.com

**Maria Lewandowicz** is an Assistant Professor of Comparative Legal History at the University of Gdańsk, Poland. She specializes in comparative legal history, private law, and gambling law. She is the principal investigator of the National Science Centre of Poland research project, Swiss Civil Code from 10 December 1907: Goals and Methods, pursued at the Faculty of Law and Administration of University of Gdańsk (2017–2021). Email: lewandowicz@prawo.ug.edu.pl

**Stephen Riley** is a Lecturer in the Law School of the University of Leicester, UK. His research is in the philosophy of law, in particular, the legal and philosophical significance of human dignity, and the relationship between legal, moral, and political conceptions of justice. Email: stephen.riley@leicester.ac.uk

**Michał Rupniewski** is Assistant Professor of Law and Philosophy at the University of Łódź, Branch in Tomaszów Mazowiecki, Poland. He specializes in comparative law, political philosophy, and jurisprudence. He is Director of a research project, Human Dignity as the Foundational Value of Law: A Personalist Explanation, pursued at the Faculty of Law and Administration of the University of Łódź (2017–2021). Email: michal.dru@gmail.com

**Jan Tryzna** is Assistant Professor at the Department of Legal Theory and Legal Doctrines at Law Faculty of Charles University (in Prague). He specializes in methodology of legal interpretation and argumentation including the role of legal principles in legal orders. He is a leader of a Specific University Research Project titled Legal Aspects of Influence of Institutional Changes with Respect to Principle of Division of Powers at National, International and Supranational Level pursued at Charles University (2017–2019). Email: tryzna.jan@seznam.cz

**Ian Turner** is Reader in Human Rights and Security at the Lancashire Law School, the University of Central Lancashire, Preston, UK, where he is responsible for PhD students. Ian has taught undergraduate and graduate modules in constitutional law, human rights, security, and counter-terrorism for a number of years, and has been published widely in these areas, particularly on matters relating to the killing and torture of terror suspects. He is an Editor of the *International Journal of Human Rights*, and a member of the Editorial Boards of *Democracy and Security* and *Studies in Conflict and Terrorism*. Email: IDTurner@uclan.ac.uk

**Eva Weiler** is a Research Associate in Philosophy at the University of Duisburg-Essen. She is writing her thesis on the justification of property rights with a focus on common property and natural resources. Her research fields are philosophy of law, legal pluralism, and democratic theory. Email: eva.weiler@uni-due.de

# Introduction

## Legal change and political philosophy[1]

*Maciej Chmieliński*

The perspective that is central to this book is that of political philosophy. Thus, the investigations presented here are not directly focused on the formal validity of law, researched by legal dogmatics, or simply on social acceptance of legal rules, researched by social sciences. Rather, we examine the area situated *in between* legal validity or social acceptance of law and its change: the area of reasons supplying its philosophical and political justification. In such an approach, legal change can be understood broadly, and the law that is of interest here can be of different fields (e.g. constitutional law, international law, or private law). The adopted concept of legal change embraces, therefore, formal changes made by amendments, passing new laws or issuing formal decisions and court judgments, as well as informal changes, such as those emerging from changing interpretation of the existing rules by the bodies applying the law. Theoretical distinctions, however, such as those between formal and informal change, or different fields of law, do not have a significant role to play; the research conducted in this book emerges from a belief that in all practical processes of change the justifying reasons are a point of reference for the debate, even if appearing only implicitly. It is assumed, and systematically demonstrated in this volume, that this normative background – examined by political philosophy – is inevitable for deep understanding of legal change in a democratic society.

More specifically, one might say that legal change involves political philosophy in two ways. The first way is that of politics and law – separate social institutions – vividly interacting with one another at the occasion of change in laws. The change itself is the result of political deliberation, voting, and bargaining processes in the public sphere that happen among legislative bodies, courts, executive organs, international institutions, and divergent representatives of civil society. Intellectual origins of existing laws in stable Western societies are in fact not commonly a subject of deeper reflection or intellectual revision. Most of them are respected by reason of habit. Therefore, in real social practices it is the change within laws which demands justification and inspires discussions concerning its

1 This chapter presents results of the research financially supported by the National Science Centre, Poland, as part of the project No. 2015/19/B/HS5/02522.

origins and sources. One can say that it acts as a "lens" that focuses the rationale for justifying the law.

The second way in which legal change inevitably involves political philosophy is that the general rationale for legal change in democratic societies consists of two strictly connected issues: the justification of legal changeability, and the justification of the changed law (the change in the strict sense). The principle of legal changeability is quite obvious: a democratic legal system without this principle is hardly imaginable (Schwartzberg 2007). It is, however, so general and so obvious that we only identify it at the theoretical level (Berman 2005: 18f). Nonetheless, one should bear in mind that any change in the strict sense – the change within/to particular laws – assumes changeability, and such a particular change is always a derivative thereof. As we argue in this book, political philosophy, when applied with a view to enhancing the interpretation of law, considerably enlightens both general changeability as well as the particular changes in the law.

We believe, however, that politico-philosophical enquiry into the justification of legal change should be conducted in constant dialogue with other disciplines, particularly legal dogmatics and social sciences.

As far as the former is concerned, the issue is relatively simple. In democratic societies, consistency within the legal order as a whole, understood as legal validity, is a necessary prerequisite for the legitimacy of law. Therefore, it determines the possibility of changing the law in the sense of its legal admissibility. Legal scientists examine the procedural aspects of admissibility in the legal system, that is, they examine the compatibility of the change with other positive norms: constitution, formal sources of law, and international agreements. They examine the amended regulations by the rules of interpretation, explaining their meaning and consequences for the practice of the application of law. Each legal change that is contrary to the law which is higher in hierarchy is legally unacceptable and cannot be considered valid law (Beetham 1991: 4, Wintgens 2012: 193).

From the perspective of social science, there are two important questions in considering democratic legal change: the question of the "need" vs the "ought" of change, and the question of the "can" of the change. In other words, in every legal system there is a game being played between the virtual ability on the one hand, and the philosophical justification of the need for change on the other. Following Jűrgen Habermas, one might call it an interplay "between facts and norms" (Habermas 1996). This has several levels, but on the elementary level it simply means that not all desired changes can be successfully carried out. It happens, for example, that formally correct changes do not go hand in hand with changes in the sphere of social practices, being therefore socially unacceptable. Changes can be also pernicious for social practices, or values which justify the change can be internally conflicted. As far as the possibility of the change is concerned, the main subject of social sciences is the explanation of empirical legitimacy of authority. In modern democracies the most important form of authority is the legal one, i.e., the authority based on the rule of law (Weber 1964: 131, Beetham 1991: 5f). Thus, the legitimacy of the legal authority is strictly connected with the legitimacy of law.

The social efficacy of legal change is considered by the social scientists (e.g. political scientists, sociologists of politics, social psychologists), in democratic societies at least, to depend heavily on its social legitimacy. In the "canonical", Weberian approach, social legitimacy is tantamount to the *Legitimationsglaube* – a belief shared by the community members that the change is legitimate, proper, socially useful, or meaningful (Weber 1968: 213, Simmons 2001: 131, Beetham 1991: 6). It means that broadly understood, social acceptance for the content and scope of change constitutes the most important condition for a socially efficacious change. This acceptance is ***broadly understood*** in the sense that it results from a wide range of motivations derived from various spheres. These may be motivations related to political practice and connected with support for current legislative authority ("classic" issues of legal, traditional, or charismatic authority of the power), motivations coming from the political, moral, ethical, or social worldview (conviction about equity, integrity, implementation by changing the common good or social agreement in this respect), religious motivations (e.g. Christian opposition to abortion or euthanasia connected with belief about their deadly sinful character), economical motivations (cost reduction, economic efficiency), or scientific motivations (e.g. maximal or minimal standards for strengths of materials in the building law, which result from the natural sciences – physics).

Although Weberian-oriented social science accepts moral or philosophical motivation to obey the law, the very content of the law's justification is of no significance. The examination of legitimacy by representatives of the social sciences consists merely in explaining its mechanism in order to find the starting point for studying social behavior related to change. Social sciences deal primarily with the behavior dictated by manifold motivations (Beetham 1991: 33). From this point of view, the ability to change means first and foremost the probability of a certain social process in a society dominated by certain beliefs dictating concrete behaviors of its members (potential acceptance of the proposed change by society). Thus, the examination of the ability to change would focus on the potential for acceptance of the introduced change by society members. The lack of acceptance results in the inability to introduce a change. Of course, the inability is not meant in the formal-legal sense, but in the sense of the possibly common social tendency to evade the law. When such a tendency is persistent, it may undermine – and in the long term even completely impede – the introduction of changes. For instance, it is possible to introduce an irrational speed limit on the road, i.e. restrictions in a place where the conditions allow for much faster and secure driving. Such restrictions, however, will probably not be commonly observed by drivers, unless we set a speed meter or a policeman in this place. If we do that, however, the factor determining the behavior of drivers will not be the internal conviction about the limit really making sense (social acceptance, internalization), but only the external factor: fear of punishment. Such a limitation – irrational and deprived of common social acceptance – does determine the behavior of drivers, but in a different way than intended. It must also be remembered that the legitimacy is gradable and not of "zero-binary" character. ("Legitimacy is not an all-or-nothing affair" – Beetham 1991: 19f). A change in the law is rarely supported by all society members, it can even not be commonly questioned, and its legitimacy can be of an "indirect" nature, having its source only in the *Legitimationsglaube* in the current elite, or simply the authority of the institutions introducing the new laws.

According to David Beetham, whose approach to legitimacy (being polemic to Weberian standpoint prevailing in social sciences, see Beetham 1991: 7) is accepted here, "moral-political justifiability" as the subject of political philosophy, is the additional element constituting the legitimacy of authority, next to legal validity examined by legal sciences and the social acceptance as examined by Weberian-oriented political science (Beetham 1991: 5). The philosophical and political justifiability of law appeals to the above-mentioned question of "ought" or "need" of the legal change. It is connected with "weighing" the reasons for change in light of such categories conditioning the duty such as justice, universal validity, normative legitimacy, or social utility (Beetham 1991: 5). Unlike legal validity, political justifiability is not and cannot be a condition *sine qua non* for legitimacy. The diversity of standpoints and reasons justifying them in divided, pluralistic societies, the lack of real possibility of recognizing a single standpoint as universal or at least inter-subjectively important preclude its recognition as such a condition.

There are tensions and differences between these standpoints, which make the reasons they formulate contradictory and opposite (Beetham 1991: 16). For example, the right of private property of the of production, which is considered the fundamental and inherent right in liberal and conservative thinking, is an artificial and exploitive institution from a Marxist standpoint. The legal duty to wear seat belts in the car by responsible adult people, from the point of view of moral autonomy (present e.g. in the political philosophy of Kantian liberalism or libertarianism) means a violation of the freedom of decision, while from the point of view of paternalism present in the conception of the welfare state, it is something self-evident. The diversity of standpoints is even more intensive and more visible in so-called "hard cases" that include for example: abortion, euthanasia, or medical procedures, requiring the doctor to make choices between patients who can still be helped and those who can no longer be helped. In other words, from the perspective of pluralistic and internally diverse democratic societies, there is no element in current political philosophy that could "objectify" its reasons. Such a kind of "Archimedean vantage point" can be found in the modern scientific approach (although here it is also often relativized and questioned, see, for example Feyerabend 2010).

In the social sciences, such a point is generated by the Weberian methodology based on *Legitimationsglaube*. In legal sciences the same is achieved by examining the legal procedures of changing the law. The former objectivizes its results by choosing from a wide spectrum of represented religious, moral, political, or other standpoints which are represented most often and therefore enjoy the biggest *Legitimationsglaube*. Using statistics, for example, social sciences can approximately answer the question what change in law enjoys social support or will probably gain it, and what change is, or will be, deprived of social acceptance. The legal procedures, alternatively, allow the determination of at least which of the proposed or introduced changes is consistent and which are inconsistent with the legal rules of change. Therefore, they can guarantee a relative certainty according to the legal validity of the introduced change. It seems hard to claim that political philosophy is able to offer anything similar. It is rather uncontested that this sphere is characterized by the pluralism of approaches and views (Knoll, Snyder, & Şimsek 2018). In light of the lack of objective scientific methods, the importance of moral and political reasons for the change in law may appear questionable.

From the point of view of this question, we can see that political philosophy is practiced in two ways. First, it can be treated as a discipline arguing for or against various legal solutions, but from the external perspective, being fully autonomic with regards to legal sciences. This point of view is represented, in fact, by the majority of leading representatives of political philosophy, who go "from political philosophy to law" (a similar scheme of explaining the relationship between law and philosophy is given by Zirk-Sadowski 2000), formulating "from outside" postulates regarding specific legal solutions. Among such thinkers, there are two of the greatest representatives of 20th century political philosophy: John Rawls and Jűrgen Habermas. In their approach, law appears as an indispensable element of a well-organized society, based on cooperation (Rawls 1993, 1999) or as one of the aspects of a broad and multidimensional project of "communicative actions" (Habermas 1984, 1987, 1996). This way of practicing political philosophy does not contradict the "minimal" assumption of legal positivism and analytic jurisprudence about (at least relative) separation of (political) morality from law (on the complicated relationship between law and morality in legal positivism see: Hart 1958: 250, Raz 1979: 227, Coleman 1982, Coleman & Leiter 1996, Waluchow 1994, Sebok 1998: 269). This point of view allows the perception of various affiliations and correlations between legal sciences and political philosophy, but in principle it does not need to advocate for their unity.

Second, political philosophy can be practiced as an internal element of jurisprudence, integrating legal reflection with political-philosophical reflection. In this way it has been practiced primarily by such natural law theorists such as Rudolf Stammler, Lon Luvois Fuller, or most recently John Finnis. For them, the philosophical-political reflection is an integral element of natural law. Using the methods of political philosophy, they are looking for the universal conditions of just law (the concept of "basic goods" – Finnis 1980) or a more contextualized account on the law's normative basis ("law of nature with variable content" – Stammler 1896). Fuller (1969) is seeking the conditions of "internal morality of law". The standpoint that most deeply integrates political philosophy and law is that of Ronald Dworkin (1977, 1986, 1993, 2006, 2011). According to his "integral jurisprudence", moral and political values are legal values as well; they are part of the broad interpretative context that plays a role in determining what the law is. In other words, Dworkin's interpretivism

> denies that law and morals are wholly independent systems. It argues that law includes not only the specific rules enacted in accordance with the community's accepted practices, but also the principles that provide the best moral justification for those enacted rules. The law then also includes the rules that follow from those justifying principles, even though those further rules were never enacted. Interpretivism, in other words, treats legal reasoning as I have argued in this book we must treat all interpretive reasoning. It treats the concept of law as an interpretive concept.
>
> (Dworkin 2011: 402)

Therefore, Dworkin believes that every correct interpretation of the law must appeal to the current "interpretative" culture being present in a given legal community and thus to political philosophy being an integral part of this culture. The best possible interpretation of law is firstly the most coherent interpretation from this culture's point of view and secondly the interpretation which fits best to the interpretative judiciary path for a given case (Dworkin 2011: 126).

In our approach, following Dworkin and natural law theorists, we examine political philosophy as integrated with jurisprudence, or even simply as part of jurisprudence. We believe that law is not neutral to political philosophy; rather, the deep normative structure of law contains political-philosophical elements that determine a certain "heuristic background" without which the given legal institution does not make sense. This claim is supported not only by jurisprudence itself, but also by the previously described considerations on social legitimacy by Beetham. If moral and political justifiability of laws play a role in their legitimacy and social acceptance, then the law and political philosophy are integrated simply by the token of social practice. The members of society, when making sense of and applying law, inevitably use political-philosophical ideas as a point of reference, even if implicit.

Alternatively, our approach has a completely different purpose than the approach represented by natural law theorists or Dworkin. The goal is neither to look for universally just, moral or right legal solutions and decisions, nor to seek the best interpretation of legal norms or precedents. Focusing on the legal change, we look at the underlying reasons in a neutral way. Prima facie we do not support any concrete political-philosophical position, but by examining the relationship between the new legal norms and their justification, we try to create a tool for a better understanding of law. In the perspective adopted in this book, political philosophy plays the role of a relatively neutral heuristic tool which – connected with legal dogmatics – allows for better interpretation and justification of law.

The perspective of political philosophy allows for examining the moral and political justification of legal change on the one hand without definitely answering the theoretical question about the law's nature as such, and on the other hand without giving up serious considerations of real connections between law and political morality that undoubtedly occur. In this regard, the approach adopted in this work is closer to the "distanced" view of social sciences. Political philosophy applied to considering reasons for legal change makes a bridge between legal dogmatics that essentially establishes the content of norms and social sciences that examine how these norms in work practice. Examining the justification of norms, political philosophy on the one hand sheds some light on their content (puts them in the wider context of normative beliefs) and on the other indicates some predictions as to their functioning in practice, because the functioning of the law in practice assumes that the law can be understood, applied, and internalized by its subjects (Waldron 2012: 15). This goal determines the construction of this book, which consists of three parts.

## Part I General theories

The purpose of the first part is to identify the most important focal points of the normative space (the term is borrowed from Tadeusz Biernat) which can be identified in contemporary debates about the justification of the legal change. The reasons involved come from various argumentative orders: ethics, morality, politics, economics, social sciences, and even natural sciences. In Chapter 1, Tadeusz Biernat looks at the normative space from the perspective of standards of law-making. He offers a relatively neutral theory that allows categorizing these standards in an interdisciplinary manner. In Chapter 2, Michał Rupniewski introduces what he claims to be the two leading, ordering categories of the normative space, to which every legal change inevitably refers to, at least in a democratic state. Those categories are public reason and background culture. Rupniewski refers in this regard to the "late" theory of John Rawls, however, according to Rupniewski, these categories are relatively politically neutral and independent from the represented political-philosophical position. They are a necessary part of so-called "open justification" that combines the traditional public reason theory with the recognition of background culture as an alternative source of legitimate reasons for change.

Considering traditional nation-state-centered perspectives in jurisprudence (Biernat) and political theory (Rupniewski) adopted by Chapters 1 and 2, in Chapter 3 Eva Weiler focuses on identifying fields where these categories intellectually support (and sometimes fail to support) justification for legal changes on international and transnational levels. Contrasting legal centralism and legal pluralism, she demonstrates the challenges that legal pluralism pose to contemporary foundations of democratic representation, popular sovereignty, and legitimacy. The chapter's chief perspective is a neo-republicanism that assumes equality as the inevitable value and condition of law. Law is conditioned (dependent) on equality (understood as equal participation in the law-making process) in the sense that without assuring the minimum equality, and thus non-domination, law ceases to have any authoritative claim. Although the normative claims of legal pluralism are generally rejected (particularly their resting on the notion of common good or justice), it is assumed that the empirical part of pluralism theory is correct, and the pluralization of legal bodies might in fact work for, not against, fostering freedom as non-domination.

In Chapter 4, Stephen Riley completes the view of the most important focal points for contemporary normative space by formulating basic assumptions for the theory of change in human rights and identifying the most important contemporary challenges for their change. Also, in this field, the concept of public reason and the concept of background culture turn out to play an important role. The theory of legal change conceptualized by the cosmopolitan public reason moves the normative status quo (minimum) of human rights to their extension to new spheres (maximum) that the changing human condition yields. In contrast, contemporary background culture is the source of the dominant tendency to "rationalization" of human rights, which simply means their self-limitation. Riley remarks that the current legal and intellectual background culture is averse to human rights, which results from the commonly shared legal-positivist argumentation resulting in serious problems with protecting the human rights. As an answer to this, he proposes a set of desiderata for a theory of change that could ensure human rights' ability to answer the challenges of the present day.

The considerations collected in Part I allow formulation of three conclusions that methodologically direct the research program underlying this work. First of all, the borderline between social sciences and political philosophy in justifying legal change is inevitably relative and often simply intuitive. The notion of political legitimacy used by social sciences and the notion of moral-political justification used by political philosophy are often used interchangeably both by representatives of social sciences and political philosophy (often "normative legitimacy", identified with philosophical justification is mixed with "empirical legitimacy", characteristic of social sciences – Beetham 1991: 8 – alternatively legitimacy is distinguished from legitimation – Wintgens 2012: 193). At the same time, representatives of political philosophy and jurisprudence include in their deliberations the categories drawn from social sciences, because they consider that these categories interact and complement each other. Secondly, political-philosophical justification creates a normative element about the basic legitimacy structure of the legislative authority and is an integral part of this legitimacy, making an interpretive, Dworkinian "bridge" between the legal and the social sciences. Thirdly, the categories of public reason and background culture are stable points of reference for the conceptualization of the change in law at its every level. Thus, the general conclusion is that the focus on public political culture (public reason's domain) needs to be complemented by the background culture (non-public civil society, customs, and social practices).

## Part II Paradigmatic political philosophies of legal change

The second part focuses on the particular approaches in political philosophy which offer the most distinctive vision of moral-political justification of legal change. The texts collected in this part, therefore, attempt to clarify the heuristic tools that are most useful for studying the change of law.

Searching for these tools, Maciej Chmieliński begins with a study of polemics between a broadly defined holist, conservative-communitarian model of thinking about legal change, and an individualist, liberal-contractarian model (Chapter 5). These polemics should enable a deeper understanding of the relationship between public reason and background culture, outlined in the first part. In the holist, conservative-communitarian model, thinking in terms of the background culture prevails, whereas the categories of public reason dominate the approach based on the liberal-contractarian model. Such a perspective allows a dialogical organization of the main philosophical oppositions between these two models of legal change: epistemic imperfection versus epistemic perfection, substantial common good versus aggregative/procedural common good, particularism versus universalism, nationalism versus cosmopolitanism, emanation versus creation, and finally, opposition between legal determinism and legal creationism. The last pair of opposition is the most important one, determining the two alternative approaches to legal change. Determinism assumes that human will, and thus preferences of the society's members, plays an extremely limited role in the processes of legal change. Rather, the latter process is tantamount to "decoding" the possible new law from the previous change in social practices. On the contrary, legal creationism assumes free and conscious creation of law according to the peoples will, preferences, and individual rights.

These two opposite models form a heuristic background for examining the legislative activity in a democratic state, where practical processes of change result from a dynamic synthesis of these models, and attempts to reconcile them, as explored in Chapter 5. The subsequent chapters exhibit that regardless of fundamental ideological differences, conceptualizing the change in law inevitably looks for a synthesis of holistic justification related to the background culture and individualistic justification connected with public reason. In Chapter 6, Kamil Aksiuto contrasts the communitarian category of natural law with the individualistic category of natural rights, using the theory of Alasdair MacIntyre to demonstrate this internal, important intellectual dimension of the dialectics of legal change. In Chapter 7, Michał Rupniewski demonstrates that the foundation of natural law theories based on the concept of Thomas Aquinas is also the synthesis universalism referring to the objective basis of law, which can be human nature, basic goods, or human dignity on the one hand, and on the other hand of the particularism characterizing concrete social practices in various political communities.

In Chapter 8, Eduardo Charpenel outlines the sources of the normativity of law in the conception of Immanuel Kant: the social contract, the natural right, and the principle of publicity. Charpenel demonstrates that the tension between law understood as an *a priori* rule appealing to the public reason, and the *a posteriori* circumstances to which the law in the real life must always respond. The principle of publicity, and the pursuit of public reason, as Charpenel argues, allows for the synthesis of these *a priori* principles and empirical, *a posteriori* circumstances. The reasons for changing the existing rules, therefore, might come from the demands of justice, as well as from the particular circumstances that legal communities face.

In Chapter 9, Maciej Chmieliński examines the Marxist approach to legal change in its three crucial variants: economically determinst, voluntarist, and historicist, identifying legal-creationist and legal-deterministic elements of the doctrine. This chapter confirms the thesis formulated by Chmieliński in Chapter 5 that these two models constitute a helpful heuristic tools in considering justification of legal change. However, the Marxist perspective seems to be useful only as the complementary perspective that may help in *criticizing* legal change, but not in *explaining* it in the manner adopted in this volume.

The investigations carried out in Parts I and II illustrate the complex way in which legal change is determined by the politico-philosophical heuristic background. Practical processes of legal change constitute a twofold interplay between facts and norms. On the one hand, public reason and background culture interact together in the normative space yielding new legal provisions and their interpretation. On the other hand, these provisions are always marked by the interplay between holistic legal determinism and individualistic legal creationism. In contemporary democratic societies, public reason will be most often associated with individualist and creationist thinking about law, and background culture will yield a more holistic/deterministic account. These categories are, however, not strictly assigned to each other; they may overlap and mix, creating the reach and diverse normative background of the processes of change. At the same time, it is assumed that other determining factors, such as legal validity and social legitimation, play a decisive role in these processes. Political philosophy, however, might shed additional light on their content and directions.

## Part III Practical processes

The methodological thesis about political philosophy as a bridge between social and legal sciences assumes that the theoretical and philosophical conceptions should be open for the possibility of empirical verification. Therefore, Part III begins with Marc Goetzmann's examination of the elements rudimentary for background culture in the pluralistic context of non-Western countries: customs and customary law (Chapter 10). Goetzmann shows how customs and customary laws of post-colonial societies are being confronted today by values of individualist-liberal Western culture, which are often "imported" in the legal reforms taking place in these societies. He demonstrates the reasons why the customary background culture should be taken seriously, and that legal reform based solely on a logic derived from individualist public reason can become an incomprehensible and unacceptable foreign element, or can be accepted only in a superficial way. However, Goetzmann offers an alternative solution for an effective and legitimate reform, that is, establishing a "market for norms": alternatives for the customary law offered by state authorities and non-governmental organizations. He argues that this can lead to a gradual change of the social practices embedded in customary law, rightly considered unacceptable from a Western, liberal viewpoint.

In Chapter 11, Maria Lewandowicz explores Swiss codification of civil law as the historical example of the successful synthesis of the customary, communitarian elements with a modernization dictated by the Enlightenment idea of universal standards of codification. In Chapter 12, J. Patrick Higgins suggests how the intellectual and cultural background, including traditional political pluralism and tolerance, were in deep conflict with the politically monist, totalitarian, and intolerant assumptions of real socialism, that eventually lead to the collapse of the Polish communist system. In Chapter 13, Melissa Hamilton deals with the problem of overcriminalization in the United Kingdom resulting from the new legal solution called "coercive control", which consists in criminalizing different abusive behavior in intimate relationships that does not involve physical assaults. Although being an advocate of the state responding to domestic violence, she puts this particular institution into question. Its application might turn out to disregard the subtle and delicate dynamic of relationships in the family and partnerships. As such, the coercive control statue seems to stay in conflict not only with social efficacy of law, but also with commonly accepted cultural patterns of behavior and natural family dynamics.

Finally, Ian David Turner (Chapter 14) and Jan Tryzna (Chapter 15) consider the influence that two current legal-cultural phenomena – Islamic terrorism (Turner) and growing dynamics of changes in the law (Tryzna) – have on the current theory of human rights. Turner argues that international terrorism calls into question an actual method of the protection of human rights in the Western world, which are understood above all as individual rights. Such a method can serve, and in fact it *does* serve, to protect terrorists. The only possible solution to this problem is, for Turner, to adopt the collective right to security and protection of the nation/society that under certain circumstances might be superior to individual rights. He analyses the solutions present in the African Charter on Human and Peoples' Rights (ACHPR) which can offer guidelines for a more communitarian account on human rights more generally. Jan Tryzna illustrates the growing dynamics of law in current democratic societies by examining the legislative and judicial practices with particular emphasis on the Czech Republic (Chapter 15). He suggests that the intense dynamics of legal changes and the growing role of law in contemporary democratic legal cultures imposes strengthening the regulatory status of the principle of legal certainty and its integration with the fabric of human rights law. All of these chapters illustrate relationships between communitarian elements usually connected with the background culture and the individualist connected with public reason, often being very subtle.

The main task of Part III is the confirmation of the usefulness of the heuristic tool introduced in Part I and clarified in Part II to assess the intellectual influence of the philosophico-political background on social processes of the legal change. In this volume, political philosophy is applied with an intention to help in understanding and governing these processes. It answers the call for the "research responsibility" postulated (among others) by Dworkin (2011: 99). He explicitly requires a realistic applicability of political philosophy, and that is the commitment that we share. The helpful source of inspiration to realize this task is the "social theory of law", also called "social jurisprudence". The social jurisprudence approach combines, among others, legal realism with the assumptions of the historic law school, starting from an assumption that law is essentially a historical and social fact, or a social institution (see Tamanaha 2015). According to Brian Z. Tamanaha, "the common thread that unites this jurisprudential tradition can be pared down to two propositions: law is social in nature and is best understood through an empirically-focused lens" (Tamanaha 2015: 2266).

The approach presented in this work limits the methodological inspiration derived from social jurisprudence to looking "through an empirically-focused lens", without prejudging the social nature of the law. Such an approach is possible thanks to the tools of legal, social, and historical sciences applied in Part III. What distinguishes it from social jurisprudence is the object of interest. Social jurisprudence deals first of all with the application of law. Accepting the generally realist concept of "law in action", social jurisprudence is primarily interested in judicial activity, i.e. in the activities of courts. From our perspective, the more important and straightforward field of application our theory is the law-making. This brings the adopted perspective closer to "legisprudence" of i.a. Luc Wintgens (2012, Wintgens & Oliver-Lalana 2013). However, since we consider both formal and informal changes, our approach has some relevance (as explained by Rupniewski in the Conclusion) in the judicial interpretation and application of law.

The considerations contained in Part III confirm the observation made by Harold Berman, one of the leading representatives of the socio-historical jurisprudence, that the change in law contains "the element of continuity from past to future in the development of the culture of a society, including its legal culture" (Berman 2005: 18f). A heuristic instrument derived from political philosophy allows us to fulfill this observation with concrete content and to define a change as the moment that binds the historical community with modernization. The law in contemporary democratic societies is always a compromise between community values and individual interests, and thus it combines a holistic element (common good and duties resulting from it) with an individualistic element (the interests of individuals and rights related to it) (Ihering 1979: 10f). Therefore, its change is always a result of arguments derived from historical continuity associated with thinking in terms of political community, which is an amalgam of particular customs, traditions, unique cultural factors, and long-lasting practices of specific communities, and arguments derived from the society's public reason.

The lack of perceiving one of either of these two poles and disregarding the complex relationships between them in the law-making processes can even result in undermining the legal validity of the law itself. It does not happen immediately, but has a long-term effect (often counted in decades), gradually eroding the law which does not consider the criteria of appropriateness established either by the background culture or by the public reason. Especially the lack of "sensitivity" of the legislator to community practices and institutions being deeply rooted in specific societies, such as customs, customary laws and established moral and political patterns of conduct, may result in the ineffectiveness of changes not only at the constitutional level, but also at the level of detailed areas of law. Legal changes ignoring the background culture can easily turn become a purely arbitrary manifestation of domination, despite the supporting arguments derived from public reason. The law is always applied in concrete social conditions. These conditions affect both the creation and validity of the law, as well as its interpretation and application, because validity claims being formulated by law are always more or less dependent on social facts (in the concepts of e.g. Habermas and Alexy "between facts and norms" mediates a communication medium, while in the concepts of social jurisprudence, law is simply a social fact: Habermas 1996, Alexy 1983, Tamanaha 2015).

According to the "classic" Weberian paradigm, the law is valid (the validity is distinguished here from mere existence that characterizes customs or social conventions) because there is a group of people enforcing the law (officials, judges, etc) and, secondly, because there exists the overwhelming social belief in the legitimacy of the law. Although legal validity does not necessarily need to be accompanied by moral-political justifiability (Weber strongly argues with Rudolf Stammler, who in his opinion confuses these questions – Weber 1968: 32) it does not mean that moral-political justifiability is generally irrelevant for the social efficiency of the legal change. On the contrary, the legal practices of contemporary democratic societies indicate that the law's authority is also dependent on its moral-political justifiability. Although the lack of moral-political justifiability does not directly determine the legal validity of law (Raz 1986: 46), it obviously weakens this authority and may lead to it being undermined in the long run.

The scientific procedure underlying this monography requires an examination of elements taken from normative perspective represented by political philosophy through the prism of empirical/descriptive perspective derived from social jurisprudence and from social sciences. It aims at the development of a heuristic tool able to improve the understanding of, as well as clarifying the political and philosophical background of, the legal changes. The effectiveness of this tool is verified through the examination of examples or "case studies" illustrating formal and informal legal changes first between custom and law, second in the public law, third in the private law, and at last in the sphere of human rights. Obviously, the proposed set of case studies should not be seen as fully exhaustive. It is only a compact illustration of what the application of the instrument in main legal areas looks like. The proposed scientific program is intended as supporting contemporary legisprudence and jurisprudence by using a heuristic tool that is derived, at bottom, from the philosophical-political debate between Rawls and communitarians. This debate took place during the last three decades of the 20th century, continuing into the beginning of the 21st century, and its conclusions seems to be even more important at the end of the second decade of the 21st century.

## References

Alexy, R. (1983) *Theorie der juristischen Argumentation. Die Theorie des rationlen Diskurses als Theorie der juristischen Begruendung*. Frankfurt am Main, Suhrkamp.

Beetham, D. (1991) *The Legitimation of Power*. New York, Palgrave MacMillan.

Berman, H. J. (2005) 'The Historical Foundations of Law', *Emory Law Journal*, 54, 13–24.

Coleman, J. L. (1982) 'Negative and Positive Positivism', *Journal of Legal Studies*, 11, 139–164.

Coleman, J., and Leiter, B. (1996) 'Legal Positivism', in D. Paterson (ed.) *A Companion to Philosophy of Law and Legal Theory*. Oxford, Blackwell, 244–249.

Dworkin, R. (1977) *Taking Righs Seriously*. Cambridge, Massachusetts, Harvard University Press.

Dworkin, R. (1986) *Law's Empire*. Cambridge, Massachusetts, Harvard University Press.
Dworkin, R. (1993) *Life's Dominion: An Argument About Abortion, Euthanasia, and Individual Freedom*. New York, Alfred A. Knopf.
Dworkin, R. (2006) *Is Democracy Possible Here? Principles for a New Political Debate*. Princeton, New Jersey, Princeton University Press.
Dworkin, R. (2011) *Justice for Hedgehogs*. Cambridge, Massachusetts, Harvard University Press.
Feyerabend, P. (2010) *Against Method*. 4th ed., New York, Verso Books.
Finnis, J. (1980) *Natural Law and Natural Rights*. Oxford, Oxford University Press.
Fuller, L. L. (1969) *The Morality of Law*. New Haven, Connecticut, Yale University Press.
Habermas, J. (1984) *The Theory of Communicative Actions*. Vol I, Boston, Massachussets, Beacon Press.
Habermas, J. (1987) *The Theory of Communicative Actions*. Vol II, Boston, Massachussets, Beacon Press.
Habermas, J. (1996) *Between Facts and Norms, Contributions to a Discourse Theory of Law and Democracy*. Cambridge, Massachusetts, MIT Press.
Hart, H. L. A. (1958) 'Positivism and the Separation of Law and Morals', *Harvard Law Review*, 71, 593–629.
Ihering, R. von (1979) *The Struggle for Law*. Westport, Connecticut, Hyperion Press.
Knoll, E., Snyder, S., and Şimsek, N. (eds) (2018) *New Perspectives on Distributive Justice: Deep Disagreements, Pluralism, and the Problem of Consensus*. Berlin and Boston, Massachusetts, Walter de Gruyter.
Rawls, J. (1993) *Political Liberalism*. New York, Columbia University Press.
Rawls, J. (1999) *A Theory of Justice*. Cambridge, Massachusetts, Bellknap Press.
Raz, J. (1979) *The Authority of Law. Essays on Law and Morality*. Oxford, Oxford University Press.
Raz, J. (1986) *The Morality of Freedom*. Oxford, Oxford University Press.
Schwartzberg, M. (2007) *Democracy and Legal Change*. Cambridge, Cambridge University Press.
Sebok, A. J. (1998) *Legal Positivism in American Jurisprudence*. Cambridge, Cambridge University Press.
Simmons, J. A. (2001) *Justification and Legitimacy. Essays on Rights and Obligations*. Cambridge, Cambridge University Press.
Stammler, R. (1896) *Wirtschaft und Recht Nach der Materialistischen Geschichtsauffassung*. Leipzig, Von Veit & Comp.
Tamanaha, B. Z. (2015) 'The Third Pillar of Jurisprudence: Social Legal Theory', *William & Mary Law Review*, 56, 6, 2235–2277.
Waldron, J. (2012) *Dignity, Rank, and Rights*. Oxford and New York, Oxford University Press.
Waluchow, W. (1994) *Inclusive Legal Positivism*. Oxford, Clarendon Press.
Weber, M. (1964) *The Theory of Social and Economic Organization*. Talcott Parsons (ed.), New York, Free Press.
Weber, M. (1968) *Economy and Society*. Berkley, California, University of California Press.
Wintgens, L. J. (2012) *Legisprudence. Practical Reason in Legislation*. Farnham, Ashgate.
Wintgens, L. J., and Oliver-Lalana, Daniel (2013) *The Rationality and Justification of Legislation. Essays in Legisprudence*. Heidelberg, Springer.
Zirk-Sadowski, M. (2000) *Wprowadzenie do filozofii prawa* [Introduction to the Philosophy of Law]. Kraków, Zakamycze.

# Part I

# General theories

# 1 Standards of law-making as the parts of normative space in the post-modern democratic states

## The question of justification and legitimacy of law[1]

*Tadeusz Biernat*

### Introduction

The questions of what *is* and what *should be* law have dominated the theory and philosophy of law for years. Over the last century, this debate has been extended to the specific issues concerning the creation, application, and interpretation of law. Law-making has become one of the important issues. The positions presented in this debate have been closely related to philosophical positions, trends in jurisprudence, and, to a large extent, separately shaped legal systems. There has been a mainly positivistic trend to the direction of legal considerations, such as the issues of the body authorized to make law, the coherence of the legal system (the relationship between the established normative acts and those that belong to the system), and also the role of the legal procedures in the process of law-making. My analysis of the basics of the law-making process refers to the last of the above-mentioned aspects, stressing the role of standards.

The legislative standards of the state under the rule of law are important elements of the normative space that influences law-making processes and creates new conditions of justification and legitimization of law. It is beyond dispute that the quality of the legislative process and its effects, in the form of the created laws, depends on the degree of the realization law-making standards. Rather, I would like to discuss the auxiliary thesis that it is the degree

1 This article was written as a part of the research project No. 2014/13/B/HS5/00565- financed by NCN (National Science Centre Poland). Analysis of the law-making standards as the parts of normative space in the post-modern democratic states, and their role in the processes of creation of law, is only one aspect of the planned research task, entitled "The normative sources of law in the post-modern society and law-making process". The scientific aim of the project is to investigate the relationships existing between law-making process and the elements of normative space characteristic to the contemporary, post-modern society. The purpose of the study is not only an attempt to validate the hypothesis, but also the verification of the research method in the form of a referential model of law-making analysis – the study of law-making by references to the rules to the normative sources. The proposed model of the analysis is a promising method for examining legal and non-legal normative complexity by a deep, descriptive focus on lived normativity in all its forms.

of realizing law-making standards that plays an important role in the justification of legal activity and legitimacy of law. The key concept of the study is how normative spaces describe phenomena characteristic to the post-modern democratic state.

## 1 The concept of normative space

A widely discussed attribute of post-modern democratic states is the problem of the dynamics and the complexity of social systems, a phenomenon that is described in the following way:

> It is beyond any dispute that we witness a process of growing complexity in the social sphere. We may disagree on some details of the social processes taking place nowadays, but the broad outline is uncontroversial – in principle, all societies are becoming more and more complex with the passage of time. When viewed from a historical and empirical perspective, a transition from simple societies, institutions and interactions to complex, more sophisticated ones seems to be irreversible and inescapable.
>
> (Gizbert-Studnicki & Klinowski 2009: 6)

The dynamics and complexity of the modern normative environment, both the form of the new normativities as well as the creation of the normative space itself, are consequences of these processes.

To clarify the relationship between standards of law-making and the normative space in post-democratic states, first I would like to explain in what sense I use the term "normative space". This term is sometimes used to define the space between the existing legal orders (Zirk-Sadowski 2014). This concept or similar "space of normativity" is close to the notion of the "sphere of normativity", but it differs considerably. The notion "sphere of normativity" is too general and all concepts of "ordered normativity" have their place in it. When one speaks of spaces of normativity, the discussion should aim not only at proving their existence, but also at uncovering their functions. "Thinking of spaces of normativity in contemporary law implies not only looking at the emergence of varying spaces of normativity in positive law but also considering them from non-legal perspectives" (Lixinski 2008: 2). An important feature of the normative space is that normativity can take on many forms and operate in multiple spheres creating new normative reality as examples of an emerging of normative space indicate.[2]

I use the term "normative space" in a strictly defined meaning. The use of the concept of normative space results from the proposal of a new approach to the

2 The second volume of the *European Journal of Legal Studies* (2008) was dedicated to emerging areas of law or new "spaces of normativity".

study of the functioning of law in the world of normativity. The proposed change in the research paradigm consists in abandoning the perception of law as an element of the broadly understood normative order. The proposed approach differs considerably and is more useful to describing and characterizing the normative changes of post-modern society. The point is that mainstream scientific discussion does not adequately address the emergence of new forms of normativity, nor the scope and mode of their aggregation.

The vast majority of analyses in the literature, perhaps even all of them, assume that the normative and axio-normative system, including the relationships of its parts, is expressed coherently with well-defined boundaries. This allows the system to serve as the basis of normative reality. The defining elements and relations of the system most often form hierarchical order that is culturally, temporally, and territorially designated. I propose an alternative perspective on the relationship between law and normative space (normative environment), one whose characteristic feature is its dynamics. These dynamics affect both the emergence of new normative elements, or normative sources, as well as continuously clarify their normative content. However, analyzing this phenomenon, one must remember another decisive aspect: the present day is characterized by the unlimited transfer of normative elements. Anything created in one social reality can be "transferred" to another one, quickly, effectively, and without any restrictions, as effectively demonstrated by the case of precedent.

Furthermore, the force and effects of normative elements, such as precedents, are derivative from their privileged position. We point out three aspects of precedents that yield possibilities of disseminating their content worldwide in a relatively easy and natural way.[3] First, the special position of precedents is related to the narrative formula of precedents and their mediality; in the content of the ruling and the justification of precedents, there manifests itself a history, connected with a particular event, most interesting to the media. Second, the rule expressed in the precedent by its relationship to facts is more understandable and clear than the abstract general norm. Third, in the modern world the emergence of new forms of mass communication gives unlimited possibilities of disseminating the content of precedents. Generally, the content expressed in the normative sources of one reality is not only easily accessible, but also often indicates a potential pattern in the similar social situations.

Assigning to the normative space a strictly and permanently defined structure and boundaries is difficult. Key normative elements can periodically play the most important role, but their normative functions are not always decisive. In broader terms, the notion of normative space includes more or less formalized elements

3 In some cases, the need to disseminate court judgments is emphasized officially. "It highlights the need for the dissemination of relevant decisions of the Court of Justice of the European Union (CJEU) and for an exchange of national court decisions in line with CJEU and European Court of Human Rights case-law pertaining to the provisions of the Employment Equality Directive" (European Parlament 2016, point 92).

(first of all, systems of legal principles and norms – law itself) that influence law and the creation of law. In other words, normative space is part of environment, in which the law is only a point on a normative continuum. The following well expresses and justifies my approach:

> We are normative animals, expressing evaluative judgments of appropriate claims and conduct. Normativity is thus universal. Legality isn't. Laws, as defined by centuries of Western convention, are points on a normative continuum and always rest within the wider matrix of less-institutionalized normativity. Legal norms are a subset of social norms. But if laws and norms may be distinguished in this way, they cannot be divorced. For this reason, jurists must take general normativity seriously and social scientists must respect legality's unique normative position . . . There has been no – and is now no – unified and pure legal or normative space, controlled respectively by either an all-embracing state or society. Instead, laws and norms always rest within the wider web of strong or deep legal pluralism, the totality of normative orders and more diffuse normative influences.
>
> (Donlan 2015: 8)

Given that normative statements rest within a wider web of strong and deep normative pluralism, it is justified to use various sources. Thus, in scientific studies, the selection mechanism used is of particular importance.

> The increasing complexity of society and the ever more accentuated differentiation and enhancement of merely normative perspectives require the preparation of more suitable and efficient selective mechanisms, subtracted from the momentary distribution of power, in order to maintain the level of achieved development. In ways that can be totally different in particular, systems of specific interaction are produced, the so-called procedures, with the particular task to provide binding functions.
>
> (Di Viggiano 2011: 108)

In this context, it is clear that normative statements, procedural solutions, and standards are not only an important component of the normative space, but also help shape it.

Such an approach to the normative space requires a closer characterization of the way in which I use the term "normative elements". It is not possible in this chapter to fully address the concept of "normativity", but at the least it must be stressed that normativity has different levels and forms of expression, or "the content of ought". "The use of 'should' and its normative cognates in such contexts is specified in a certain way, usually made plain by the nature of the context" (Black 1964: 176). Specific normative *contents*, expressed in different forms, are normative *elements*: they are statements that make claims about how someone *should* or *ought* to act, to behave in a social relationship. In this approach, the systematization of normative elements does not play a pivotal role, but rather it is a matter of their free aggregation carried out within the framework of doctrinal legal narrative or in the context of the practice of law. In general, the normative space consists of, most importantly: norms implicit in values; human rights; legal principles and norms; precedents; soft law norms; standards; normative statements included in the justification of judicial decisions; and normative statements included in the legal doctrine.

## 2 Legal provisions and standards of legislation

As society develops there are significant changes in normative space, including law. Laws, or more precisely the formal sources of law, are first of all procedural provisions that belong to a particular legal system and are dependent on the normative space. The same is true for all forms of legal activity, such as law-making, legal application, and the interpretation of legal acts. However, it is also true that such activity is likewise related to other normative elements. This is clearly demonstrated in the context of the law-making process, which on the one hand is governed by the legal provisions and on the other by different normative statements and standards, characteristic to the democratic state under the rule of law. Standards, being an element of normative space, determine the creation of law, and are (sometimes) more influential than legal provisions directly related to the creation of legal acts and have decisive meaning in the justification of legal activity and legitimacy of law.

The concept of "standard" has manifold meaning. Standards set the manner of conduct, the course of action. They are similar to rules as a type of directive and share all problems of normativity characteristic to that phenomenon, but they are clearly different in their broader dimension. The rules vs standards comparison is an interesting starting point for discussion:

> Thus far I have been pretending that the meanings of "rules" and "standards" are self-evident. Before defining these terms, a little background is necessary. It is possible to look at positive law (constitutions, statutes, judicial opinions, and administrative orders) as a series of directives. The formula for a legal directive is "if this, then that." A directive thus has two parts: a "trigger" that identifies some phenomenon and a "response" that requires or authorizes a legal consequence when that phenomenon is present . . . Corresponding to the two parts of a directive, there are two sets of oppositions that constitute the rules v. standards dichotomy: The trigger can be either empirical or evaluative, and the response can be either determined or guided. The paradigm example of a rule has a hard empirical trigger and a hard determinate response. For instance, the directive that "sounds above 70 decibels shall be punished by a ten dollar fine," is an example of a rule. A standard, by contrast, has a soft evaluative trigger and a soft modulated response. The directive that "excessive loudness shall be enjoinable upon a showing of irreparable harm," is an example of a standard.
>
> (Schlag 1985: 2)

The comparison of rules and standards indicates the dual nature of a standard: standards can be changed to norms by incorporating independent legal provisions or acts, while retaining directive elements that allow for its gradual evaluation:

> Indeed, our dissatisfaction with both rule-oriented and standard-oriented approaches is reflected in the tendency of rules to evolve or degenerate, depending upon our perspective, into standards, and standards to evolve or degenerate into rules. This tendency towards refinement or entropy occurs via some routine patterns:
>
> 1 Standards tend to become concretized by means of specific rules. (The meaning of a general standard is found in its specific applications.)
> 2 Rules tend to yield specific exceptions that are generated by appeal to other standards. (The meaning of a general rule is found in the standards limiting its application.)
>
> (Schlag 1985: 20)

The dual nature of standards is clearly presented in the law-making. Fundamentally, law-making standards are expressed by provisions in legally binding acts. In the broad context, law-making standards are the normative statements that obligate actors to fulfil their actions in the most proper way at the highest level. The law-making process is affected by standards in two aspects. In the first dimension, standards of law-making are the parts of legal acts related to the organization of the law-making process. Specifically and importantly, this dimension is strongly connected to the rule of law, precisely to the *state* under the rule of law. In this situation, the precise definition of the content of the rule of law principle is of particular importance. The problem of understanding the concept of rule of law was underlined in Resolution 1594 of the Council of Europe:

> The Parliamentary Assembly draws attention to the fact that in some recent democracies in eastern Europe, the main trends in legal thinking foster an understanding of the "rule of law" as "supremacy of statute law". . . . Such a formalistic interpretation of the terms "rule of law" and Etat de droit (as well as of Rechtsstaat) runs contrary to the essence of both "rule of law" and prééminence du droit. Certainly in these cases there is an inappropriate lack of consistency and clarity when translating into the legal terms used in member states.
>
> (Council of Europe 2007: Resolution 1594, *The Principle of the Rule of Law*: point 4)

Taking as a background Resolution 1594 (2007), the Venice Commission elaborated the Report on the Rule of Law adopted at its 86th plenary session (Venice Commission 2011), including the proposed definition of the rule of law to help international organizations and both domestic and international courts in interpreting and applying this fundamental value. The Commission has assumed that this definition should therefore be of a nature that allows practical application.

Thus, part of the report was a "checklist" for evaluating the state of the rule of law in single states. The next checklist developed by the Venice Commission was adopted at its 106th Plenary Session (Venice Commission 2016). The idea of this checklist was inspired by the observation that rule of law has not been conceptually developed in legal texts and practice as much as the other pillars of the Council of Europe: human rights and democracy. Human rights are at the basis of an enormous corpus of constitutional and legal provisions and of case law, at national as well as at international levels, while democracy is implemented through detailed provisions concerning elections and the functioning of institutions. Legal provisions, referring to the rule of law, both at national and at international levels, are of a very general character with spare details.

The presented checklist is intended to build on these developments and to provide a tool for assessing the Rule of Law in a given country from the viewpoint of its constitutional and legal structures, the legislation in force, and the existing case law. The checklist aims at enabling an objective, thorough, transparent and equal assessment, and it is mainly directed at assessing legal safeguards. However, the proper implementation of the law is a crucial aspect of the Rule of Law and must therefore be taken into consideration, which is why the checklist also includes certain complementary practical benchmarks. The checklist consists of three parts: the introductive part, benchmarks, and selected standards. The second part is the core of the checklist and develops the various aspects of the Rule of Law identified in the 2011 report: legality, legal certainty, and prevention of abuse of powers, equality before the law, non-discrimination, and access to justice. The third part lists the most important instruments of hard and soft law addressing the issue of the Rule of Law. For our purposes, the most important will be the second part with the checklist with benchmarks: legality, law-making procedures and legal certainty,[4] and the accessibility of legislation.[5]

## 3 Standards as ideological reference point

The law-making process is embedded in the political and legal culture in each country, and cultural substrate has an impact not only on the adopted organizational solutions and legislative standards, but also, and perhaps above all, on the law-making practices. Though it is particularly emphasized in the cultural characteristics of the legislation, this relationship can take many forms, as will be discussed below. The cultural aspect of the law-making organization is combined

4 Regarding law-making procedures and legal certainty, five questions are important: is the process for enacting law transparent, accountable, inclusive, and democratic? Are there clear constitutional rules on the legislative procedure? Is parliament supreme in deciding on the content of the law? Is proposed legislation debated publicly by parliament and adequately justified (e.g. by explanatory reports)? Does the public have access to draft legislation, at least when it is submitted to parliament? Does the public have a meaningful opportunity to provide input?

5 Considering the accessibility of law, we must ask: are all legislative acts published before entering into force? Are they easily accessible, e.g. free of charge via the Internet and/or in an official bulletin?

with important issues of the standards of legislation, which are the basis of actions and postulate the relatively high level of their fulfilment. The concept of such type of standards refers to the patterns of, and, at the same time, constitutes a kind of ideological reference point for the undertaken actions. Such ideological reference points are visible in which particular law-making models are preferred.

The law-making models are correlated to the type of political and legal system. In democratic states under the rule of law, the voluntaristic model is rejected in favor of rational and discursive models of creating law. The discursive model, which is based on the concept of communicative rationality, has a special position today, where communicative rationality is a derivative of the discourse, by social actors in the process of law-making and decisions based on consensus. The fundamental problem is whether such a consensus is possible.

A critical analysis of law-making models leads to a more thorough characterization of making law as a special kind of decision-making process that progresses via phases and stages, particularly the pre-legislative and legislative. The first phase includes the activities that involve making political decisions, initiating the creation of law, as well as the actions leading to the drafting of a normative act. The second phase includes operations aimed at producing an act. The latter consists of the following stages: a) identification of the conflict/problem to be solved; b) articulation of goals and courses of action; c) determination of the scope of legal intervention, e.g. a bill; d) legislative initiative and conducting legislative procedure; e) publication of the act of law; and f) assessment of its constitutionality.

The nature of the decisions depends on the phase of law-making process, and therefore, the differentiation of the various typological stages of law-making decisions, facilitates their recounting and analysis. The decisions defining the scope of legal intervention, as well as subsequent decisions undertaken in the legislative phase are strongly associated with the rational model of the law-making process and related standards.

An important and widely discussed issue concerns the decisions made at the pre-legislative phase. Who makes decisions at this stage? At this stage, it is resolved that one of the politically determined goals will be realized with the use of legal instruments. The outcomes are often the result of succumbing to social pressure, media influence, and they do not have much in common with a rational political choice. An example might be the phenomenon of "penal populism". The identification of problems/conflicts in social, political, and economic matters is a political action. Politicians, as they perform roles and hold specific positions within the political system, shape the occurrence of the legislative impulse.

Impulses of another type may occur at the event of a conflict/problem taking place within the legal system; undertaking legislative action may be purely legal, justified by the consistency and coherence of the system, by the problems of the application and interpretation of law, or by the changes taking place in the environment of the legal system (international law, European Union law). From the subjective point of view, the identification of the internal problem, i.e. the problem forming the element of the legal system, is the domain of lawyers. In practice, it is important to formulate *de lege ferenda* demands.

The next step in the pre-legislative phase is the decision to define the scope of legal intervention, where impulse is transformed into a draft of specific legislation in order to achieve certain objectives. This decision involves the choice of both selecting the type of normative act, as well as preparing the draft. The decision-making process, especially at these early stages, is very complex; the undertaken decisions, as presented above, should be considered oversimplified. These processes are accompanied, as a rule, by many auxiliary/complementary decisions: a) the characterization and evaluation of the policy in the area of regulation; b) the characterization and evaluation of the normative environment (legal environment and the environment of the remaining normative systems, for example, moral or religious, taking into account the trends); c) the characterization and evaluation of social discourse; and d) description and evaluation of the constitutional standard. The correlation of the distinguished areas of the basic and auxiliary/complementary decisions in the law-making process determines the level of the effectiveness of law.

My thesis is that the quality of the legislative process and its effects, as evidenced by the form of the created laws, depends on the degree to which the standards are realized compared to the proposed models of law-making in the practice of legislation elaborated by the community of democratic states. The implementation of *good* legislation and the ensuring of a relatively high quality of laws created thereby requires not only that the adopted organizational solutions will guarantee the intent of the law-making process, but also respect standards determined by the models of this democratic consensus. Accordingly, this is concerned with the demands stated by the strongly preferred discursive model and in the practice of preparing draft laws, where what proves to be ultimately important is how the social actors participate in the law-making process.

The broadest forms of participation of the social actors in the law-making process are consultations, which take various forms and have different status in the organization of law-making, which, in turn, affects the legal basis for their implementation. Abiding by the principle of consultations (which is not equivalent to taking into account the results of the consultations) is the responsibility of the legislator, but only for the implementation of certain types of legislative drafts. The implementation of statutory regulation on lobbying into the Polish legal system constituted an important step in formalizing the participation of social actors in the legislative process. Another important institution was that of public hearing (Biernat 2016).

Actual analysis, however, shows at least considerable gaps in our thesis, if not sometimes the exact opposite of it. Numerous examples point to a lack of correlation between the standards derived from the theoretical model of law-making and the actual practice of law-making process in Poland. The quality of the legislative process and its effects in the form of the created laws depends on the implementation of the canon of a correct/proper legislation. Ensuring a relatively high quality of the created laws requires at least such level of adjustment in which the adopted organizational solutions will guarantee the postulated mode of action, designated by the adopted theoretical model. The indicated features include:

transparency and collegiality, manifested in the accepted principles of arrangement, assessment, and cooperation, integrity, professionalism, and openness, manifested in complex possibilities of consultations. In such a system, we can talk about the fulfilment of the condition of adapting the organizational solutions to the implementation of the proper legislation model.

The undertaken actions go, however, in a different direction, and the adopted solutions are largely irrelevant. It is enough to trace the real law-making decisions. The list of the draft laws submitted to the Sejm during two months (from 14 April to 14 June 2016) includes a total of more than 80 assigned with the number of printing: 30 projects were submitted by the government and more than 50 by the deputies. A considerable part of the latter was submitted by the deputies representing the parliamentary majority, namely the government. The drafts submitted by the deputies, due to the solutions within the organization of law-making, are not subject to the rigors applying in case of the drafts submitted by the government. In the Polish system only that second path assures the implementation of the standards of legislation. Consultations are not needed whenever the deputies of the ruling parliamentary/government majority receive specific instructions to implement the legislative initiative. One decision, usually declaring "we let it go through the parliamentary group", reduces, by its very definition, a more sensible legislative path (Biernat 2016).

For this very reason, the quality and content of law is widely criticized. An overwhelming number of regulations are incoherent due to lack of a clear axiological basis and reliable knowledge, leading to inaccuracy of legal solutions. The fact that they are complicated and uncommunicative has amounted to such a level that there have arisen unsolvable problems and situations, or to quote the words of the Supreme Court judge, "such situations in which even courts cannot manage" (Wronkowska 2000: 11). Such critical assessments concerning legislative process in states during the transformation period do not apply strictly to Poland. A. Bröstl, when, writing about Slovakia, points out a similar phenomenon: "First of all, the kind of parliamentary malpractice changing into routine should be critically analyzed, when legal acts (ordinary legislation) are 'produced' like industrial goods for consumers without sufficient preparation" (Bröstl 2000: 79).

Law-making standards are the normative statements which obligate actors to fulfil their obligations in the most proper and at the highest level of the subject of that activity. Such a dimension and the role of legal standards in the law-making process depend on contextual elements and draw our attention to the different meaning of standards. This was also highlighted in the Venice Commission report as follows:

> The contextual elements of the Rule of Law are not limited to legal factors. The presence (or absence) of a shared political and legal culture within a society, and the relationship between that culture and the legal order help to determine to what extent and at what level of concreteness the various elements of the Rule of Law have to be explicitly expressed in written law. Thus, for instance, national traditions in the area of dispute settlement and

> conflict resolution will have an impact upon the concrete guarantees of fair trial offered in a country. It is important that in every State a robust political and legal culture supports particular Rule of Law mechanisms and procedures, which should be constantly checked, adapted and improved.
>
> (Venice Commission 2016, point 42)

## 4 On justification and legitimacy of law

Does law require legitimacy? In contemporary legal discourse the fundamental premise is the assumed necessary legitimacy as an element constituting the law, and more precisely, as the element constituting the relationships between law and legal actors in a democratic social system that guarantees a certain level of the autonomy of these entities. The concept of legitimacy is necessary to describe and explain these relationships. A number of studies about the legitimacy of law particularly highlight the relationship that exists between the approach to law and its legitimization. The positivist approaches replace legitimacy with the concept of legality.

> Positivists certainly have a point in insisting that law needs to be made by competent lawmakers. However, they are wrong in maintaining that these lawmakers are not bound by any other norm than the legal norms issued by higher legal authorities. Their theory does not account for legal values and principles, as a basis for criticizing legislation and legal decisions like judicial decisions, for lawmakers are bound by legal principles. Therefore, besides the concept of legality we need the concept of legitimacy to explain the authority of law and the citizens' duty of obedience to the law.
>
> (Gribnau 2002: section 5)

In the approaches that differ from positivist ones, legitimacy of law is treated as a necessary element. The reconstruction of Dworkin's position presents this issue as follows:

> In Dworkin's account validity, if it plays any role in his account at all, is the least important of the four: validity for him is the conclusion of the inquiry, not its starting point. On this view the starting point for the inquiry is legitimacy, for our concern is to distinguish between law and non-law, and for Dworkin the basis is the distinction between legitimate and illegitimate use of force. All aspects of the law, from identification of sources to, most centrally, questions of interpretations are built around the question of legitimacy. Rather than (potential) legitimacy being the product of norms having the right content, legitimacy is the central element in determining the content of legal norms.
>
> (Priel 2011: 22)

Although the justification of law is the part of its legitimacy, the understanding of the latter differs significantly, and not always is justification a constitutive element thereof (Wintgens 2012). Regardless of which form of legitimacy is being emphasized, the entire process takes place at two levels: epistemological and axiological. A crucial remark about legitimacy is contained in the following statement: "Legitimacy is a generalized perception or assumption that the actions of an entity are desirable, proper, or appropriate within some socially constructed system of norms, values, beliefs, and definitions" (Suchman 1995: 574).

The key problem, associated with the legitimization of law, results from law-making process and its "dual nature", its double roots: political and legal reality. The political dimension "complements" the requirements of the general theory of law. The proposal to complement and to strengthen the democratic legitimacy of the legislator aims at defining the conditions that legitimize the key decisions of the legislator, which can be adopted in the law-making process. The relationships outlined above are suggestions to contemporary answers to questions of legitimacy and are often based on arbitrary interference into "the chain of legitimacy relationships". When referring to law, for example the constitution, as a form of legitimizing state authority, we break this legitimacy chain without any justification. We do not attempt to sufficiently justify the "moment of entering" this holistic structure of legitimization.

In general, legitimization is understood as addressing potential arbitrariness, as the attempt to explain the paradoxes and contradictions and to justify the adopted course of action (Biernat 2014). In this process, the actors are placed in different locations throughout the social structure with own preferences. Taking into account the general characteristics of conceptualizing the defining of legitimacy, and especially the indicated dilemmas connected with the adopted theories of law's legitimacy, it is justified to seek a new legitimization formula, while taking into account the contemporary conditions of legitimacy. I have analyzed some aspects of this issue elsewhere, suggesting a diverse way of treating legitimization (Biernat 2000). The principles of the proposed analytic paradigm rely on the thesis that the legitimization of a given object is related to an independent individual who accepts and justifies this object from the viewpoint of his own autonomous orientation. Such autonomous orientation means a permanently renewed process of recognizing social reality, understanding, and attribution of the senses. The suggestion of the research paradigm is derived from the following basic question: is, and in what conditions, the legitimization process analytically possible? It is defined as a gradual legitimating situation (Biernat 2000). This is determined by the "normative minimum", which, contemporarily, is usually law-based in nature. This normative minimum is the one that could be found in the principles of democracy. Situations in which the legitimization is possible are only the "starting point" in the processes of legitimating law. The key processes occur in the frame of complicated relations with various aspects of "real law, its creation and application".

Law is at all times continuously "defined" by the actions of those involved in legal relations. Legal decisions that are taken determine the position of the specific actors who thus become "full" participants in the game. At the same time, they experience law and each of these overlapping experiences renews and modifies the systems of meanings that can be found in it. The relations between the actors, shaped by the mechanisms that stimulate their activity, under certain "legitimizing" conditions, take the form of an interactive game in which every movement and reaction encounters a specific response. It is a peculiar kind of discourse, based on actual actions in the sphere of law. Such relations are crucial for determining the legitimacy of law, since they take into account the different motives of its legitimization and emphasize the dynamics of this process. I suggest referring to this type of legitimacy as the constitutive legitimacy. In terms of the latter, there is a combination of two aspects: the legitimizing situation, i.e. the conditions of legitimization, and the mechanisms that stimulate the social actors involved in this process.

Under the proposed model, legitimacy is understood as a kind of game of social actors within the selected aspects of the political and legal system, if the actors are willing and able to participate in this game and when they meet with proper conditions to be involved in it. In this game we use well-known patterns, such as what is legal, correct, righteous, fair, just, moral, etc., but we do not have a prescription which would tell us how to reach the legitimate legal system of a whole, or what are the conditions under which a "comprehensive" legitimacy is possible. The game can take place by means of a discourse, both the traditionally understood one as well as the one that applies specific legal decisions and facts. The discourse is not only a directive or a postulate. It is a potentially possible and significant fact, when it actually takes place, whose effect and significance come down to creating such legitimacy of law that would be proper for contemporary complex systems.

The proposed model and approach to the legitimacy of law substantially define its functions. In addition to the function defined as basic and traditional, which inspired this study, one can point at two more. The traditional function is interpreted as a justification and clarification of a particular type of rule-based pattern contained in law. This is understood as breaking the arbitrariness of law. One additional functions of legitimacy can be determined as follows: one is treated as a peculiar "reserve" of law. It refers to the specific content of law, broadly defined as the content of provisions, norms, and legal institutions. This function is confronted by the sense of the latter and by the possibility of attributing sense in the process of cognition and validation, thus it determines a potentially accepted scope of meanings. Another function is formed or "activated" when legal decisions are paramount in determining the position of specific actors. This is the accommodative function which provides the foundations for the authority of law. When considering this function, legitimacy profoundly changes and transforms the relations within law. It does not change the substance of law, but it defines different "internal" relations in which the most decisive round in the game of law's legitimacy takes place.

Adherence to standards by law-makers, both legal and derivate, from the proposed law-making model, knowledge such standards in society, and the ability to control their applications can play an important role in the game that decides the "legitimacy of law".

## References

Biernat, T. (2000) *Legitymizacja władzy politycznej. Elementy teorii [Legitimisation of Political Power. Elements of the Theory].* Toruń, Wydawnictwo Adam Marszałek.

Biernat, T. (2014) 'Complexity of Contemporary Legal Systems: Dilemmas and the Paradoxes of Law's Legitimacy', in *Towards Recognition of Minority groups. Legal and Communication Strategies*, edited by Marek Zirk-Sadowski, Bartosz Wojciechowski and Karolina M. Cern, Farnham, Ashgate, 261–271.

Biernat, T. (2016) *Legislacja. Analiza procesu. [Legislation. Process analysis].* Kraków, Oficyna Wydawnicza AFM.

Black, M. (1964) 'The Gap Between "Is" and "Should"', *The Philosophical Review*, 73 (2), 165–181 www.collier.sts.vt.edu/5424/pdfs/black_1964.pdf [accessed 30/01/19].

Bröstl, A. (2000) 'On Preparation and Impact of Legal Science in Legislation and the Judiciary: Focusing on Slovakia', in *Legal Research in Dynamic Society*, edited by Krzysztof Pałecki and Aleksander Peczenik, Kraków, Ratio, 74–86.

Council of Europe (2007) *Resolution 1594 (2007)*, Parliamentary Assembly, Council of Europe.

Di Viggiano, P.L. (2011) 'Evolutionary Forms of Law and Social Systems', *Curentul Juridic, The Juridical Current, Le Courant Juridique*, 45, 102–112.

Donlan, S.P. (2015) *To Hybridity and Beyond. Reflections on Legal and Normative Complexity.* www.academia.edu/2078759/To_Hybridity_and_Beyond_Reflections_on_Legal_and_Normative_Complexity [accessed 30/01/19].

European Parliament (2016) *Report on Application of Council Directive 2000/78/EC of 27 November 2000 Establishing a General Framework for Equal Treatment in Employment and Occupation* ('Employment Equality Directive') (2015/2116 (INI)), A8-0225/2016, point 92, European Parliament.

Gizbert-Studnicki, T. and Klinowski, M. (2009) 'Complexity of the Social Sphere and the Judicial Decision-Making Process', *Archivum Iuridicum Cracoviense*, XLII, 5–25.

Gribnau, J.L.M. (2002) 'Legitimacy of the Judiciary', *Electronic Journal of Comparative Law*, 6.4, www.ejcl.org/64/art64-3.html [accessed 30/01/19].

Lixinski, L. (2008) 'In Normative Space', *European Journal of Legal Studies. Spaces of Normativity*, 2 (1), 2–8.

Priel, D. (2011) 'The Place of Legitimacy in Legal Theory', *McGill Law Journal*, 57 (1), 2–35 https://digitalcommons.osgoode.yorku.ca/cgi/viewcontent.cgi?referer=&https redir=1&article=2127&context=scholarly_works [accessed 30/01/19].

Schlag, P.J. (1985) 'Standards', *UCLA Law Review* 33, 379, 1–28.

Suchman, M.C. (1995) 'Managing Legitimacy: Strategic and Institutional Approaches', *The Academy of Management Review*, 20 (3), 571–610.

Venice Commission (2011) *Report on the Rule of Law*, Venice Commission.

Venice Commission (2016) *Rule of Law Checklist*, Venice Commission.

Wintgens, L.J. (2012) *Legisprudence. Practical Reason in Legislation*, Farnham, Ashgate.

Wronkowska, S. (2000) 'Zagadnienia procesu legislacyjnego' ['The Aspects of Legislative Process'], *Przegląd Legislacyjny* [*Legislative Review*], 1, 32–45.

Zirk-Sadowski, M. (2014) 'Flexible Normative Space Between the European Law and the Member State Law as a Source of Constitutional Identity', in *Towards Recognition of Minority groups. Legal and Communication Strategies*, edited by Marek Zirk-Sadowski, Bartosz Wojciechowski and Karolina M. Cern, Farnham, Ashgate, 237–260.

# 2 Public reason, background culture, and the justification of legal change[1]

*Michał Rupniewski*

## Introduction

In today's world it is uncontroversial, or even obvious, to think of law as an instrument in the hands of different norm-setting actors. These (state and non-state) actors are responsive to various demands articulated in the public sphere, economic challenges, or technological development, and the law follows up their agenda. As a result of this, legal change has become an inevitable, and problematic, feature of most jurisdictions. Given that, this book as a whole tries to demonstrate that the integrity and certainty of law, as well as social cohesion and stability, seem to depend heavily on good governance of the processes of change. In my view, this may be achieved only if preceded by thorough politico-philosophical investigations; a sound philosophy of legal change can and *should* help sort out the prudential and practical concerns. Political philosophy, then, might serve not merely as a particular justificatory framework for a particular law or judgement, but rather as an interpretative tool, helping to understand (and thus govern) the background conditions of the actual processes. The fact that legal change has been shaped by philosophical conceptions has been generally overlooked.

In this chapter, I provide an outline for one such philosophical framework, based on the distinction between public reason and background culture, introduced by John Rawls (1996) in his *Political Liberalism.* The key idea is that background culture should be acknowledged as an independent source of justification, different from public-political justification that public reason yields. Therefore, I propose a view I call the Open Justification Model, which is an alternative to Rawls and public reason liberalism,[2] while sharing its main categories and commitments. This model interprets legal change and its justification as

1 This chapter presents results of the research financially supported by the National Science Centre, Poland, as part of the project No. 2015/19/B/HS5/02522.

2 My point of reference is the "consensus view" of public reason: that a rule is considered justified if members of the relevant public share the same justificatory reasons. I do not directly engage with an alternative account of public reason – the "convergence view" – that proposes the weaker condition that each member have *a* sufficient, though not necessarily shared, reason for justification (Gaus & Vallier 2009). Instead of convergence, I propose an alternative account that takes non-arbitrariness as the crucial feature of open justification, which might overlap with the convergence view but should not be conflated with it.

an interplay between values and principles inherent to public reason and background culture.

## 1 Public reason and background culture: A Rawlsian-inspired framework

*Public reason* and *background culture* are technical terms of the later Rawls's philosophy, and we shall examine some details of their meaning more deeply later in this text. For now, suffice it to say that public reason and background culture refer to two opposite (though reconcilable) spheres of social and political life. Public reason is "the reason of equal citizens, who, as a collective body, exercise final political and coercive power over one another in enacting laws and amending their constitution" (Rawls 1996: 214). Thus, the sphere of public reason embraces values and principles that operate on the level of constitutional essentials and basic justice: equal citizenship, fair distribution of primary goods, individual liberties, and (political) autonomy. Rawls believes those values and principles, inherent to the public political culture, might be widely shared in a society that is marked by disagreement in other important spheres: morality, religion, and philosophical worldview. In order to respect and sustain this disagreement, which is a natural outcome of human reason freely operating within conditions of freedom, citizens impose certain restrictions on each other when arguing or deciding within public institutions. Rawls says that it is a moral duty – the duty of civility (Rawls 2001: 577). As far as citizens exercise political (coercive and final) power on one another, they are bound to offer reasons grounded in non-divisive, public values and principles. Such restrictions are nonbinding in the pluralistic background culture, which is the sphere "of the social, not the political. It is the culture of daily life, of its many associations: churches and universities, learned and scientific societies, and clubs and teams, to mention a few" (Rawls 1996: 14).

In a background culture, then, no legal coercion is directly involved, and thus the constraining rules of public reason do not apply, or at least do not apply that strictly. It is important to emphasize that Rawls envisages a democratic society as one in which people's comprehensive views are not in straightforward opposition to the public values (Rawls 1996: 269), and citizens endorse public institutions also from within their own comprehensive doctrines. As the duty of civility requires, however, in the context of public political forum and coercive political power, they should offer reasons potentially accessible to citizens generally, and not to individuals as members of some particular groups or associations.

For example, churches, as part of background culture, may impose strict illiberal rules on their members, insofar as those rules do not violate their basic status as free citizens. Breaching the discipline of fasting, at certain times of the year, is considered an offence by the Catholic church. As long as the punishment for that offence is of purely religious nature (like penance prayers), and one is generally free to leave the church, it stays compatible with basic liberties required by public reason. Therefore, there is no straightforward opposition to one having status as a free and equal citizen and being simultaneously a believer in the Church. Also, the Catholic church requires helping the poor, and recommends some forms of state action dealing with these issues. Many solidarity policies applied by the state might therefore be endorsed by Catholics from within their own worldview, but at the same time Catholics are able to accept and endorse public reason arguments, considered "eligible" at the public political forum from a Rawlsian perspective, such as basic fairness in distributing the primary goods.

The example above, however instructive, is trivial; one could obviously find many cases that entail problems and conflicts, and reveal the uneasy relationship between public reason and background culture, or even reveal the very distinction as pretty blurry. Are we really able to discern public reasons from non-public ones in real-life debates? Consider the arguments for liberal abortion law: is there any reasonable method to determine whether these arguments are rooted in public reason, and not merely in a comprehensive doctrine, say, atheistic utilitarianism?[3] Another question: at what point does public reason legitimately require an intervention in the background culture? Is legally banning a full-face veil that some Islamic women wear a necessary condition of maintaining equality of men and women, for example?[4]

These and similar problems have triggered strong criticism (Waldron 2007; Finnis 2011: 256–276), and it seems dubious indeed whether an operation of distinguishing reasons as *a priori* "eligible" or "ineligible" in the public realm can escape arbitrariness.[5] It is also unclear what theory of reason and reasonableness is the ground of Rawls's account, and whether or not it constitutes another comprehensive doctrine, as this would obviously render the whole project self-contradictory.[6] In this chapter, however, we are at a somewhat fortunate condition: we are not looking for the full solution to be adopted by a political liberal as an answer to many possible objections. Instead, I will argue that

3 It is important to recall that, for Rawls, public reason is not a form of secular reason. As far as secular-comprehensive reasons are concerned, "a central feature of political liberalism is that it views all such arguments the same way it views religious ones, and therefore these secular philosophical doctrines do not provide public reasons" (Rawls 2001: 588).

4 One prominent political liberal, Martha Nussbaum, has argued against banning the burqa (Nussbaum 2010).

5 As Jeremy Waldron rightly points out, justification – at least taken in the abstract – should be open to all reasons to be rational, at least *prima facie* (Waldron 2007: 116). Perhaps this is why Amartya Sen criticizes Rawls for introducing "closed impartiality" which may threaten objectivity and fairness (Sen 2010: 126–135).

6 For his public reason theory to work, Rawls must ascribe certain moral powers to citizens, and consider them rational and reasonable. The latter feature enables citizens to endorse principles of justice for their own sake, and not merely as means (like in the Hobbesian scheme, for instance). It is unclear to me how this claim can be put forward in isolation from some substantive theory of practical reason. Since citizens are not merely utility maximizers, using nothing but basic instrumental rationality, who are they? Rawls claims that reasonableness, as part of the political conception of the person, is an implicit idea of democratic culture rather than a metaphysical feature of persons. This, however, seems to lack explanatory power.

the Rawlsian scheme, although modified, seems attractive in a limited sphere of inquiry, that is, in investigating legal change. There are many different factors influencing legal systems, and many justification strategies applied in the actual public realm. To sort it out, conceptually and normatively, one may borrow from the fundamental distinction offered by Rawls in *Political Liberalism*. This chapter focuses on finding a model of public reason and background culture working together in the law, particularly in case of legal change. I do not claim to offer an adequate interpretation of Rawls's works. Rather, I am trying to provide a useful, Rawlsian-inspired *instrument for interpreting and evaluating legal change*.

## 2 Open justification

### *2.1 The concept and why it is needed*

Before giving a more detailed explanation of the Rawlsian distinction, I must clarify and explain some crucial assumptions about open justification as understood in a technical sense. First of all, I assume that legal change (in democratic polities at least) must be, and in fact *is being*, justified to the public – the relevant community of citizens regarded as reasonable, free, and equal agents. Law is not merely a product of some norm-setting authority, but also a publicly known and justifiable norm laying claims to rightness or correctness (Alexy 2008). This is perhaps best visible when the law is being changed by the relevant actors (legislators or judges). Just as the law itself might be examined apart from the authority issuing it, *justification* of its change can and *should* be examined apart from law's *legitimacy* in the strict sense. Whereas the latter is to be associated with the law-making entity, the former pertains to law's merits, its content, which either does or does not have good reasons standing behind it. In political practice, as well as in many theories, these two dimensions go hand in hand. But they mean different things: for example, one might imagine a new law that is well-justified – there are sound reasons for it – but is produced by an illegitimate regime, or suffers from some serious procedural flaws that occurred in the legislative process. Moreover, one can surely imagine a perfectly legitimate regime producing law that in many instances is unreasonable or ill-conceived or superfluous.

For the sake of clarity, then, I propose a *prima facie* distinction: 1) justification as a content-related virtue of law; 2) legitimacy in the strict sense, as credentials of authority setting the norms;[7] and 3) overall legitimacy of law, which obtains when the two former elements are in some reasonable conjunction. The subject of this chapter is justification in the sense stipulated above.

7 Where these credentials come from is an extremely complex issue which will be omitted here as this chapter focuses on justification as a content-related virtue of law. However, it is important to bear in mind, as most thinkers and not only legal positivists agree, that law may have a normative force taken from elsewhere, even when failing in some important content-related respects. Almost everyone (libertarians and anarchists excluded) acknowledges that the mere fact of a legitimate authority issuing a norm is a sound and content-independent, but of course not absolute, reason to obey (Shapiro 2002).

More specifically, I deal here with *open* – as opposed to *public or political* – justification. The two last terms are often taken to be synonyms (Chambers 2010), albeit Rawls took pains to discern them in a peculiar way (Rawls 1996: 385–388). In order to emphasize the difference between the approach proposed in this chapter and most of the literature on the topic, including Rawls's account, I propose to introduce another, technical term of "open justification". As it is widely accepted among public reason liberals, the principle of public justification[8] says that a rule (in our case – legal change) is publicly justified *when all members of the relevant public have sufficient reasons to accept it.*[9] Different equivalents to "accept" are used, like "internalize" (Gaus 2011: 263), "endorse" (Rawls 1996: 137), but their meaning is similarly strict and demanding. Namely, they all seem to mean at least that publically justified rules are such that all members of the relevant public have a content-related reason, and thus are morally bound to develop a full commitment to obey.[10]

Although this chapter is highly inspired by public reason liberalism, I see the principle of public justification as too strict when applied to legal change, particularly when not limited to merely constitutional change. In the former case, perhaps, the foundational nature of constitutional amendments might render the public justification scheme adequate. But since even this has been contested (Greenawalt 1995), it seems obvious that in case of such instruments of legal change as ordinary legislation and ordinary courts' jurisdiction,[11] it is not flexible enough and not realistic to require public justification at all times. Commitment toward law, including accepting legal change, surely happens to be more complex that "having sufficient public reasons to endorse it". First, in many cases, citizens obey, apply, or accept new law *despite* the fact that they believe it doesn't go in the best direction, or that it adopts wrong means to right ends. And second, the reasons that are given to justify the change in law appeal to public reasons *as well as* to spheres like the nation's history, normative precepts derived from religion, or comprehensive conceptions of the good. To theorize legal change, then, a more flexible concept of justification should be adopted; one that could capture

8 Rawls uses different terminology which can be misleading. To clear up the terms, let us emphasize that public justification in the sense adopted in this chapter equates with what Rawls calls either political justification or liberal legitimacy.

9 Here I paraphrase Fabian Wendt (forthcoming: 2). As Wendt rightly points out, the principle of public justification does not necessarily mean that laws justified otherwise are illegitimate, and can be in itself detached from public reason liberalism and work as part of comprehensive liberalism, for example.

10 As the pluralism regarding conceptions of the good is taken for granted, one is permitted to use only the special class of reasons that count as a public justification and therefore produce the abovementioned duty of commitment. The reasons appealing to widely shared democratic ideals like equal citizenship, individual freedom, autonomy, welfare, or capabilities, are considered non-divisive and likely to be shared among the relevant public. Other arguments are questionable as coming from comprehensive doctrines rather than from public political ideas implicit in a democratic society. This is a very well-known and widely commented aspect of public reason theory, and thus we need not to discuss it.

11 It is important to note that in continental Europe courts do not have authority for judicial review. In the relatively common model (Poland included) only a specialized body – constitutional tribunal – is entitled to judge a law non-constitutional. Therefore in Poland, for example, even the Supreme Court, as distinct from Constitutional Tribunal, does not deal directly with constitutional change.

these complex relations. For the purposes of this chapter, then, I propose to speak of "open justification of legal change", understood as a technical term. Using this technical term, the following principle of open justification is proposed:

> Legal change is justified when each citizen has a sufficient, content-related reason to obey it, seeing it as not merely arbitrary but justifiable to a minimally sufficient extent.

Although the word "obey" is used here, one might use also "accept", but in a very weak sense of the word, similar to this when we accept an invitation, even if we are not really happy in having received it. Just as courtesy or respect makes us accept invitations to gatherings we have neither interest nor delight in attending, open justification allows and requires us to accept laws which fail to meet our own well-considered criteria for just or optimal law. Unlike in cases of public justification, open justification includes situations when the law in question is primarily backed by a comprehensive doctrine that one does not share. Nevertheless, according to the political justification principle, this acceptance is still content-related and has a moral dimension. This might sound paradoxical at first glance, but I believe it is not: it simply goes a step further than public reason liberals want to go with their view on justification.

What is this step? Public reason liberals have conceptualized commitment despite disagreement. It was not limited to disagreement about the comprehensive conceptions of the good, but extended to public values too. For instance, Rawls accepted a family of differing (but all liberal) conceptions of justice operating under a constitution that meets the requirements set by the liberal principle of legitimacy. Liberal legitimacy, which equates with public justification in the sense adopted in this chapter, was not supposed to replace but rather to complement justice (Weithman 2015). Under such a model, then, even when laws have deficiencies with regard to justice (say, do not follow Rawls' difference principle), they might still be justifiable, in the sense of meeting the criteria of justifiability and reciprocity embodied in constitutional essentials. For public reason liberalism, then, the criterion of "justifiability" is less demanding than one of "justice". But still, according to this doctrine, laws (for Rawls – constitutional essentials and laws regulating the question of basic justice) might be justified only from one particular standpoint, that is, the public-political standpoint of free and equal citizens (Freeman 2004: 2047).

In the face of what has been said before in this chapter, as well as alternative models of justification that political philosophers not adhering to political liberalism propose, it might seem a little dogmatic. I claim that even if laws have not been or cannot be successfully justified publically, this does not automatically render them arbitrary or having no justification whatsoever. Therefore, the concept of open justification I propose tries to extend the idea of commitment despite disagreement and recognizes different sources of justification than public reason.

But what of the "endorsement" criterion? Of course, "to justify" a rule is to give reasons of justice, rightness, truth, or goodness that stand behind it and make others morally bound to endorse it. But since open justification focuses on non-arbitrariness, the problem of endorsement of such reasons is still important, but not central. Despite endorsing a set of reasons (A) for *p*, appealing to me very strongly, I acknowledge that my fellow citizens might follow a different set of reasons (B), which I do not share, and those reasons make them opt for *q*. What is the status of B? For a political liberal, it depends on whether or not B comes from public reason. If it does not, then it is nothing but an illegitimate coercion. But is it really that easy to conclude this? Following Jeremy Waldron (1999), I assume that, as members of democratic society, citizens are obliged to respect the choice thoroughly made at an institutional level, and obey a new law as the law of their legal community, even if far from perfect.[12] If that is taken seriously, then perhaps the alleged non-publicness of reasons should not be the only decisive factor automatically overruling a duty to respect and show some commitment toward law backed by reasoning that one does not entirely endorse. After all, the decisions on legal change have been made by people, our fellow citizens, to whom we owe respect. If B is coming from a comprehensive conception of the good that we think is fundamentally mistaken, we nevertheless must acknowledge that our fellow citizens may have a rational commitment to it. Trying to engage with their view and understand them in political terms seems a duty as strong as their duty to present their view in a publically accessible way.

Such an approach might sound anti-Rawlsian, and in fact rejecting political liberalism in its pure form. Am I proposing a hybrid theory, then? I will deal with this issue later, when I briefly consider the problem of priority: even if open justification does welcome comprehensive doctrines as source of justifying reasons, it does not say how to weight those reasons. So it still might turn out that open justification view is compatible with public justification in the sense that the latter has general priority in the justificatory framework for legal change. To determine this, I must first show what I take to be the sound sources of justification, in order to show how these different sources work in public reason and background culture in the processes of legal change.

## *2.2 Sources of justification*

As we have seen, the principle of open justification requires a "minimally sufficient reason" to comply with a law as not merely arbitrary. The first, basic conditions of non-arbitrariness that come to mind are procedural virtues, like publicity and transparency of legislation. These are matters of institutional design and good practice that, according to the distinction introduced in this chapter, constitute legitimacy in the strict sense rather than a source of justification. Certainly,

12 For instance, in *Dignity of Legislation* Waldron writes: "[t]o think about institutions and politics, I must be willing at least part of the time to view even my own convictions about justice – however true or important I take them to be – as merely one set of convictions among others in society, and to address in a relatively neutral way the question of what we as a society are to do about the fact that people like me disagree with others in society about matters on which we need a common view" (Waldron 1999: 91).

overall legitimacy requires justification, and justification of law must take place in legitimate institutional environment, without which it ceases to make sense, so these spheres are intimately intertwined. But this chapter focuses on substantive reasons rather than credentials of the authority setting the norms, and procedural virtues fall into this second category.

As far as substantive reasons are concerned, open justification is comprised of divergent kinds being brought up in legislative or judicial processes of change. But what are they? One strategy to identify this would be empirical research and some generalizations made afterwards, according to methods of sociology of law. This cannot be done within this project, but, as one might see in this volume, legal practice is heavily influenced by political philosophy. Therefore, basing on political philosophy providing models of justification, one may identify the following sources of substantive justification: a) economic efficiency, b) public justifiability c) historical roots, and d) the comprehensive morality. Sociology is surely able to falsify the list, but I suppose that its general lines would survive such a test.

Economic efficiency is quite obvious: most of new law nowadays is oriented at producing wealth (gross domestic product), improving the state's budget or solving socio-economic problems so that social welfare is improved. Therefore, economic efficiency is an important factor used in justification, and economically efficient laws usually gain vast social acceptance. For some philosophers, such as James M. Buchanan or David Gauthier, economic efficiency is the ultimate justification also in philosophical terms. Public reason theorists challenge this and say that apart from instrumental reason (rationality), there is a reasonableness that moral agents share, which results in the possibility of endorsing principles of justice or reciprocity for their own sake. This is the public justifiability of law. What public reason theorists do not affirm is that historical roots of a particular legal community constitute distinct and important source of justification. For example, law of succession in each country is not merely a set of rules that should work efficiently and could be changed into some new system if this new system turns out more efficiently. Rather, in many if not in all countries, law of succession emerges from a particular judicial tradition and cannot be interpreted nor amended in terms of economic efficiency or public justifiability only. So, in many cases, historical roots matter independently from other factors. This approaches goes back to Friedrich Carl von Savigny in 19th century Germany, but nowadays seems to be widely acknowledged among communitarian political philosophers such as Alasdair MacIntyre. The comprehensive morality, however, also must be taken into account. The values that go beyond public reason in the strict sense, as long as they depend on some vision of human good, are nevertheless supported by strong social commitment and engagement, oriented toward common good.[13]

13 Michael Sandel, for example, argues that direct reference to comprehensive views in civic discourse "could provide a stronger, not the weaker, basis for mutual respect. Rather than avoid the moral and religious convictions that our fellow citizens bring to public life, we should attend to them more directly – sometimes by challenging and contesting them, sometimes by listening to and learning from them" (Sandel 2010: 268).

For the sake of discussion, we might call the first two the contractarian sources of justification, whereas the last two are communitarian-conservative sources. Now, the key idea of this chapter is that those rival or alternative sources are not as rival and alternative as it has often been assumed. Of course, seeking to reconcile these traditions in one cohesive moral theory might be a wrongheaded project, but in this volume we deal with the philosophy of legal change. Thus, we are allowed (and I think obliged) to listen to the empirical world in which different strategies overlap and are being used simultaneously. In this limited and distinct sphere of enquiry, the different sources of justification might be integrated in one model of public reason and background culture working together. Whereas contractarian sources stand for public reason, communitarian-conservative sources belong to background culture. To explain why and in what sense I think the latter has an autonomous justificatory power, and how it stands toward public reason, I shall move to the next section.

## 3 Public reason and background culture: A model of legal change

### *3.1 Recognizing background culture*

At the first glance, the following picture appears to result from a political-liberal perspective: public reason, and legitimate democratic law coming from its exercise, sets the framework for citizenry activities. Some of those activities take place in the background culture, rooted in commitments coming from different religious or philosophical (in the broad sense of both terms) views. Therefore, the only sphere of interest in investigating legal change is public reason: the work of institutions is to improve the conditions of basic justice, liberties, and equal citizenship. If this were the right scheme, then the background culture, as regarding the deeper – philosophical and moral – identity of individuals and groups, would be out of the picture as a part of general conditions or circumstances in which law operates, not being at the same build into the very normativity of law, at the public level. Each citizen would naturally use his comprehensive views to fully justify laws *for himself*, but legal change as an institutional process would boil down to exercising public reason and realizing its values or urges in the changing conditions.

I think this would be too rushed. While there are public reason theorists who seem to offer such schemes (Gaus 2011: 481–487), Rawls takes a different path. As mentioned, the duty of civility obliges citizens to put forward public reasons to justify laws in the public political forum, but it does not bind in every possible social situation to be solved in legal terms. It is basic justice and constitutional essentials that are the subject of public reason and require the limitations of public justification. As Rawls writes, “[m]any if not the most political questions do not concern those fundamental matters, for example, much tax legislation and many laws regulating property; statutes protecting the environment and controlling pollution” (Rawls 1996: 214). As Rawls admits in the same passage, those and similar political questions may involve public reason, but in an indirect way. Although the line may be very blurry, this seems a right intuition: it makes space for justifications other that these of public justifiability, for open justification. Basing in it, one recognizes background culture as an inevitably justificatory component, at least of these laws which are not fully covered by the public reason but involve different concerns. Using such Rawlsian-inspired framework, we should see public reason and background culture as providing "checks and balances" for each other. Legal change can be seen as a result of an interplay between those two, and not limited exercise of public reason.

Recall that background culture is the sphere of social life where "many and diverse agencies and associations with their internal life reside within a framework of law that ensures the familiar liberties of thought and speech, and the right of free association" (Rawls 2001: 576). It can be said that recognizing these associations as having a say in justification of legal change acknowledges the communitarian element present in the later Rawls. According to this reading, different communities forming the society's background culture have their own normative and cultural traditions and they are entitled to introduce them into laws. Dealing with issues that do not directly regulate constitutional essentials or basic justice, the constraints of public justification do not apply directly, so comprehensive views are fully legitimate in justifying legal change. In constitutional/basic justice cases the legitimacy of comprehensive doctrines is provisional – one is obliged to reconcile comprehensive with public reasons, and offer the latter in due course (Rawls 2001: 591–593).

The approach I am proposing disagrees with Rawls and with political liberalism generally in two important points. First, according to the principle of open justification, the arguments coming from background culture (historical roots and comprehensive morality) should be recognized as having justificatory power. More precisely, citizens, when arguing from within their comprehensive views, should also be recognized as having equal civic standing.[14] Therefore, in my approach, the duty of civility requires not only trying to present one's arguments in publicly justifiable terms (which still is extremely important), but also trying to engage with others in a way that makes one able to recognize their comprehensive reasons as reasons, and not as mere arbitrary demands. Whereas in the Rawlsian version of the duty of civility the burden of proof seems to be on the one who is arguing (she must take pains to present her view in terms of public reason in due course), I propose to reverse it: the one who is denying a

14 The closest Rawls gets to recognizing the civic standing of citizens as individuals holding comprehensive doctrines is the idea of public justification (in a special, technical meaning different from this of political justification which, as I have said, equates with public justification in the sense put forth in this chapter). "Public justification happens when all the reasonable members of political society carry out a justification of the shared political conception by embedding it in their several reasonable comprehensive views. In this case, Reasonable citizens take one another into account as having reasonable comprehensive doctrines" (Rawls 1996: 387). But this clearly requires everyone endorsing the same political conception of justice (an overlapping consensus) which makes the recognition conditional and as fragile or unlikely as an overlapping consensus is.

justificatory force of a comprehensive argument should show why and how it threatens fundamental values protected by public reason. Second, one should take into account that background culture influences the way citizens interpret and apply public reason. As Gerald Gaus puts it:

> [C]omprehensive conceptions and the freestanding justification are apt to interact in complex ways. Once people are aware of their full range of values . . . even if they continue to affirm the conclusions of the freestanding argument they are apt to disagree on how its abstract principles are to be interpreted.
>
> (Gaus 2011: 42)

Therefore, one cannot separate those two spheres too sharply but rather see them as "diffusing" into one another.

### *3.2 Checks and balances*

Given what has been said above, legal change (perhaps including constitutional change) is best understood as a process of an interplay between contractarian (public justifiability and economic efficiency) and communitarian-conservative (historical roots and comprehensive morality) factors, each having an independent justificatory power. In this perspective, law is a device of social cooperation, certainly influenced by traditions and historically evolved practices, but at the same publicly rational and open to the current, actual needs of cooperating individuals and groups. It might be called the Open Justification Model (OJM).

Such an eclectic account on justification presupposes a likewise eclectic general vision of society, namely, neither as an organic whole (like in communitarian thinking), nor a mere association of independent individuals (like in contractarian thinking). The middle-ground idea is that of the social union of social unions which Rawls takes from Humboldt (Rawls 1974: 520–529). Members to this kind of community see the intrinsic value of cooperation and institutions securing it, but only insofar as it is at the same based on equal respect to each citizen. As I have already said in this chapter, if equal respect is to be taken seriously in a model of justification, it should acknowledge that citizens are inhabitants of "two cultures" at the same time. On the one hand, a citizen is committed to the political principles present in a constitution; on the other, she holds a comprehensive view, or at least partially comprehensive view, of some kind. Therefore a democratic, pluralistic society consists of many different communities at one level, and one political community at the other level, the latter governed not by a comprehensive conception, but by public reason. Yet the two spheres are not completely separate; public institutions do form the worldviews that citizens have, and citizens do form the institutions according to the worldviews they have (Rawls 2011: 90).

The OJM is aimed at reconciling the two spheres by recognizing each as providing "checks and balances" for the other. One example that may illustrate the proposed approach is the issue of European Civil Code, a project that once was aimed at embracing all European Union (EU) countries with a unified civil law system. Although the idea has a relatively long history, and did receive some support from politicians and scholars, nowadays it is officially abandoned by the European Commission. Instead, some soft law instruments have been introduced, like the Common Frame of Reference (Schmid 2012). Setting the details of EU law mechanisms aside, one might ask a more general question: why is such an ambitious project so unlikely to succeed in the near future? Certainly, assuming that the EU is a political community of some sort, a project for European Civil Code does not violate its public reason; the basic ideas of civic equality and individual autonomy would be protected, and member states would have to accept it one by one. Therefore, it seems that the question of justifiability of such a deep legal change cannot be resolved within public reasons only. Rather, one must look at the background culture – tradition, common views, and tendencies in society. Note that the argument here is not only of prudential nature: if the background culture in Europe is not ready for unification of civil law, and it seems it isn't, introducing a civil code would be an arbitrary imposition rather than legitimate development of the EU law.

Alternatively, the OJM allows and legitimizes volitive creation through law, as the idea of public reason presupposes. Thus, interventions in the background culture, if the latter significantly breaches the public values, are considered legitimate. Each case would be considered separately, and individual circumstances would heavily influence the particular decisions (say, of judges or legislators). As a general principle, when equal civic standing or some other fundamental value of public reason is fundamentally threatened by some practices in the background culture, then the public reason has a legitimate claim to change this through legal acts. Again, but this time due to prudential concerns, such acts should take into account the background culture they will appear in (like Goetzmann in this volume shows). Another influence that public reason surely has on background culture is the long-term one: as Rawls supposes, and common experience confirms, public institutions do have power to transform comprehensive worldviews present in the society, and some once revolutionary solutions (e.g. voting rights for women) are now more than obvious almost for everyone.[15]

### *3.3 The question of priority*

The serious trouble that OJM may face is the question of priority or ordering in justification. One of the hopes of public reason theory was to adjudicate different claims coming from various positions in a pluralistic society. If open justification

15 Rawls believes that this long-term impact of public reason on citizens' views would (as one might reasonably expect) lead to an overlapping consensus, that is, everyone affirming one political conception of justice (Rawls 1996: 164–168). Elsewhere (Rupniewski 2018), I argue that this is inconsistent with the Rawlsian idea of the burdens of judgement, and the idea of an overlapping consensus might be replaced by some weaker forms of civic bonds, social stability still being possible.

allows divergent reasons to be counted, is it able to provide a scheme of weighing them? Even in the original Rawlsian scheme the issue was not fully clear. In *Reply to Habermas*, he clearly stated that political (that is – public) justification is only *pro tanto*, and should be complemented by a full justification that every citizen is considered able to carry out for herself, according to the comprehensive doctrine that one has. Since "[t]the political conception gives no guidance in such questions", the political justification "may be overridden by citizens' comprehensive doctrines once all values are tallied up" (Rawls 1996: 386). The OJM is even more radical about it, since comprehensive doctrines may count as sources of justificatory reasons.

One solution (which would lead the OJM quite close to Rawls' political liberalism) would be that public justifiability is a necessary element of justification as far as constitutional essentials and basic justice are concerned. In other spheres (say, ordinary legislation), there is no such requirement, but since all laws must not violate constitutional essentials, the congruence of norms is assured. In this sense, a kind of priority of public justifiability is an element of the OJM.

There are, however, important issues that make a self-confident and self-constrained use of this idea in practice, particularly of legal change, very fragile. The analysis carried out in this chapter seems to confirm Kent Greenawalt's doubts:

> We should be suspicious of the idea that analysis of the conditions of liberal democracy in general will yield any fairly precise line between constitutional essentials and ordinary issues and will also yield some subtle demarcation of how far comprehensive views can figure in the development of positions based on public reasons. Perhaps on these points all liberal democracies are sufficiently similar, but I do not suppose that the constraints appropriate for a homogenous society like Sweden will necessarily be the same as those appropriate for a country as diverse and contentious as the United States.
>
> (Greenawalt 1995: 1317)

The reason why this suspicion seems right is that the interplay between public reason and background culture certainly takes place also at the highest level of constitutional essentials. Principles such as freedom of conscience or equality before the law are embodied differently in different times and places precisely because their content and its interpretation is heavily influenced by the relevant background culture.

## Conclusion

Despite possible doubts and shown weaknesses (that each conception inevitably contains), I argue that the Rawlsian-inspired framework, with its focus on the distinction between public reason and background culture is needed, not only for proper understanding of modern legal orders, but also for prudent politics of legal change therein. On the one hand, it shows that the face of contemporary processes is manifold, thus the respect and recognition of the background culture of a given democratic society is both a prudential necessity and a legitimate moral requirement. On the other hand, it hopefully gives intellectual tools to critically engage with the processes of legal change, in which the virtue of non-arbitrariness should be the first concern. If the latter claim is true, then the law that lacks justification, to a minimal sufficient degree and upon the OJM, automatically loses its legitimacy. The justification of law constitutes the necessary (but not sufficient) condition for its legitimacy, even when resting on reasons that not all citizens share. Although political justification is always open to controversies and counter-arguments, and in this sense may never be fully neutral, it constitutes non-arbitrariness, and thus opens a way to legitimacy, rather than closing it.

## References

Alexy, R. (2008) 'On the Concept and Nature of Law', *Ratio Juris*, 21(3), 281–299.

Chambers, S. (2010) 'Theories of Political Justification', *Philosophy Compass*, 5(11), 893–903.

Gaus, G. (2011) *The Order of Public Reason: A Theory of Freedom and Morality in a Diverse and Bounded World*. Cambridge: Cambridge University Press.

Gaus, G. and Vallier, K. (2009) 'The roles of religious conviction in a publicly justified polity: The implications of convergence, asymmetry and political institutions', *Journal of Law, Philosophy and Culture*, 35 (1–2), 51–76.

Greenawalt, K. (1995) 'Some Problems with Public Reason in John Rawls', *Political Liberalism' Loyola of Los Angeles Law Review*, 28, 1303–1377.

Finnis, J. (2011) *Reason in Action: Collected Essays, Volume One*. Oxford: Oxford University Press.

Freeman, S. (2004) 'Public Reason and Political Justifications', *Fordham L. Rev*, 72, 2021–2066.

Nussbaum, M. (2010) 'Veiled Threats?', *The New York Times*, The Opinion Pages, https://opinionator.blogs.nytimes.com/2010/07/11/veiled-threats/ [accessed 31/01/19].

Rawls, J. (1974) *A Theory of Justice*. Cambridge, MA, Harvard University Press.

Rawls, J. (1996) *Political Liberalism: With a New Introduction and the 'Reply to Habermas'*. New York, Columbia University Press.

Rawls, J. (2001) *Collected Papers*. Cambridge, MA, Harvard University Press.

Rupniewski, M. (2018) 'Citizenship, Community, and the Rule of Law: With or Without Consensus?' in M. Knoll, S. Snyder, and N. Simsek (eds) *New Perspectives on Distributive Justice*. Berlin and Boston, de Gruyter, 275–290.

Sandel, M. (2010) *Justice: What's the Right Thing to Do?* London, Penguin Books.

Schmid, D. (2012) '(Do) We Need a European Civil Code (?)', *Annual Survey of International & Comparative Law*, 18(1), 263–293.

Sen, A. (2010) *The Idea of Justice*. London, Penguin Books.

Shapiro, S. J. (2002) 'Authority' in J. Coleman and S. Shapiro (eds) *The Oxford Handbook of Jurisprudence & Philosophy of Law*. Oxford, Oxford University Press, 382–493.

Waldron, J. (1999) *The Dignity of Legislation*. Cambridge, Cambridge University Press.

Waldron, J. (2007) 'Public Reason and "Justification" in the Courtroom', *Journal of Law, Philosophy and Culture*, 1(1), 107–134.

Weithman, P. (2015) 'Legitimacy and the Project of Political Liberalism' in T. Brooks and M. Nussbaum (eds) *Rawls's Political Liberalism*. New York, Columbia University Press, 73–112.

Wendt, F. (forthcoming) 'Rescuing Public Justification from Public Reason Liberalism' in D. Sobel, P. Vallentyne, and S. Wall (eds) *Oxford Studies in Political Philosophy* 5, https://marcsandersfoundation.org/wp-content/uploads/Wendt_Rescuing-Public-Justification-from-Public-Reason-Liberalism.pdf [accessed 05/01/2019].

# 3 The moral, the political, and the legal

## Changing patterns of justification in a world of legal pluralization

*Eva Weiler*

## Introduction

In liberal democracies, the rule of law is secured by two elements: first, sovereignty and therewith legislation lies with the parliament as the representative of the people and their will; and second, the law's generality hinders misuse of this sovereignty as well as misuse of private power (see Neumann 1953: 80–85). Within this conception, changes of the law are legitimate when issued by the sovereign, i.e. the parliament, and the legitimacy of the decisions of parliament is measured by the inclusiveness of the political process, the quality of political deliberation in the public sphere etc. But sovereignty has its limits: the norms issued by the parliament are only permissible if they conform to the (written or unwritten) constitution – even the sovereign, even the political power is bound by the law.[1] The law itself is and has to be conservative, since legality and generality can only be guaranteed if every new norm is issued according to a given norm-setting process, prescribed by existing norms (Neumann 1953: 82, 86).

Rule of law, not of man – as the liberal republican tradition would have it, social and political relationships can be "tamed" when transferred into legal relationships. What shall be excluded by the generality of the law is the exercise of mere power, where power is defined as the ability to enforce one's own partial interest against the others' will by disposing over relevant resources (Weber 1980: 542ff). If the reason for entering into a political community is overcoming the state of mere power, that reason has to be fulfilled for each and every individual. Those who are excluded from the legal relationship, those whose status as a legal authority is constantly ignored, have no reason to be bound by the law (Kant 1977: 345, Niederberger 2009: 21f). Legal change would therefore have a double boundary: it cannot be the enforcement of a merely partial interest, and

1 Insofar as the sovereign can change the constitution itself this is only true for everyday legislation that can be subject to constitutional review; there cannot, strictly speaking, be any limit to sovereign political power. However, constant changes of the constitution or parts of it would lead to a severe loss of trust in the political power, since it would be proof of a lack of willingness to make itself accountable.

it cannot strip individuals or groups of individuals from their status as a potential rights-holder.

But formal generality does not guarantee that individuals or groups of individuals are safe from being discriminated against, as we know from several historical and current examples (see Neumann 1953, Gowder 2016). This is due to the fact that, first, even general norms can regulate issues so specific they only apply to certain individuals, and, second, social, economic, and cultural differences make it the case that applying general rules can mean very different things for different people. It is, as Anatole France stated in 1894, "the majestic quality of the law which prohibits the wealthy as well as the poor from sleeping under the bridges, from begging in the streets, and from steeling bread" (France 1910: 87). It is for this reason that democratic states have, on the one hand, a system of checks and balances and separation of powers, and, on the other hand, social systems that try to facilitate at least a minimum of social and political inclusion and security.

However, there appears to be a growing disappointment and discontent with liberal democratic systems. There are multiple reasons for that which shall not be explored here. In this chapter, I want to focus on a line of critique that questions the basis of the concept of liberal democratic states, namely its sovereignty, founded on the idea of *legal centralism*. The growing literature on *legal pluralism* is highly sceptical to the question of whether the legislative is in fact the only norm-setting body within the state and whether a separation of powers as envisaged by the ideal of the republican state can be achieved to a satisfactory degree. There are, pluralists claim, private actors like corporations and associations, but also collective actors like cultural or religious communities, especially in former colonies, that do effectively issue legal norms. Adding to this, state-law increasingly conflicts with international and transnational law as well as with the norms of international private actors such as corporations, banks, and non-governmental organizations (see Berman 2007, Michaels 2009, Tamanaha 2011, Meder 2015).

To give an account of legal change we must explain the conception of law we refer to as well as the criteria with which we are judging the legitimacy of legal norms and/or legal orders. As a critique of legal centralism, the account of legal pluralism has, unsurprisingly, an understanding of the law and of what makes legal norms legitimate that differs from the one given above. In fact, I want to claim that it is this understanding of the law as evolving out of society as an expression of both the lifeworld and the normative principles operating within a legal community (see Gailhofer 2016, Meder 2015), which is the starting point of a *political* endeavour to effectively change the functioning of the law itself. Thus, those who do not understand the pluralization of norm-setting authorities as a perversion of the law hold a normative claim: since liberal democracies as we know them might not fulfil the promise of democratic representation, either in general or for certain groups, a pluralization of norm-setting actors might actually lead to a democratization of those states.

This is especially the case in post-colonial societies, where the official legal system is often less effective than the non-official systems and sometimes regarded as illegitimate or ill-suited for the lifeworld of those subject to it (see Tamanaha 2011, Berman 2007). Legal pluralists are therefore often promoting a stronger role of legal sociology and legal anthropology for legal theory, sometimes negating the distinction between the normative and the empirical, or grounding the normative in social facts (see Meder 2015, Seinecke 2015, Shah 2014).

Obviously, there are strong implications for the question of legal changes, if the pluralistic model is right. Whereas the centralized model can perceive of legal changes only as changes issued by parliament or within the well-defined boundaries of judicial discretion, for the pluralistic model changes are much more likely to occur within the every-day practice of certain groups or actors, which are then often taken up by the judiciary and molded into state law. Likewise, the legitimacy of legal change within the centralized model depends on the well functioning of political and legal procedures, and can therefore be identified with legality as such, whereas legitimacy in the pluralistic model would depend to a greater extent on the adequacy of the rules to the judgements and practices of those subject to them.

In this chapter, I want to claim that this conception of legitimacy ultimately presupposes either a shared understanding of the common good or the validity of moral claims as such. The conception of pluralism I am going to examine in section 3 of this chapter has, I want to ague, a liberal understanding of the (state) law as functioning as mediation or management between co-existing, relatively autonomous legal entities. Law as mediation is only convincing if there is a common standard – the common good or inherently given normative standards of functional systems – to judge by. The conception of pluralism I am examining in section 4 focuses on presumed moral laws; there has to be a plurality of legal entities because every moral or cultural community is inherently valuable. This conception, which is almost libertarian in effect, cannot, I want to claim, be justified in a post-metaphysical world and it is bound to produce manifold normative conflicts. Thus, both conceptions of pluralism are, despite making valid points, unconvincing in light of the problem they want to solve – the pluralization of legal bodies and normative orders. To demonstrate this, I will first outline what I take to be the normative foundation of the law, namely a neo-republican account of non-domination (section 1). I will then go on to examine the two conceptions of pluralism, one given by Stephan Meder in his book *Doppelte Körper im Recht* (section 2), the other given in an examination of the rulings of the Inter-American Human Rights Court by Dina Shelton (section 3). Since I take the pluralists to make important observations from an empirical perspective, I will be sympathetic to the account of Meder which I deem to be partly compatible with the concept of non-domination.

The second account, observed in the findings of Shelton but also in theories like those of Werner Menski, Masaji Chiba, Brian Tamanaha, and Prakash Shah, shares at least one element with Meder – the emphasis on a major, more independent role of the judiciary. As I will argue, it is especially these accounts that have an agenda not only to change certain norms within the existing order, but also to change, if possible, the order as a whole. The request for change stems from a justified critique of the current situation within legal orders, but the direction chosen leads, I want to demonstrate, to a moralization and politization of the law that might be detrimental to the law's normative foundation and its function to replace power with binding norms. I will conclude with a reaffirmation of the principle of non-domination as the criterion for the legitimacy of both the legal order as a whole and of legal change. As a last step, I will concretize this principle with an account of the rule of law based on equality as given by Paul Gowder, to describe which kind of reasoning we might want to term "legal" and which to exclude from legal-political arguments.

## 1 Two concepts of political freedom

Political freedom both in the centralistic and the pluralistic perspective can be linked to the concept of political self-determination. Within the liberal tradition, starting with Locke, the political state is understood as emerging out of a social contract, based on more or less extensive (liberal) fundamental rights that have to be secured within the political community. The original texts of social contracts might or might not have had a concept of political rights and political participation (see Tuck 2015), but, especially since the 20th century, democracy cannot be detached from the idea of a political community determining its own laws and ways of life. There have of course been authors challenging this conception of freedom on the grounds that first, this goal cannot be achieved within today's complex societies and second, it is normatively problematic with regard to other groups or societies that might be strongly affected by sovereign decisions (see Kelsen 2006, 2008). Accounts from critical theory, radical democracy, and cosmopolitanism have, among others, pointed to the fact that within monopoly capitalism economic power cannot be controlled anymore and so the rule of law gets perverted (see Neumann 1953), that there is no such thing as a common will but only agonistic forces within society (see Mouffe & Laclau 2012), or that national self-determination is highly problematic in a globalized world (see Held 2010, Niederberger 2009).

One answer to this critique was to rethink the notion of freedom that shall be enabled and secured by political communities with the notion of non-domination, coined by Philip Pettit (1997). For accounts of non-domination, the liberal tradition that associates freedom with the exercise of liberal rights and political self-determination of sovereign nations becomes problematic insofar as it stresses unilateral behaviour towards others. The normative problem lying at the basis of non-domination with regard to the law is that the law can be *enforced*. Since the law is something that can be forced onto others, it has to be justified to them. However, even a justification that has come about in a democratic process can become incomprehensible over time, or for a newly constituted group – therefore there have to be mechanisms to contest and possibly change the existing law (see Pettit 2012, Niederberger 2009, 2011).

The concept of non-domination is a gradual one; there can be more or less arbitrary imposition of force and there can be more or less room for possibly dominating relations. Minimizing them would mean first establishing rules and a respective institutional setting, but it would go on to emphasize that the rules themselves and the authorities interpreting and executing them would have to have the least "arbitrary" form possible – legal norms and competencies have to be clear and transparent, i.e. there should be as little room for discretionary power as possible.

The best we can do to minimize arbitrariness and establish non-domination is of course to build a republic, implement a strong separation of powers and strong democratic mechanisms, checking on the application of norms through contestation, making sure that officials are being held accountable for any actions deviating from their prescribed competency, and enabling citizens to actively participate in political processes. The main institutional feature of non-domination would be that citizens are in control, that they can shape the outcomes of political processes by means of contestation, political participation, vote etc. (for a more extensive account see Niederberger 2009: Chapter 4).

As Philip Pettit emphasizes, non-domination is not judged by the legal order being just or being a just representation of "the people‘s will" (Pettit 2012: 60). Legitimacy in this account is not defined by the question whether the people as a whole could in principle agree to certain settings, processes, or acts, but whether these settings and processes have been in accordance with the ideal of non-domination in how they were brought about. Note that this also means that a given regime can become legitimate even when at its beginning it wasn't. We do have good reasons to accept even an unjust and partly illegitimate system as long as its rules are binding on all sides and as long as there are mechanisms in place to change it over time. In fact, as there will always be laws and regulations that we will deem to be unjust and thereby judge "dominating" by their content or effects, it is of high importance that we look for the legitimacy of the regime, not for the quality of each of its norms (Pettit 2012: 60).

With its emphasis on the separation of powers and strict limits to legal discretion, the neo-republican account is of course a proto-type of legal centralism. It is also based on the assumption of a vast and "deep" pluralism that cannot be overcome by reference to a shared general will or a shared understanding of justice (see Niederberger 2009: Chapter 2). Defining political freedom as non-domination is grounded in the assumption that there is neither a general will that exceeds the merely formal criterion of a constituted legislative nor any grounding conditions of justice that could be defined prior to the legislative process to determine which acts of coercion are justified.

## 2 Pluralism: Democratization and control?

As an account of legal centralism, the neo-republican concept of non-domination might seem to be incompatible with any normative account of legal pluralism. Just as an account that appears to stress self-determination, possibly without accounting for the dominating relation between self-determined communities, pluralism might appear incompatible with non-domination. I want to claim, however, that we might find interpretations of pluralist's accounts that are compatible with non-domination. If so, we could take on the empirical diagnosis given by pluralists and then incorporate the normative claims for democratization of both the creation and alteration of the law into the account of non-domination.

In his book *Doppelte Körper im Recht* (Meder 2015),[2] Stephan Meder develops an account of pluralism based on the theories of German 19th century authors Otto Giercke and Friedrich Karl von Savigny as well as British early 20th century, Harold Laski and Ernest Barker. In his reading of the pluralist tradition and his description of actual legal practices, Meder claims that instead of focusing exclusively on the ideal system to regulate relationships between agents, more weight should be given to how legal rules are *de facto* often created (see Meder 2015: Chapter 9). Legal rules are, according to Meder, more often than not the result of a practice of those subject to them, eventually turned into "proper" law by state authorities, that still have priority in the case of conflict between non-state legal entities (Meder 2015: 168). Apart from that, there are a variety of norms being set, first, by private actors who do have officially granted norm-setting competencies and, second, by international and transnational legal entities like the European Union.

There is, following Meder, both a problematic and a normatively valuable aspect to the fact of the plurality of legal sources. Especially in the area of private and contract law, powerful private actors are veiling as mere contracts what should actually be recognized as legal norms; when Google issues general terms and conditions, agreeing to them cannot be described as an exercise of private autonomy without severely distorting this concept (Meder 2015: 245). There is no possibility to negotiate the terms agreed to and only one party has the status to change the terms and conditions – which makes it a unilateral, uncontrolled exercise of legal competence. Alternatively, the legal autonomy of cooperatives, municipalities, and cities gives them the opportunity of self-regulation. Since smaller units are better suited to represent their members' interests, this autonomy can facilitate more democratic decision-making. But *self-regulation* does not refer to *self-determination* as much as to the exercise of control. By giving norm-setting capacity to smaller units, the norm-setting competence of bigger units is limited (Meder 2015: 152ff). Apart from the more empirical claim for a limitation of power through the dispersion of it, Meder advocates a concept of "inner constitutionalization" of norm-setting entities. Like the state, legal bodies should be constituted in a way that gives effect to democratic principles such as transparency and responsiveness (Meder 2015: 31f, 249ff). Cooperatives would in many cases already at least partly fulfill these criteria; the codes of Corporate Governance would be a further example as well as Rough Consensus and Running Code, the consent systems used to create new systems and codes on the internet (Meder 2015: 263ff).

2 The title "Double bodies in law" is a reference to Horowicz' *The Kings Two Bodies.*

Meder's emphasis on the means of democratic control like transparence, participation, and the possibilities of appeal (Meder 2015: 269) read like a paraphrase of Pettit's account of non-domination. One could describe his account of pluralism as the attempt to flesh out a political and legal order under the conditions of the growing pluralization and the weakening of the sovereignty of nation states according to the principle of non-domination. The focus on the creation and the ever-changing character of the law would fit with Pettit's gradual picture of non-domination and with the refusal of neo-republican thought to link the concept of freedom to that of self-determination and justice.

Coming back to the question of legal change, the combined accounts would read as follows: according to the concept of non-domination, the law is a mechanism to control power, comprising two elements. First, the formal element of a set of procedures to ensure that the equal status of each and every individual is secured in the decision-making process and, even more importantly, that there are mechanisms for contestation so that rulings that have dominating effects can be renegotiated. Negotiation is not formal. Therefore, there has to be a second element in place, namely mechanisms and procedures to deliberate the content of political and legal decisions and their effects. Accordingly, legal changes would be legitimate if they are brought about within the formal mechanisms agreed on and if the decision-making process has been inclusive to respect the equal status of each and every individual. A legal *order* is legitimate, if it provides contestation mechanisms so that dominating effects that have not been foreseen or that occur due to external changes can be addressed. Questions of justice, shared values, etc. arise only within the deliberative process. What is important about them is that while they can be raised and discussed within the public and political sphere, the legitimacy of the outcome does not depend on the content but on the process that it has been reached by. Meder's version of pluralism sketched out above would fit with this account and complement it in a world of pluralization of legal bodies; giving relative legal autonomy to certain agents might facilitate effective control and strengthen democratic processes. His account could even be understood as compatible with legal centralism – Meder needs the figure of the state as the last arbiter because he is well aware of the potential "tyranny of groups" (see Meder 2015: 195). We need the state to secure fundamental rights that might be threatened by smaller collective units.

It is the concept of the arbiter that distinguishes Meder's account from legal centralism and brings him closer to two developments of the law and legal pluralism that are incompatible with non-domination. The pluralism described so far in this text would consist mostly in granting a norm-setting competence within rather well-defined limits to certain actors. To strengthen the role of the judiciary and to conceive of the state and its institutions as arbiter, moderator, or management (Meder 2015: 15) is only possible if we presuppose a neutral ground, i.e. a common good, or the possibility of proving the validity of moral norms that are brought before the courts because of their *limited* reach (being moral norms for only *this* religious/cultural group within a plurality of groups).

Addressing change is one of the main concerns of legal pluralism, especially those theories that argue from a standpoint of either international legal developments or from post-colonial societies want to point to the fact that the given legal order/s is/are not suited to reflect the changing functioning and self-perception of the international sphere or post-colonial societies. In the next section I want to argue that what these accounts are ultimately promoting might amount to a qualitative change of the law itself – or, as I want to argue, that what they are ultimately talking about pertains to the sphere of morals and politics, not to law.[3]

## 3 Pluralism: Moralization and politization of the law?

Until now, what I have been describing could be termed changes *within* the law – I always started from the assumption that there is something like a constitutional state and a legislative process that, even in the case of law that is recognized subsequently, can determine what the law is by reference to pre-existing legal norms. There are three sometimes distinct and sometimes interconnected changes in the legal context that could be termed changes *of* the law, where the change would refer to a qualitative alteration of the function and concept of the law. All of them, I want to argue, are concerned with changing existing norms and legal orders that are perceived as morally wrong or too rigid to cope with the problems of today's world. The first one, which I will name only briefly, is what could be called the escape from the law: international economic arbitration that creates a sphere that is regulated by those party to it, but not controlled by political power (Fischer-Lescano & Teubner 2004). This development might be the most problematic one; it is also the most silent one, taking place fairly unnoticed. It points to institutional and democratic deficits at the transnational level and will most probably either result in the establishment of something like an actual transnational (economic) legal order or continue to be power-politics veiled by legal phrasing.

The second development could be called the moralization of the law. It is the, often strategic. use of the language of rights to achieve certain societal or political results. I call it moralization because it alludes not necessarily to existing law but to moral rights or frames the granting of existing (human) rights as a moral issue (see Niederberger 2014). The politization takes place at the institutional level: courts taking up the task of determining which (moral) claim should be given effect to are ultimately making political decisions. Both these aspects become most clear where they are meant to remedy politically dysfunctional systems with a weak enforcement of fundamental rights. But they are also brought up in the discussion about allowing cultural or religious minorities to use their legal norms within European societies (see Shah 2014).

To illustrate what I mean by moralization and politization, I want to shortly outline a case ruled by the Inter-American Court for Human Rights (IACHR). In her paper on "The Inter-American Human Rights Law of Indigenous

3 I do not want to claim that a clear distinction between those three notions is always possible, I just want to draw attention to different rationales that are linked to them.

Peoples" Dinah Shelton (2013) describes the development of human rights law in America and cites some of the most important rulings of the IACHR that try to strengthen indigenous communities against state atrocities. To give effect to the rights that could help shield them against violation, the Commission and the IACHR adopted "several overriding principles of interpretation to give effect to what they see as the object and purpose of the human rights instruments they apply". Among those doctrines are an "evolutionary approach or rule of dynamic interpretation", part of which is the "application of the American Declaration and 'other international acts of the same nature' as well as 'other rights or guarantees that are inherent in the human personality or derived from representative democracy as a form of government'" (Shelton 2013: 943f). The first development with a major effect on the status of indigenous peoples was a series of court rulings that lead to the recognition of a broadened understanding of the legal term "property" as used in article 21 of the American Convention on Human Rights. An "originalist" reading would have meant limiting the term to private property and therewith excluding communal ownership as practiced by indigenous peoples. Although communal ownership is recognized as a form of property in most constitutions of the signatory states of the Convention on Human Rights, the court referred to the International Labour Organization (ILO) Convention no. 169 to decide that "property" in Article 21 must be understood to include communal property to be in accordance with other international law (Shelton 2013: 945, 954).

The second development with a strong effect on indigenous rights is the understanding of property as a culturally defined term. To further strengthen the right to property and indigenous' claims to the restitution and acknowledgement of their property, the Commission and the Court have developed a line of argument that directly links the right to property to the right to culture. The right to culture is provided as part of the right to self-determination, stated in the United Nations Declaration on the Rights of Indigenous Peoples, so the argument starts from the right to self-determination, picks out the right to determine one's own culture, and then identifies the ancestral land of indigenous' peoples as an indispensable element of those peoples' cultural identity (Shelton 2013: 957).

There are two tendencies within international human rights law that foster such a development. First, one could argue, as soon as the IACHR adopts an "evolutionary approach or rule of dynamic interpretation" it is bound to "make sense" of legal terms, rationales etc. in a way that allows for a coherent understanding of the body of international human rights law. "Finding" underlying principles and "harmonizing" norms will almost certainly lead to a broadened normative understanding of the respective principles and norms that have been enacted for specific contexts by specific actors with a specific legal practice and will therefore be "narrower" in their original meaning and scope. Second, the Commission and Court are trying to remedy a situation where states are regularly violating basic rights of citizens and minorities – i.e. where the political control of state and private actors and institutions is weak. The law has become the most effective way to do politics, which is exactly what the Court has come to do.

To do so, the Court and those who come before it have adopted a moral rights language. The rationale behind this language is no longer to determine legal competence and to apply the norms that have been set by democratic governments with a certain intent, meaning, and scope. It is about *moral claims* of the individual or certain groups that are deemed to be legitimate by reference to the *moral status* of the individual or group.

This change of rationale has a major effect on democracy: self-determination as the Court uses it is shifted from political self-determination that would include the *political and legal competence* to determine the relevant areas of one's own political community, to a conception of the *maintenance* of an *authentic cultural identity*. Similarly, the concept of democracy is no longer based on political rights, political institutions, and political procedures to facilitate the negotiation of claims and interests brought forward in the social and political realm. In the Court's understanding, democracy means that everyone or every group gets their interests to be *effectively* heard *as their particular interests*. The institution to ensure this representation is, consequently, not the parliament but the court.

The conception of legal change this account is based on is one of the appropriateness of legal rulings in light of certain moral norms and principles and an assumed common good – in this case, the common good of the international community, stated in human rights law. It can still be regarded as a positivist understanding of the law in a Dworkinian sense (see Dworkin 1982). However, in a multi-level jurisdiction the political element of the law emphasized by Dworkin becomes even more clear and even more problematic. Lawyers must construct the reality of indigenous groups – or, in the European case, of religious or cultural groups – the overall reality of the political community those groups live in, and they have to (re)construct the moral and political basis to judge the inadequacy of existing legal norms and rulings and to prove the adequacy of the change.

One does not have to deny the fact that judges and lawyers cannot but interpret the norms they are dealing with to understand that adopting an "evolutionary approach or rule of dynamic interpretation" (Shelton 2013: 943), where the basis of that interpretation are moral reasons, could in the end be detrimental to the legal sphere. If the law is a means to create binding decisions that are backed by force but not brought about by force, the underlying condition that has been stated over and over again in a long tradition of republican thought is the non-partiality of the legal ruling. There is no reason to accept a norm or ruling as binding that has been imposed unilaterally or is grounded on reasons incomprehensible to one of the parties. The concept of an impartial *judge* only makes sense if there is a "neutral ground", i.e. a shared understanding of justice. When Locke, for example, evokes that figure he does so against the background of *natural law* (Locke 2004: 351). However, if we do not believe in natural law, the "impartial judge" can only be understood as the judge who applies norms that have been brought about in an impartial manner. Impartiality in a non-metaphysical world belongs to the political process where it is translated into equal status of each and every person – something we won't find in Locke, where the status of a person is determined by her rationality (Locke 2004: 309).

The recourse to moral reasoning in a situation of the pluralization of both legal bodies and normative orders can therefore not be convincing. It operates with an account of plurality that is bound to fail for logical reasons: in the absence of a shared universal moral order, every moral claim brought up in court is but a partial reason that claims validity *because of its partiality*. Certain reasons shall apply because they belong to a certain group and this group only (see Shah 2014, Shelton 2013). But if I take my own law or, for that matter, my own moral claims to be the only valid or decisive claims, even just for a specific situation, then "law" or "morals" stop at my border, be it physical or political. If the law or moral reasoning is bound to the limits of a group's cultural definition of it, an outsider who does not share the underlying values or definitions has no reason to regard them as binding – unless he voluntarily recognizes them as valid claims (Kelsen 2008: 145). Legal decisions based on moral claims could therefore either be perceived as the illegitimate enforcement of only partial claims and be rejected – as has been the case in a 2011 ruling of the IACHR against Brazil, after which Brazil suspended its payments to the Commission and the participation in the Court for one year (MercoPress 2011); or, they depend on the goodwill of those recognizing them. Politicizing the law in this way will most likely erode its binding force and lead to more conflict.[4]

## Conclusion

In his book *The Rule of Law in the Real World*, Paul Gowder gives an account of the rule of law based on equality (Gowder 2016). Gowder shares one important element of critique with the pluralists, namely that the rule of law as a principle of mere formal generality is blind to the effects legal norms may have on different groups of people. His definition of the rule of law therefore broadens the concept of generality: to be general, a norm must not presuppose that any of the parties involved or affected by a norm issued in parliament or ruled by in court is inferior to any of the other parties (Gowder 2016: 29ff). Equality with regard to the law is defined as equal access to the law and equal control of it. Everybody has to be able to take part in those procedures that bring about or inform legislation and everybody has to be able to contest breaches of the law or effects of it that lead to an inequality and are, therefore, dominating (Gowder 2016: 58ff, 142). This has an important consequence for the reasons that can be given within the legal realm. It does not exclude exceptions or special norms for specific groups – it might even demand them to facilitate actual equality. Yet, it does exclude claims that are based on reasons that are reasons only for certain groups, such as religious

4 I don't want to argue against all legal practices involving the concept of the "impartial judge". The procedures of reconciliation practiced in African customary law can be practicable in a number of cases – as long as the respective communities are relatively homogenous and as long as the cases are not "hard cases" (see Ndulo 2011).

or cultural reasons. That does, of course, not mean that those reasons are not and could not be the basis for legislation. But the process of legislation is a *political* one; the fight for change of certain legal norms, a new legislation, or an alteration of the legal order or parts of it has to be a political one as well.

If we take Gowder's account of the rule of law as a descriptive account, we could say that any situations that involve partial reasons are in fact *political* situations. Indigenous groups as well as religious or cultural groups in Europe or even big corporations trying to implement their norms fight a political fight for the recognition of their causes or the effective enforcement of their interests. The question that could be raised in cases like those of certain indigenous populations in South America or the Afro-American population Gowder is referring to is therefore also a political one: if we can demonstrate that these groups are constantly excluded from political and legislative processes, if they are constantly prevented from access to and control of the law, then there is no normative reason for these groups to regard themselves to be bound by the law. In such cases, as well as with regard to the more or less uncontrolled legal power of economic agents, political resistance would be legitimate.

Thus, pluralism can teach us to see the legal and political power some agents have or lack, but, I want to maintain, it cannot provide us with a convincing conception of either the creation or the alteration of legal norms or legal orders. Neither the reference to a common good nor the – in fact deeply liberal – claim to accept partial moral reasons for their partiality can be justified in a non-metaphysical, plural world where agents cannot but affect and thereby possibly dominate each other in multiple ways. To presuppose a common good will have paternalistic effects (Niederberger 2009: 89ff), shielding communities from certain legal changes and facilitating others, whereas the change brought about by the enforcement of partial interests might be dominating towards others, both with regard to single rulings and to structural changes. But it is not only the paternalizing or dominating effects of legislation and legal rulings that are problematic. It is also the fact that, within a globalized, pluralistic world, alluding to the common good (that can, contrasted against a global background, only be partial) or to partial moral reasons as a justification of the *law* deprives the law of its binding force. This binding force is the result of inclusive political processes, i.e. of the way legal rules are created. In a pluralistic world, it cannot be the result of a just outcome – not until we politically settle on a definition of what the word "just" would entail and translate it into institutions and legal norms that can be constantly contested.

## References

Berman, P. S. (2007) 'Global Legal Pluralism', *Southern California Review*, 80, 1156–1237.

Dworkin, R. (1982) 'Law as Interpretation', *Critical Inquiry*, 9 (1), 179–200.

Fischer-Lescano, A. and Teubner, G. (2004) 'Regime-Collisions: The Vain Search for Legal Unity in the Fragmentation of Global Law', *Michigan Journal of International Law*, 25 (4), 999–1046.

France, A. (1910) *The Red Lily*. New York, Current Literature Publishing Company.

Gailhofer, P. (2016) *Rechtspluralismus und Rechtsgeltung*. Baden-Baden, Nomos.
Gowder, P. (2016) *The Rule of Law in the Real World*. New York, Cambridge University Press.
Held, D. (2010) *Cosmopolitanism. Ideals and Realities*. Cambridge, Polity Press.
Kant, I. (1977) *Metaphysische Anfangsgründe der Rechtslehre*. Frankfurt am Main, Suhrkamp Verlag.
Kelsen, H. (2006) 'Vom Wesen und Wert der Demokratie', in Hans Kelsen (ed.), *Verteidigung der Demokratie*, Tübingen, Mohr Siebeck.
Kelsen, H. (2008) *Reine Rechtslehre*. Tübingen, Mohr Siebeck.
Locke, J. (2004) *Two Treatises of Government*. Princeton, Princeton University Press.
Meder, S. (2015) *Doppelte Körper im Recht*. Tübingen, Mohr Siebeck.
Merco Press (2011) 'Brazil furious with Human Right Commission decision cuts all relations', 20 April, http://en.mercopress.com/2011/04/30/brazil-furious-with-human-rights-commission-decision-cuts-all-relations [accessed 8.23.2018].
Michaels, R. (2009) 'Global Legal Pluralism', *Annual Review of Law & Social Science*, 5, 1–35.
Mouffe, Ch. and Laclau, E. (2012) *Hegemonie und radikale Demokratie. Zur Dekonstruktion des Marxismus*. Wien, Passagen Verlag.
Ndulo, M. (2011) 'African Customary Law, Customs, and Women's Rights', *Indiana Journal of Global Legal Studies*, 18 (1), 87–120.
Neumann, F. (1953) 'Zum Begriff der politischen Freiheit', in Franz Neumann (ed.) (1967) *Demokratischer und autoritärer Staat*, Frankfurt am Main, Europäische Verlagsanstalt.
Niederberger, A. (2009) *Demokratie unter Bedingungen der Weltgesellschaft? Normative Grundlagen legitimer Herrschaft in einer globalen politischen Ordnung*. Berlin, New York, De Gruyter.
Niederberger, A. (2011) 'Freiheit und Recht. Zur philosophischen Bedeutung der Demokratie', *Philosophisches Jahrbuch*, 18 (1), 21–38.
Niederberger, A. (2014) 'Are Human Rights Moral Rights?', in Mattihas Lutz-Bachmann and Amos Nascimento (eds), *Human Rights, Human Dignity, and Cosmopolitan Ideals. Essays on Critical Theory and Human Rights*. London, Routledge.
Pettit, P. (1997) *Republicanism. A Theory of Freedom and Government*. Oxford, Oxford University Press.
Pettit, P. (2012) 'Legitimacy and Justice in Republican Perspective', *Current Legal Problems*, 65, 59–82.
Seinecke, R. (2015) *Das Recht des Rechtspluralismus*. Tübingen, Mohr Siebeck.
Shah, P. (2014) *Legal Pluralism in Conflict. Coping with Cultural Diversity in Law*. New York, Routledge.
Shelton, D. (2013) 'The Inter-American Human Rights Law of Indigenous Peoples', *University of Hawai'i Law Review*, 35, 937–982.
Tamanaha, B. Z. (2011) 'The Rule of Law and Legal Pluralism in Development', *Hague Journal on the Rule of Law*, 3 (10), 1–17.
Tuck, R. (2015) *The Sleeping Sovereign*. Cambridge, Cambridge University Press.
Weber, M. (1980) *Wirtschaft und Gesellschaft. Grundriss der verstehenden Soziologie*. Tübingen, Mohr Siebeck.

# 4 Human rights

## Desiderata of a theory of change

*Stephen Riley*

### Introduction

A less explored challenge for human rights theory is to provide a theory of change. Law makers and judges need to make human rights responsive to new circumstances and emerging threats. They cannot, however, simply create new human rights or radically alter our institutional arrangements without sound justification. There needs to be principled continuity in both the identification of human rights and in our institutional approaches to them. This chapter analyses the grounds for change amongst human rights and the theoretical context in which such an analysis must take place.

Human rights law bears similarities and dissimilarities to other fields of law. Societies create and amend law to accurately reflect and govern their practices. Equally, rapid radical change in any field of law is undesirable in the light of law's coordinating function. Unlike other fields of law, however, calling for change in human rights is to face resistance on specific practical and principled grounds. Human rights practice is established and tolerably successful, or at least sufficiently successful to make us hesitant about root-and-branch reform. Theories of human rights posit an underlying principle guiding the development and interpretation of the law, a foundational principle which may well be ambiguous about the possibility and nature of change. Indeed (as we will see) there is already considerable pressure towards the narrowing or reducing of the scope of human rights rather than expanding them, arguments grounded in the distinctive origin and foundations of human rights.

In this chapter I argue that change is properly conceptualised on the basis of commitment to cosmopolitan public reason but also responsiveness to threats to the human condition. I argue that other competing human rights theories which seek to justify only the *status quo* are theoretically incoherent. And I conclude that, given pressing drivers of change, there is no alternative but to develop, on the basis of certain desiderata, a revised, dynamic, and substantial account of human rights and their institutional realisation. Section 1 gives examples of the justifications for change in human rights. Section 2 provides an outline, then criticism, of "rationalisation" as a more restrictive position on change. Section 3 moves to a more positive concern with the desiderata of a theory of change.

## 1 Drivers of change

Three models of change will serve here as possible reasons for, or drivers of, legal change. I call these sociological change, institutional change, and existential change. The first requires a change in the substance and scope of human rights law. The second requires rethinking the institutions overseeing human rights. The third requires constitutive change in the international order, change in institutions, *and* change in the substance of human rights to maintain the very possibility of human rights. These models can overlap. And these are not necessarily uniquely significant for human rights. Nevertheless, they are important classes of reasons for changes to the fabric, the governance, or the implementation of human rights. In each case, I argue, certain kinds of demands for "fidelity" to existing conceptions and practices of human rights are inappropriate or indefensible.

First, *sociological change* can be thought of as change in the practices that the law was intended to govern. This can denote changes in positive morality where, for example, certain practices cease to be perceived as sufficiently wrongful to merit criminalisation. Sociological change also denotes fundamentally practical or technological phenomena whereby certain social practices come into existence or go out of existence. As an example of sociological change we can consider the law of privacy. The very idea of privacy has been mutating because of our relationship with information technology, the governance of data, and the breaking down of a strict division between public and private authority. Human rights laws, in turn, have been radically changed by a revolution in our relationship with privacy. Indeed, human rights law has been used to expand the protection of privacy in systems where the law has been under-developed, for instance in the UK and US where explicit constitutional provisions were otherwise absent (Solove & Schwartz 2014). But the substantive human rights law in this area remains orientated to a pre-technological conception of state-based threats to private correspondence and is orientated towards state intrusion into the physical private sphere. The typical text of the law in this area speaks of protecting "correspondence" and speaks of the sphere of "family life" as if it were a closed physical, social, and informational space. The law of Article 8 of the European Convention on Human Rights is amongst the most complex areas of Convention law, covering much that is unexpected, and failing to cover practices we might have expected (Wheeler 2017). The law of the European Union (EU) focuses on official use of data but until recently has done so in relative isolation from widespread social practices relating to the sharing of private information (European Commission 2017) and even now fails to cohere with wider changes in our conception of the private and the private sphere. These laws, then, fail to match the sociological reality that they are intended to govern. We cannot expect human rights to be offer a timeless expression of a right to privacy – rights and privacy are diachronic – but we can expect our existing laws and institutions to be adapted or reformed to map substantial sociological change.

How should we change the law to better reflect these challenges? Fidelity to the *idea* of the human right promulgated in 1948 would be wrong-headed if construed as slavish adherence to the *text* of the Universal Declaration of Human Rights (UDHR) of 1948. Human rights are intended to be the positive legal correlates of underlying principles able to guide regulative and constitutive change in the face of radical challenges. Such principled interpretation would require us to rethink our expression of the right for the twenty-first century. From this perspective, there is no principled barrier to reform of the human rights law relating to privacy beyond those normally relevant to law reform (i.e. avoiding excessively frequent change). On the contrary, there are good reasons for systematic reform of the substance of positive law. What is required is a move towards data protection principles on the one hand and the presumption of innocence on the other. We need to link privacy and data in way that reflects the technological conditions we inhabit (see Polčák & Svantesson 2017). And we need to link privacy and protection against abuse of our online activities; in particular we need assurance that the tendencies of modern governments to collect and farm data are checked in a way consonant with the presumption that we are free citizens, not objects of suspicion (Kerr & Earle 2013). In essence, the underlying sociology that gives the law its meaning and function has changed, and so too must the fabric of human rights law.

Second, *institutional change* relates to the need for reform of our human rights institutions to confront novel and acute intra-statal challenges, challenges that have become abundant and pressing in Europe and beyond. Mass migration, allied to frequent related humanitarian emergencies and compounded by poor distribution of responsibilities between states, is a human rights crisis. Human rights *laws* are engaged at the level of basic humanitarian entitlements, treatment in detention and processing, and in social and economic rights including citizenship. Human rights *institutions* are not built to regulate at this level of complexity. The European Court of Human Rights (ECtHR) has been able to adjudicate on only a slim cross-section of these issues (Dembour 2015). The division of competence and normative focus between the ECtHR (with civil and political rights) and the EU's contingent concerns with welfare and borders (derivative of its economic functions) only obscures a solution. The necessary change lies in the question of subsidiarity in the widest sense: identifying who can best solve problems and how power can be best distributed. Rethinking the problem through subsidiarity might yield a clearer drive for states themselves to better deal with migration, it might demand a novel institutional arrangement, and it might require better international cooperation beyond Europe's borders. These are not simple judgements or adjustments. But if we consider human rights relevant to the problem, then we must find concrete institutional arrangements that properly realise them.

Note that, as with sociological change, fidelity to the existing fragmentary system is not only conservative but also an abnegation of responsibility. At its crudest level, the idea that we should not challenge the existing competencies of institutions in order to avoid jeopardising their existing successes is a triumph of pragmatism and institutional inertia over principle (for analysis see Breakey 2017). The idea that the competence of institutions is pre-given and written into their founding documents is of more weight. Institutions are rarely competent to alter their own basic functions. This means that institutions tend to be inherently conservative. But, by the same token, we should not therefore be surprised that radical change or radical alternatives to our institutions might be necessary. At the very least, where there are systematic threats to the lives and well-being of substantial numbers of people, dramatic rethinking of institutional competence is necessary as are the interpretive practices within those institutions.

Third and finally, *existential change* relates to threats to humanity itself or widespread and systematic damage to normal human practices. These are threats to the very conditions of the possibility of human rights. Climatic threats (or other core threats to sustainability) threaten the very possibility of delivering human rights. That is, not only would human rights suffer within any emergency resource allocation process, but also human life itself would take on a different value where "population bottlenecks" force a decision between quality or quantity of human lives (Mulgan 2011). They require international action encompassing both sociological and institutional grounds of change: a rethinking of the substance of human rights themselves to better reflect the physical and environmental conditions of human existence, and reform of institutions (including the principles of subsidiarity and power distribution) necessary to maintain human rights in international practices and institutions.

Fidelity to the existing system and instruments of human rights is inconsistent with the reforms necessary to maintain human rights in circumstances of dire physical and institutional pressures. The physical and resource demands of a large class of rights – rights concerning protection of our environmental, economic, or cultural heritage – may become impossible to fulfil, at least without concomitant costs for other morally important practices. Indeed, the physical and social infrastructure for other rights may be erased too, such that complex rights – due process, education, group rights – are impossible to respect because of our physical conditions. To some extent, these problems seem well served by accounts of human rights that seek to align human rights with *humanitarianism*, i.e. acute threats to humanity as opposed to "merely" broad human entitlements. On that assumption human rights were never intended to intrude on distributive decisions and should be seen as speaking only to basic or minimal demands. But we should note that this conception of human rights is likely to result in an abnegation of responsibility to consider more fundamental alteration of our human rights systems. "Humanitarianism" is a set of practices working in parallel to respecting human rights. "Humanitarianism" should not, conversely, mean jettisoning large swathes of human rights laws as the first casualty of difficult social and political circumstances.

In sum, these grounds of change are not wholly distinguishable. The sociological mixes with the institutional and the wider political and environmental context in which human rights have to function. These models are not intended to denote discrete problems to be solved with new rights or new treaties. They require consciousness of a particular kind of horizon for human rights thinking, one that is future orientated rather than over-determined by certain originary crises or atrocities. And they require a particular attitude to human rights thinking: seeking principled change to human rights to protect the underlying principles and core rights.

In each case it has been suggested that a particular kind of fidelity to the past is problematic. It should be added that the proposed horizon for human rights thinking is also challenged by a theoretical parsimony which would guard against introducing too much additional theory (political, moral, or legal) into our thinking. This counsels us to be wary of any approach to human rights that is too theoretically expansive. At an extreme it would deny that these are properly human rights considerations at all; arguably democratic decision-making about our institutions would be lexically prior in any normative or practical deliberations about these issues. These kinds of commitments are a barrier to a rethinking of human rights and change. But they are not all of the same force, clarity, and intelligibility. Accordingly we should analyse and defuse these criticisms before going any further.

## 2 Rationalisation

### *2.1 Forms and objectives*

"Rationalisation" is an ideal type created from common features and resemblances found across modern human rights theory. Elements could be found, for instance, in Griffin's influential work on human rights (2008), in Hopgood's work (2013; also Hopgood et al. 2017), but also in that of theorists as different as Beitz (2011) and Moyn (2010). I use the term "rationalisation" to connote the idea of "rationalizing", meaning a "careful preservation" or sometimes "necessary reduction in" the use of human rights. It suggests circumstances where something valuable must be rationed for there to be enough, or as good, for others to receive in the future. But it also suggests that human rights must be "made to fit" an existing set of assumptions or commitments. Rationalisation reflects the common assumption that human rights are over-expansive or intrusive relative to our established constitutional rights. It is a project of conditioning human rights that is congenial to both critics of human rights as well as to some general theorists of law who, while not hostile to human rights law, want a theory of human rights that will not prove inconsistent with legal positivism and constitutional conservatism (a position particularly associated with Rawls's late work *The Law of Peoples*, 2001). It is distinguished by certain objectives and methodological commitments.

Rationalisation's objective is reduction in the *influence* of human rights by conditioning human rights. Such conditioning requires properly disciplining human rights law in line with our other positive legal norms, and it means systematically limiting the influence of human rights within a constitution and within political and legal thinking more generally (Beitz 2011: 44–47). On the assumption that the valid norms of our legal systems carry special force in the determination of rights and responsibilities, existing norms should be given priority in the event of clashes and the normal canons of interpretation should be applied equally to human rights laws (Griffin 2008: 37). Moreover, while some kinds of foundational claims may be conceded to human rights those foundational claims should be used to limit, not expand, the identification and influence of human rights (Moyn 2010: 13). The foundations of human rights should limit the scope of human rights to interests of crucial importance. We should, it is argued, be suspicious of human rights claims that do not relate to absolutely bedrock issues of human interests and human vulnerability (Hopgood 2013: 5–6). Thus, while rationalisation of human rights is a project of insisting upon the conditioning human rights by *external* normative commitments (political or legal systems), one important recurrent theme is the *internal* limits or internal thresholds to human rights claims, stressing that human rights or human rights theory have a certain self-limiting scope because of their concerning only urgent, acute, or especially basic human concerns (Rawls 2001: 79–80).

Whether the source of limitation is internal or external to human rights law, the underlying common-denominator of rationalisation is the placing of a burden of proof on human rights. Regardless of the validity of human rights law, we are invited to assume that human rights stand in need of justification. Human rights (laws and institutions) need to show proof of their protecting core or primary interests only. And such a burden is justified by certain standards. First, theoretical *parsimony*: that we should be suspicious of expansive elaborations of the moral force of human rights and we should prefer justifications made in terms of basic or pressing (often "humanitarian") urgency. This can usually be supported by selective appeal to international instruments and practices which seem to reflect pressing interests and be related to humanitarian concerns (Beitz 2011; Rawls 2001). Second, the burden of proof against human rights requires a certain *fidelity* to focal instruments, institutions, and interpretive assumptions. It can, in some cases, be fidelity to the international human rights system created in the post-war period. While this is often the object of criticism (over-expansive instruments and over-reaching institutions), the creation of new instruments and institutions is presumed to be inconsistent with the prevailing consensus on what constitutes human rights. Alternatively, it could be fidelity to a domestic system or instrument (particularly bills of rights) that are taken to be more valid, authentic, or authoritative expressions of basic rights (Kateb 2011: 28).

This assortment of commitments and assumptions encompasses a sizeable proportion of contemporary human rights theory. Nevertheless, "rationalisation" is an ideal type useful for conceptual exploration, being more specific in its objectives and standards than the demand for "human rights within non-ideal theory" or a "political account of human rights". It contains elements of both of these types of human rights theory, revealing elements shared by both. The ultimate attraction of any such rationalising project is its conservative function. Its conservation of important elements of legal justice, particularly longstanding constitutional practices. Preservation of national independence including dualism relative to international law. But also its preserving the central "moral force" of human rights in a certain limited sense, namely as the humanitarianism of international legal discourse and practice.

### *2.2 Rationalisation as over-demanding*

Each of these objectives and standards are questionable or defeasible in their own terms but especially in the light of the demand to understand change in human rights.

In the first instance, the problem of rights inflation (the repeated or excessive designation of certain important entitlements as human rights) turns on whether we accept a theory of human rights as relating to "basic interests". In the absence of a complete theory of human rights that justifies such minimalism (in the face, amongst other things, of the expansive scope of UDHR rights), "rights inflation" lacks any critical force.

The problem of "disruption of settled practices" is more challenging insofar as it is fuelled by legitimate concerns related to the rule of law. We should not amend our core norms (norms with far reaching implications for actors and institutions) without due care. The rule of law, in other words, rightly demands certain checks on the rapidity and scope of legal change. But there is no reason why human rights should be singled out as excessively problematic in this respect. Conversely, we expect commitment to such entitlements to have far-reaching constitutional implications and therefore there is no *a priori* reason why the burden of proof should not be shifted *to* constitutional norms if they conflict with human rights.

Accordingly, the burden of proof we associate with rationalising projects is partly questionable and partly reversible. Questionable regarding the tying of human rights to an opaque quota of legitimate human rights. Reversible because of human rights' intended far-reaching scope. Human rights are *meant* to be constitutive, in the sense of changing the conditions of the creation and enforcement of norms within a system. This in turn points to reasons why parsimony and fidelity will not serve to maintain the burden of proof against human rights.

The assumption that our theoretical commitments regarding human rights should be parsimonious is driven by partly plausible concerns about controversial assumptions in theorising, either to protect human rights from theoretical vulnerabilities or to ensure that justificatory accounts of human rights can be legitimated by consensus. Parsimony is attractive as a theoretical virtue. But we should demand specificity as to what kind of parsimony is desirable in this context. "Jurisprudential parsimony" might be accomplished if we only adopted as much theoretical commitment as is necessary to explain our present legal practices. This is, of course, a highly constraining (and defeasible) methodological commitment because it demands explanation rather than justification of human rights and is therefore unconcerned with how we might create new practices. "Normative parsimony" might be thought to demand that we limit the scope of human rights to certain kinds of moral claims preventing human rights from colonising all of our normative discourse or challenging the authority of our legal systems. Applying normative parsimony to human rights is, however, ambiguous because it leaves undecided whether the source of the limitation is internal or external to human rights. Are the moral limits to the scope of human rights internal limitations related to a foundational principle, or external limitations related to what can be justified by consensus? Neither limitation is necessarily parsimonious in terms of the quantity and scope of human rights claims that they produce. Jurisprudential parsimony is arguably a supportive factor in efforts to limit human rights to basic *constitutional* rights given their proven efficacy in legal discourse. Normative parsimony is arguably found in efforts to limit human rights to basic *humanitarian* interests given their efficacy in international political discourse. But these require independent, and complete, defences of the priority of constitutionalism or of humanitarianism in a *praxis* of human rights. The force of either of these positions is far from self-evident.

The insistence that somewhere in our theoretical accounts of human rights we need or must have fidelity to certain kinds of established practices is also ambiguous. Its ambiguity can be captured in four points. First, the ambiguity of whether this is fidelity to domestic (constitutional) or international (human rights) practice. Second (assuming the international expression of human rights is focal) whether it is the Universal Declaration alone or the whole range of international instruments that are models of "authentic" human rights. Third, whether we should understand international human rights as broadly signalling a conception of human rights to which we should show fidelity, or whether there is a more precise commonality within the international rights that can be reconstructed. In other words, it is unclear whether we should be showing fidelity to the specific aims and foci of individual rights (perhaps all and only those rights now considered customary international law), or showing fidelity to the overall endeavour of international human rights law. Fourth, and finally, there is an ambiguity in much human rights theory as to whether our fidelity is to an underlying *principle* or rather to a particular function or vision arising from an originary *historical event* or trauma. In other words, to give particular importance to certain legal instruments need not mean that human rights are meaningful only in relation to the historical events or epoch that gave rise to that instrument.

Regarding fidelity, the special significance of *international* human rights discourse creates distinctive concerns. From the outset we granted a special status to the UDHR as a model for the scope of human rights law. The UDHR is generally accepted as the paradigm example of a modern menu of human rights, but this will not satisfy those who believe that older bills of rights have better claim to be models of rights (Kateb 2011). Differently, international law has produced "generations" of rights (really as accidents of treaty drafting), generations that seem to imply a hierarchy within human rights; international practice, then, appears to support the prioritisation of a certain class of rights in our practice and in our theorising. But such prioritisation was never envisaged by the drafters of the international bill of rights. And the practice of the international arena is questionable as a model for human rights enforcement given its embeddedness in a legal system as idiosyncratic as the international system.

More widely, any fidelity to a model or expression of certain principles raises a more general, jurisprudential, question about whether interpreters of law should show fidelity to a certain kind of institutional *practice* or certain doctrinal *products* of those practices. So, questions around the centrality of the international regime in our thinking are not just a question about the special function, and special idiosyncrasies, of public international law but an interpretative question of how we expect human rights to be understood as a class.

In essence, rationalisation represents hostility to certain kinds of change, is obscure on the sources of possible change (how our systems and instruments should become better responsive to certain specific problems), and silent on how it might be possible to reform our human rights systems to better confront fundamentally human problems.

## 3 Desiderata of a theory of change

### *3.1 Frameworks of practical reason*

In dissolving the challenge of rationalisation, we partially clarify the desiderata of a theory of change in human rights law and institutions. Good theorisation of change requires not only fidelity to the letter of certain instruments, but also creative and principled response to threats. Such theorisation is not parsimonious minimalism, but must be better theorisation of the foundation of human rights and law itself such that the normative force of human rights law *and* the force of existing law are given due weight. We should reject, ultimately, a burden of proof against human rights because of their putative tendency to have expansive implications in legal systems. Rather, we need to modify human rights law mindful of their principled core and mindful of the institutional context in which they need to function.

In better conceptualising these commitments, along with the drivers of change and their application to human rights, I will draw upon two ideas (both used, and refined by, Rawls but without here seeking to explicate Rawls' use), namely the claims of "public reason" and the "circumstances of justice" (Rawls 2001). These, together, should be treated as the structures necessary to make a coherent overall judgment about change in human rights.

On the one hand, human rights form a certain kind of claim about public reason, about the reasonable boundaries to what is politically and legally justifiable for any system or polity. On the other hand, human rights must be responsive to the circumstances of justice, i.e. the "givens" of social and political theory, the inescapable human and environmental constants that make legal justice and distributive justice necessary. The interplay of the two ideas give us structures for analysis because they force us to consider our normative relationship with both the "normal" demands of justice and "extreme" challenges to human entitlements and human institutions.

They also assist in clarifying what is unique and what is general in this context. Human rights share a general need, with other areas of law, to acknowledge the circumstances of justice as conditioning any normative claims, not only in formal sense of "ought implies can" but also in the sense of "minimum content of natural law", the need for systems to reflect certain factual constants in human affairs in order to avoid burdens or regulations that threaten a society's own existence

(Hart 2012). Human rights, conversely, have their own relationship with the basic "coordinates" of law, i.e. of time and space. They require cosmopolitan public reason, i.e. concern for entitlements that transcend state boundaries. And they demand an orientation to the future, i.e. maintaining the conditions of the possibility of human rights, not merely within one polity but any future polity. The framework of practical reason that is appropriate for human rights does not relate to any putative universalism of "human nature" but rather to a universality in temporal and territorial scope.

### *3.2 Public reason as cosmopolitan reason*

Public reason gives us the principles, and constraints, intended to guide change both in the substance of law and its institutional realisation. Public reason is associated with civil society and the structures of governance within a state (Rawls 2001), it represents the "ground rules" of political and social practice within which a range of legitimate policies and practices are permitted (Dworkin 1977). But in the context of human rights this state cannot be thought of as a particular civil society. Indeed, the effort to insist that human rights be viewed from the perspective of fidelity to a particular constitutional order is, as we have seen, indefensible from the point of view of theorising about human rights. Human rights, simultaneously at a domestic and international level, assist in defining what is reasonable, and defining the basic adjudicative and legislative boundaries within which laws and institutions will function. The position of human rights in public reason therefore inhabits the *cross*-jurisdictional space of shared constitutional ideals, and the *transnational* space connecting national and international law.

Public reason, in the context of human rights is, then, cosmopolitan public reason. It concerns the entitlements that flow from individuals possessing rights simply as humans, and it concerns the fact that such entitlements will have direct regulatory implications (international human rights laws) and institutional and constitutive implications (the rule of law). This has three more specific but related meanings. It means that the justification of institutions and practices are always to be judged in part (if not exclusively) by their contribution to the protection of individual rights. It means that domestic jurisprudence on human rights should be informed by international jurisprudence on human rights. And it means that far from constitutional orders and their territorial boundaries conditioning the meaning and function of human rights, human rights should take normative priority over the contingencies of sovereign and territorial difference. This in turn explains how our obligations, to the extent that they are cosmopolitan, are *universal*; they are claimable regardless of time and place even if, de facto, they are not made enforceable by particular states.

But they are also, importantly, *conditioned*. They are conditioned (like any norms) by "ought implies can", that obligations must be *capable of being fulfilled*. They are conditioned by their own internal principles of *qualification*: limits related to public order, public morality, and the conditions necessary for the reconciliation of competing rights claims. And they are conditioned by *subsidiarity* i.e. the need for power to be distributed properly relative to expertise and authority. Thus cosmopolitanism, while making states' authority conditional, does not negate the state because of the state's contribution to a system of common but differentiated responsibilities. The desideratum for human rights theory is a structural differentiation of human rights responsibilities which is not merely the adoption of human rights by individual states, but a subsidiarity marrying the domestic and international in a relationship of good order. Put another way, human rights have to be understood as conditioned, not by contingent or arbitrary choices relative to political cultures, but rather by their being a shared body of principles and norms that transcend territorial boundaries and which must govern, as well as reflect, change.

By extension, public reason, in the context of human rights, implies what has been called the "indivisibility" of human rights. "Indivisibility" is not immutability, it is international community's commitment to a *set* of rights. Without such an assumption we can make no sense of international instruments and institutions. That is, there is no hierarchy of human rights in international law and (*pace* Rawls) no "core" or "primary" humanitarian rights in relation to which all other human rights are secondary. Human rights laws (in the sense of the plural, and sometimes heterogenous norms and instruments found at national, regional, and international levels) are, and should continue to be, norms relevant to all aspects of humans' social, physical, and economic lives. This means that public reason, as it relates to our commitment to human rights, is concerned with delineating reasonable demands regarding civil society, economy, and the entitlements of marginalised or vulnerable groups. Efforts to treat the "intrusion" of human rights into issues of distribution or social justice as illegitimate are wrong-headed, at least where such a critique is intended as rationalising critique putatively applying human rights' own internal limitations. The desideratum for human rights theory is the integration of each generation of rights and progressive realisation of human rights as a whole. Any changes to the law of human rights must, therefore, reflect new and emerging social and economic practices and will not respect division between the legal, moral and political "spheres".

Ultimately public reason in the context of human rights demands a distinctive orientation to time and space. To the extent that there are differences between polities, those differences are framed or conditioned by obligations that transcend borders. And the scope of reasonable governmental action is also bounded by a fundamental entrenchment of human rights within our national and international orders, i.e. they, and their conditions of possibility, must be preserved into the future. The desideratum of a theory of change is determination of those grounds where sovereign inviolability can be negated, without this being tied to circumstances of atrocity or crisis, but rather tied to the social and physical grounds of human rights' continuation into the future.

### *3.3 From the circumstances of justice to the human condition*

The brute factual background against which we have to understand human rights is the "human condition". In Arendt's sense, the human condition is the set of inescapable background conditions against which our normative discourse takes its meaning and encompasses the environmental and agentic horizons of human existence (Arendt 2013). Being the inescapable factual conditions of human activity, this is where we find the source of or demand for change in the fabric of human rights law, the sources of dynamism. As the physical context in which humans live changes, our discourses of justice will begin to change too. Accordingly, the human condition relates to the concerns we have brought under "sociological change". It, also, however offers a way of explaining how it is that sociological, institutional, and existential change are related.

We have to amend the traditional understanding of the circumstances of justice which insists that the root of justice lies in moderate scarcity (Hubin 1979). As moderate scarcity turns into a deeper and irresolvable scarcity, our core notions relating to justice – property, the needs of persons – will change (Mulgan 2011). We should also be aware that implicit accounts of human nature – the moderate selfishness or moderate sociability assumed by the contractarian tradition – will be challenged by both urgent humanitarian claims arising from existential threats and indeed by the sociological and institutional changes that will flow from them. In essence, no theoretical presuppositions about the grounds of justice and reasonable human behaviour are immune from alteration given existential change. The desideratum for our theories of human rights is finding ways for human rights to intervene in our distributive and rectificatory discourses and rearticulate justice in the light of a changing and threatened human condition.

The importance of appeal to the human condition also lies in the fact that it does not claim to be a theory of human impulses or human limitations, but a *generic* concern with human action as it interacts with the agency of others and the wider environment. Classical natural law, along with contractarianism, has taken this to be exhausted by general claims about human sociability or human selfishness. We, in contrast, should be concerned with the generic conditions of human agency and in particular changes in the physical and social environment that may affect that agency (Lutz 1995). The desideratum for human rights theory remains (as it has long been maintained (Gewirth 1978)) to explore the generic elements of our agency and well-being to generate direct economic and social obligations.

Clearly amongst the concerns that flow from the human condition are the *necessary* demands of material subsistence. The inclusion of these within human rights law are important because without them human action becomes impossible. But one implication of human rights theory is that we should pay particular attention to the importance of the *contingent*. That is, the contingencies of the physical world and human lifeworld, both of which are influenced by human agency but neither of which are wholly controlled through conscious human agency. This presents political and institutional problems with normative dimensions: the maintenance of a sustaining environment (sustainability), confronting natural or humanly created emergencies (humanitarianism), and resisting irrationalism in politics (nationalism and other forms of anti-cosmopolitanism).

These bring contingency and irrationalism into conflict with the ideas of plurality and reasonableness characteristic of universal public reason. However, it should not be assumed that all contingency is unwanted or problematic. The desideratum for defence of human rights is inclusion of concern for contingency, i.e. we need to keep the future open, and erasing contingency in human affairs is undesirable if it means colonisation of the human lifeworld (Habermas 1985) to the exclusion of change and liberty. In sum, we should look for links between the institutional, sociological, and existential in the ways in which our lives are potentially harmed by technological and environmental change. Human rights concerns – and changes to human rights – will arise where these start to reduce the potential for self-determination in individual conduct, broader patterns of change in social life, and self-determination at the level of the species as a whole.

Part of the challenge facing human rights is to give better recognition of the human condition in terms of a sustainable future as a human right in itself, but also better recognition of the threats that irreversible intervention in the environment will pose to the human condition. But we should also be aware that work and labour are inevitably part of that condition and susceptible to radical changes over time; work and labour have always had the potential to be degrading, but we need human rights to better chart the mutation in forms of work and labour that diminish human agency (Dupré 2016). Regarding human action itself (in Arendtian terms, the possibility of making decisive intervention in social affairs and in particular to begin again in our social practices) is also threatened by increasing (re-)stratification of societies and imbalances of wealth (Arendt 2013). These are not simple, discrete, "political", or "economic" issues and existing human rights cannot address them with such simple categories. The desideratum for a theory of change is capturing these problems as human rights problems and confronting them via institutional as well as substantive change.

### *3.4 The desiderata*

The desiderata of a theory of change, then, must not only identify specific problems and then translate these directly into material changes in human rights law (e.g. creating new human rights to a healthy environment or to water). A concern with the underlying principles necessary for the substantive law and the relevant institutions must encompass our conventional understanding of human rights' foundations (typically human dignity) but must also consider the cosmopolitan context in which change is necessary and desirable. Moreover, the desiderata of a theory of change will include an account of human dignity as the basic principle of human rights, discrimination between different putative drivers of change to decide which should be acted upon, and a theory of how public reason and the human condition *interact* such that this principle, these drivers, and these frameworks of practical reason can be reconciled.

With this said, there are certain ways in which public reason and the circumstances must be combined or mediated between. On the one hand, the unifying principle sitting between these ideas must be human dignity as human rights' foundation, but as this is not univocal, a coherent view of change must specify the institutional and not just normative implications of human dignity (see Riley 2017).

On the other hand, there is the persistent importance of coherence in our normative orders, i.e. ensuring that the important differences and legitimate tensions between law, morality, and politics are always resolved in such a way as to maintain the basic status of individuals. While a seemingly intuitive or self-evident desiderata of any normative theorising, human rights as constitutive commitments to good governance are precisely the discourse through which we express the importance of coherence in our normative orders of law, morality, and politics. The tendency to see human rights as purely legal or political or moral phenomena obscures this crucial aspect of human rights function and meaning.

## Conclusion

What is change in human rights and how is it best undertaken? Approaching change cannot simply be fidelity to existing legal institutions or political practices. It cannot be fidelity to the substance of the post-war instruments and institutions and nor can it be fidelity to national constitutional orders. These are evasions of normative questions (the normative force of human rights vis-à-vis our other normative commitments) and they are inherently conservative. Equally, a certain kind of parsimony in theorising about human rights (as about anything) is no doubt desirable but we cannot generate a theory of change out of non-ideal theory; this either collapses into the kind of fidelity already shown to be inadequate or begs the question. Any hopes for the theoretical and practical "self-limitation" of human rights are wrong-headed. We cannot simply hope that human rights shrink (under the weight of their own limited moral scope) to produce a progressively neater fit with our prevailing institutions.

We must accept the breadth of human rights claims as they arise from our changing societies and practices. And we must find ways to allow principled change in human rights law. These principled grounds for change are found partly in existing human rights discourse, particularly foundational claims about human rights. But the wider frameworks of ideas necessary for understanding change are extrinsic to legal human rights discourse. They are ideas like public reason, cosmopolitanism, and the human condition which point to the dynamics underlying and demanding change, and point to the institutional conditioning that is proper to human rights as constitutive commitments.

This discussion of desiderata has, then, been a predominantly theoretical analysis of how human rights discourse should link to wider concerns in moral, legal, and political philosophy. Nonetheless, is also shows how we should engage with contemporary trends in political discussion of human rights. Recent critique of Europe's human rights regime has expressed a simple opposition between "top-down" human rights protection and more cooperative or "subsidiarity-based" protection of human rights (see the Draft Copenhagen Declaration 2018). This only varies the familiar theme that a burden of proof should be levelled against human rights where (potentially any) democratic institution can claim normative priority over a "non-indigenous" norm. What is essentially opposition to human rights in the name of a majoritarian conception of democracy should be resisted in itself and as a model of change. Articulating and pursuing principled change in human rights law – whether it be by law makers, state signatories, or civil society – should begin with the question of how it is humanity's shared condition is under threat and how we preserve humanity through those changes by altering the substance, but not the priority, of human rights law.

## References

Arendt, H. (2013) *The Human Condition.* Chicago, University of Chicago Press.

Beitz, C. R. (2011) *The Idea of Human Rights.* Oxford, Oxford University Press.

Breakey, H. (2017) 'It's Right, It Fits, We Debated, We Decided, I Agree, It's Ours, and It Works: The Gathering Confluence of Human Rights Legitimacy', *Law and Philosophy*, 37(1), 1–28.

Dembour, M.-B. (2015) *When Humans Become Migrants: Study of the European Court of Human Rights with an Inter-American Counterpoint.* Oxford, Oxford University Press.

Draft Copenhagen Declaration (2018) 'Declaration of the High Level Conference meeting in Copenhagen on 12 and 13 April 2018 at the initiative of the Danish Chairmanship of the Committee of Ministers of the Council of Europe, dated 5 February 2018', https://menneskeret.dk/sites/menneskeret.dk/files/media/dokumenter/nyheder/draft_copenhagen_declaration_05.02.18.pdf [accessed 30/01/19].

Dupré, C. (2016) *The Age of Dignity: Human Rights and Constitutionalism in Europe.* Oxford, Bloomsbury Publishing.

Dworkin, R. (1977) *Taking Rights Seriously.* London, Duckworth.

European Commission (2017) 'Reform of EU Data Protection Rules' http://ec.europa.eu/justice/data-protection/reform/index_en.htm [accessed 30/01/19].

Gewirth, A. (1978) *Reason and Morality.* Chicago, University of Chicago Press.

Griffin, J. (2008) *On Human Rights.* Oxford, Oxford University Press.

Habermas, J. (1985) *The Theory of Communicative Action. Vol. 2.* Boston, Beacon Press.

Hart, H. L. A. (2012) *The Concept of Law.* Oxford, Oxford University Press.

Hopgood, S. (2013) *The Endtimes of Human Rights.* London, Cornell University Press.

Hopgood, S., Snyder, J., and Vinjamuri, L. (eds) (2017) *Human Rights Futures.* Cambridge, Cambridge University Press.

Hubin, D. C. (1979) 'The Scope of Justice', *Philosophy & Public Affairs*, 9(1), 3–24.

Kateb, G. (2011) *Human Dignity.* Harvard, Harvard University Press.

Kerr, I., and Earle J. (2013) 'Prediction, Preemption, Presumption: How Big Data Threatens Big Picture Privacy', *Stan. L. Rev. Online*, 66, 65.

Lutz, M. A. (1995) 'Centering Social Economics on Human Dignity', *Review of Social Economy*, 53(2), 171–194.

Moyn, S. (2010) *The Last Utopia: Human Rights in History.* Harvard, Belknap.

Mulgan, T. (2011) *Ethics for a Broken World: Imagining Philosophy After Catastrophe.* London, Routledge.

Polčák, R., and Svantesson, D. J. B. (2017) *Information Sovereignty: Data Privacy, Sovereign Powers and the Rule of Law*. Cheltenham, Edward Elgar Publishing.

Rawls, J. (2001) *The Law of Peoples: With, The Idea of Public Reason Revisited*. Harvard, Harvard University Press.

Riley, S. (2017) *Human Dignity and Law: Legal and Philosophical Investigations*. London, Routledge.

Solove, D. J., and Schwartz, P. (2014) *Information Privacy Law*. New York, Wolters Kluwer Law & Business.

Wheeler, M. (2017) 'The Unruly Article 8', 1 Crown Office Row Publication, www.preview2.1cor.enstar.net/1155/records/1186/mw%20talk.pdf[accessed 02/02/19].

# Part II

# Paradigmatic political philosophies of legal change

# 5 Legal "determinism" or/and legal "creationism"?

## Conservative-communitarian versus contractarian approaches to legal change[1]

*Maciej Chmieliński*

### Introduction

The main goal of this chapter is to denote the conceptual opposition between two models of justification of legal change that are present in the political practices of current democratic societies: justification derived from the assumption that law is a passive reflection of some higher order that is followed by the people, and justification assuming that law results from aggregated – rational or/and reasonable – creation of the society members. I want to focus on the pivotal aspect of justification, which is the role of legal authority in the process of change. Looking from this perspective, the first type of justification is generally questioning any active role of the authority, boiling it down to the deeply limited and determined choice between previously existing dispositions or "habits of the heart" (as we can call it following Bellah, Madsen, & Sullivan 1985). On the contrary, the second type affirms the free creation of law as fundamental for legal change. While in the first the freedom of lawmaking is totally cast into doubt by the assumption of predetermination of legal change by communitarian habits and dispositions, in the second one the change in law seems to be dictated solely by the actual and aggregated will of the members of democratic society. I claim, and intend to demonstrate, that taking the first approach "too seriously", one can end up excluding the justification of all changes that are not deeply connected with the habits, traditions, and customs of the society (cultural, religious, moral, and the like). Alternatively, the radical form of the second point of view can lead to a legal system being totally isolated from the deep sources of its identity and historical experience, which can undermine the stability and certainty of law by changing it too easily, perhaps even in a "revolutionary" way (Finnis 2011). The two kinds of justification result from the dialectically oppositional conceptions of the human condition as well as oppositional approaches to rationality. Like Weberian "ideal types", they obviously never exist in real legal practices. These practices always approach one or the other standpoint, being a "mix" of them.

1 This chapter presents results of the research financially supported by the National Science Centre, Poland, as part of the project No. 2015/19/B/HS5/02522.

The main task of this chapter is to identify and precisely describe the antithetic models as points of reference that may yield a heuristic tool. The reason for this is that adopting various legal solutions in contemporary democratic societies draws from both models.

The two "hard" methodological assumptions are necessarily connected with the above thesis. First, each change in the law in democratic society is of a profoundly political character. All the economical, religious, moral, technical, or security reasons for change are considered as factors balanced by the politics of law that aims at reaching an equilibrium between the common and the individual interests. I understand politics here in the special way, i.e. as the meta-perspective for factors resulting from all these fields. It does assume the general primacy of politics over the other fields (as primacy of theology in the Middle Ages), but only its "cumulative" character, which allows including into political debates many diverse reasons. However, I do not reduce politics to this "cumulative" character. My approach is limited only to the particular aspect of politics that is connected with legal change. Also, assuming the political character of legal change, I am not interested in settling between legal positivism (Hart, Raz), legal interpretivism (Dworkin), iusnaturalism (Finnis, Stammler, Fuller), or other actual standpoints of jurisprudence or legal theory. I am interested in the structure of the political argument for change, independent from its relation to the concept of law. Although the latter may differ among theoretical standpoints, the persistence of the political moment in law is of empirical, rather than theoretical, nature.

Second, I assume that being of profoundly political character, legal change always demands some philosophical justification. Legal practices of most current democratic societies indicate that it is not enough to justify the change of law only by reference to its pedigree from a democratically elected legislature, public court, legitimate government, or proper international institution (positivist's "test of pedigree" – see Austin 1995: 166, and positivists critique of it: Hart 1994: 81). Such a pedigree can be the sufficient condition for a positive legal validity or for descriptive legitimacy. However, for politically, religiously, morally, and economically diverse (and divided) democratic societies, which are at the same time highly egalitarian (at least historically comparing), such a justification seems to be simply not enough. Members of these societies always demand convincing justification, without which the change in law can be called "partisan" (Waldron 1990: 12), burdened with a "democratic deficit" (Marquand 1979: 64), or simply characterized by a bureaucratic or an "administrative absolutism" (Hayek 2011: 365). In other words, the lack of justification can make the changed law "defective" with regards to the extra-legal aspects, and if such an objection is accompanied by real political power, the "defective" change can be even canceled.

I believe that politics in this aspect cannot do without philosophy. It is the political philosophy that provides the law-changing authority with the tools to balance these various reasons either by the more individual-right-centered prism or by the more community-centered one. It can be either a "popular" philosophy used by ordinary citizens or more "academic" philosophy to which representatives of the intellectual elite (i.e. judges, politicians, academics, journalists) may and should refer. Parliamentary amendments, acts of local and international parliaments, decisions of local and international governments, as well as judges' decisions, are always, at least implicitly, based on philosophical considerations. According to the main thesis of this chapter, the philosophical reasons for change are always being derived from social holism and social individualism, constituting an interplay between individual rights and common interests. That is why, in my perspective, these two philosophical categories have an extremely important heuristic value.

## 1 Social holism and social individualism: Historical sources of legal determinism and legal creationism

The "legal determinist" standpoint is historically connected with the ontological natural law theory presented by a part of ancient Greek thinkers such as Aristotle and especially the Stoics, for whom the ontologically understood natural law always determines the positive law. Similar assumptions can be found in some Christian conceptions (Thomas Aquinas's for instance), and partly also in theories created by some conservative thinkers like Edmund Burke (1951) or Joseph de Maistre (1819, 1884). In the modern era, although the ontological aspect of legal determinism is no longer accepted in the classical way, one can find considerable legal-deterministic themes in the conservatism of Michael Oakeshott or Roger Scruton, as well as in the communitarian approach of Alasdair MacIntyre (1989, 2007a, 2007b), Michael Sandel (1982) or Charles Taylor (1985, 1989a, 1989b, 1991). Also, some elements of this approach to law are present in the legal doctrine of F.A. von Hayek (2011).

The "legal creationist" approach is in turn generally connected with the contractarian wing of social contract theory, and with various versions of legal positivism, where law is considered to be solely an effect of volitional creation by the current human legislator and where the norms of natural law are generally not an integral part of the valid legal order. The historical predecessor of such an approach was Thomas Hobbes, whose conception excluded the natural law as a real, active motivation for human behavior. Recall that he assumed that "covenants, without the Sword are but Words, and of no strength to secure a man at all" (Hobbes 1651: 103). Such an assumption can be found also in the early utilitarianism and legal positivism of Jeremy Bentham (1931, 1945, 1970) and John Austin (1995). Another important source of inspiration for contractarianism is the conception of David Hume, insofar as it questions the metaphysical underpinnings of the social contract and connects it with conventions and bargaining (Hume 2008). The current version of this approach is most characteristic in the modern contractarianism of J.M. Buchanan (1962, 1975, 1985, 1991), D. Gauthier (1986, 1990), and I. Narveson (1988), stemming from the Hobbesian-Humean line of social contractarian thought. They refer to economic rationality and game theory, in which the law finds its source in dynamical historical contracts, dictated essentially by maximization of individual utility. The alternative social contract theories that may be called "contractualism" (as opposed to "contractarianism"), especially Kantian theories of J. Rawls (1971) or T. Scanlon (1982, 1998), are seen by the contractarians as a quite distant wing of social contract theory (Narveson 1988: 131, 148, Hampton 1991: 33). From the point of view taken up in this chapter, the contractual wing is indeed not "pure enough" as mixing the holist and individualist assumptions (see, for instance, Charpenel in this volume).

Now, the two opposite visions of the source of law – deterministic and creationist – result from the dialectically oppositional conceptions of human condition. The first one we can call "social holism" and the second one "social individualism" (on that distinction, see Rau 1995, Chmieliński 2004: 7).

In social holism, human nature is of "social" character" (Aristotle 1959: 5), which means that human individuals are "deeply rooted" (M. Sandel 1982: 21) in a concrete community, and therefore they are socially and culturally determined. The community, the social whole, enjoys methodological and – at the end of the day – also axiological priority to the human individual that is seen merely as a member of community. The human individual is created by community: its culture, values, ethics, norms, and customs (MacIntyre 2007a: 444, Taylor 1989: 183). The participation in social practices, and not some abstract individual human nature, constitutes the human being that therefore inevitably needs to identify with some real community as the point of reference. "Real" needs and goals of human individuals are therefore derived from needs and goals of the community (Aristotle 1959: 9/10). Such a standpoint assumes an "organic" type of social organization, close to what Ferdinand Tönnies called *Gemeinshaft* – "communal society" (Tönnies 2002: 33).

Unlike social holism, in the case of individualism the human individual is perceived as socially and culturally undetermined by the community, and therefore it has a methodological priority to the community (Buchannan & Tullock 1962: 11). The methodological individualism transforms in these conceptions into the *social* individualism, where needs, preferences, and goals of human individuals are always seen as the central values and fundamental points of reference for each community. Social needs and preferences are never of autonomous value, because they are only an effect of aggregation of individual needs and preferences. The conflicts between particular needs and preferences are solved by bargaining procedures. Thereby the community can be seen only as an aggregate of human individuals; it is being created by them and fully subordinated to the aggregated needs, preferences, and goals of its members (Bentham, Buchanan, Gauthier). It results in a kind of a "mechanic" type of social organization, similar to that which Ferdinand Tönnies described as *Gesellschaft* – "community" or "associational society" (Tönnies 2002: 33/34).

## 2 Epistemic imperfection versus epistemic perfection

The above-described picture of relations between the human individual and the society results in two opposite assumptions concerning human knowledge about how society is functioning. If we generally assume that the human individual is deeply rooted in community, then the community is prior to the human mind. Therefore, in social holism, the possibility of finding some *a priori* universal standards of being rational and reasonable is generally excluded; the standards are always particular and characteristic of concrete communities (MacIntyre 1989: 103). According to the holist approach, people learn how to be rational and reasonable throughout all life taking part in the community practices. Their most important intellectual power called "*phronesis*" (MacIntyre 1989: 103–145) means the ability to learn from such experiences and thus recognize what is good or just. The relevant social knowledge cumulates such an experience and has primarily "practical" character, as called by Michael Oakeshot in his distinction between "practical" and "technical" knowledge. Based on the accumulation of experience, social knowledge is essentially not the knowledge of an individual mind, but rather that of many past and current generations (M. Oakeshot 1962: 7).

We can distinguish two aspects of such knowledge: "quantitative" and "qualitative". In its "quantitative" aspect, wisdom of generations means a collective knowledge of "many brains" (using the James Surowiecki's notion, it is "the wisdom of crowds", 2005). In its "qualitative" aspect, it assumes the historical wisdom of many generations. Therefore, such an accumulation, combining both "qualitative" and "quantitative" aspects, involves not only knowledge about how the social institutions are functioning in the moment, but also the wisdom concerning the ways they functioned in the past. However, it is important to bear in mind that knowledge in its "qualitative" aspect is not simply information that can be taken from historical books or from different historical narrations. The social knowledge or wisdom is "accumulated" in long-existing institutions such as culture, customs, or traditions, and in the long-lasting political and legal institutions of the concrete community. It essentially differs not only from the individual knowledge, but also from the collective knowledge. Its communitarian character means something more than only aggregated – collective – wisdom. It means that such a knowledge is as much of the collective as of the "generational" character (it connects past and current generations). This assumption results in two important consequences.

First, it intellectually excludes and undermines thinking in any universal, cosmopolitan categories and acting according to universal, cosmopolitan values. As parts of a bigger whole (concrete community), human beings are rooted in that community to the extent that it completely determines and designs their patterns of thinking and behavior. What is more, people whose behavior would be determined by some alleged cosmopolitan standards are considered to be "defective" in some way: their perspective of evaluating activity and behavior is somehow flawed as their ability to apply the categories of justice is deprived of the necessary context (MacIntyre 1989: 103ff, 2016: 188). Justice is learned through gaining the communitarian virtue of *phronesis*. Abstract formulas of justice, as for example the formula "to give someone their due", remain empty without the concrete social content. Justice means different things depending on whether it is a slave, oligarchic, monarchic, democratic, or any other type of community. The rationality of social institutions, as well as justice and laws, is created by the social whole and the assumption of the substantial good of this whole. People cannot be just outside of the whole, as they are – in the aspect of them enjoying practical reason, virtues, or even capability of esthetical appreciation – a product of the whole.

Second, the communitarian nature of knowledge strongly relativizes something we can call the "social-epistemic capacities" of the human reason. "Encoded" in community institutions, the wisdom is also deeply "esoteric" and hidden from the eyes and minds of average individuals, which is the result of wisdom being heteronomous and external to the individual human mind (MacIntyre 1989: 103–145, Oakeshott 1962: 7, similarly, Hayek 2011: 77). It is impossible for an individual as well as for the ahistorical-collective human mind to fully "catch" the "real substance" of community, and these minds are always fundamentally and essentially imperfect in respect to the multi-dimensional wisdom of community. It results in the pessimist vision of "the limits of (individual) human reason" (as Vermeule (2009) calls it): the epistemic imperfection of the human mind, being unable to individually recognize all the "wisdom of community". The proper cognition of the community's wisdom is a challenge not only to foreigners; even the insiders may face "epistemic" problems in this respect.

It is worth stressing that such a methodology of the socially rooted human being is not merely a description of the human condition, but it inevitably concerns values. The description above of the human condition and the epistemic capacity yields the highest status of communitarian and/or national values such as traditions, customs, and other historically and culturally determined patterns of behavior. The respect for existing institutions is derived from a high evaluation of the long-term evolution of the multi-levelled, often very complicated and multi-dimensional, social practices that cannot be rationalized in the simple categories of the actual human will.

The model of the individualist standpoint begins questions about human reason and social knowledge from obviously opposite assumptions. If we assume that the community is nothing more than the aggregate of individuals, human mind must be prior to it. It means that there are, and must be, *a priori* universal standards of public reasonableness and rationality, which are common to all, being essentially similar in each part of the globe. According to the contractarians, the absolute minimum of these standards creates the naturalist assumption of a maximization of a personal interest limited by reciprocal maximization of the interest of the other individuals (optimization) (Gauthier 1991: 16). It is thus the kind of economic rationality that at least constitutes the essential, and in some way "inborn", substance of the universal human reason. Economic rationality is seen as the common denominator of all human behavior, even if this behavior is only subjectively motivated: "Reduced to its barest essentials, the economic assumption is simply that the representative or the average individual, when confronted with real choice in exchange, will choose 'more' rather than 'less'" (Buchanan & Tullock 2004: 17). Reasonability of these standards is always determined by rationality understood as the ability of counting and ordering all the human world and maximizing the preferences and needs. People are naturally (i.e. "self-evidently" – in the sense of Hume) equipped with the above-mentioned standards; their most important intellectual power is thus an ability to use the "inborn" economic rationality in the right way.

If so, then the important social knowledge is the wisdom about general principles of the economic efficiency of current social institutions. The historical dimension of social experience involving culture, traditions, and customs, is tantamount to a result of evolutionary social games dictated generally by the economic rationality of individuals. Some aspects of the social experience can be of course forgotten throughout the development of a society because of diversity and specific nature of particular historical circumstances, but generally the customs can be revealed, reconstructed, and evaluated using economic rationality. The standards that come from customs are generally of an ethical-naturalist character. What is more, there is no need to reveal and reconstruct them in every situation. As results of the historical evolutionary bargaining processes based on the economic rationality, customs and traditions lower the "transaction costs" by enabling the actors to save intellectual labor simply by behaving according to custom (North 1992: 5). Therefore, the community practices are not treated as some superior order to be respected for its own sake, but rather as ample instruments of coordination and pursuit of individual interest.

The instrumental approach towards community practices is possible exactly because they are considered the results of aggregated individual actions based on the economic rationality. Following the Enlightenment, the contractarians believe that in principle we can understand our social institutions by means of our individual mind, which is the ultimate source of them and which is of universal character. From the point of view of the above-mentioned Oakeshot distinction between practical and technical knowledge, all the relevant knowledge in this model is of "technical" character. It results in the optimist vision of relatively "unlimited human reason". There is no fundamental epistemic imperfection of our knowledge, because the same or very similar standards of maximization are autonomous and internal to each individual human mind. Such intellectual egalitarianism makes possible the methodological cosmopolitanism and thinking in universal and globally common categories.

The above-mentioned opposite anthropological and epistemological assumptions result in two radically opposite standpoints in political philosophy. The social holism that characterizes the communitarian-conservative model results in a strong substantial vision of common good. In this vision, common good, i.e. the good of a particular community, has an objective, external and higher status in relation to the good of individual members of the community. If this taken in the conjunction with the epistemic imperfection of individual human reason, it results in the problem of how to decide about the substance of the common good and how to determine its content. Because of the imperfection of reason and the above-described status of common good, the substance of the common good cannot be revealed simply by an aggregation of individual preferences and needs. All one can do, therefore, is trying to recognize the common good in the existing institutions – to "encode" it from therefrom.

The substantial vision of the common good can require even the slavery of community members. For instance, for Aristotle slavery was the self-evident part of the common good of the ancient Hellas. Slaves were "assistants in the class of instruments of action" and "parts of property" (Artistotle 1959: 17ff), and what we consider today as objectification of some human beings was natural for the ancient Greeks. The institution of slavery was necessary for leading a "good life" by the others – the free members of such society. Deep differences in social status are therefore inscribed in such a community that is fundamentally perceived in analogy to an organism, where social groups are parts of an "organic" social body. An important consequence of this approach is therefore an assumption that people are not equal and free "by nature", but their social status, such as equality and freedom in contemporary societies, is always derived from the concrete community as an outcome of its institutions and practices. Freedom, equality, and social position are therefore "given" by the community.

The political *universum* of the human being is here always the horizon of a concrete, particular community. Each community differs from each other, which results in a strong political relativism. A nationalist standpoint is naturally rooted in the communitarian point of view, not only in its methodological, but also in its social and political aspects. We can only compare institutional solutions inside of the national/cultural community, but we can't evaluate legal or ethical standards of one community from the point of view of another. There is only the particular-communitarian (national, ethnic, religious) and never a universal-cosmopolitan perspective of evaluation of each political order. People don't voluntarily create social institutions because they are methodologically secondary to them; institutions spontaneously evolve from the historically cumulated social practices and traditions, customs, and social patterns.

Unlike in the conservative-communitarian model, there is no substantial, "objective" common good in the individualist model represented by the contractarians. The only form of common good can be derived from an aggregation of individual needs and preferences through bargaining procedures and it fully depends on it. Any "metaphysical", transcendent perspective of an imagined and "esoteric" higher substantial order is excluded. Being an outcome of aggregation of individual preferences and needs, the common good is of purely formal character because it can emerge only from procedures of such an aggregation. The common good is tantamount to the aggregated good of individual members of society. They must be fundamentally equal and free "by nature", because it is the "temporal", "mundane" aggregated good of them, which can be the only point of reference. Their social status and social roles are of secondary character if people are primarily taken to be autonomous individuals.

If the human individual is methodologically prior to the community and common good is of the aggregative character, fundamental social standards have to be universal. As mentioned above they are at least of an economic character. If so, people's political *universum* is not limited to a concrete community, but is of the universal-cosmopolitan character. It does not always have to involve an explicit assumption of "cosmopolis". However, the possibility of such an assumption is always there in the intellectual background. The "reductionist" economic character of these standards causes that the main metaphor of this approach is the metaphor of contract, which in the context of social institutions – morals, law, or political institutions – is called "the social contract". It means that all social institutions result from processes of naturally evolving mutual agreements, which takes place between people equipped with minimal common economic standards of behavior. Because the contract here is often seen as the historical one, the social institutions in different societies do not have to be identical. The assumption of universality of economic standards does not necessarily entail that an effect of using human will must always bring the same results. Rather, the universality I have in mind here means that we are always guided by logic based on the same fundamental assumptions, but it does not mean that the effects of using this logic are always the same. In this approach, ethical and political categories are ordered by and subordinated to economic categories, and ethics and politics are dominated by the logic of economics. However, various conditions and conceptions of politics or economics cause that institutional solutions dictated by the same assumptions differ from each other in different societies.

## 3 Justification of change in the law: Legal determinism versus legal creationism[2]

These contrasting general assumptions of political philosophy determine opposite concepts of law. According to the first – conservative-communitarian model of law – the legal order is an emanation of a concrete, particular community. Law, like any normative system, is the accumulation of long-lasting historical experiences of various particular communities. Positive law is not actively created by the will of the members of this community, but only passively "recognized" or "decoded" from the higher, originally existing community order. The main mark of the law is the difference, which means that we can compare norms derived from different legal systems, but we cannot weigh or evaluate them in any way from any external, i.e. neutral, perspective of the "impartial spectator", because such a universal perspective simply does not exist. MacIntyre perfectly puts it in regard to rationality:

> it is an illusion to suppose that there is some neutral standing ground, some locus for rationality as such, which can afford rational resources sufficient for enquiry independent of all traditions. Those who have maintained otherwise either have covertly been adopting the standpoint of a tradition deceiving themselves and perhaps others into supposing that theirs was just such a neutral standing ground or else have simply been in error.
>
> (MacIntyre 1989: 367)

2 This distinction is not tantamount to one between judicial activism and judicial retreat, because activism and retreat are connected with judicial activity, whereas determinism and creationism are above all connected with legislation. On the judicial activism vs retreat, see: Barnett 1987, Wolfe 1997, Kmiec 2004, Green 2008, Berlatsky 2012.

Although MacIntyre refers here not to legal order but to rationality, rationality as such is for him the starting point for justice, and the combined visions of rationality and justice are inevitably a reference point for the concept of the legal order of a concrete community. The law is not taken from nowhere, and its material sources are the standards of rationality and justice commonly adopted in a given community. Thus, it seems legitimate to carry out an analogy between the concrete legal order, on the one hand, and, on the other, a tradition of rationality and justice. We must, therefore, assume that the legislator, both in a concrete community and in a specific lawmaking tradition, must be determined by this rationality and by the commonly adopted visions of justice. As a member of a specific community and legislative tradition, the legislator cannot escape from the concepts of rationality and justice that are characteristic to them. The use of such analogies leads to the conclusion that in the determinist model these are the factors that fully determine the content and nature of existing laws.

Unlike in the conservative-communitarian model, in the contractarian model legal order is created by people's agreements, being an effect of a long-term bargaining based on the economic "calculus of consent" (Buchanan & Tullock 2004). For Buchanan, law is an effect of some kind of consent, which has to be unanimous on the constitutional level (Buchanan & Tullock 2004: 91), and on lower levels of law it needs not be unanimous, but has to meet the requirements of the "contractarian test" (Buchanan 1977: 33). The latter creates the ahistorical procedure appealing to the social contract theory and seems to be similar to a Kantian way of testing rules (on this procedure, see: Chmieliński 2013: 815). As Buchanan explains, "we may evaluate any element of the existing legal structure in terms of its possible consistency with 'that which might emerge' from a genuine 'social contract' among all persons who are involved in the interaction" (Buchanan 1977: 33). Social contract is a heuristic tool here, a tool that serves in testing the law against the universal contractarian criterion of agreement. As Buchanan adds, arguing against Hayek:

> This test applies equally to those elements of legal structure that may have evolved without conscious design or intent and to those elements which may have been quite explicitly "laid on" for the achievement of a particular purpose at some time in the past. The evaluative analyst must test all "law" on such "as if" contractarian criteria.
>
> (Buchanan 1977: 33)

The contractarian procedure assumes a particular kind of constructivism that Buchanan distinguishes from "constructivist rationalism" in Hayek's understanding. For Buchanan, the individualist contractarian position

> seems clearly to fall within the constructivist category in the sense that it does "provide a guideline for deciding whether or not existing institutions were [are] to be approved". But the position is not at all rationalist in the sense that rationality norms, as such, are applied to the group.
>
> (Buchanan 1977: 33)

As he explicitly stresses to clear his contractarian position

> If properly qualified and interpreted, the contractarian position offers plausibly acceptable alternative to both Hayek's implicit attribution of efficiency to whatever institutions emerge from an evolutionary process and to the rationalist conception which posits the existence of a group mind.
>
> (Buchanan 1977: 33)

In the polemic with Hayek (crucial for his conception of law), Buchanan rests his theory of law on a rejection of Hayek's assumptions of spontaneous order and invisible hand as the proper perspectives for law's evaluation. He thereby rejects the assumption of the historical evolution of law, and makes his concept ahistorical and anti-evolutionary. According to this perspective, even if law in fact "emerges" from such a spontaneous order in the way similar to the invisible hand and even if there is a spontaneous historical evolution of law, we always must have an external instance which helps us to evaluate the outcome of this process, because there is "no reason to expect that the evolution of law made by independent judges insures efficiency or optimality" (Buchanan 1977: 37). Historical legal evolution cannot always be considered the guarantor of best legal solutions. If historical evolution were such a guarantor, historically longer-evolving legal solutions or legal systems would have to be always better than those having evolved for a shorter time. For instance, according to Hayekian evolutionary logic, European laws (at least English) would have to be always better than American ones. Such an assumption is for Buchanan obviously counterfactual: "The historically determined institutions of legal order need not be those which are 'best'. Such institution can be 'reformed', can be made more 'efficient'" (Buchanan 1977: 31). For Buchanan, Hayek represents the standpoint characteristic of "the European classical liberal", being impossible to accept at least from the point of view of the American constitution which

> was deliberately constructed in large part by James Madison and his compatriots. Theirs were no invisible hands. They set out to construct a constitutional framework for the "good society", which they defined implicitly as "free relations among free men". For two centuries their construction has stood the test.
>
> (Buchanan 1977: 38/39)

Rejecting the idea of historical evolution, Buchanan's "creationism" must recognize that each national or concrete law can be evaluated from the perspective of similar economical standards, and that these standards are universal for different countries and communities. In the creationist standpoint so conceived, *similarity* is the main starting point for evaluation of law. Differences are accepted if and only if they are acceptable from this universal point of view.

The above-described fundamentally opposite conceptions of law and legal order, present in the conservative-communitarian and the contractarian models, yield the two opposing concepts of legal change. The conservative-communitarian justification of change begins with the substantially understood common good. Only such change can be justified which improves the common good. If common good is strictly connected with the moral substance of community, the most important question concerning legal change is what the content of this substance is. As community members, we can know this content only from our *phronesis*, i.e. from practical learning and studying of institutions, which are deeply rooted in a concrete community. However, limits of our individual reason as well as limits of reason of the legislator make all our potential decisions never fully informed and thereby always imperfect. We can be never sure whether the introduced changes will be efficient or socially effective. Epistemic limitations of reason mean that it is impossible to predict many of the important consequences of the legal authority's decision-making process and thus, also of the legislative actions taken by this authority.

This is the reason why a legislator has to be always very cautious and "conservative" in his decisions, and the main values of the legal system are consistency and conservation. Legal change is rather an exception, and far-going or revolutionary changes are totally excluded. Evolutionary communitarian way of reforming laws seems to rest on a strategy of resilience, which "is a capacity to cope with unanticipated dangers after they have become manifest, learning to bounce back" (Wildavsky 2017: 77). The opposite strategy – the strategy of anticipation (called also "strategy of interception") – should be strictly limited or even excluded in the conservative-communitarian model, because "anticipation is mode of control by a central mind; effects are made to predict and prevent potential dangers before damage is done . . . Anticipation attempts to avoid hypothesized hazards; resilience is concerned with those that have been realized" (Wildawsky 2017: 77). Roger Scruton, one of the most recognizable English conservative thinkers appeals to this strategy *inter alia* in his "green philosophy" convincing that "in confronting the day-to-day problems of stewardship, resilience may often be more reasonable than interception" (Scruton 2012: 131). Obviously, resilience isn't the only conservative-communitarian strategy of the legal change, but it is the "most natural" one, because it seems to be closest to the Aristotelian *phronesis*.

From the conservative-communitarian point of view, empirical reasons and directions of legal changes are "encoded" in existing historical legal institutions. In this model, the role of the legislator is not to create something new, but rather to "decode" and "read" these reasons and directions from the existing institutions. The legislator's perception is directed not only to the future change, but also to the past, and "the past" is much more important than "the future", because it allows for a better recognition of historical patterns and rules of the gradual legal evolution. According to Hegel's famous sentence, "The owl of Minerva spreads his wings only with the falling of the dusk" (Hegel 1979: 178), which means that being epistemically limited, we can only draw lessons from the history; only the history familiar enough and only the past are sure.

If reasons and directions of changes are "encoded" in community institutions and the legislator has only to "decode" their content, then the role of the will of the democratic sovereign in the process of legal change is not the primary question.

The primary question is whether the change is consistent with community patterns and logic of its institutions or not. Reforms can be accepted if and only if they are consistent with the historical substance of community – with the internal "logic" involved in its institutions. It is this "logic" which contains the substantial common good of the community. Thus, the sovereign's and thereby also the legislator's will is fully determined by this logic, and the legislative activity is rather of a passive and reactive character than of an active one. The legislator does not create the law independently, but he recognizes it only "walking on the path" of the collective, historical legal evolution. In its "vertical" dimension, this model is of the "historical" character. In its "horizontal" dimension, it is of the "collective" character, but without the optimist assumption of Enlightenment that reason is universal, that the collective and the individual reason are in fact the same, and that the collective reason can be understood by means of the individual reason. The will of legislator is determined not only by actual collective needs and preferences of the democratic society, but first of all by the inner "esoteric" logic of existing institutions – by existing "status quo". Each amendment or judiciary decision which aims to change and transgress this logic is seen as revolution against the community itself and as such it is totally excluded.

The limited ability for an autonomous creation of legal values and rules excludes every form of "revolutionary" and centrally planned changes. The assumption of "the limits of human reason" is tantamount to the impossibility of foreseeing the social consequences of a legislative action. Such an assumption suggests that all changes made by parliaments or judges are fundamentally dangerous, given the limits of human reason. The question remains, therefore, if any change can be justified in such a model.

First, one needs to emphasize that the relatively simple "aggregative" answer, natural for modern democracies, is strongly excluded. Such an answer boils down to the assumption that more human minds are involved, the better the change will be. If this were to be accepted, then the best solution would be tantamount to the unanimity solution. Or, in other words, the quantity of supporters of the legal change would determine the quality of it. For representatives of the conservative-communitarian standpoint this cannot be a proper solution, because there is no space for the famous (materialist but inspired by Hegelian dialectics) Marxist law of transformation from quantity into quality (Engels 1987: 110ff). The problem of epistemic limitations concerns not only the individual human reason, but also the human reason as such, which always remains only the *human* one and thus is limited, regardless of the individual or collective level. An aggregated answer is volitional, because it appeals only to the current will of numerous people.

There are however many methodological problems with aggregation and determining the content of the general will (for instance, Arrow 1963). In fact, this is the reason why many conservative-oriented thinkers appeal to the religious assumptions as the ultimate basis of political decisions (Burke 1951: 88f, Maistre 1819, 1884, 1994). The order created by the "Higher Being" can be paradoxically the easiest answer here, and for hundreds of years such a justification has been used as ultimate. But even for those who evoke the Higher Being in the present day, such a theological answer is not considered sufficient. Searching for the best laic justification of the "higher order", they find community, seen not only in its simple collectivist and horizontal dimension, but also in the vertical, historical, and cultural plane. Such a conservative-communitarian model appeals to the Burkean affirmation of the connections between generations, and the necessity of respect for the cultural, social, and political heritage. Such a vertical dimension of historical community creates a resource from which legislators and judges should draw reasons and contents of legal changes. Each legal change must be "decoded" from a complexity of social practices that determine and create its rationality, characteristic only of concrete, historical communities. According to this model, even legislators in statutory law systems do not strictly speaking create law; rather, they always search for law that is rooted in both horizontal and vertical dimension of community. Therefore, a justified type of change is thus determined simultaneously by these dimensions. It is not the legislator's or sovereign's will to change law, making free decisions about change, but the objective necessity coming from both collective and historical dimensions of the concrete community.

The opposite, contractarian approach assumes that the key factor justifying a legal change is an agreement based on maximization or optimization of aggregated preferences and the needs of the current society's members. As we can see, in the above-mentioned "contractarian test", two perspectives of evaluation are internally connected: the economic rationality and the political contractarian procedure.

Economic rationality means that a legal change is justified if and only if it efficiently provides social needs and preferences, maximizing or optimizing them. If so, efficiency is the important factor in the evaluation of legal change. Such an economic evaluation can be made before as well as after the change, because the efficiency measure is of the universal and ahistorical character. Even if representatives of the contractarian approach take into consideration traditions, customs and historical factors, economic rationality can "integrate" these factors essentially as social institutions lowering transaction costs (North 1992: 5). As we saw above, traditions or historical evolution cannot be the proper source of evaluation, according to Buchanan. It is rather the other way around: it is legal traditions and the historical evolution of law that is being evaluated. Thereby, the contractarian position reverses the direction of communitarian *phronesis* and begins with aprioristic categories.

The contractarian test essentially serves the economic evaluation of change. Buchanan's postulate to test law on an "as if" contractarian criteria is tantamount to the hypothetical, aprioristic answer to the question of whether legal change will or will not be socially efficient. The question remains, however, what happens if the commonly agreed legal changes are not economically effective? In other words, can people agree for the economically inefficient solutions, or is economic efficiency the external limit determining the will of the legislator? The question is important, because it concerns the problem of economic determination or indetermination of the legislator's will. We can answer this question "yes and no" at the same time. "Yes", because the legal solution has to be socially efficient and at the end of the day there is no other measure of efficiency than the "minimalist" economic measure. Alternatively, we can say "no" at the same time, because the economic rationality is something essential to each individual and thus – according to the individualist methodology – also to each kind of the lawmaker. Thereby we have substantially no external limitation in such an individualist "marriage" of economic and political elements.

Alternatively, if economic rationality provides consequences unacceptable under the contractarian test (which can be rarely possible), the individualist point of view excludes following the economic rationality. It results from the contractarian doctrine of rights. Violating human rights and important human goods by economically effective solutions is excluded by the individualist character of the contractarian perspective. Conception of human rights substantially differs from the conservative-communitarian assumption of natural law. The content of natural law is tediously "encoded" from diverse historical practices of concrete communities, whereas natural right is simply "given in advance" by individualist universal methodological priority of human individual and the optimist assumption of the relatively unlimited human reason resulting therefrom. Using one's reason, one can universally assume that every human individual in every latitude wants at least two things: to live and to possess. "The principle to be emphasized, however, is that some structure, any structure, of well-defined rights is a necessary starting point for the potential trades that are required to remove the newly emergent interdependence" (Buchanan 1977: 97). Property rights are especially important for this perspective, because without property there is simply no economics and economic rationality.

Therefore, economic rationality is subordinated to the contractarian procedure. There are some standards drawn from basic rights that the legislative authority must respect, regardless of the reasons provided by economic authority. However, in such a legal positivist standpoint, it is only the legislative authority that creates the duty to obey the rule. Unlike in the conservative-communitarian model, law and legal changes are voluntarily created directly by legislators using individualist contractarian procedures to look for the optimal solutions for providing needs and preferences of democratic society. It is not directed towards the past but looking into the future. The desired virtue of change, therefore, is its ability to adapt actual social contracts based on the mutual maximization of dynamically changing needs and preferences. Law can be voluntarily created by lawgivers and the only limitations for such lawgiving activity are contractarian procedures (with basic rights embedded therein) and standards of economic rationality that are, in certain sense, internal to the human individual. Thus, such a model can be called "creationist", because it depends only on free agreement of individual members of the society, being a question of their efficiently aggregated will regarding preferences and needs.

## Conclusion

The above presented, Weberian-mode "ideal types" never exists in real political and legal practices that can only get close to the one or another standpoint. For instance, in the East European, post-communist countries, after the collapse of communism, where the legal change was connected to deep, systemic institutional and political transition, "revolutionary" changes were not total, and some laws and statutes remained unchanged or only partially changed. It proves that in real social practices the total legal change is not only unnecessary, but also undesirable, even in the processes of the legal and political transition. Detailed analysis of two above presented opposite models show the following:

(1) The above-described models of justification can be always considered as complementary points of reference, building together the relatively complex justification of law. In justification of legal practices some elements of both – determinist and creationist – models are always present. Obviously, the two kinds of justification are used in many various ways, and that the relationships between them are sometimes very complicated and uneasy to understand, but it confirms a thesis that they are always used in legal practices.
(2) Our considerations show that justification as complex as this in current democratic societies cannot escape drawing from both the determinist and the creationist model. Historical communitarian values always supply a necessary continuity and identity to the concrete legal change, at least in the higher, constitutional level. The figure of volitional creation taken by an aggregate will of the democratic society is in turn necessary to make the law an institution of a democratic character and "the people" – subjects and not only objects of law. Additionally, the "creationist", economic rationality secures one of the clearest (though not always most useful) criterion of evaluation of the change of law as such, i.e. its economic efficiency.
(3) It seems that any dynamic synthesis of these opposite elements which constitutes the goal of real-life justifications cannot totally exclude either of the poles. At the end of the day, they are taken not as opposite but as complementary. In real life, both the conservative-communitarian and contractarian models supply the justification of change in law. As a result, the legal change: (a) cannot be fully "alienated" from culture, customs, and traditions of the legal community in question, and generally needs to reach some consistence and equilibrium with it; (b) cannot be extremely sudden and revolutionary; and, at the same time, (c) can be relatively well adjusted to the actual needs of society. Disregarding any of these three elements always makes the change hardly feasible and susceptible to criticism. Taking them into consideration does not automatically eliminate such a criticism, but it can limit it. Of course, such a complex justification can be (and is) complemented also by other important conceptions as for example by conceptions of autonomy or dignity and it always has an open character.

## References

Aristotle (1959) *Politics*, Cambridge, Harvard University Press.
Arrow, K. J. (1963) *Social Choice and Individual Values*, New York, Wiley.

Austin, J. (1995) *The Province of Jurisprudence Determined*, Cambridge, Cambridge University Press.

Barnett, R. (1987) 'Judicial Conservatism v. A Principled Judicial Activism. Foreword to Symposium on Law and Philosophy', *Harvard Journal of Law & Public Policy*, 10: 273–294.

Bellah, R., Madsen, R., and Sullivan, W. M. (1985) *Habits of the Heart. Individualism and Commitment in American Life*, Berkeley and London, University of California Press.

Bentham, J. (1931) *A Fragment of Government*, London, Oxford University Press.

Bentham, J. (1945) *The Limits of Jurisprudence Defined*, New York, Columbia University Press

Bentham, J. (1970) *Of Laws in General*, London, The Athlone Press.

Berlatsky, N. (ed.) (2012) *Introduction to Judicial Activism: Opposing Viewpoints*, Farmington Hills, Greenhaven Press.

Buchanan, J. M. (1975) *The Limits of Liberty. Between Liberty and Leviathan*, Chicago, University of Chicago Press.

Buchanan, J. M. (1977) *Freedom in Constitutional Contract. Perspectives of a Political Economist*, College Station Texas, A. & M. University Press.

Buchanan, J. M. (1991) *The Economics and the Ethics of Constitutional Order*, Ann Arbor, University of Michigan Press.

Buchanan, J. M. and Brennan, G. (1985) 'Modelling the Individual for Constitutional Analysis', in J. M. Buchanan and G. Brennan (eds) *The Reason of Rules. Constitutional Political Economy*, Ann Arbor, University of Michigan Press.

Buchanan, J. M. and Tullock, G. (2004) *The Calculus of Consent – Logical Foundations of Constitutional Democracy*, Ann Arbor, University of Michigan Press.

Burke, E. (1951) *Reflections on the French Revolution*, London, J. M. Dent & Sons, and New York, E. P. Dutton & Co.

Chmieliński, M. (2004) 'Wstęp' ['Introduction'] in *Atomizm a indywidualizm. Rozważania nad myślą polityczną i prawną Wilhelma von Humboldta* [*Atomism and Individualism. Deliberations on Political and Legal Thought of Wilhelm von Humbold*], Wydawnictwo, Uniwersytetu Łódzkiego Łódź.

Chmieliński, M. (2013) 'Deliberatives Rechtsetzungsverfahren als Gewährleistung der juridischen Autonomie nach Immanuel Kant', in Stefano Bacin, Alfredo Ferrarin, Claudio La Rocca and Margit Ruffing (eds) *Kant und die Philosophie in weltbürgerlicher Absicht Akten des XI.Internationalen Kant-Kongresses*, Bd 3, Berlin/Boston, De Gruyter.

Engels, F. (1987) 'Anti-Dűhring', in *Karl Marx, Frederick Engels Collected Works*, Vol. 25, New York, International Publishers.

Finnis, J. (2011) 'Revolutions and Continuity of Law', in J. Finnis (ed.) *Philosophy of Law*. Collected Essays Vol IV, Oxford, Oxford Scholarship.

Gauthier, D. (1986) *Morals by Agreement*, Oxford, Oxford University Press.

Gauthier, D. (1990) 'David Hume, Contractarian', in David Gauthier *Moral Dealing: Contract, Ethics, and Reason*, Ithaca, New York.

Gauthier, D. (1991) 'Why Contractarianism?', in Peter Vallentyne (ed.) *Contractualism and Rational Choice. Essays on David Gauthiers Morals by Agreement*, Cambridge, Cambridge University Press.

Green, C. (2008) *An Intellectual History of Judicial Activism*, ExpressO, https://works.bepress.com/roger_craig_green/1/ [accessed 30/01/19].

Hampton, J. (1991) 'Two Faces of Contractarian Thought', in Peter Vallentyne (ed.) *Contractualism and Rational Choice. Essays on David Gauthiers Morals by Agreement*, Cambridge, Cambridge University Press.

Hart, H. L. A. (1994) *The Concept of Law*, Oxford, Clarendon Press.

Hayek, F. A. (2011) *The Constitution of Liberty. The Definitive Edition*, London and New York, Routledge.

Hegel, G. W. F. (1979) *Werke*, Frankfurt am Main, Band 7.

Hobbes, T. (1651) *Leviathan or The Matter, Form and Power of a Common-Wealth Ecclesiastical and Civil*, printed for Andrew Crooke, at the Green Dragon in St-Pauls Church-Yard, London.

Hume, D. (2008) 'Of The Original Contract', in Raymond Geuss and Quentin Skinner (series eds) *David Hume. Political Essays*, Cambridge, Cambridge University Press.

Kmiec, K. D. (2004) 'The Origin and Current Meanings of Judicial Activism', *California Law Review*, 92(5), 1441–1478.

MacIntyre, A. (1989) *Whose Justice, Which Rationality*, 11, Notre Dame, University of Notre Dame Press.

MacIntyre, A. (2007a) *After Virtue*, Notre Dame, University of Notre Dame Press,.

MacIntyre, A. (2007b) *Ethics and Politics. Selected Essays. Volume 2*, Cambridge, New York, and Melbourne, Cambridge University Press.

MacIntyre, A. (2016) *Ethics in the Conflicts of Modernity. An Essay on Desire, Practical Reasoning, and Narrative*, Cambridge, Cambridge University Press.

Maistre, J. de (1819) *Du Pape*, Lyon, Rusand.

Maistre, J. de (1884) 'Etude sur la souverainete, part I, X, Vol I', in Colin Lucas (ed.) (1989) *The French Evolution Research Collection/Les Archives de la Revolution Francaise*, Oxford, Pergamon Press.

Maistre, J. de (1994) *Considerations on France*, Cambridge, Cambridge University Press.

Marquand, D. (1979) *Parliament for Europe*, London, Jonathan Cape.

Narveson, J. (1988) *The Libertarian Idea*, Philadelphia, Temple University Press.

North, D. (1992) *Transaction Costs, Institutions, and Economic Performance*, San Francisco, International Center for Economic Growth.

Oakeshott, M. (1962) *Rationalism in Politics and Other Essays*, London, Methuen & Co.

Oakeshott, M. (1995) *Experience and its Modes*, Cambridge, Cambridge University Press.

Rau, Z. (1995) 'Introduction', in *Contractarianism versus Holism. Reinterpreting Locke's Two Treatises of Government*, New York and London, University Press of America.

Rawls, J. (1971) *A Theory of Justice*, Cambridge, Belknap Press.

Roosevelt, K. (2008) *The Myth of Judicial Activism: Making Sense of Supreme Court Decisions*, New Haven, Yale University Press.

Sandel, M. (1982) *Liberalism and the Limits of Justice*, Cambridge, Cambridge University Press.

Scanlon, T. M. (1982) 'Contractualism and Utilitarianism', in A. Sen and B. Williams (eds) *Utilitarianism and Beyond*, Cambridge, Cambridge University Press.

Scanlon, T. M. (1998) *What We Owe to Each Other*, Cambridge, Harvard University Press.

Scruton, R. (2012) *Green Philosophy: How to Think Seriously About The Planet*, London, Atlantic Books.

Surowiecki, J. (2005) *The Wisdom of Crowds*, New York, Anchor Books.

Taylor, Ch. (1985) 'Atomism', in *Philosophy and the Human Sciences*, New York, Cambridge University Press.

Taylor, Ch. (1989a) *Sources Of The Self*, Cambridge, Harvard University Press.

Taylor, Ch. (1989b) 'Cross Purposes: The Liberal-Communitarianism Debate', in N. Rosenblum (ed.) *Liberalism and the Moral Life*, Cambridge, Harvard University Press.

Taylor, Ch. (1991) *The Ethics of Authenticity*, Cambridge and London, Harvard University Press.
Tönnies, F. (2002) *Community and Society. Gemeinschaft und Gesellschaft*, Mineola New York, Dover Publications.
Vermeule, A. (2009) *Law and the Limits of Human Reason*, New York, Oxford University Press.
Waldron, J. (1990) *The Law*, London and New York, Routledge.
Wildavsky, A. (2017) *Searching for Safety*, London and New York, Routledge.
Wolfe, Ch. (1997) *Judicial Activism. Bulwark of Freedom or Precarious Security?* New York and Oxford, Rowman Littlefield.

# 6 Natural law ethics and the issue of legal change[1]

*Michał Rupniewski*

## Introduction

Although the term "natural law" has multiple meanings in jurisprudence, two main tendencies in understanding this term can be discerned. According to the first one, every legal theory affirming an internal connection of law and morals, or even regarding the two as being in fact one normative system, can be labeled ***natural law***. Ronald Dworkin, by endorsing a "tree structure" of morality, politics, and law, can be called a natural law theorist in this sense (Dworkin 2011: 405–407). Alternatively, the emphasis can be put on the affirmation of ***a substantive vision of a human being, and the good of community*** as the core commitment in natural law thinking.[2] When understood in this second way, natural law theorizing does not primarily focus on definitional issues (e.g. what is law?), but rather attempts to answer: (1) what is the objective ground for both morals and law? And (2) what good is to be attained through legal institutions and practice? Such an approach might be called "natural law ethics", as opposed to "natural law jurisprudence".[3]

Since this book aims at examining the values and principles that determine processes of legal change, investigations of natural law ethics seem a more promising area of interest. According to the terminology adopted in this volume, issues such as the controversy concerning the conceptual relation of law and morals belong to legal theory rather than legal philosophy; the latter focuses on law's justification, and thus on values and purposes of law, whether internal or external to the legal system.

1 This chapter presents parts of the results of the research project *Normative Models of Political Legitimation of Change of Law in a Democratic State* – project number 2015/19/B/HS5/02522 – supported by the National Science Centre (Poland). Also, I am grateful to Marek Piechowiak for reading the draft of this chapter and for helpful comments on it.

2 The second way of defining natural law theory is more specific: only theories closely connected to the tradition of Aristotle and Aquinas, that is, to the tradition affirming the substantial and real foundation for natural law, would count as natural law ones. Dworkin and Fuller, although being non-positivist, are far too "procedural" and "neutral-liberal" to be called natural law thinkers in this second, stricter sense.

3 This distinction has been proposed by Robin West (2011). She argues that natural law, understood as natural law ethics, can become a powerful tool of normative legal critique, conducted within the progressive-liberal intellectual framework. Therefore, she focuses on the issue of human good to be attained through law.

Thus, legal philosophy and natural law ethics overlap: to examine philosophically the dynamics of change that (I will argue) are embedded in natural law theory, one needs to answer precisely the questions posted in the previous paragraph.

Of course, as natural law tradition is extremely rich and multi-layered, it is not possible to arrive at conclusions that would be true for natural law ethics taken as a whole; one must narrow down the investigations in some way. Undoubtedly, the most comprehensive and influential account on natural law was given by Thomas Aquinas. His thought is still a point of reference for many contemporary philosophers and political theorist working in the natural law tradition. Therefore, this chapter will attempt to identify an Aquinian account of legal change, as far as the natural law and the human (i.e. positive) laws are concerned. However, this is not an exegetical paper, strictly speaking; restraining myself to the *Summa Theologiae* (1947 edition) I will attempt to work up a model of legal change that follows from Aquinas's account on law and natural law. I also intend briefly to show how this general model of thinking is present among contemporary scholars working in Aquinian tradition.[4]

The general conclusion is the following: reason constitutes the foundation for human law, and the law is a reasonable decision of a legislator, informed by cognition of the relevant part of reality that is to be ordered. The extra-legal reality (that is, the reality of the human beings as well as concrete communities in question) determines the common good, and thus human good that is to be attained through legal institutions. For Aquinas, the starting point of any practical reflection is provided by human nature. His followers (Finnis 2011 [1980], Maritain 1951, Piechowiak 2016) modify that, and take up either the dignity of the person or human goods as the objective-real grounds for law, and thus legal change.

## 1 Law's reasonable orientation toward the common good: An aquinian model

### *1.1 The source of law's normativity: Cognition through reason*

Christine Korsgaard, in her famous Tanner lecture *The Sources of Normativity*, suggested that the titular problem is urgent only for modern philosophers. The pre-modern accounts on ethics

> seem to support the idea that human life has a purpose that is or only can be fulfilled by those who live up to ethical standards and meet moral demands. And this is supposed to be sufficient to establish that ethics is really normative, that its demands on us are justified.
>
> (Korsgaard 1992: 23–24)

4 I quote the *Summa Theologiae* as *ST*. I follow the conventional mode of citation, indicating the part of the *Summa* in roman numerals, then indicating the question (q.), and article (a.). If the quote comes from an objection, I add an indication "sc.". For a reply to objection (that each article contains), I add an indication "ad".

In other words, Korsgaard seems to suggest that pre-modern philosophers take normativity for granted together with the teleological metaphysics they commonly share, and thus do not need to delve into the nature of normativity as a separate issue. I doubt if this is really the case. Aquinas gives us many reasons for this doubt. The part of *Summa Theologiae* (hereinafter *ST*) dealing directly with law starts with the question whether it pertains to will, or to reason. Aquinas answers that the latter is the case, and thus his treaty on law might be read as providing an alternative to the voluntarist claim that "*quod placuit principi, legis habet vigorem*" (*ST*: I–II, q.90 a.1 sc.3). Therefore, the starting point of my inquiry is explaining in which sense reason is the source of law's normativity, or, in other words, how law is based on natural reason.

According to the definition offered by Aquinas in *ST*, law, understood in abstract terms as every "rule and measure" (*regula et mensura*) of acts, is "an ordinance of reason for the common good, made by him who has care of the community, and promulgated" (*ST*: I–II, q.90 a.4). This general definition embraces all main kinds of law: the eternal, the natural, the human, and the divine. In this chapter, we are interested mainly in the middle two: the human (positive) law as a result of human legislation, and the natural law as a foundation thereof, and a special way in which the eternal law is present in the human being as a reasonable being. The eternal and the divine law, coming directly from God's acts, are situated beyond the scope of legal philosophy and pertain to respectively to philosophical (natural) theology and to theology proper.[5] Asking about the objective basis for the eternal and divine law is superfluous, as the answer is obvious: it is God (perfectly reasonable, absolute Being) who is its direct source. The picture gets more complicated in case of the natural and the human law, where God (and thus the eternal law) leaves space for human freedom, agency, and choice. The crucial role is played by natural, human reason, and the "reasonableness", rather than the "naturalness", of law becomes its crucial feature, although the two do not stand in a strong opposition to each other.

Perhaps a good way to explain this is to consider an example of a legal institution. Let us take marriage, which is backed by natural law, according to Aquinas. He writes:

5 Recall that the eternal law embraces all of creation, as an act of the divine reason, or His reasonable plan, and not merely His will. It is, therefore, the rule and measure God uses in the act of creation, containing the ideas for all the beings in the universe, similar to those that an artificer has for pieces of art he would produce (*ST*: I–II, q.93 a.1). Every being (including the non-rational ones) has inclinations proper to their nature, according to the eternal law. However, human beings, as reasonable creatures having free will (as the eternal law prescribes), are not only passive creatures being measured and governed, but are also capable of acts of measure and governance. Thus, a special way in which human beings are measured by the eternal law is them having practical reason, making them capable of free decisions informed by the natural law as principle of acts (Baur 2012: 248). The divine law – the Old and the New Testament – is a necessary complementation of natural law and natural reason. Among other things, it directs human acts not only toward the terrestrial, but also toward the eternal happiness (*beatitudo aeterna*), and it eradicates the doubt that might occur when applying unaided natural reason.

> A thing is said to be natural in two ways. First, as resulting of necessity from the principles of nature; thus upward movement is natural to fire. In this way matrimony is not natural, nor are any of those things that come to pass at the intervention or motion of the free-will. Secondly, that is said to be natural to which nature inclines although it comes to pass through the intervention of the free-will; thus acts of virtue and the virtues themselves are called natural; and in this way matrimony is natural, because natural reason inclines thereto
>
> (*ST*: Supp., q.41 a.1)[6]

Marriage is natural *because* it is reasonable, and reason is not a "supernatural" power transcending the nature. Rather, the inclinations coming directly from reason constitute human nature together with other inclinations, like those coming from sensitive apprehension, which we share with other (nonrational) animals. Our rational nature, then, extends to all aspects of humanity – our inclinations and powers are all of one substantial form, constituting rational human person (*ST*: I, q.76, a.1).[7] As Aquinas writes, "reason is one in itself, yet it directs all things regarding man, so that whatever can be ruled by reason, is contained under the law of reason" (*ST* I–II, q.94, a.2 ad 3). Therefore, in the case of marriage, all aspects of marital life are perceived in the context of the human person fulfilling her natural dispositions, and thus cultivating natural reason. Reason is a power enabling a free choice of ends; it is to provide an understanding of ends, and thus provide an objective basis for intentions determining human acts.[8] Analogically, legal institutions that are backed by natural law are determined by reasonable ends, or goods, that they serve. In case of marriage, one might identify the two: the good of the offspring and the good of the spouses (*ST*: Supp., q.41 a.1). The children, having a definite mother and father sharing the household, are not only brought up into this world, but also function in an environment potentially providing education and leading towards virtue. The spouses, living together in an enduring relationship of fidelity (*fides*), lead a community life characterized by certain "fellowship", or "friendship" (*ST*: Supp., Q.55 a.1), according to their natural inclinations.

6 It is important to remark that this quote comes from the *Supplementum*, most probably written by the disciples of Aquinas, on the basis of their notes and Aquinas' commentary on Sentences (Torrell 2012: 21). However, since in this chapter I am looking for a model of Aquinas's thought, and nothing in the account on marriage presented in the *Supplementum* seems to contradict the rest of Aquinas's practical philosophy, I am taking a liberty of using this as a starting point.

7 Thus, Etienne Gilson rightly points out that:

> It would be completely foreign to the Thomistic perspective to regard the material universe as the result of some calamity, and the union of the soul and body as the consequence of a fall . . . The body is not the prison of the soul, but a servant and instrument placed in its service. The union of soul and body is not a punishment of the soul, but a salutary bond through which the human soul will reach its full perfection.
>
> (Gilson 2002: 222)

8 Although intention (*intentio*) is, properly speaking, an act of the will, and not reason (*ST*: I–II, q.12 a.1), the will in the proper sense is present in the agent only via reason (*ST*: I–II, q.6 a.2). Freedom, as a *liberum arbitrum*, consists in choosing between goods to be pursued. To discern and understand the goods, one needs to apply reason (see Williams 2012).

The structure outlined above can be observed in other legal and governmental institutions. It is always a human good embraced by reason, and then pursued or protected through the rules of the law, whether natural or human. Therefore, the central tenet of natural law ethics is the following: law has an objective basis in extra-legal reality, and that basis can be cognized through natural reason. For Aquinas, arguably, that basis is provided by human nature (essential properties of man), to the extent that it can be known to us (Lisska 1997: 120–126). The crucial implication of this, for reconstructing an Aquinian model of legal change, is that the legislation guided by natural law does not consist simply in applying abstract first principles to the particular cases, but in actively examining the (human) reality that calls for ordering via legal norms and institutions. After reflection and deliberation (see Finnis 1998: 62–72), a reasonable decision is to be made by the lawgiver, according to what is known and understood through natural reason. And this is the source of law's normativity, according to natural law ethics.[9]

### *1.2 Common good: The personalist interpretation*

As we have seen, law is essentially connected to natural reason, which cognizes the good. Now, the good that is organizing and ordering for law is the common good. Although the individual good is embedded in and protected by the common good, it is the latter that constitutes the *raison d'être*, and the criterion to evaluate legal arrangements. The common good is a shared end (some kind of perfection, as for instance justice[10]) that may be enjoyed by a state or community (*civitas*). Aquinas writes:

> He that seeks the good of the many, seeks in consequence his own good, for two reasons. First, because the individual good is impossible without the common good of the family, state, or kingdom . . . Secondly, because, since man is a part of the home and state, he must needs consider what is good for him by being prudent about the good of the many. For the good disposition of parts depends on their relation to the whole
>
> (*ST*: II–II, q.47 a.10 ad 2)

9 Returning to Korsgaard's essay, natural law ethics obviously falls into the category of moral realism (Korsgaard 1992: 30–49). It is noteworthy, however, that this (pre-modern) form of realism escapes the most common modern argument against realism. The argument goes that realism rests on the assertion of the existence of objective values (such as "the good") as separate entities that can be intuited, and thus lacks explanatory power. As we have seen, there is no need to assume that "values" or "obligations" exist as separate entities or quasi-platonic Forms.

10 Aquinas explicitly says that the common good is that of justice and peace (*ST*: I–II, q.96 a.3). On other occasions he also mentions God as the ultimate common good of the universe (from the perspective of the eternal law). He also uses a military victory as an example. A more limited common good is the good of the children for their parents (for the Aquinian references, see Baur 2012: 240).

The commitment toward the common good is thus underlined by the metaphysical claim that the whole is prior to the parts; in this case, the political whole is prior to the individual parts (citizens) forming it (Baur 2012: 238–244). The state is one of the many natural communities that human beings participate in. It has a distinguished place, though, as being self-sufficient: "the good of one man is not the last end, but is ordained to the common good; so too the good of one household is ordained to the good of a single state, which is a perfect community" (*ST*: I–II, q.90 a.3). However, this does not mean that the community is absolute, or requires special respect as an end in itself. Although the common good might require some sacrifice on behalf of individuals pursuing their good,[11] Aquinas offers a model in which the common and the individual goods are not in strict opposition. It is important to bear in mind that human beings are individual substances, and therefore perfect wholes (endowed with existence, which is a separate metaphysical category in Aquinas's system). The state is not a substance, and is a whole only *per analogiam*, insofar as it is ordered and structured. Therefore, although Aquinas says that the law should seek perfection of the state, the ultimate purpose of this perfection is not the state itself. Rather, as indicated above, it is the perfection of the individuals (Piechowiak 2012: 106–117). Likewise, the perfection of individuals is the ultimate purpose of positive law. As Aquinas writes, "in order that man might have peace and virtue, it was necessary for laws to be framed" (*ST*: I–II, q.95 a.1). According to the Aristotelian metaphysics of finality that Aquinas accepts, the flourishing of a human being heavily depends on the autarkic (and, in this sense, perfect) political community (*ST*: I–II, q.90 a.2). This is the reason why one seeking the good of the many seeks in fact his own good too.

From the perspective taken up in this volume, one might see this view as a middle-ground position between social holism and individualism. On the one hand, Aquinas accepts the social-holistic legacy of Aristotle: the whole is prior to the parts, and therefore law "is ordained to the common good of the multitude" (*ST*: I–II, q.96 a.3). On the other hand, the true purpose of the community is not the community as an end in itself.[12] As we have seen in the case of marriage (which is a community with its own, though limited and not perfect, common good), the main purpose is the offspring: their life, upbringing, and virtue. Analogically, as far as a perfect community

11 A famous example offered by Aquinas is that of capital punishment. Since, according to Aquinas, putting thieves to death is required by justice, it pursues the common good. The family members of the sentenced, however, might want him to live, for the sake of the good of their family. And even though their will is therefore not a bad will, it must not be pursued. The judge, as the guardian of the common good, and for the sake of the common good, should put the criminal to death (*ST*: I–II, q.19 a.10). It has also important theological implications that are not of our concern here (see MacInterny 1992: 96).

12 On the contrary, the idea that human beings exist as ends in themselves, being naturally free, is present already in Aquinas (*ST*: q.64 a.2 ad 3). I owe this important observation to Marek Piechowiak (Piechowiak 2016: 76).

(the state) is concerned, the main purpose is the citizens: the common good provides the circumstances that enable their flourishing. However, the political community does not constitute the ultimate point of reference for the human person. As Aquinas puts it, "[m]an is not ordained to the body politic, according to all that he is and has" (*ST*: I–II, q.21 a.4 ad 3). In other words, the political community does not embrace the whole reality of the human individual. Although man is indeed a social and political animal, natural reason makes one naturally free in the community. Therefore, arguably, the human fulfillment rather than the community's fulfillment is the main concern of the common good (Finnis 2018).

## 2 The universal, the particular, and legal change

### *2.1 Natural law: The first principles and their conclusions*

Having identified the grounds for law, that is, natural reason and common good, we can now proceed to the issues of legal change. Aquinas directly addresses the problem whether law may change, both in case of the natural (*ST*: I–II, q.94 a.5) and the human law (*ST*: I–II, q.97). In the case of a natural law that orders and directs human action towards fulfillment, it is unchangeable as far as the orientation toward the good is a feature of every human will, and reason measuring the will. Therefore, "the precepts of the natural law are to the practical reason, what the first principles of demonstrations are to the speculative reason; because both are self-evident principles" (*ST*: I–II, q.94 a.2). The first principles of speculative reasoning[13] are not a product of deduction, but enable any sort of theoretical judgment, as axioms. The first principles of practical reasoning reflect the basic inclinations of the human nature, and therefore are "starting points" (MacInterny 1992: 108) enabling any reasonable reflection on means and ends. Since the good (self-fulfillment) is an end of every human being, and constitutes the purpose of every action, the first principle of natural law is that "good is to be done and pursued, and evil is to be avoided." (*ST*: I–II, q.94 a.2). Just as the cognition of being (as being) is implicitly present in any act of theoretical cognition, the cognition of the good is implicit in any practical judgment, that is, a judgment oriented toward an end. Despite the fact that, as Thomas believes, there is one ultimate human good, which is God himself, he accepts a multitude of first principles of practical reason. Some other goods are necessary to achieve the ultimate good, and therefore are apprehended "naturally as man's good" (*ST*: I–II, q.94 a.2). These other, more specific precepts are grounded in human nature, and the set consists of: preserving one's being, establishing a family life, acquiring knowledge (about God in the first place), and peacefully living in society (*ST*: I–II, q.94 a.2).

The first precepts of natural law constitute a foundation of any practical judgment and thus cover both ethics and law. They are unchangeable and therefore universal (*ST*: I–II, q.94 a.4). What should be emphasized is that their validity

13 Strictly speaking, practical and theoretical reason are not two distinct powers, according to Aquinas, but one intellectual power (*ST*: I, q.79 a.11).

is limited neither to Christians, nor to any other cultural community, as they stem from human nature, which is a nature of the species, and thus common to all humans, and commonly known. However, the universalism that Aquinas has in mind should not be too easily conflated with modern universalism, so severely and famously criticized by Bentham. The first precepts of natural law are neither abstract, *a priori* principles, nor substantive values existing in a manner of Platonic Forms. Rather, they are present in the reason of the concrete acting person, insofar as this person performs acts realizing her nature. Therefore, they are always open to specification, and always operate in a social context of the common good and the positive law of a concrete community.[14]

The first precepts of natural law are further specified by natural reason in "certain matters of detail" by what Thomas calls "proper conclusions" (*ST*: I–II, q.94 a.4). For instance, a general precept of natural law is that one should live according to reason, as a rational animal. As a proper conclusion from this, it follows that "the goods entrusted to another should be restored to their owner" (*ST*: I–II, q.94 a.4). Analogically, we can say that all that one might easily infer as a conclusion from the general precepts has this status; for instance, one shall not kill, or one shall not commit adultery. For these proper conclusions to be determined, no human legislation is needed; their content is present in the reason of the acting person insofar as they are inferred from the first precepts. Therefore, proper conclusions may change natural law "by way of addition", never subtracting anything from the natural law, but supplementing its content (*ST*: I–II, q.94 a.5).[15] Whereas the first precepts are universally binding also in the sense of allowing no exception, a proper conclusion "may be changed" in the sense of allowing an exception in extraordinary circumstances. One example Aquinas gives is if one claimed his weapon held in deposit "for the purpose of fighting against one's country", it would be contrary to reason, and thus to natural law, to realize that request (*ST*: I–II, q.94 a.4).

As Czesław Martyniak rightly observes, there is another category of conclusions from natural law to be examined. He calls them "second-order" rules, as they are serving the secondary aims of a practice or institution in question (Martyniak 2006: 112).[16] Since each social practice or institution is rooted in natural human inclinations, they constitute their ends. All rules serving the primary end of a relevant practice or institution go into the category of proper conclusions; for instance, since it is a natural inclination to preserve one's being,

14 For instance, when Aquinas writes about discipline that law fosters and requires, he asserts that it should be required "according to human customs" and "adapted to place and time" (*ST*: I–II, q.95 a.3). There is, therefore, no abstract, rational political and legal order that could be substantively determined, according to Aquinas. Each social order, though measured and order by reason and law, is always concrete and unique.

15 In an ordinary course of events, the proper conclusions would go into the fabric of positive law, and therefore Aquinas writes here about positive law (together with Divine written law) changing the natural law by way of addition (*ST*: I–II, q.94 a.5). However, the proper conclusions do not require juridification to be binding in conscience, thus we can say that they themselves change natural law by way of addition.

16 The distinction between primary and secondary ends that Martyniak applies here, comes from another work by Aquinas, *Summa Contra Gentiles* (Martyniak 2006: 166).

the rule forbidding murder is a proper conclusion from a more general rule that one should do no harm to others. But in certain matters of further detail, and secondary end, the natural reason also operates, deriving even more detailed rules from the first precepts. An apt example is a rule of monogamous marriage. As we have seen in this text, the primary end of marriage (the offspring having definite mother and father) may be achieved in a polygamy (but not in polyandry, as the father would be indeterminate). Therefore, monogamy is not a proper conclusion, but a second-order rule. Despite this, polygamy is "against the law of nature", Aquinas argues, giving numerous reasonable arguments in favor of a monogamous marriage, referring mostly to faithful relation between spouses as an important good attained through marriage (*ST*: Supp., q.65 a.1). However, if the circumstances were different (for instance, there would be very few men in comparison to the number of women), the monogamous marriage rule could be changed. Therefore, in the second-order conclusions, the natural law may "vary according to the various states and conditions of men" (*ST*: Supp., q.41 a.1).

As we see, even natural law, which is universally binding in its first precepts, is nevertheless open to specification by the particular conditions of the societies in question, as far as secondary rules are concerned. Therefore, it seems, natural law may be affected by social changes or changes of custom. It is also a matter of virtues and vices present in the society. It might turn out unreasonable to require from a barbaric society what can be inevitable in a society of the just and virtuous. Some institutions, such as election of representatives, might be suitable for a virtuous people, and then become unreasonable as the same people gets corrupted (*ST*: I–II, q.97 a.1). Given what has been said before, we might say that the natural law, although being universal in its first precepts, is always "contextualized" and possibly changing in the matters of detail. This feature of law being rooted in a particular social reality is even more obviously to be observed in case of the human (positive) law, to which we now shall proceed.

### *2.2 Human law:* Ius gentium, ius civile, *and custom*

Although natural reason is capable of ordering human affairs and resolving cases on its own, Thomas acknowledges that the common good calls for proper legislation, that is, positive law introducing abstract norms binding in a relevant legal community (*ST*: I–II, q.95 a.1 ad 2). As he writes, "[t]he general principles of the natural law cannot be applied to all men in the same way on account of the great variety of human affairs: and hence arises the diversity of positive laws among various people" (*ST*: I–II, q.95 a.2 ad 3). However, the positive law must not violate the natural law, and is always in some sense derived therefrom. More precisely, there are two modes in which the human legislator uses the natural law in the law-making process. First, a positive law may be a "juridified" conclusion from natural law, like in case of law forbidding murder mentioned in the previous section.[17] Second, a positive law might be a further specification of the natural law in ordering maters of detail. In this mode, the legislator operates by determination, using the general rules of natural law (embedded in natural reason) as guidelines. In case of law concerning murder, "the law of nature has it that the evil-doer should be punished; but that he be punished in this or that way, is a determination of the law of nature" (*ST*: I–II, q.95 a.2). A rule establishing a punishment for murder is derived by conclusion, and then introduced into the fabric of positive law. All the specifics of the particular punishment, in a given legal community, constitute a derivation from positive law by determination.

Following this twofold mode, Thomas divides the human law into the *ius gentium* (law valid across nations), and the *ius civile* (law of a state), the former being a result of conclusion, the latter of determination. As shown by the example of a law against murder, the *ius gentium* is more general and more closely connected to the natural law. However, it needs a specification through the positive law proper, that is, through the *ius civile*, almost at all times. The latter is compared to the arts; one might understand it as the way through which the legal good is to be attained in the social reality. In a manner similar to that of a craftsman, the legislator "gives a particular shape" to the generalities found in her natural reason. The shape of legal institutions is then left to a free, though principled, decision of those having authority to frame the laws for a community. (*ST*: I–II, q.95 a.2). Such legislative decisions are never made to last in perpetuity, in other words, are always *pro tanto* decisions. They are naturally open to reasonable changes, erasing the deficiencies and achieving greater perfection. Also, as the "condition of man" changes, the law should reflect it, accordingly to its commitment to common good, which, as we have seen, concerns the citizens in the first place (*ST*: I–II, q.97 a.1).

However, the comparison to arts is limited, as far as law is not merely a technical instrument. Rather, the law is by its very nature rooted in customs of a concrete community whose members have their own ways of thinking, patterns of social interaction, and cultural commitments. As he writes:

> Rules of art derive their force from reason alone: and therefore whenever something better occurs, the rule followed hitherto should be changed. But "laws derive very great force from custom," as the Philosopher states (Polit. ii, 5): consequently they should not be quickly changed.
>
> (*ST*: I–II, q.97 a.2 ad 1)

The legislative decision that fails to take these social roots of human law into consideration will not be able to serve its primary function, which is fostering

17 Although there have been some doubts here (Legarre 2012) in my view a rule forbidding murder has a twofold status. It may be a rule of positive law (when properly posited by authority), or a rule of natural law present in natural reason as a proper conclusion from a first precept.

the common good of a particular community. Interestingly enough, Aquinas acknowledges custom as one of the ways through which human reason and will manifest itself, and thus a common custom may be a source of a binding force of human law (*ST*: I–II, q.97 a.3). Therefore, if a law is being commonly questioned by customs, no longer being useful for the community, it should be changed (or is changed already solely by the custom), insofar as the human condition in question has undergone a reasonably justified change (*ST*: I–II, q.97 a.3 ad 2).

## Conclusion: The presence of Aquinas in contemporary discourse

Although the medieval world was obviously different from ours, the relevance of Aquinas's thought for the present discussions is not questionable. In my view, one can point at three moments in law (and therefore jurisprudence) that are, to certain extent, inspired by Aquinas: (1) reasonable content, (2) teleology, and (3) realism. The idea that law is grounded in natural reason, that is, that the law is reasonable, is present among many jurisprudential schools, even rivals to Thomism. As we have seen, Aquinas does not argue that the natural law is "out there" in the universe. It is present in natural human reason, as a structure of practical reflection and human action. Thus, the two modes for deriving legal rules depicted above can be understood as two modes of argumentation for law's reasonable, content-related justification. The role that natural law theory plays in "taking the reasons for action seriously", has been reaffirmed in the twentieth century (George 1999: 35). A re-engagement with Aquinas's doctrine might shed new light on the theory of reasonable justification that seems to have Aquinas as one of founders. The less common moment, though still present in contemporary discourse, is the teleological structure of legal argumentation. The modern law has been closely connected to deontology, emphasizing that law's primary function is a coordination of external freedom that is enjoyed equally by all. Despite that important commitment, many scholars continue to work within teleological tradition, pointing at the human good and fulfillment as the chief function of law.[18] Both the reasonability and teleology of law provide important guidelines for justifying legal change: the idea that the possible problems arising from introducing a new law should be outweighed by the benefit to the community comes directly from Aquinas.

Finally, and most controversially, there is moral realism. Today, as the possibility of theoretical metaphysic has been heavily questioned, the appeal to human nature and its finality, in the classical form, tends to be rejected, even

18 The most influential, and arguably closest to Aquinas, is the theory of Germain Grisez and John Finnis, famously presented by the latter in his *Natural Law and Natural Rights* (2011 [1980]). Another examples are Jacques Maritain (1951) or Martha Nussbaum (2008).

by the followers of Aquinas. Instead of appealing to human nature, the natural law ethicists ground their reflection either in basic human goods (Finnis 2011 [1980]) or in the dignity of the human person (Maritain 1951). On the former view, some basic human goods can be identified, and each individual is naturally free and entitled to pursue those goods. In the latter view, human dignity is the basis of the moral duty to affirm and respect the human person. At the same time, the precise answer to the question of what exactly pays that debt is left open to discussions. This bears important consequences for the issues of legal change. Whereas the appeal to human nature tends to legal entrenchment, both human goods and human dignity leave a vast space for a pluralistic discussion on legal change and its directions. The shape of legal institutions for realizing the human good and expressing the respect for the human person is not presupposed. Rather, despite realism and teleology present in natural law ethics, it depends on the practice, background culture or, as Aquinas would call it, on human customs shaped by reason and will.

## References

Aquinas (1947) *The Summa Theologica* (Benzinger Bros. edition 1947), translated by Fathers of the English Dominican Province, https://dhspriory.org/thomas/summa/index.html [accessed 30/01/19].

Baur, R. (2012) 'Law and Natural Law' in B. Davies and E. Stump eds, *The Oxford Handbook of Aquinas*, Oxford, Oxford University Press.

Dworkin, R. (2011) *Justice for Hedgehogs*, Cambridge: The Belknap Press of Harvard University Press.

Finnis, J. (1998) *Aquinas: Moral, Political, and Legal Theory*, Oxford: Oxford University Press.

Finnis, J. (2011 [1980]) *Natural Law and Natural Rights*, Oxford: Oxford University Press.

Finnis, J. (2018) 'Aquinas' Moral, Political, and Legal Philosophy', *The Stanford Encyclopedia of Philosophy (Summer 2018 Edition)*, E. N. Zalta ed. https://plato.stanford.edu/archives/sum2018/entries/aquinas-moral-political/ [accessed 31/01/19].

George, R. P. (1999) *In Defense of Natural Law*, Oxford: Oxford University Press.

Gilson, E. (2002) *Thomism: The Philosophy of Thomas Aquinas*, transl. L. K. Shoot and A. Maurer, Toronto: Pontifical Institute of Medieval Studies.

Korsgaard, Ch. (1992) 'The Sources of Normativity', The Tanner Lectures on Human Values, https://tannerlectures.utah.edu/_documents/a-to-z/k/korsgaard94.pdf [accessed 31/01/19].

Legarre, S. (2012) 'Derivation of Positive from Natural Law Revisited', *Scholarly Works*, Paper 1086 http://scholarship.law.nd.edu/law_faculty_scholarship/1086 [accessed 31/01/19].

Lisska, A. (1997) *Aquinas's Theory of Natural Law: An Analytic Reconstruction*, Oxford: Oxford University Press.

MacInterny, R. (1992) *Aquinas on Human Action: A Theory of Practice*, Washington: The Catholic University of America Press.

Maritain, J. (1951) *Man and the State*, Chicago: University of Chicago Press.

Martyniak, Cz. (2006) *Dzieła [Works]*, Lublin: Wydawnictwo KUL.

Nussbaum, M. (2008) 'Human Dignity and Political Entitlements' in *Human Dignity and Bioethics: Essays Commissioned by the President's Council on Bioethics.* https://bioethicsarchive.georgetown.edu/pcbe/reports/human_dignity/chapter14.html [accessed 30/01/19].

Piechowiak, M. (2012) *Dobro wspólne jako fundament polskiego porządku konstytucyjnego [Common Good as the Foundation of the Polish Constitutional Order]*, Warszawa: Biuro Trybunału Konstytucyjnego.

Piechowiak, M. (2016) 'Thomas Aquinas: Human Dignity and Conscience as a Basis for Restricting Legal Obligations', *Diametros* 47, 64–83.

Torrell, J. P. (2012) "Life and Works" in B. Davies and E. Stump eds, *The Oxford Handbook of Aquinas*, Oxford: Oxford University Press.

West, R. (2011) *Normative Jurisprudence: An Introduction*, Cambridge, Cambridge University Press.

Williams, T. (2012) 'Human Freedom and Agency' in B. Davies and E. Stump eds, *The Oxford Handbook of Aquinas*, Oxford: Oxford University Press.

# 7 Natural law against natural rights in the thought of Alasdair MacIntyre

*Kamil Aksiuto*

## Introduction

While few would deny the importance of Alasdair MacIntyre's contribution to contemporary ethics and philosophy, he remains an eminently controversial figure. To someone who is not familiar with his whole body of work, MacIntyre will most likely be associated with a hostile and dismissive attitude towards concepts that occupy a central role in modern social and political life, such as natural rights.

Over the course of this chapter I would like to argue that MacIntyre's rejection of natural rights is closely related to an underappreciated shift in his thinking. This shift consists in him adopting an account of natural law as an alternative to the idiom *human* rights. I begin with examining MacIntyre's reasons for doubting the existence of natural rights. Then I proceed to argue that while following those reasons MacIntyre encountered difficulties, which in turn led him to embrace natural law. In the subsequent parts of the chapter I then examine his account of natural law in greater detail. I will also demonstrate how this account of natural law allows MacIntyre to expand on his critique of natural rights. Finally, I try to sketch the normative structure of a community whose shared life would be informed by precepts of natural law. In this context, I will also attempt to draw implications from MacIntyre's views for the issue of legal change, although what he explicitly says about the latter is very limited.

## 1 Natural rights in *After Virtue*

In *After Virtue* (2007) Alasdair MacIntyre presented a radical diagnosis of the impoverishment of modern morality. One of the most notorious aspects of this work is his dismissive rejection of rights belonging to individuals simply in virtue of their humanity. In the 18th century this category of rights was most commonly referred to as natural rights and in the contemporary world are they named human rights (henceforth, for simplicity sake, I will be referring to them as natural rights). MacIntyre rather (in)famously asserted in his book that: "there are no such rights and belief in them is one with the belief in witches and in unicorns" (MacIntyre 2007: 69). Natural rights are nothing but an instance, albeit a very important one, of the moral fictions with which modern morality is populated.

What justifies such a strong and undoubtedly controversial claim? One of the main reasons emerges from the section of *After Virtue* where MacIntyre criticizes the conception of rights put forward by Alan Gewirth. To claim that one is in possession of certain right is to perform an action. MacIntyre contends, however, that such action can only be intelligible if it presupposes the existence of social institutions and practices conferring specific rights on individuals participating in those institutions and practices.[1] So individuals can intelligibly claim rights not in virtue of their humanity, but *qua* bearers of particular social identities. Hence, MacIntyre concludes that: "Lacking any such social form, the making of a claim to a right would be like presenting a check for payment in a social order that lacked the institution of money" (MacIntyre 2007: 67).

What the above-mentioned argument establishes is that natural rights could not have been intelligibly claimed in all societies, independent from their historical context. Obviously, it does not justify the conclusion that there are no rights of this kind. Yet, MacIntyre in *After Virtue* remains unshaken in his scepticism. In a revealing passage he claims that:

> The best reason for asserting so bluntly that there are no such rights is indeed of precisely the same type as the best reason which we possess for asserting that there are no witches and the best reason which we possess for asserting that there are no unicorns: every attempt to give good reasons for believing that there are such rights has failed.
>
> (MacIntyre 2007: 69)

Simply put, all the arguments that have thus far been made to justify natural rights have failed. As we will see, this thought also resurfaces in his later works.

## 2 Natural rights and moral absolutes

Not long after the first edition of *After Virtue*, MacIntyre revisited the topic in his Charles F. Adams lecture *Are There Any Natural Rights?* The lecture, which was subsequently published (MacIntyre 1983), offers a more careful and detailed examination of arguments mounted by supporters of natural rights as well as the exposition of MacIntyre's objections. Furthermore, it represents a transitional period in his thinking on the subject. It expands on his critique of natural rights while also introducing some new considerations and foreshadowing the future developments of his philosophical stance.

In *Are There Any Natural Rights?* MacIntyre first tries to present, for the sake of argument, a case for slavery that is as strong as possible. The details need not concern us here, but he readily admits that a defensible form of slavery could not be based on racial supremacy doctrines, rather it should be limited only to those

1 MacIntyre allows for the fact that there are rights arising from promises as well as from positive law, but for the sake of the clarity of the argument I do not consider them here.

with criminal and parasitic inclinations while simultaneously granting them legal protection against murder, rape, and certain kinds of punishment. Were we to reject such a type of slavery, we would have to show that slavery as such is not only inherently evil, but also deserves absolute moral condemnation. MacIntyre is convinced that the only grounds which would justify this conclusion are either appealing to natural rights or to the law revealed by God. He then proceeds to argue that, thus far, all the theories of natural rights have failed. Over the course of the extended analysis, MacIntyre draws on the argument described in the previous section. Natural rights belong and must have belonged to human beings in all places at all times, even when and where the linguistic idiom of such rights was still not yet available. Yet, historically, rights have been typically ascribed, claimed, exercised etc. within the framework of specific institutional and social arrangements. Obviously, rights of the latter kind cannot be timeless and universal. However, MacIntyre also draws attention to two other features of the most influential theories of natural rights which he sees, or saw at the time, as particularly problematic: natural rights are supposed to be self-evident and they are so strong as to override all other considerations.

First, natural rights cannot be derived from any more fundamental beliefs, but are self-evident and immediately perceived as true by any rational human being. This conviction was expressed by Thomas Jefferson in the *Declaration of Independence* in the famous passage: "We hold these truths to be self-evident: that all men are created equal; that they are endowed by their Creator with certain unalienable rights; that among these are life, liberty, and the pursuit of happiness". MacIntyre's discussion of the self-evidentness claim is much too brief, but it is clear that at this stage of his thinking he was not prepared to grant that any such claim can be vindicated. To be more precise, he maintained that the property of evidentness can indeed be ascribed to a statement, but only insofar as it presupposes the truth of a set of other background statements which are not themselves evident (MacIntyre 1983: 15).

Second, natural rights are supposed to have an overriding character which trumps all other considerations (for instance considerations of the greatest happiness of the greatest number). However, if this were indeed the case, political community would have to be exclusively based upon voluntary acts of consent of rights-bearing individuals. MacIntyre maintains that things are the other way round, the very act of consent necessarily presupposes the existence of political community with a certain normative structure, so the former cannot be constitutive of the latter. Indeed, were natural rights to possess such an overriding character, the logical conclusion would be that: "the notion of a just political society is the notion of an impossible society" (MacIntyre 1983: 17). This was, according to MacIntyre, quite inadvertently demonstrated by Robert Nozick's *Anarchy, State, and Utopia*.

Due to the above-mentioned reasons, MacIntyre finds all theories of natural rights that have been advanced thus far irredeemably flawed. And since he also believes that there is no good reason to expect that a new argument in favour of natural rights will be discovered, he draws the conclusion that there are no such rights (MacIntyre 1983: 18). It is dubious whether MacIntyre indeed managed to demonstrate what he thinks he did, but what is more important is the conclusion of the argument which also harkens back to the beginning of the chapter. It started with an assertion that if slavery was to be unconditionally prohibited it would have to be either in virtue of natural rights or in virtue of the law established by divine legislator. Since MacIntyre discards natural rights, it follows that either God's law condemns slavery in any form or that indeed there is no reason to prohibit it unconditionally. This conclusion is presented to a reader as a dilemma, not as an affirmation of the divine origin of at least some fundamental moral rules. Yet, it is tempting to assume, although to the best of my knowledge there is no textual evidence for this, that the formulation of this stark alternative prompted MacIntyre himself to search in a new direction. The choice was between acknowledging that either certain unbreakable moral rules can be rationally grounded or else even the most cruel and inhumane actions could in some circumstances be justified, and MacIntyre was certainly not inclined to embrace the latter proposition.

## 3 The justification of the natural law

The need to defend the existence of certain moral absolutes at the very least coincides with a gradual transition within MacIntyre's thought from a broadly Aristotelian perspective to a specific Thomistic interpretation of the former. In his subsequent writings the notion of the natural law gains an increasing prominence.

Nevertheless, MacIntyre is aware of at least some of the challenges that any attempt to revive the natural law tradition faces in the contemporary world. He identifies at least two requirements that any defensible theory of the natural law must satisfy:

> [F]irst . . . it must furnish an adequate explanation of the failure of the natural law to secure widespread assent in some cultures, especially in the cultures of the advanced modernity such as our own, and second that it must identify the grounds for assent to the precepts of the natural law, which are in fact available to all rational persons . . . even if those grounds are in very large part either flouted or ignored.
>
> (MacIntyre 2000: 104–105)

These two conditions are obviously related, since a whole range of moral disagreements that persist in the contemporary Western societies (MacIntyre 2006b: 67f), often described as their irreducible pluralism, is usually taken to be a quite conclusive evidence against the existence of the natural law that in normal circumstances should be recognized by any rational agent. Therefore, MacIntyre's task is both to explain the sources of the contemporary moral disagreement and to argue that this disagreement can somehow be explained by a theory of natural law without sacrificing the universal validity of the latter. It is the second part of that task that I will be preoccupied with in the following section.

MacIntyre follows Aquinas and Jacques Maritain in maintaining that human beings are "essentially sociable" (MacIntyre 2000: 108). What he has in mind is not an obvious fact that individuals need to cooperate to achieve certain goods that they would not be able to secure on their own. Those goods, for instance security and education, are typically referred to as public goods and contemporary political and economic theorizing has no problem with recognizing their importance. MacIntyre, however, is after something more than public goods. In everyday, practical life individuals function simultaneously within various social contexts, in a family, in a workplace, in a political community etc. It is a mistake to conceive of their identities as *prior* to those social relationships. It follows that when one is deliberating about his or her own individual good, its content cannot be determined independently of the good of those "social wholes" to which one belongs. Consequently, to the notion of individual and public goods a third notion should be added, that of a common good. MacIntyre's argument here closely resembles Charles Taylor's distinction between "irreducibly social goods" and public goods, the latter of which cannot be provided to an individual without also benefiting others (Taylor 1995: 127–145). Common goods are obviously various, depending on a social unit to which the concept applies. But what they have in common is that the good of a particular association: "cannot be constructed out of what were the goods of its individual members, antecedently to and independently of their membership in it" (Knight 1998: 240).[2] In other words, common goods are constitutive of the good of an individual person.

But how is the content of our individual and common goods to be determined? MacIntyre's answer to this question points to the importance of continuous, rational deliberation with various others, deliberation which typically emerges and is carried on in the context of everyday, practical life. We can only discover what are our relevant individual and common goods through the common enquiry with family members, colleagues at work, fellow citizens, and sometimes also with complete strangers. Thus, practical reasoning is essentially a social activity (MacIntyre 2006b: 179). MacIntyre follows both Aristotle and Aquinas in arguing that: "the central deliberative questions are not of the form 'What should I do here and now?' and 'How should I live?,' but of the form 'What should we do here and now?' and 'How should we live?'" (MacIntyre 2006b: 72). Why is this so? The crucial distinction to be drawn here is between goods and desires. The objects of desires are multifarious, although money,

2 Furthermore, it is important to notice that if there are indeed common goods in such a strong sense, they do not give rise to the well-known dilemma of "free-riding" which applies to public goods. It can be argued, if a typical notion of instrumental rationality is applied, that it is indeed irrational for a given individual to bear certain costs required for the maintenance of those public goods when it would be possible for him or her to avoid those costs. But to act against what common good requires would be equivalent not only to harming others but also to harming oneself. An egoist, therefore, is not acting rationally. Consequently, an initially egoistic individual, who however understands that his or her good is not independent of the various common goods, should be motivated to respect the duties arising from the common goods. Eventually such a person might in this way overcome his or her egoism.

pleasure, power, and/or social status frequently appear as a common denominator, yet in the course of practical life we learn (or fail to learn) to distinguish what we desire from what is genuinely good for us. Desire in itself does not constitute a reason to act in one way rather than another (MacIntyre 2016). But we never learn to make that distinction once and for all. Therefore, we rely on critical and objective evaluation of our moral (or even broader, evaluative) judgements from the standpoint of others.[3] Only in this way it is possible to identify and correct the limitations and mistakes involved in our individual perspectives and avoid mistaking our desires for genuine reasons.

Yet, here a question arises: what requirements have to be met in order to sustain such continuous deliberation? In MacIntyre's view the end towards which common enquiry moves is truth, in the classical sense of "*adaequatio rei et intellectus*". This requires participants in the deliberation to distance themselves from the desires for pleasure, money, and power, and related interests. What is needed is a form of "intellectual and moral asceticism" (MacIntyre 2006b: 77f). Moreover, we must trust those with whom we deliberate, e.g. trust that they will not use physical force against us or threaten us with it, that the will refrain from trying to deceive us and employing other forms of non-rational persuasion, that they will keep their promises, etc. There are certain norms which constitute the "ethics of enquiry" and which are embodied in the social relations in which genuine deliberation (not a *simulacra* of it) takes place.

It is unsurprising that the content of such norms, according to MacIntyre, is identical with what traditionally was identified as first precepts of the natural law: norms forbidding murder, theft, fraud, breaking of promises, and so on. MacIntyre once again follows Aquinas in claiming that the first precepts of the natural law are: 1) universal in scope 2) exceptionless 3) identical for everyone, and 4) not inferred from more basic premises or beliefs. Their universality means that they apply to every person, independent of the social *milieu* he or she happens to belong to. In conjunction with their exceptionless character this implies that first precepts constitute an unchanging moral standard. It is, however, the last of these characteristics that is particularly important, since it amounts to revision of MacIntyre's position on self-evidentness. That the first precepts of the natural law are self-evident does not mean that they are to be characterized by clearness and distinctness of the Cartesian ideas, neither are they analytic judgements that could be known to be true *a priori* (MacIntyre 2006a: 159). They will not be equally evident to every person satisfying minimal requirements of rationality (MacIntyre 2006a: 147–148), moreover, the knowledge of the first precepts can in various ways be obscured or distorted.[4] But nevertheless there are "first principles of practical reason":

3 Needless to say, deliberation with other people can be not only the source of correction, but also of corruption. This happens when our interlocutors lack the "virtues of objectivity". Think of characters such as Lady Macbeth or Iago, or about their real life, usually less dramatic, counterparts.

4 I describe some of the causes of the failures to recognize the first precepts of the natural law in the subsequent section of this chapter.

> in adopting the attitudes of rational enquiry we discover that we have already – implicitly, characteristically, rather than explicitly – had to accord them authority. They cannot be but presupposed and are therefore the necessary starting point for any enquiry that pursues the truth about goods or good in order to pursue goods or good.
>
> (MacIntyre 2006b: 79f)

This allows us to identify the crucial contrast between natural rights and the natural law. Mark C. Murphy points out that natural rights theories are individualistic, at least in the sense that the locus of justification of rights is placed in the individual human being. The individual's good or choice is supposed to justify protection against certain kinds of treatment. Natural law theories also grant individuals immunities from harm and abuse, but: "The reason for recognizing these immunities is that their recognition is essential for the carrying out of common projects. The normative force of the immunities is borne by the common good, not some individual's private good" (Murphy 2003: 169–170). First precepts of the natural law as MacIntyre understands them are "enabling rules" (Murphy 2003: 167) that allow individuals to share in rational deliberation about their individual and common goods.

## 4 Moral disagreement and the theological supplement

Let me now return to the issue to which I have already alluded: according to MacIntyre, first precepts of the natural law are self-evident. Also note that knowledge of them does not require divine revelation, so their acknowledgement should not be conditional on where one stands with regard to the existence of God. How is it so, then, that for many inhabitants of late modernity the precepts of the natural law seem unconvincing?

The answer that MacIntyre has to offer can, I think, be divided into several parts. First, there is a relatively straightforward case of someone violating the natural law due to succumbing to certain desires. As mentioned before, we are never entitled to assume that our judgements about what is good for us are infallible. The desire for pleasure, money, power etc. can operate in very subtle disguises and we are always liable to yield to it, even though we might be convinced that we are pursuing our goods, rather than merely desires. Thus, temporarily in many instances we might be blinded to the moral requirements of the natural law.

The second case is a good deal more complex than a moral lapse. MacIntyre repeatedly stresses that common deliberation, and consequently also the education of desire, typically takes place in the context of practical life (MacIntyre 1999: 135f). However, what he has in mind is a specific type of collective activity, the one which is directed towards the achievement of the goods internal to a given practice. Playing chess is a practice in the MacIntyrean sense, while making money is not. One can only become a great chess player through playing that game, while there is no single corresponding activity through which one could become rich (MacIntyre 2007: 187–196). Suppose, however, that many practices either vanished, like many traditional crafts, or were weakened by the harsh realities of the modern life. Those who were not lucky enough to be initiated into a well-functioning practice would be deprived of an opportunity to learn about their individual and common goods through a shared, rational deliberation with others. Moreover, they would most likely not understand that unconditional obedience to certain rules is necessary for the sustained character of such deliberation. In MacIntyre's view this is indeed the situation of many individuals nowadays. When confronted with many competing accounts of morality and their own desires, they begin to see individual choice as morally sovereign (MacIntyre 2000: 112ff). Thus, the precepts of the natural law are bound to be perceived by them as arbitrary limitation of individual freedom.

Finally, it will surely turn out that the explanation offered thus far for the failure of natural law to generate universal assent is itself controversial. Committed utilitarians, for instance, certainly will not be swayed by it, and this is largely because they operate with a different conception of practical reason than the Aristotelian-*cum*-Thomistic account of MacIntyre. So the disagreement extends from the question of the authority of natural law to the very nature of practical reasoning (MacIntyre 2009a: 3–4). This brings us to the topic that MacIntyre revisited frequently in his works: that of a fundamental disagreement between rival moral and philosophical traditions (MacIntyre 1988: 349–369, 2006a: 3–23). Since the examination of this issue is beyond the scope of this essay, let me just register the peculiarity of MacIntyre's position: while he is prepared to admit that traditions such as Thomism and utilitarianism cannot appeal to any set of neutral standards to resolve their disagreements, at the same time he maintains that it may still be possible for one tradition to vindicate its rational superiority over the other. This can be achieved if proponents of one tradition can imaginatively identify with the standpoint of the other and, drawing on the resources of their own tradition, explain why certain problems had to arise for the rival tradition and why the latter must fail, by its own standards, to solve those problems. Yet, nothing guarantees that proponents of the other tradition will acknowledge their defeat, e.g. the impetus theorists for instance failed to accept the superiority of Newton's physics (MacIntyre 2009a: 32–37).

Traditional natural law theories claimed that precepts of natural law can be known by natural reason and therefore independently of the divine revelation. Yet, the theistic background in which those theories were couched is obvious. I think it is fair to say that over the years MacIntyre has been hesitant about how much Christian beliefs should inform his account of natural law. What I presented above is the justification of natural law which deliberately avoids controversial religious assumptions. But things are more complex than it might seem at first sight. MacIntyre notes that it is not an accident that Aquinas' treatment of natural law in *Summa Theologiae*: "is immediately preceded by an Augustinian discussion of sins and vices, in which sins are characterized as 'transgressions of reason' . . . in the context of a complex account of human evil" (MacIntyre 2006b: 82). This passage finds an interesting counterpart in one of MacIntyre's most recent statements. While emphasizing the need for theological explanation of hostile criticism of the natural law he claims that:

> The kind of theological account that we need will have to draw upon the resources of that theological anthropology, at its foundations biblical and Christological . . . an anthropology that provides a perspective without which we cannot understand the relationship between the powers and limitations of reason.
>
> (MacIntyre 2009b: 350)

It seems then that it is not the knowledge of the natural law that requires theological support, it is the failure to assent to its precepts. If I understand MacIntyre correctly, to fully comprehend the sources of moral disagreement regarding the natural law, what is needed is a theological account of the defects in practical reasoning as resulting from human sinfulness.

## 5 Natural rights as ideology

There is a historical narrative that has been retold by MacIntyre in various versions since *After Virtue* that is supposed to explain, among other things, the displacement of the *natural law* by the idiom of *natural rights.* The details of this account cannot be fully examined here, but the crux of the narrative is fairly straightforward. Premodern societies were "imperfect"[5] embodiments of an ideal of community in which mutual trust was reinforced by shared allegiance to a certain conception of ultimate human good. However, with the advent of modernity the belief in trustworthiness of others as well as in the single vision of ultimate human good was gradually undermined or even destroyed (MacIntyre 1991: 100–101). What are the consequences of this great social transformation? First, the possibility of engaging with others in rational deliberation of a type I tried to describe above shrank dramatically. Second, modern individualism conceives of individuals as having certain presocial moral rights emerged, which is unsurprising, since in a society where one cannot generally speaking trust others, "a new need would arise for norms whose central purpose would be protective: to defend each person from becoming merely an instrument for the achievement of someone else's desires, preferences, and will" (MacIntyre 1991: 101). This is how, according to MacIntyre, natural rights entered the scene.

The individualism that underpins natural rights, however, bedevils the whole enterprise. No agreement was reached about the grounds of justification of

5 This seems to open MacIntyre to a charge that has been often raised against him: that he is a nostalgic reactionary or a descendant of romantic critiques of modernity. Admittedly, there are clear traces of nostalgia for a lost world in MacIntyre's views, but I do not find that charge convincing, at least in its most straightforward form. While he clearly admires ancient Athens or Christian Europe from the Middle Ages, he is quite aware of their grave flaws, be it slavery or medieval antisemitism. More importantly, MacIntyre has repeatedly stated that it is impossible to turn back the clock of history. Instead, he tries to envision the forms of contemporary social life that would inevitably be very different from *polis* or Gregorian *ecclesia*, but in which what was admirable about these could be revived.

natural rights as well as about the content of the catalogue of those rights. This makes the claims to rights in contemporary culture "essentially contestable" (MacIntyre 1991: 104) and ready-made to be used as an instrument of ideological deception (or self-deception) in various power struggles. From the American and French revolutions until contemporary times, the invocations of natural rights have been made on *ad hoc* basis and without any regard for consistency (MacIntyre 1983: 19).

In my view, there are two features of contemporary rights rhetoric which worry MacIntyre the most. First, in creating a semblance of rational debate it undercuts the possibilities for authentic rational enquiry, at least those still left in modern societies. When claims to rights are advanced by one party against the other, quite often also claiming certain rights, or when rights are competing against the considerations of general welfare, what is really happening is not a rational deliberation, but the clash of interests, powers, and wills (MacIntyre 2006b: 211f). The self-righteousness of contending parties is a mirror image of the fact that they are not trying reason with each other, but rather to secure "the assent of those who already agree with the particular conclusions argued" (MacIntyre 1991: 106). The outcome of such struggles will be determined in most cases by who owns more resources like money and influence upon political elites, which is precisely what the rhetoric of rights disguises.

Second, MacIntyre remains distrustful of the functioning of rights in contemporary moral and political discourse due to his conviction that they makes us more vulnerable to the coercion and domination by various sorts of bureaucratic authority. One of the distinctive features of traditional natural law theories was that they were supposed to offer a public and shared standard by which any system of positive law could be evaluated (MacIntyre 2000: 103). However, the extent of moral disagreement in modern societies makes it increasingly difficult to rely on common, widely shared moral views to resolve the disputes between individuals or groups. Characteristically, this disagreement is only deepened by the multiplication of claims to the possession of rights. Unsurprisingly, in these circumstances, the contending parties often end up in the courts. "Incessant litigation" has become an endemic feature of modern societies (MacIntyre 2000: 114). It is the state apparatus in the first place which benefits from the widespread popularity of claims to rights, since:

> Generally and characteristically they are used to present continually renewed challenges to what is taken by those who present them to be institutional *status quo*, challenges designed to dissolve the bonds, and undermine the authority, of all institutions intermediate between the individual on the one hand and the government and the justice system on the other: such institutions as families, schools and churches.
>
> (MacIntyre 1991: 105)

In these circumstances, the only resort of citizens against the coercive actions of the state apparatus is, often enough, relying on lawyers, who offer expert knowledge well beyond the reach of plain persons. But in MacIntyre's view this amounts to entering a relationship which is all too often manipulative. Already in *After Virtue* he described contemporary culture as a combination of individualistic and bureaucratic elements (MacIntyre 2007: 24–31), echoing Max Weber's characterization of modernity. The claims of various representatives of bureaucratic authority are based on them possessing relevant expertise and their alleged objectiveness. Contrary to this, MacIntyre maintains that: "Ours is a culture dominated by experts, experts who profess to assist the rest of us, but who often instead make us their victims" (MacIntyre 2000: 91). Arguably, among those experts one can quite often find the lawyers.

## 6 The normative structure of the Aristotelian community

Is there any alternative to the contemporary domination of the natural rights rhetoric and its consequences? MacIntyre places his hopes in small-scale communities, which we might call Aristotelian, which could avoid the pitfalls of mainstream societies. While this still is a project, and a sketchy one, rather than social reality, it is nevertheless important to ask what would be the normative structure of such community?

It is of primary importance for an Aristotelian community to be bound by a shared conception of the ultimate human good. It directs the members of the community towards their common good of the highest order[6] and provides them with a normative standard, supposedly independent of preferences and interests of individuals and groups, which is one of the preconditions of rational deliberation. MacIntyre is at pains to stress that allegiance to the communal conception of the ultimate human good is "compatible with the occurrence of extended and significant disagreements" (MacIntyre 2006b: 38). He also allows for the possibility of reformulation and modification of said conception, at any moment parts of it are open to critical reflection and questioning through the process of shared deliberation. However, what cannot be questioned at any moment, at least not from within the community, is this conception of the ultimate human good as a whole, i.e. that even though individuals may challenge specific instances or parts of this conception, there are limits as to what can be challenged while remaining a member of the community.

The overarching conception of the ultimate human good is the end towards which other normative aspects of the Aristotelian community are directed, and due to the importance of common rational enquiry members of this association should recognize the authority of the first precepts of the natural law as exceptionless and universal. MacIntyre also assumes that such community is going to have its own legislation or positive law. One of the

6 What I have in mind when speaking about "common good of the highest order" is that various individual goods and common goods of smaller social units (common goods of family life, common goods of a workplace etc.) are accorded their due rank within the overall vision of the human flourishing.

crucial lacuna in MacIntyre's account is that he never elaborates on how that legislation is supposed to be related to the law issued by the state and to the institutions of the state that are responsible for the review and enforcement of the latter.

It is nevertheless clear that intra-communal legal rules are only binding on its members as long as their content is informed by the natural law or at the very least does not conflict with it (Knight 1998: 247). It can therefore be safely inferred from the previous considerations that the first precepts of natural law set the limits of what is amenable to legal change. Legislation that would violate those precepts, even if enjoying considerable political support, in this view would be unjust and devoid of normative force. Similarly, the logic of MacIntyre's argument seems to warrant the conclusion that members of the Aristotelian community can make legitimate claims based on the natural law and addressed to those holding political office in the community. For, although law will be typically promulgated on behalf of the whole association by its representatives, ordinary members of the Aristotelian community will be capable of judging whether legal rules are in accordance with the natural law (MacIntyre 2006b: 48–49). Whether they could make similar claims addressed to the political institutions of the state is, however, much less clear.

As already mentioned, MacIntyre follows Aquinas in characterizing the first precepts of the natural law as unchanging and unchangeable (MacIntyre 2006b: 65). However, the secondary precepts of the natural law are always a matter of application of the first precepts to particular circumstances and therefore can legitimately vary. This allows for a considerable degree of flexibility when it comes to legal implementation of secondary precepts. Yet it is necessary to proceed with caution, as the authority of legal rules is at least partly based on habitual obedience. MacIntyre in his essay *Natural law as subversive: the case of Aquinas* (2006b) emphasizes the anti-establishment features of the views of the "Angelic Doctor". One of the crucial aspects of Aquinas's position was his defence of local customs which can have the force of law against the legislative aspirations of the monarchic powers, feudal aristocrats, and even ecclesiastical authority (MacIntyre 2006b: 51). This seems to imply that even in a completely different social context, when the first precepts of the natural law are not at stake, legislation should still treat customary rules with due respect. Legislative innovation merely for the sake of innovation is not a virtue.

Two additional points are worth noting here. First precepts on the natural law are unbreakable, yet they also have a point and purpose which consists in enabling the common pursuit of the ultimate human good. In order to apply them intelligently in contingent circumstance, members of the community need the acquisition of virtues. MacIntyre mentions the virtues of prudence, temperateness, courage, and justice. It is the virtue of prudence (Aristotelian φρόνησις) which is crucial in order to avoid mere fetishism of rules. Furthermore, the primary function of law in the Aristotelian community is to contribute to moral education. Legal norms are supposed to not only prevent certain types of conduct, to provide additional motivation to those who lack firm moral character, but also to foster the acquisition of virtues among the members. It does not follow that this educational function of law justifies the goal of legally imposing a wholesale moral code. To illustrate this point, MacIntyre contrasts the account of law by Aquinas with opposing views of liberals and puritans. MacIntyre maintains that Aquinas: "Like those puritans and unlike those liberals . . . understands the law as an instrument for our moral education. But, like those liberals and unlike those puritans, he is against making law by itself an attempt to repress all vice" (MacIntyre 2006b: 47). This is mainly because any attempts to impose the requirements of virtue unrestrictedly through legislation are self-defeating.

Finally, central to the Aristotelian community is also a conception of justice which is inseparable from the shared conception of the ultimate human good. Justice is not about the protection of rights belonging to individuals simply *qua* individuals; justice specifies what members of the community owe to each other in the light of the common good they are trying to achieve. Therefore, justice is both about (just) deserts and needs. In his earlier writings MacIntyre used to emphasize the importance of desert, as contemporary theories of justice lack place for any such notion (MacIntyre 2007: 246–251). However, in his later works a significant shift occurred, arguing that *before* it is possible to justify deserts, i.e. to recognize and honour those who are making a particularly valuable contribution to the common good, we must first secure various minimum needs: of the poor, of the educationally disadvantaged, of the disabled (MacIntyre 1999: 130, 136–140). These are not just miseries which adversely affect individual wellbeing, but they deprive those afflicted by them of an opportunity to contribute to the common good. MacIntyre even explicitly identifies oppression with: "any form of social relationship that denies to those who participate in it the possibility of the kind of learning from each other about the nature of their common good that can issue in socially transformative action" (Knight 1998: 250). Therefore, the task of the participatory community lies in the reversal of the sequence that Marx envisioned for the transition from socialist to communist society: justice is to be understood as moving away from "From each according to her or his ability, to each according to his or her needs" to "From each according to her or his ability, to each according to his or her contribution" (MacIntyre 1991: 107).

What follows from this is that justice in the Aristotelian community is compatible with ascribing rights to individuals. Yet, those rights are understood not as attaching to them simply *qua* human beings, but *qua* members of the community, for instance in virtue of special needs or desert. In other words, they are analogous to what *jura* were in Roman law, norms structuring social relations within a particular community (MacIntyre 1991: 100).

## Conclusion

MacIntyre's account of the natural law surely leaves many questions unanswered (or not even posed). It is also bound to be rejected from various philosophical standpoints, some of them perhaps not that far removed from MacIntyre's own.[7] Moreover, in MacIntyre's view this outcome is to be expected. The point of his enterprise is, however, not to present another academic moral theory: it is rather to articulate the moral and philosophical commitments embedded in a practical life of a very specific community. Moral theory can ultimately vindicate its superiority over rivals only in the context of the practical life of such a community, once it becomes another academic position it is doomed to become a culturally marginal exercise of argumentative skills entangled in unresolvable controversies that populate the academic landscape. MacIntyre believes that there was a tradition of communal life, manifesting itself in various forms in different historical contexts, in which moral theory and practice were united. He is also convinced that this tradition can be revived. It is indeed controversial whether such a tradition existed in the past. It is even more problematic whether it has any future. But yet, it appears that MacIntyre's attempt to argue that there is natural law, that there are rules that bind us unconditionally but at the same time which are not justified on individualistic grounds, should be interpreted as a part of this larger project.

## References

Knight, K. (ed.) (1998) *The MacIntyre Reader*. Notre Dame, University of Notre Dame Press.

MacIntyre, A. (1983) *Are There Any Natural Rights?* Brunswick, President and Trustees Bowdoin College.

MacIntyre, A. (1988) *Whose Justice? Which Rationality?* Notre Dame, University of Notre Dame Press.

MacIntyre, A. (1991) 'Community, Law and the Idiom and Rhetoric of Rights', *Listening: Journal of Religion and Culture* 26 (2), 96–110.

MacIntyre, A. (1998) 'Politics, Philosophy and the Common Good', in Knight, K. (ed.) *The MacIntyre Reader*. Notre Dame, University of Notre Dame Press, 235–252.

MacIntyre, A. (1999) *Dependent Rational Animals*. Chicago and La Salle, Carus Publishing Company.

MacIntyre, A. (2000) 'Theories of Natural Law in the Culture of Advanced Modernity', in McLean, E. B. (ed.) *Common Truths: New Perspectives on Natural Law*, Wilmington, Isi Books, 91–115.

MacIntyre, A. (2006a) *The Tasks of Philosophy. Selected Essays, Volume 1*. Cambridge, Cambridge University Press.

MacIntyre, A. (2006b) *Ethics and Politics. Selected Essays, Volume 2*. Cambridge, Cambridge University Press.

7 I am thinking here for instance about the accounts of natural law by such contemporary Thomistic thinkers as John Finnis and, recently deceased, Germain Grisez.

MacIntyre, A. (2007) *After Virtue. A Study in Moral Theory.* Notre Dame, University of Notre Dame Press.

MacIntyre, A. (2009a) 'Intractable Moral Disagreements', in Cunningham, L. S. (ed.) *Intractable Disputes About the Natural Law. Alasdair MacIntyre and Critics.* Notre Dame, University of Notre Dame Press, 1–52.

MacIntyre, A. (2009b) 'From Answers to Questions: A Response to the Responses', in Cunningham, L. S. (ed.) *Intractable Disputes About the Natural Law. Alasdair MacIntyre and Critics.* Notre Dame, University of Notre Dame Press, 313–351.

MacIntyre, A. (2016) *Ethics in the Conflicts of Modernity. An Essay on Desire, Practical Reasoning, and Narrative.* Cambridge, Cambridge University Press.

Murphy, M. C. (2003) 'MacIntyre's Political Philosophy', in Murphy, M. C. (ed.) *Alasdair MacIntyre.* Cambridge, Cambridge University Press, 152–175.

Nozick, R. (2001) *Anarchy, State, and Utopia.* Oxford, Blackwell Publishers Ltd.

Taylor, Ch. (1995) *Philosophical Arguments.* Cambridge and London, Harvard University Press.

# 8 Kant's conception of legal change

*Eduardo Charpenel*

## Introduction

As is very well known, the interest in Kant's practical philosophy has grown enormously in the English-speaking world due to the impact of John Rawls' 1971 classic and groundbreaking work, *A Theory of Justice*. Rawls' theory of justice argues that there are fundamental principles that should be followed by political institutions in order to achieve fairness within the social structure and to secure its members a set of primary rights. Rawls was inspired by Kant's rejection of consequentialism as well as by the latter's general philosophical outlook, which appealed to formal procedures of practical reason rather than to material ends.

Rawls conceived his own project as a practical alternative that radically differed from both intuitionism and utilitarianism, the two dominant views in the philosophical landscape of his time. However, it is particularly noteworthy that his appropriation of Kant's thought for political philosophy rested not so much on Kant's own political thought, or the premises contained therein, but rather on key notions of his moral philosophy.[1]

Thus, even with the renewed interest for Kant that Rawls gave rise to, one could still claim that for a period of time Kant's political and legal thought remained poorly known and discussed despite of the renaissance of his philosophy. Yet, this has dramatically changed over the last three decades, with extensive scholarly work having been carried out in Kant's political philosophy, which is now one of the most widely discussed branches of his philosophy.[2]

1 In a very similar way, Habermas and Apel rehabilitated in the German-speaking world many ideas of Kant's moral philosophy within the political and social philosophies they developed, neglecting thereby to some extent Kant's political and legal thought. Nonetheless, in the case of Habermas, even if the above is true, it would be unfair to affirm that he has completely overlooked Kant's legal philosophy in his writings, since texts of his such as *Between Facts and Norms* (1996) and "Kant's Idea of Perpetual Peace, with the Benefit of Two Hundred Years' Hindsight" (1997) do exhibit an important acquaintance with it. For a very detailed discussion of Rawls', Apel's and Habermas' appropriation of Kant see the thorough monograph of Höffe (2002: 215–288).

2 In general terms, it could be said that the scholarly debates concerning Kant's political philosophy start from the question of whether Kant grounds his political philosophy in his moral philosophy or

Due to this "rediscovery" of some Kantian legal and political notions, several Kantian topics are now being analyzed from different and novel angles.

In what follows, I will offer an account of how Kant conceived the topic of legal change in a legal framework. Before doing that, however, I will reconstruct what I take to be Kant's core sources of legal normativity. Characterizing them in some detail will allow me to provide an adequate account of Kant's conception of legal change in realms such as international and constitutional law. In dealing with this subject, I will stress Kant's emphasis on the attention one should pay to the context in question in which a legal development or change is called for – something that displays his concern for divergent historical and cultural circumstances while framing and implementing the law. Then, I will reconstruct the legitimate ways in which, according to Kant, we ought to proceed when we embark upon the project of changing laws, thereby pointing out the ethical motivation that political actors should have in order to do this. Lastly, I will make some concluding remarks regarding the actuality of Kant's legal thought.

## 1 Sources of legal normativity in Kant

### *1.1 Kantian contractualism*

The resources that Kant employs to ground legal normativity are diverse, but let us first revise one which paradigmatically has drawn a lot of attention from Kant's readers. In his major political works of the 1790s, Kant appeals to the notion of the social contract, which, as is well known, played a central role in the political

not. Both in the German and the English language Kantian scholarship this question tends to sharply divide the interpreters. Whereas scholars such as Höffe (2002), Maus (1994), Ludwig (1993) and Guyer (2000) defend a reading in which Kant does directly and robustly ground his political and legal philosophy on the categorical imperative, giving rise thereby to a continuous normative order that would only differ in its application to the external (legal) and internal (moral) dimensions of human action, scholars such as Willaschek (2009), Ripstein (2009) and Wood (2002) in turn hold the thesis that, despite textual evidence that could suggest otherwise, Kant establishes in the political and legal spheres a quite different normative order, which has distinctive principles and norms of its own and leads to particular conceptions of law and authority that are qualitatively different, and to a rather large extent independent, from those found in the moral realm.

In the present text, I will not be able to argue in depth for my own reading, which, in a way, aims towards an intermediate and conciliatory position between the two extremes of the debate. The position I hold could be fleshed out in the following way: on the one hand, I claim that Kant tries to make the sphere of right as compatible and harmonic with the sphere of morals as possible, and that both ultimately originate in human freedom. Even if each of these spheres relates to the external or to the internal dimension of human action more eminently, neither of them is articulated in a way that neglects the existence of its counterpart or precludes the possibility of its counterpart's realization. Furthermore, right is importantly informed – albeit not determined – by key notions of morality, and it is at least in some levels the goal of the former to establish the conditions of possibility which enable the full realization of the latter. On the other hand, I sustain as well that the normative resources to which Kant appeals in the realm of law at the very best resemble, but are not in any case identical to, those in the realm of morals.

thought of Hobbes, Locke and Rousseau. However, unlike other contractualist thinkers who considered the establishing of the social contract as a historical or factual event, Kant clearly conceived it solely as an ideal of reason which demands from us the instauration of a judicial order of a particular kind. As he writes in "On the Common Saying 'This May Be True in Theory, But It Does Not Apply in Practice'" [*TP*] with regard to the nature of the social contract:

> It is in fact merely an *idea* of reason, which nonetheless has undoubted practical reality; for it can oblige every legislator to frame his laws in such a way that they could have been produced by the united will of a whole nation, and to regard each subject, in so far as he can claim citizenship, as if he had consented within the general will. This is the test of the rightfulness of every public law.
>
> (*TP* 8: 297)[3]

Furthermore, the contract is associated there with some *a priori* principles which for Kant are: "1. The *freedom* of every member of society, as a *human being*. 2. The *equality* of every member with every other, as a *subject*. 3. The *independence* of every member of the commonwealth, as a *citizen*" (*TP* 8: 297). As Kant himself explains, these principles are not promulgated by the state, but are rather the conditions by which a state can rationally function and be founded on intersubjective grounds.

Kant goes through great efforts to elucidate what is implied by each of the above mentioned principles. Summarizing, we could say that freedom, in its legal sense, implies that each member of a state has a right to self-determination and to embrace the way of life he deems correct as conducive to happiness – insofar, of course, this does not unlawfully collide with the personal projects of others. This equality conveys the idea of equal standing before the law that each person has – which implies something relevant in Kant's times, namely, the dubious character of nobility and aristocracy – and that independence is linked with the right of members of a commonwealth to be co-legislators and have their voice heard in law-making procedures – although, in this regard, Kant makes some highly questionable remarks about how economic independence would be a criterion for full-citizenship (cf. *TP* 8: 290–296).

In a way that is consistent with the contractualist tradition, the social or original contract is for Kant also a source of fundamental judicial and political legitimacy: it establishes certain fundamental conditions in order to consider a human group as properly confirming a political state, to ascribe lawfulness to the actions the state undertakes, and to ascertain the duties that the state must fulfill in the present as well as in the future. In other words, a civil constitution is a union that must be regarded as an end in itself. This union

3 I will quote Kant indicating in each case an English abbreviation of the work I am referring to, the volume of the Academy Edition (*Akademie Ausgabe*) where the work in question appears, and the corresponding page. I will quote directly from the English translations contained in the final bibliography. All the English translations were contrasted with the German original texts.

> which is therefore the unconditional and first duty in any external relation of people in general, who cannot help mutually affecting one another, is to be found in a society only insofar as it is in the civil condition, that is, constitutes a commonwealth.
>
> (*TP* 8: 289)

In this translation, it is important to notice, however, that "affecting" does not mean a violent collision of interests as Hobbes may have had it – the original reads "*in wechselseitigen Einfluss auf einander zu gerathen*" – but rather the fact that, given the conditions in which we live our lives, we must inevitably interact with other human beings and establish certain patterns of reciprocity in our conduct in order to secure our freedom. Even if we would pose a golden age quite different than the gloomy scenario of the Hobbesian state of nature, it would be still, as Kant affirms in the *Metaphysical Elements of the Doctrine of Right* [*DR*] of the *Metaphysics of Morals*, "a state of society in which justice is absent and one in which, when there is a controversy concerning rights (*ius controversum*), no competent judge can be found to render a decision having the force of law" (*DR* 6: 312).

From the above it follows that the reason why we deem it necessary to establish it is not at all a particular feature of human nature such as, say, an alleged proclivity to aggressiveness or to impose our will upon others, or a dictate of our inextricable wish to reach happiness, but rather the legitimate, rational demand of having secured one's own freedom properly. This foundation, in turn, calls for the protection of everything I can legitimately claim as mine and explains the great efforts Kant takes to define property rights. That this is ultimately a claim for political freedom, i.e. external freedom, becomes clear when Kant enunciates the Universal Principle of Right: "Every action is right that in itself or in its maxim is such that the freedom of the will of each can coexist together with the freedom of everyone in accordance with a universal law" (*DR* 6: 230; cf. *TP* 8: 289–290).

### *1.2 Natural right*

Kant's appeal to the social contract has led many interpreters to label his political philosophy as primarily contractualist,[4] although there are some complications with this reading, at least if one takes it straightforwardly. For one thing, Kant does not renounce natural law principles in his legal thought. This is particularly noteworthy in the case of the *DR*, where, for instance, Kant seems to link in a very substantial

4 An interpreter who has endorsed a strong contractualist reading of Kant is Howard L. Williams (1983, 2003). For a critical view of overemphasizing this motif in Kant see Onora O'Neill (2015).

In this context, it is important to remark that the nature of the social contract at a national level differs considerably from that of the social contract at an international level. The social contract at the national level is not a historical fact but rather an ahistorical concept of pure reason as a legitimate ideal, which entitles an agent to force other individuals to enter into a civil condition with him even against their will; by contrast, the international contract, which aims to guarantee perpetual peace, must take place at some point in history and be agreed upon by the different states.

way the validity of the system of rights that he proposes with a certain view of natural right. To be sure, the kind of natural right that one finds in his writings differs significantly from the kind of natural right that one can find in medieval scholastic authors. In the medieval tradition, natural law is more often than not discussed in a theological framework so that every principle or norm is either varyingly compatible with Scripture, or is at least modified, in a more rationalist way, so that it is coincident with what Scripture teaches. For Kant, in turn, the principles of natural right or natural law are cognizable by pure reason alone, and they have a hierarchy over positive law (cf. *DR* 6: 225). Furthermore, if it were not because of the aid that these principles provide, it could be said that law and right as such could never acquire a solid rational status (cf. *DR* 6: 229). In Kant, however, as it can be expected, these principles are conceived as being *a priori* and grounded in pure reason, but their application presupposes some knowledge about the nature of human beings and of the empirical conditions in which they have to interact with each other.

What is the scope of natural right in Kant? This is to some extent a complex issue. For when Kant introduces the General Division of Rights he claims that natural right depends exclusively on *a priori* principles and that positive rights depend on the particular acts of a legislator, but then he proceeds to discuss another division between innate and acquired rights and affirms that there is only one right that is innate, namely:

> *Freedom* (independence from the constraint of another person's will), insofar as it [this freedom] is compatible with the freedom of everyone else in accordance with a universal law, is the one sole and original right belonging to every person by virtue of his humanity.
>
> (*DR* 6: 237)

This could certainly raise the impression that the innate right to freedom is the only natural right, but many things speak against this. On the one hand, in the prior division, he already introduces some fundamental natural rights by appealing to the three formulae of the Roman jurist Ulpian: 1) be an honest person (*honeste vivere*), 2) do no one injustice (*neminem laedere*), and 3) *suum cuique tribuere*, which according to Kant should not be translated literally but rather be interpreted as "Enter into a condition in which each person has what is his guaranteed against everyone else" (*DR* 6: 236–237). However, property and acquisition rights are also conceived as being part of natural right. The claim that one can legitimately raise before others regarding something as one's property in the state of nature is, in the Kantian conception, one based on natural law. In the same line, one could say, just to mention another example, that Kant's conception of marriage – which is also, in many of its aspects, highly controversial – also derives from natural law premises, which are only fully guaranteed once the natural state is abandoned and the civil state is established. Other similar arguments could be drawn from the particular legal issues Kant discusses throughout his treatise.

One could extract from these and other cases the radical consequence that, since *DR's* main purpose is to lay out all the *a priori* principles on which right must rest, and since Kant is not by any means embarking upon a project of simply suggesting what a good system of positive laws should contain, then the entire *DR* must be read rather as a treatise of natural right as some interpreters have suggested.[5] Undoubtedly, if this were the case, there would be principles within natural right which would have more weight than others[6] – the above-quoted Universal Principle of Right being the most eminent and hierarchically superior of them. But even granting that, it could be possible, at least on the grounds of *DR*, to say that, in this text, the importance of the original contract has been to some extent downplayed, since it does not perform any fundamental role in the derivation or establishment of natural rights and its appearance is comparatively marginal and only occurs at the rather advanced stages of Kant's argument (cf. *DR* 6: 267, 315, 340). Again, with regard to this topic, there exist some controversies as whether Kant substantially modified his theory throughout his different writings. Given the scope of our discussion, it is impossible to delve into this question, but regardless of how one might want to deal with this issue, I think it is clear that Kant recognizes both in the social contract and in natural law two different sources of normativity which, even if they are compatible, are not to be entirely conflated with each other. Even at the late stage of the publication of the *DR* Kant does not eradicate the concept of the social contract from his theory and, although less frequently, he still appeals to it in ways that are consistent with what was established in *TP*, so that gives us important grounds to think that these are different normative sources that serve different justificatory and explanatory purposes in Kant's legal thought.

### *1.3 Publicity principle*

The panorama becomes even more complex in light of a third source of legal normativity that appears in a very eminent way in one of the writings we have not discussed so far, namely "Towards Perpetual Peace" [*PP*]. There, in the last section of the text, which bears the title "On the agreement between politics and morality according to the transcendental concept of right", Kant defends the idea that, unlike what theorists such as Machiavelli affirmed, the exercise of political and legal power is not ruled by a set of categories and principles which stand in opposition to morality. On the contrary, what Kant claims is that a legal disposition, in order to be truly lawful, must be evaluated against a principle that he calls the ***transcendental principle of right*** and which in the scholarly discussion is commonly referred to as the ***publicity principle***. He offers two formulations of

5 In a paradigmatic way, Mulholland (1990) has developed an interesting interpretation of Kant that places him much closer to the natural law tradition than to the contractualist one. Other authors who suggest something in this line are Byrd and Hruschka (2010: 16). In their commentary to the *DR*, they stress the fact that Kant held lectures for twenty years using Achenwall's *Jus naturae in usum auditorium* as a handbook.

6 This, however, does appear to be the case in *TP* with regard to freedom, equality and independence, that is, the principles we previously discussed. Even though Kant does not refer explicitly to them in *TP* as having the status of natural rights, they could be rightfully interpreted as such in light of the *DR*.

this principle: 1) "All actions that affect the rights of other human beings, the maxims of which are incompatible with publicity, are unjust" (*PP* 8: 381); and 2) "All maxims that *require* publicity (in order that they not miss their aim) are in agreement with both politics and right" (*PP* 8: 386).

After having announced the first formulation of it, Kant affirms that the publicity principle must be understood both as an *ethical* and as a *judicial* principle – this, to my mind, is something that should be taken into account when dealing with interpretations that separate the grounding of ethics and right in Kant too sharply. Although Kant does not explain why exactly he considers the publicity principle as an ethical principle, some reasonable conjectures can be made in order to elucidate why this principle would have an important ethical salience. On the one hand, Kant suggests that a ruler who must be silent and who must hide his purposes in order to act – provided that, if he were to unveil these purposes to the public, these would be inevitably thwarted – would be behaving unethically insofar as his maxims would collide with those of the citizens of a state. In dealing with the responsibilities that belong to his office in this way he would be manipulating the freedom of his subjects, and thus he would be behaving immorally (cf. *PP* 8: 381).

On the other hand, it seems that, not in relation to others but on an individual level, his conduct itself would be highly questionable due to the casuistry in which such a ruler would incur. A ruler who employs equivocal terms purportedly, attributes to his enemies fantastic evil intentions and considers actions such as invading another state minor faults would clearly be incurring, in Kant's eyes, in some serious ethical faults, which the philosopher even equates with the negligence of duties such as philanthropy and the right of humanity (cf. *PP* 8: 385). Certainly, even if a ruler were to behave like this, the subjects would not have any coercive rights against the head of a state or the rulers in question. Yet, the fact is that this moral wrong, in the exercise of this office, would nonetheless be censurable by practical reason.

From a judicial point of view what is important to stress about the publicity principle is that it does not indicate what the best course of legal action is. On the basis of its first formulation, the publicity principle can only show which actions would be unjust, but it does not determine which policy among those that are not censured by this principle ought to be followed. In this formulation, as Kant himself remarks, the publicity principle is a negative one, because it simply tells us what ought not to be done (cf. *PP* 8: 381–382). On the basis of the second formulation, however, the publicity principle acquires a more positive dimension. In this case, all projects and purposes that ought to be dealt publically within a state in order to be implemented are – in virtue of that very same publicity they have to comply to – *eo ipso* in accordance with right. Again, the principle seems *prima facie* to allow for different legal courses of action to be taken, but Kant thinks that, given that these projects would have to be subjected to the scrutiny of the subjects, these projects would be, to a greater or lesser degree, in accordance with the subjects' own conception of happiness, and thus would be promoting the unity of everybody's ends within that state (cf. *PP* 8: 386).

The sources of legal normativity to which Kant resorts are manifold, and it is difficult to determine if they all have the same strength in all different contexts or if one could establish a hierarchy among them. The task of elucidating this cannot be carried out here. In what follows, I will succinctly revise some of the discussions Kant addressed that imply changing of laws. By discussing them, we can at least gain an idea of what the normative force is of each of these principles in Kant's own thought.

## 2 Kant's account of legal change

The main scenario in which Kant addresses the topic of legal change is in the context of his theory of international relations, which in turn entails a theory of how political states should be shaped in order to achieve perpetual peace. To be sure, Kant considers in general that laws regarding different contingent matters may and will change in the course of time, since they depend on empirical facts and on very particular circumstances, and for that reason they are not the direct object of philosophical analysis. Taking into account what he affirms in the beginning of *DR*, there are many levels of what right encompasses, and his principal aim as a philosopher is to determine the *a priori* principles that are the foundations on which a rational system of law should be grounded – these and only these principles can guarantee that right operates as a science (*iurisscientia*) (*DR* 6: 229).

Thus, the way in which Kant first and foremost conceives the practice of legal change pertains to the modification of the existing factual political and judicial arrangements so that they can conform to the principles that practical reason ensues. In a much neglected passage of his (in)famous essay on lying, Kant explains what the relationship is between the *a priori* normativity of right and the different realms of its application:

> Now, in order to progress from a *metaphysics* of right (which abstracts from all conditions of experience) to a principle of *politics* (which applies these concepts to cases of experience) and, by means of this, to the solution of a problem of politics in keeping with the universal principle of right, a philosopher will give 1) an *axiom*, that is, an apodictically certain proposition that issues immediately from the definition of external right (consistency of the *freedom* of each with the freedom of everyone in accordance with a universal law); 2) a *postulate* (of external public *law*, as the united will of all in accordance with the principle of *equality*, without which there would be no freedom of everyone); 3) a *problem* of how it is to be arranged that in a society, however large, harmony in accordance with the principles of freedom and equality is maintained (namely, by means of a representative system); this will then be a principle of *politics*, the arrangement and organization of which will contain decrees, drawn from experiential cognition of human beings, that have in view only the mechanism for administering right and how this can be managed appropriately. Right must never be accommodated to politics, but politics must always be accommodated to right.
>
> (*On a supposed right to lie from philantropy* 8: 429)

Existing arrangements and the laws that validate them should be corrected so that they can comply with normative standards that are binding for all actors. Two important factors play a role here. First, the application of the pure principles of law takes into account the peculiarities of the context in question; in other words, the application of *a priori* right is not conceived by Kant as straightforward, but as something mediated by context sensitivity. And second, political actors ought not to make right comply with their own private interests and agendas. They should rather orientate themselves by what the principles of pure right prescribe in order to change the laws and practices within a particular society.

The way this approximation towards principles of pure right ought to be carried out depends on the nature of the practices themselves to be ruled – some practices should be stopped and legally forbidden immediately, since they seriously threaten the establishment of decent and peaceful relations among the states. Other practices should also be urgently stopped but the effects and consequences they have had historically – when their acceptance was widespread – admit, due to particular historical, social and economic impediments, a more gradual correction. Arrangements that fall under this case are according to Kant in *PP* the colonization and acquisition of states, the existence of military forces and groups, and taking advantage of the economic indebtedness of one state to one's own (*PP* 8: 343–347). They fall, in Kant's terminology, under the domain of permissive laws (*leges permissivae*), which, even though may seem to have a peculiar and paradoxical character – since laws are ensued *prima facie* to prohibit something, not to permit it – actually do condemn that practices of this kind continue to be carried on. The reason why these practices – which, in themselves, are censurable – are legally tolerable is that they have had an impact upon factual political, social and even economic arrangements, which may be at present not so easy to modify.

In a very similar vein, Kant deals with the measures that should be taken in order to improve the functioning of governments. For Kant, the most distinguishing feature of a government is not how many people partake in political power and hold offices –what he calls the form of sovereignty (*forma imperii*), of which there are only three possible variants: monarchy, aristocracy and democracy – but how the government preserves the rule of law and treats its citizens, that is to say, what he calls the form of government (*forma regiminis*) (*PP* 8: 352). This latter feature of governments only admits of two possibilities: despotic and republican. Despotic governments are those which either treat their citizens paternalistically and make decisions for them, pretending to know what their true self is, or those which manipulate the citizens or make instrumental use of them in order to serve the interests of those in power by, for instance, waging wars in order to acquire wealth. In turn, republicanism is for Kant a form of government in which there is a constitutional division of powers and, more importantly, in which laws are framed as if the citizens could have given to them their assent.[7] Republican governments abide by the principles of freedom, equality and independence that characterize

7 The latter is the most important aspect of Kant's conception of republicanism. See Ripstein (2009: 175ff).

Kant's conception of the original contract, acknowledging thereby the dignity of the members of the commonwealth and their free rational nature. Furthermore, only republican governments are fitted to create a league of nations by means of which the conflicts between the different state members can be solved peacefully instead of belligerently.

Despite the importance of introducing a republican government among the states, Kant considers that doing this untimely or inadequately could be something counterproductive and undesirable. The next passage describes in detail how Kant understood the practice of constitutional changes:

> A state can *govern* itself in a republican manner, even if it still possesses a despotic *ruling power* according to its present constitution, until the people gradually become able to be influenced by the mere idea of the authority of the law (as if it exerted physical force) and hence are found capable of their own legislation (which is originally based on right). Even if the impetuosity of a *revolution* provoked by a bad constitution were to bring about a more lawful one illegitimately it should no longer be deemed permissible to return the people to the previous constitution, even though under the old constitution any person who had violently or maliciously participated in that revolution would have rightly been subject to the punishment accorded rebels. But as concerns the relation to other states, one cannot demand of a state that it abandon its constitution, even if the latter is despotic (which indeed makes it a stronger one with regard to foreign foes), as long as the danger exists that it could be swallowed up by other states. It must therefore be permissible to delay the carrying out of such a change of constitution until a more fitting opportunity arises.
>
> (*PP* 8: 372–373)

In light of the above, one could affirm that for Kant acknowledging the pertinence of a principle of right does not amount to having sufficient grounds to carry it out or enacting it straightforwardly. Particularly difficult circumstances call for a rather prudential and cautious implementation of the principles of right that would lead to a republican constitution. In the hypothetical case that Kant envisions, the condition to be met in order to do this is to have a well-educated people who would comply with their duties as citizens not only due to the authority of the monarch or of the state, but also because they are enlightened and autonomous enough in order to do this out of conviction. Here it is particularly important to emphasize that it is not the consequences which validate the principle; the principle of right claims validity independently if circumstances allow for its full implementation. Contrary to what many have interpreted, Kant does make important room in his philosophy for the consideration of outcomes and empirical contingencies, but these considerations do not pertain as such the validity of the principles of practical reason in question whether ethical or judicial – as it happens in consequentialist theories – but rather their most adequate execution in face of the non-ideal conditions we must constantly deal with.

## 3 Space for the demands and exercise of public reason

A final important aspect of legal change in Kant's thought concerns the ways in which the demands for such changes can be made. In order to clarify this point, it is necessary to take into account one of the most controversial aspects of his political theory: his theory of revolution. As is well known, Kant denies that there is such a thing as a legitimate right to take justice in our own hands and start a revolution. According to Kant, to grant revolutions a judicial legitimacy could either mean that the people who rebel against the supreme authority are in fact the supreme authority and not the latter, or that there is a higher authority than the supreme authority that can decide whether the people or the supreme authority is right, which also leads to the absurd conclusion that the supreme authority of the government is not at all such, but rather that very instance that is entitled to issue a judgement upon it and sanction it (cfr. *TP* 8: 300; *DR* 6: 319–320). However, if that were the case, then the search for a true supreme authority would inevitably lead to a *regressus in infinitum*.

This is not the place to judge the pertinence of Kant's position in this regard.[8] What is interesting to note, however, is one of the most important reasons for holding this posture: only by abiding by the rule of law – even in non-ideal conditions – we are able, in Kantian terms, to have a particular kind of agency, that is, the proper and distinctive agency of citizens. And citizens, according to Kant, have at their disposal particular ways of expressing their particular views and even their discontent regarding public affairs, which can lead to the correction of the laws or of some specific application or interpretation of them. As citizens, we are entitled to act as learned scholars who, taking notice of what we consider to be defects and misdoings of the government, decide to emit publicly a critical judgement upon it, with the aim of contributing to change things for the best. Furthermore, any prohibition to the exercise of such right and liberty would be contrary to the very ends of the state. As Kant puts it:

> Accordingly, since every human being still has his inalienable rights, which he can never give up even if he wanted to and about which he is authorized to judge for himself, while, on that assumption, the wrong that in his opinion is done to him occurs only from the supreme power's error or ignorance

8 In the light of many totalitarian experiences and political catastrophes of the 20th and the 21st centuries, it does seem unsound and highly counterintuitive to affirm that a people never have a right to a rebellion or a revolution. Even though we may grant that one cannot stipulate in a judicial system that there could be a legal right to a rebellion, we find difficult to accept that Kant never conceded as such a *moral* right to carry out one in extreme, unbearable scenarios. The only thing of the like he stated – very much in the fashion of his controversy with Benjamin Constant regarding the alleged right to lie because of philanthropic concerns – was that those who initiate a revolution must bear all the positive and negative consequences of their actions, which implies that if they fail they can appeal to no right which would excuse or condone them, and that if they succeed in their enterprise then the new order they create ought to be respected. For a detailed discussion on Kant's views on revolution see Korsgaard (2008).

> of certain consequences of his laws, a citizen must have, with the approval of the ruler himself, the authorization to make known publicly his opinions about what it is in the ruler's arrangements that seems to him to be a wrong against the commonwealth.
>
> (*TP* 8: 304)

Like Hobbes, Kant believes that citizens cannot overthrow the government, but, unlike him, Kant thinks that citizens could indeed be wronged by the laws and decrees of a state. "The people", Kant says, "have inalienable rights against the head of state, although these are not coercive rights" (*TP* 8: 303). And one of this fundamental rights consists in being able to express one's own thoughts in order to promote what is best for the commonwealth – or, in other words, to contribute to its progress in the rule of law. To exert this right is something that is legitimized and even furthered by what the social contract as an idea of reason demands. This is consistent with the spirit of one of Kant's most famous short pieces, "What is Enlightenment?" [*WE*], where he argues for a public use of reason by means of which different practices, norms and institutions should be scrutinized and, when possible, improved, taking always into account that changes should not be radically and unilaterally implemented, especially when one is holding a particular office and one must comply with the specific duties pertaining to it (cfr. *WE* 8: 38ff).

Particularly in the case of legislators and politicians themselves, Kant holds that, when they identify the necessity of making this changes, they have the duty:

> to focus on remedying it as soon as possible and bringing it into compliance with natural right, as the latter presents itself as a model to us in the idea of reason, even if this should require sacrifices of their egoism.
>
> (*PP* 8: 372)

Thus, Kant portraits the figure of what he calls a ***moral politician*** – an actor who does not treat politics and morality as if they were intrinsically opposed, and who does not twist morality in order to make it more compatible with other interests of his own. In this sense, Kant's enduring lesson can be taken to be that all true improvements of law that count as such, besides of aspiring to a greater clarity and internal coherence, are always motivated by the will of someone who wants to see the rule of right prevailing over other motivations. For as he states in *DR*: "If legal justice perishes, then it is no longer worthwhile for humans to remain alive on this earth" (*DR* 6: 332).

## 4 Concluding remarks

Kant's legal thought is very diverse and complex, and offers many intellectual challenges to his readers, both in terms of scholarly hermeneutical analysis in order to evaluate his views and in terms of the systematic way in which one may try to apply Kant's ideas to our contemporary predicaments. To be sure, there are many ways in which one could appropriate his philosophical thought, as the plurality of recent studies of Kantian inspiration that deal with property rights, international law, fair trade and human rights clearly bears witness to.[9] More often than not, as this happens with great authors of the philosophical tradition, one is compelled to go beyond Kant in order to be truly coherent with the spirit of his philosophical intuitions and doctrines, transcending thereby the limitations of his context and some of his underlying ideological biases. Such a task, if done pertinently, however, can only be carried out with a solid knowledge of what his texts actually say. In this sense, as I pointed out in the Introduction, it is only relatively recently that we have gained a more informed knowledge of his legal and political philosophy through the closer study and attention that have been paid to texts that were for a long time neglected; it is therefore only to be expected that if his moral philosophy by itself nourished some of the most prominent political philosophies of recent times, our political and legal imagination will be further stimulated by the direct discussion and engagement with what Kant actually had to say in regard to those particular realms. His distinction between different legal normative sources, his regard for the dignity of both the law-makers and citizens, the formal criteria of law that he puts forward, and his insightful considerations about the implementation of law and the ethics that govern this practice constitute a perennial legacy with which we must come to terms in order to envision more inclusive political and legal systems and a world in which rights enhance the rational freedom of all human beings.

## References

Byrd, B. S. and Hruschka, J. (2010) *Kant's Doctrine of Right. A Commentary.* Cambridge, Cambridge University Press.

Guyer, P. (2000) *Kant on Freedom, Law and Happiness.* Cambridge, Cambridge University Press.

Habermas, J. (1996) *Between Facts and Norms. Contributions to a Discourse Theory of Law and Democracy.* Cambridge, MIT Press.

Habermas, J. (1997) 'Kant's Idea of Perpetual Peace, with the Benefit of Two Hundred Years Hindsight', in Bohman, J. and Lutz-Bachmann, M. (eds) *Perpetual Peace. Essays on Kant's Cosmopolitan Ideal.* Cambridge, MIT Press, 113–154.

Höffe, O. (2002) *Categorical Principles of Law. A Counterpoint to Modernity.* University Park, Pennsylvania State University Press.

Kant, I. (1900ff.) *Gesammelte Schriften.* Vol. 1–22 Preussische Akademie der Wissenschaften, vol. 23 Deutsche Akademie der Wissenschaften zu Berlin, from vol. 24 onwards Akademie der Wissenschaften zu Göttingen, Berlin.

Kant, I. (1999) *Metaphysical Elements of Justice.* Indianapolis/Cambridge, Hackett Publishing Company.

Kant, I. (2006) *Toward Perpetual Peace and Other Writings on Politics, Peace and History.* New Haven/London, Yale University Press.

9 A brilliant collection of essays that addresses many of these Kantian topics from a contemporary perspective is to be found in the recent volume edited by Krasnoff, Sánchez Madrid, and Satne (2018).

Korsgaard, C. (2008) 'Taking the Law into Our Own Hands: Kant on the Right to Revolution', in *The Constitution of Agency. Essays on Practical Reason and Moral Psychology*. Oxford/New York, Oxford University Press, 233–262.

Krasnoff, L., Sánchez Madrid, N., and Satne, P. (eds) (2018) *Kant's Doctrine of Right in the 21st Century*. Cardiff, University of Wales Press.

Ludwig, B. (1993) 'Kants Verabschiedung der Vertragstheorie. Konsequenzen für eine Theorie sozialer Gerechtigkeit', *Jahrbuch für Recht und Ethik/Annual Review of Law and Ethics*, vol. 1, 221–254.

Maus, I. (1994) *Zur Aufklärung der Demokratietheorie. Rechts- und demokratietheoretische Überlegungen in Anschluss an Kant*. Frankfurt am Main, Suhrkamp.

Mulholland, L. A. (1990) *Kant's System of Rights*. New York, Columbia University Press.

O'Neill, O. (2015) 'Kant and the Social Contract Tradition', in *Constructing Authorities. Reason, Politics and Interpretation in Kant's Philosophy*. Cambridge, Cambridge University Press, 170–185.

Rawls, J. (1971) *A Theory of Justice*. London/Cambridge, Harvard University Press.

Ripstein, A. (2009) *Force and Freedom. Kant's Legal and Political Philosophy*. Cambridge/London, Harvard University Press.

Willascheck, M. (2009) 'Right and Coercion. Can Kant's Conception of Right be Derived from his Moral Theory?', *International Journal of Philosophical Studies*, vol. 17, 49–70.

Williams, H. (1983) *Kant's Political Philosophy*. Oxford, Basil Blackwell.

Williams, H. (2003) *Kant's Critique of Hobbes. Sovereignty and Cosmopolitanism*. Aberystwyth, University of Wales Press.

Wood, A. W. (2002) 'The Final Form of Kant's Practical Philosophy', in Timmons, M. (ed.) *Kant's Metaphysics of Morals. Interpretative Essays*. Oxford, Oxford University Press, 1–22.

# 9 Economism, voluntarism, and materialist historicism

## Three faces of the Marxist instrumental approach to legal change[1]

*Maciej Chmieliński*

### Introduction

From the Marxist point of view, the law, similar to the state, is inscribed into the base and superstructure, as the crucial element of the latter. The law and the state are central parts of the superstructure, most directly serving to maintain the existing social-economical relations. As analytical Marxists assume, it is the capitalist order which constitutes the law in particular; indeed, law is "the need" of capitalism (Cohen 2001, Altvater 1978).[2] The superstructure (such social institutions as art, morality, law, or state) is generally determined by the economic base (the organization of economic production). According to Marx and Engels:

> The material life of individuals . . . is the real basis of the state and remains so at all the stages at which division of labour and private property are still necessary . . . These actual relations are in no way created by the state power; on the contrary they are the power creating it. The individuals who rule in these conditions . . . have to give their will, which is determined by these definite conditions, a universal expression as the will of the state, as law, an expression whose content is always determined by the relations of this class, as the civil and criminal law demonstrates in the clearest possible way.
>
> (Marx & Engels 1976: 348)

Material relations in the base determine the social structure and power relations, inevitably characterized by class domination. The dominating class produces the ideas that are "nothing more than the ideal expression of the dominant material relations . . . of the relations which make the one class the ruling one" (Marx & Engels 1976: 67). Therefore, political and legal ideas, general frameworks, and

1 This chapter presents results of the research financially supported by the National Science Centre, Poland, as part of the project No. 2015/19/B/HS5/02522.

2 Unlike other elements of superstructure as for instance art, morality, or philosophy, which are also historically and economically determined, the law and the state are to disappear in the transition from socialism to communism (Bodenheimer 1952: 66). For more on analytical Marxism, see Bertram in Bidet and Kouvelakis (2008: 123f).

particular laws, are interpreted as generally determined by historical-economic relations of production (Wetherly 2005: 109), and as an instrument used (consciously or not) by the dominating class to maintain power. Law legitimizes the economic power of the state, and both law and the state serve the interests of the dominating class (Wetherly 2005: 151).

Granted, although Marxism provides one of the most characteristic perspectives of the economic-political evaluation of law, at the same time it does not create a genuine, autonomous theory of law. The central aim of the Marxist jurisprudence was neither – as in its investigations in economy – building the new foundations for it, nor offering a new comprehensive theory of it, but as Collins explains it was "to criticize the centre-piece of liberal political philosophy, the ideal called the Rule of Law" (Collins 1982: 240). Therefore, theorizing about law in this paradigm is always the "construction[s] of what Marx or Marxism would or should say about the subject" (Krygier 1990: 648) rather than systemic *reconstruction* of what they actually said. A similar approach should be applied when one is interested in a Marxist account of legal change. Therefore, instead of delving into the original doctrine of Marx and Engels, I will concentrate on its most characteristic developments present in twentieth-century Marxist jurisprudence.

One may identify three characteristic tendencies that help approach the question of legal change in Marxism: "economism" (or "economic determinism"), "voluntarism", and the third one, which may be called "historicism". They reflect three crucial aspects of the Marxist doctrine: economic determination of the superstructure, the idea of class struggle, and the assumption of historical materialism. These three aspects, all present in the original theory, are foundations of the competing, and often very radically conflicted, tendencies belonging to Marxist jurisprudence.[3] The best examples of the first and the second tendency can be found in early Soviet legal thought.[4] Examining the early Soviet Union's legal system, one may see that the economistic tendency was historically prior to the voluntarist standpoint that subsequently prevailed in the Stalinist period (Sharlet 1977: 165). Both economistic and voluntarist tendencies were in turn criticized as not taking the historical materialism seriously enough by some representatives of the third – historicist – standpoint, connected primarily with contemporary Western Marxist thought.

Concluding each section, I will indicate similarities and dissimilarities between the reconstructed approaches to legal change and the models of legal creationism and legal determinism presented in Chapter 5 of this book. The main goal of such comparison is to demonstrate that the collectivism characterizing of the

3 As Kouvelakis points out, this resembles the internal dynamics of Marxism in historical social dynamics, where crises are inscribed in Marxism itself and show the "creative potential of the crisis for Marxism itself" (Kouvelakis 2008: 26).

4 In the Western world, the main texts of the representatives of the Soviet jurisprudence are available, for instance in the selection of Soviet authors edited in 1951 by John N. Hazard and translated by Hugh Babb: *Soviet Legal Philosophy* (Babb & Hazard 1951).

Marxist conception significantly differs not only from the individualism present in the contractarian approach, but also from communitarianism. Although the latter is similar to collectivism insofar as it is a socially holist approach, there are important disagreements with regards to the nature of social knowledge and the way social practices determine the law. As a result, I will argue, the fundamentally different way the justification of law is treated in Marxism allows one to treat this doctrine as a complementary, rather than decisive, perspective on the philosophy of legal change.

## 1 Marxist economic determinism:[5] Stuchka and Pashukanis

The economic-deterministic tendency was represented, among others, by Soviet legal theorists Peter I. Stuchka (Latvian: Pēteris Stučka) and Evgeny B. Pashukanis. This tendency, as Nicos Poulantzas puts it, "regards law *as a system or order of social relations* ratified by the state", where "social relations" are understood primarily as those between commodity owners (Poulantzas 2008: 26, emphasis original). In other words, law's function boils down to mirroring the economic system, which makes the law nothing but a passive reflection of the conditions present in the base. The most important starting point of the economist interpretation of law as developed by Pashukanis is the following passage from *Capital* of Karl Marx:

> [I]t is plain that commodities cannot go to market and make exchange of their own account. We must, therefore, have recourse to their guardians, who are also their owners . . . In order that these objects may enter into relation with each other as commodities, their guardians must place themselves in relation to one another, as persons whose will resides in those objects, and must behave in such a way that each does not appropriate the commodity of the other, and part with his own, except by means of an act done by mutual consent. They must, therefore, mutually recognize in each other the rights of private proprietors. This juridical relation, which thus expresses itself in a contract . . . is a relation between two wills, and is but the reflex of the real economic relation between the two.
>
> (Marx 1996: 88–89)

For Pashukanis, the fundamental type of relationship in the capitalist law is that of commodity exchange happening between participants in the market economy. The law defines the participants as abstract parties to contracts. The concept of contractual commodity exchange is, according to Pashukanis, the central heuristic tool in understanding the capitalist law. It is the economic relationship of the contractual commodity exchange between parties that creates the model of legal relationship in general, and transforms the parties into

5 On Marxist "economic determinism" in the broader sense, see Wood 2004: 63f.

abstract legal subjects. As Pashukanis points out: "At the very same time that the product of labour is taking on the quality of goods and becoming a bearer of value, man acquires the quality of a juridic subject and becomes the bearer of a right" (Pashukanis 1951a: 162). Or, as he stresses in another work, "The general theory of law and Marxism":

> Only with the complete development of bourgeois relationships does the law acquire an abstract character. Each man becomes a man in general, labour of every sort is reduced to socially beneficial labour in general and every subject becomes an abstract juridic subject.
>
> (Pashukanis 1951b: 169)

As we can see above, this is true not only for – most importantly in capitalism – private laws, but also for public law and therefore even for criminal law, where relation of commodity exchange is seen as analogous to the relation between crime and punishment.[6]

Similarly to Pashukanis, Stuchka defines law as "a system (or order) of social relationships which corresponds to the interests of the dominant class and is safeguarded by the organized force of that class" (Stuchka 1951: 20). Bodenheimer maintains that Stuchka puts special emphasis on the first part of this definition, seeing law primarily as "a system of social relationships". Under the interpretation of Bodenheimer, the true law for Stuchka is a kind of social "natural law", whereas the statutory law "called by Stuchka the law of 'volitional imperatives', is regarded by him merely as the shadow or reflection of the actual social and economic activities of human beings" (Bodenheimer 1952: 54).

It is important to emphasize that, according to the "economic" interpretation, the law has a more fundamental role than being a mere instrument of class oppression: it is an indispensable ingredient of capitalist exchange of commodity (Krygier 1990: 654f). For Pashukanis legal relation is always internally connected to economic relation, and law in the capitalist society is always the more or less visible element of these relations.

> It must be noted that the legal [juridische] viewpoint is incomparably more remote from the consciousness of the ordinary man than is the economic viewpoint, for the reason that when the economic relationship is carried into effect simultaneously as a legal relationship too, it is nevertheless the economic side of that relationship which has reality for the participants therein in the vast majority of cases, whilst the legal element remains in the background, and emerges in all its definiteness only in special and exceptional cases (legal proceedings, a controversy concerning the law).
>
> (Pashukanis 1951a: 121)

6 This is the reason why, for Pashukanis' new Soviet criminal law, capitalist criminal justice has to be replaced by purely utilitarian "measures of social defence", which according to Krygier led to the factual "legal nihilism" of the Soviet criminal justice. See Krygier (1990: 656).

However, the internal structure of law is indirectly derived from the current mode of production and has no autonomy with regard to the historical form of economic relations. As Richard Kinsey clarifies:

> The economist interpretation puts forward the law as a simple and immediate reflection of economic relations. There is a direct correspondence between the needs of capital and the content of the law – law is merely "appended" to the economic order . . . the study of law is reduced to the pure "science of the economic" and law is denied any status as "a theoretically constructed and specific object of scientific investigation" in its own right.
>
> (Kinsey 1978: 207)

In this sense, law is "encoded" in the current economic relations and can be only very cautiously "decoded" from these structures by the legislator. The role of the legislator is thus different from simply following the representatives of the dominating class and introducing the solutions that are most appropriate to their interests and will. The role of legislative authorities consists in seeking the "objective", economic elements underlying law, inscribed into the intellectual-economic background of capitalism, but also of each form of the actual society, including the socialist one (in communism there will be no law, in socialism law still exists, but in its residual, "withering" form).

The role of legislator in "scientific" Marxism is similar to that of a social-economic scientist. The legislator "researches" the economic relations of the commodity circulation and tries to "recognize" the proper legal regulations as most suitable to these relations. According to the economistic standpoint, each change in the law has to constitute a reflection of the previous change in the base.

At a first glance, it may seem that the role of the law-changing authority in the Marxist-economistic tendency is close to the role of this authority in the conservative-communitarian model described in Chapter 5. However, there is a fundamental difference which excludes treating the Marxist economic determinism simply as a variation of legal determinism as developed in Chapter 5. First and foremost, the Marxist conception of human reason is opposite to the one adopted by the communitarian-conservative approach. The Marxist theory of central economic planning is based on the optimist assumption that one can usually predict the consequences of actions (Hayek 2011: 107f). If it is possible to plan in the economic sphere, it is also possible to predict the important consequences of legal changes that resemble the economic changes (i.e. changes in the base). The legal sphere is an element of superstructure and as such is derivative of the economic base. The logic of change in Marxist economic determinism is thus more similar to the optimist epistemic assumption of the creationist model developed in Chapter 5.

## 2 Marxist's legal voluntarism: Reisner and Vyshinsky

The voluntarist tendency is also deeply rooted in Marx's and Engels' approach to law. We can find its founding assumptions in the following citation from the "Communist Manifesto":

> Don't wrangle with us so long as you apply, to our intended abolition of bourgeois property, the standard of your bourgeois notions of freedom, culture, law, etc. Your very ideas are but the outgrowth of the conditions of your bourgeois production and bourgeois property, just as your jurisprudence is but the will of your class made into a law for all, a will whose essential character and direction are determined by the economical conditions of existence of your class.
>
> (Marx & Engels 1973: 83)

In this passage, Marx and Engels emphasize the second important characteristic of capitalist law, namely, its subordination to the interest of the dominating class. The necessary assumption that can be derived from this is the conscious, volitional creation of law by the capitalist state authorities. In comparison to economic determinism, the law has a less important role to play here: it is simply more contingent. The ruling class shapes the legal relations according to their will, and the law protects the existing social arrangements; but at the same time it is "not a fundamental social arrangements itself" (Kamenka 1983: 49).

Marx and Engels gave no direct and detailed answer to the question of how law is supposed to express the economic relations in the socialist phase of social transition to communism, where the new economic and legal reality is to be born. In other words, they did not describe law in the process of economic transition in a detailed way. After the Bolshevik revolution, the answer to this question became the first necessity of the new, Soviet state. Whereas in the first post-revolutionary and New Economic Policy (NEP)[7] period, answers by Pashukanis and Stuchka were considered acceptable, after the Stalinist "nationalist" shift they became insufficient for the new Soviet legal policy. The new, voluntarist approach emphasized the active role that law has to play in introducing the new social order. It was represented by such Soviet jurists as Mikhail A. Reisner, Paul F. Yudin, and Andrei Vyshinsky, the Soviet procurator general.

Voluntarism grew out of strong criticism of Pashukanis and Stuchka. As Vyshinsky pointed out:

> It is . . . incorrect to define law – as Stuchka did – as a system of social relationships. As everyone knows, Stuchka's viewpoint prevailed at the first Congress of so-called Marxian political scientists and for a number of years thereafter. In reducing law to economics, Stuchka and his followers put an end to law as a specific and particular social category they drowned law in economics and robbed law of its active and creative role. From the viewpoint of such an understanding of law, the independent study of law as a special science loses every sort of meaning.
>
> (Vyshinsky 1951: 330)

7 On the Soviet New Economic Policy (Novaja Ekonomiceskaja Politica) see for instance Davies (1991) and Fitzpatrick (1991).

According to Vyshinsky and Yudin, the law obviously has to disappear in the economic development taking place after the Soviet revolution, but it does not mean that Soviet law can be treated solely as a "special" or "transitional" form of the capitalist law, as it was conceived by Pashukanis and Stuchka. Quite to the contrary, it must be treated as an expression of the will of the Soviet proletarian state, which is tantamount to the expression of the will of the people – "the proletariat". In other words, socialist law must indirectly serve the interest of the economically dominant group of the Soviet society, which, after the Russian revolution, was the "proletariat". By the same token, the socialist law was considered a new, better form of law, and the disappearance of law as such was deferred (Bodenheimer 1952: 61).

Unlike in economic determinism, where the law is considered to passively mirror the conditions in the base, the voluntarist tendency conceives of the economic base as "an inert field 'energised' by the will and human consciousness" (Kinsey 1978: 207). In the voluntarist standpoint, law is consciously created and changed by the legislator that works in a concrete form of the state. It is assumed that the legislator always represents the interests and will of the ruling class. In the capitalist state, it is the will of the bourgeoisie, in the socialist state – the will of the proletariat. Legal change and law are therefore never "neutral", always serving the economic interests of the dominant class as a tool of class struggle. The legislator, that is tantamount to the state, is merely the class instrument; its role is reduced to securing the interest of the concrete class. Therefore, making and changing law is considered as an expression of the collective will of the social class. The same role is played by the judges, the administration, and all the public authorities. There is nothing that can limit these authorities in modifying the law, provided that the new law corresponds to the will of the ruling class.

Marxist voluntarism seems to be similar to the creationist model of law presented in Chapter 5, in which the will of the democratic sovereign (the people) is also crucial to the legal change. However, the Marxist assumption of the non-neutrality of the legislator, and the vision of the legislator as representing solely the interests of the ruling class, does not fully harmonize with the creationist assumptions. The aggregated preferences of the sovereign in the creationist model cannot be treated as preferences of the ruling class only. Social contract, used by thinkers such as J. M. Buchanan, is obviously not the contract only between the members of the bourgeoisie, but between all citizens. The already-mentioned Marxist analysis of the capitalist society fairly demonstrates that liberal individualism is founded on the assumption of a common character of equal liberty, without assumptions of class division and class domination. The contractarian test assumes, similarly to the Rawlsian veil of ignorance, that all the hypothetical members of society would agree on the rules, at least at the constitutional level. It is derived from an assumption of individual rights, which – as we remarked in the Chapter 5 – imposes a limit on the consequences of the contractarian "economism". Unlike the creationist model of legal change, in Marxism there is no such individual-rights-limitation. Even in his early writings, Marx criticized individual rights as being based on the liberty "of man as an isolated monad who is withdrawn into himself" (Marx 1975: 229). Therefore, Marx argued:

> [t]he right of man to freedom is not based on the association of man with man but rather on the separation of man from man. It is the right of this separation, the right of the restricted individual, restricted to himself.
>
> (Marx 1975: 229)

Excluding the "atomizing" of individual rights, Marxism assumes that economic rationality always dominates the individual rights and there is nothing that could defend the individual against the economically rational, but at the same time individually harmful, legal change. Marxist legal constructivism, unlike the contractarian one, is founded on the strong assumption of the central economic planning. In this aspect it simply means that if the plan dictates something contrary to the individual rights, human freedom, or tolerance, the legislative authority is not bound to limit itself.

As noted above, in the Marxist, voluntarist approach, law is limited to the will of the ruling (or the revolutionary) class, which is taken into account by the legislative authority. Thus, harm done to the representatives of the hostile class (such the Bourgeoisie in a socialist country) is not only possible, but even, in the extreme version, self-evident or required. The consequences of such a legal voluntarism of the ruling class were explicitly seen in the Soviet Union and in the Eastern European countries, being a part of the Eastern Block (Krygier 1990: 656). If so, the Marxist, voluntarist solution seems to be closest to the model of the fully partisan model of legal change (compare Waldron 1990: 12). The partisan model means that laws are created according to interests of certain pressure groups that have, at the certain moment, enough power to force change pursuing their interest. Similarly, as in the "partisan" model, in Marxist legal voluntarism the law is created and changed only by the state, and there is no law beyond the state. The law is treated strictly instrumentally, and economic rationality is tantamount to the economic interest and needs of the ruling class.

## 3 Marxist legal historicism: Poulantzas

The third pillar of the Marxist approach to law, as mentioned above, is connected to the assumptions of historical materialism. The "materialist-historicist" character of Marx's and Engels' doctrine was an aspect of Marxist jurisprudence that has been developed in Western Europe. It was part of the critique of the two orthodox Marxist-Leninist tendencies described above.[8] Certainly, the most well-known representative of the "materialist-historicist" approach was an Italian thinker, Antonio Gramsci. His conceptions have inspired many ideas,

8 About the general development of Marxism in the Western Europe from the Soviet, Marxist-Leninist approach to the many of internally differentiated conceptions, see Tosel (2008: 39f).

including those of jurisprudence. In my view, the most instructive illustration of how "materialist historicism" was used in Western Marxist jurisprudence is found in the conception developed by a Greek student of Louis Althuser, Nicos Poulantzas.[9] He was, on the one hand, deeply "rooted" in political debates that took place in Western Marxism of the 1970s, and, on the other, he remained close to the "canonical" Marxist notions and categories – his legal theories were fundamentally formulated before his structuralist turn, and remained unchanged after the influence of Althuser.

Poulantzas starts developing his own account with the polemic against economism and voluntarism. As he argues, both are "deformations" of the original Marxist theory of superstructure, because "neither of these tendencies would appear to have succeeded in capturing the precise meaning of the fact that the juridical and state level pertains to the superstructure" (Poulantzas 2008: 25). In his opinion, it results from "a misconception of the relation between base and superstructure, denying specific effectivity of, and the dialectic between, the various 'levels' of this 'decentred unity'" (Kinsey 1978: 207). For Poulantzas, "taking seriously" Marx's and Engels' assumption of historical materialism, the concrete content of base-structure relationships fully depends on the particular time and space in which they emerge, whereas both economism and voluntarism result in fact in an "ahistorical" point of view, inconsistent with the dynamical view that was created by Marx's historical materialism.

He points out that all domains involved in the superstructure, which

> comprise a normative ensemble – morality, religion, law and the state, even art (albeit in a different sense) are . . . genetically structured, and must be methodologically grasped, according to the concrete historical values themselves engendered from the base, that they embody.
>
> (Poulantzas 2008: 26f)

It results from historical values, which determine "the condition of existence of a rule or institution at the juridical-state level" (Poulantzas 2008: 27). Such rules and institutions only express these values. Juridical rules and institutions are therefore "historical realities" and can be examined only "genetically" as an effective expression of the concrete social axiology of a particular time and place (Poulantzas 2008: 27). The failure of the voluntarist tendency is assuming that the institutions are "already structured objects" (Poulantzas 2008: 27), and not parts of historical processes, whereas "the process of genesis of historical values represents the mediator between the economic base and these superstructures" (Poulantzas 2008: 28). Thereby, the voluntarist approach ends up fully separating the law from the concrete economic base. In turn, the "simplistic economism"

9 Poulantzas' approach to law was criticized and interestingly developed by the member of the English "left realism", Richard Kinsey, an English author much less known than Poulantzas. For an interpretation of Poulantzas by Kinsey, see Kinsey (1978).

of Pashukanis and Stuchka is too reductionist: law and the state are reduced to the relations in the base. As a result, the economic determinist "disregard their specific character as a coherent system of norms and thus completely ignore their relative autonomy" (Poulantzas 2008: 28).

As Poulantzas points out, the historical specificity of the social-economic formation of the late capitalism in the second half of the twentieth century is expressed by an assumption of "individualistic voluntarism" of law (Poulantzas 2008: 32), which is expressed in a concrete set of values: private property, formal equality, and formal liberty. These values indirectly resemble the current character of economic relations depending on free exchange of commodities. Being of formal and abstract character, both equality and liberty enable the universality of capitalist law, which is crucial to secure the two features, important for the mature capitalist societies contemporary to Poulantzas, that is, calculability and forecasting. According to to Poulantzas:

> In these societies, the operation of justice, legislation and administration must take the form of predictable acts, judgements and decisions, and thus be calculable in advance. This need is itself created by, and manifest in, current infrastructural realities – a society of monopolies and concentration of large capital; the importance of the interests at stake; the accumulation characteristic of this capital; the increased amount of initial investment as a result of technical progress and the need to recover it macro-chronically; the rigidity of fixed capital, machines, and so on – capital which, on account of the high degree of its technical specialization, becomes difficult to switch between the various spheres of production; the need to determine the cost of production and the sum of wages in advance; and so on.
>
> (Poulantzas 2008: 35)

Reducing unpredictability and uncertainty in the activity of the judiciary system, and law in general, provides relative stability of the superstructure, which in current democracies is necessary for providing effective commodity exchange, and more generally for secure and convenient accumulation of capital in a highly complicated economy such as in Western countries. Predictability and certainty are resembled in the structure of the legal norm which is:

> (a) general, contrary in this respect to individual dispositions that only concern a specific case or person; (b) abstract, constructed by means of concepts that are autonomous from concrete reality; (c) formal, stripped of concrete, "material" content; and (d) *strictly codified*: by this we mean the specific structuration whose goal is to preserve the existence – and thus also guarantee the predictability – of a normative order, by allowing for its "complete reversibility".
>
> (Poulantzas 2008: 36, emphasis original)

It results in the deep systematization and axiomatization of law, which becomes a highly abstract institution. As Poulantzas argues, this results in maintaining the economic *status quo ante* of the late form of capitalism present in the egalitarian democratic state of the end of twentieth century. However, in Poulantzas' opinion, it contradicts the interests of the working class (proletariat, or wider – all these, who are not owners of means of production). Following Marx and Engels, he points out that abstract liberty and equality are internally contradicted: securing the capitalist order, they in fact help to preserve social inequalities and hindering of real liberty, which is supposed to be the essence of the capitalist order. There is a vivid internal contradiction between formal equality and real equality, as well as between formal freedom and real freedom, and that fundamental tension characterizes late capitalism.

This is precisely the point at which Poulzantzas' critique of capitalist law begins. His method is strictly connected to the idea of the dialectical synthesis between internal and external perspectives of evaluation, as characterized in the following passage:

> This particular aspect of a dialectical examination of the juridical and state sphere can be characterized as an "internal-external" process of analysis, with the relations of inferiority and exteriority – relations (as Hegel demonstrated) of totality – being conceived in accordance with the Marxist dialectic and totality. Given that this sphere constitutes a formally coherent system of rules, institutions and hierarchies of powers – internal viewpoint – aimed at exploiting the oppressed classes through repressive state power – external viewpoint – any particular norm or institution, generated out of concrete infrastructural realities - external viewpoint – will be integrated into it by embracing the specific characteristics of this sphere and being inserted into its modus operandi – internal viewpoint.
>
> (Poulantzas 2008: 39)

In other words, the state evaluated from such a mixed perspective is the synthesis of – on the one hand – the indirectly economically determined organization of "universal" rules and standards and, on the other hand, the tool of the class oppression. As Poulzantzas points out:

> From an internal point of view, the state emerges as the axiological-normative order of juridical rules and institutions taken as a whole (state as organization). From an external point of view, the state is the repressive force which, through juridical rules and institutions, is directed towards class exploitation (the state as body or instrument).
>
> (Poulantzas 2008: 42f)

The methodological conception of the internal-external perspective allows for a presentation of Poulantzas' general approach to legal change, with a caveat that he does not directly address the issue in the sense presented in this book. It is only my reconstruction, developing his general approach to law. As noted above, from the external point of view, state and law are regarded as the "tool of class oppression", which is connected to the above-described Marxist voluntarism. At the same time, dialectically, from the internal point of view, state and law are seen as a relatively autonomous element of the superstructure, being indirectly – through the abstract ideas of formal equality and liberty inscribed in the law – determined by the economic base. The will of the dominating class in the process of legal change is thus strictly limited through the abstract values of formal equality and liberty, content of which is dependent on the level of historical-economic development. Each legal change in a modern democratic state has to be consistent with these abstract ideas. This determines the role of legal authorities – the judiciary, the legislative, or the administrative – participating in the process of legal change. Fully and straightforwardly "partisan" changes are excluded, as well as a straightforward promotion of the class interests through law. A general-abstract and codified character of legal rules and norms simply limits the voluntarist tendency of legal processes. The process, however, still pursues the interest of the dominating class, but in a more sophisticated way, where class coercion is located at the deeper level of the social system, and is not connected to the direct and coercive protection of the ruling class.

Such a less observable class struggle and class coercion in late capitalism undermines and strongly reduces Marxist legal voluntarism, moving the role of administration, judiciary, or legislator to the pursuit of abstract ethics and judicial/legal morality. According to Poulantzas, the role of trade unions and working class organizations representing the interests of the ruled class in the late capitalism is therefore to "impart to the 'democratic' values of liberty and equality, negated by the contemporary state and its division from civil society – the base – a concrete, material content and meaning that are 'human' and 'true', extending to all levels" (Poulantzas 2008: 43). In my interpretation, Poulantzas saw trade unions and working-class organizations as having a fundamental historical role to play: to fill the abstract values of late capitalism with the concrete substantive content of real liberty, and real equality.

Certainly, this does not make Poulantzas a revisionist or reformist in a manner of Karl Kautsky, Eduard Bernstein, or Karl Renner; for Poulantzas, the strategies and tactics of the working class have to be differentiated and adjusted to the concrete historical circumstances. Therefore, besides the reformist, democratic way, the revolution also comes into play, if the historical circumstances permit or require. In this sense, Poulantzas does not absolutize neither reformist nor revolutionary way of social changes, being indeed committed to the idea of historical determination of changes in the superstructure. However, considering the relatively "gentle" character of the late capitalism, and a relative improvement of the situation of the working class, the coercive-revolutionary way does not appear necessary. As Poulantzas points out, strategies of the working class should be rather proportional to the concrete, historical form of capitalism.

Now, the important similarity between the conservative-communitarian model and the Marxist-historicist model is the reference to history and historical determination. Both the conservative-communitarian and the Marxist approaches to legal change are of historical character. However, the central Marxist assumption of the relatively unlimited epistemic disposition of human reason makes the process of legislators "learning" or "research" much easier than in conservative-communitarian approach. According to Marxism, it is not an esoteric wisdom rooted in the community institutions that are not fully transparent, but rather discoverable knowledge This extends not only to Marxists' revolutionary approach to common traditions and customs, but this aspect also excludes the possibility of a Burkian relationship between past and current generations, or Oakeshot's differentiation between technical and practical wisdom. Marxism is a deeply positivist – and thus modernist – conception based on scientific foundations. The dialectical historical materialism of Marx and Engels treats history as a field ruled by the same fundamental economic laws in all periods, at least since the period of slavery. Therefore, the law-changing authority does not need to "research" any "esoteric" historical institutions and practices in all aspects of the society, but only the historical-economic relations between the classes. The historical character of these relations means that the legislator must only meet the current economic needs of the dominant/revolutionary class as precisely as possible. Thereby, what is important is only the collective, horizontal dimension of human wisdom, assuming the two classes being in constant conflict. Legal authority in this conflict cannot be impartial, but is always on the side of the dominant class.

## Conclusion

As noted above, the three main tendencies of Marxist jurisprudence resemble three central assumptions of Marxism: economic determination of the superstructure by the relations in the base, the assumption of class struggle, and historical materialism, that is, economic materialism consequently applied to evaluation of human history.[10] It can be argued that they resemble three "moments" of Marxist dialectics in the legal sphere: determination as thesis, voluntarism as anti-thesis, and materialist historicism as synthesis of the two opposite poles. One might argue that it was the historical need of Marxism to use the law in such a twofold way, and finally to synthesize it in a historical-materialist manner. Economism and voluntarism were used appropriately to the historical social needs of the post-revolutionary Soviet society. In the period of building the very foundations of the new socialist state, and in the NEP period, it was economism that was more appropriate. In turn, in the period of the "sharpening of the class struggle" and "cleansing" the Soviet society from the persisting capitalist elements – legal voluntarism was more useful and efficient. Marxist legal historicism, which dialectically includes both economism and voluntarism as dependent on the actual needs of the dominating class, is in fact the current need of Marxism connected to the situation of the Western societies, which in the last decades of the twentieth century have undergone deep changes in the egalitarian direction. These are no longer the nineteenth-century societies with a

10 As in Cohen's "technological reading" of this assumption regarding history (Cohen 2001: 31f).

14-hour working day. The democratic values such as equality and equal freedom considerably improve the situation of the working class, which should be taken into account in the legal analysis.

However, the synthesized Marxist approach to law and legal change, as Poulzantzas shows it, confirms the deeply instrumental and strategic use of law in the class struggle which has been the *leitmotiv* since the founding Marxist texts. Whatever theoretical position is taken in a Marxist-inspired jurisprudence, the law remains an instrument of the ruling class, and therefore may be changed either in the revolutionary-voluntarist way, or in the gradual-determinist way, in the pursuit of the class interest, and accordingly to the circumstances. In the historicist approach, the working-class cause may be realized even by paying tribute to some selected democratic values, however they must be filled-in by a substantive content eliminating or reducing exploitation (Quigley 2007: 10). Even this, however, confirms the generally instrumental approach to law characteristic of Marxism, explicitly expressed by Marx and Engels on many occasions. As a result of such an instrumental approach, the *justification* of law may not be free-standing, and thus cannot be regarded as yielding genuine, universal reasons for action. Rather, from the external perspective, it is always attached to the underlying partisan class interest. As a result of this, from the point of view of the philosophy of legal change as developed in this volume, Marxism remains a complementary perspective that may help in *criticizing* legal change, but not in *explaining* it in the manner adopted in this volume.

## References


Altvater, E. (1978) 'Some Problems of State Interventionism', in Holloway, J. and Picciotto, S. (eds) *State and Capital: a Marxist Debate*, London: Edward Arnold.

Babb, H. and Hazard, J. N. (eds) (1951) *Soviet Legal Philosophy*, Cambridge: Harvard University Press.

Bertram, Ch. (2008) 'Analytical Marxism' in Bidet, J. and Kouvelakis, S. (eds) *Critical Companion to Contemporary Marxism*, Leiden Boston: Brill.

Bidet, J. and Kouvelakis, S. (eds) (2008) *Critical Companion to Contemporary Marxism*, Leiden Boston: Brill.

Bodenheimer, E. (1952) 'Impasse of Soviet Legal Philosophy', *Cornell Law Review*, 38 (1) 51–72.

Cohen, G. A. (2001) *Karl Marx's Theory of History. A Defence*, Expanded Edition, Princeton: Princeton University Press.

Collins, H. (1982) *Marxism and Law*, Oxford: Clarendon Press.

Davies, R. W. (ed.) (1991) *From Tsarism to the New Economic Policy: Continuity and Change in the Economy of the USSR*, Ithaca: Cornell University Press.

Fitzpatrick, S., Rabinowitch, A. and Stites, R. (eds) (1991) *Russia in the Era of NEP*, Bloomington: Indiana University Press.

Hayek, F. A. (2011) *The Constitution of Liberty*, Chicago: University of Chicago Press.

Kamenka, E. (1983) 'A Marxist Theory of Law', *Law in Context*, 1, 49–63.

Kinsey, R. (1978) 'Marxism and the Law: Preliminary Analyses', *British Journal of Law and Society*, 5 (2) 202–227.

Kouvelakis, S. (2008) 'The Crises of Marxism and the Transformation of Capitalism', in Bidet, J. and Kouvelakis, S. (eds) *Critical Companion to Contemporary Marxism*, Leiden Boston: Brill.

Krygier, M. (1990) 'Marxism and the Rule of Law: Reflections After the Collapse of Communism', *Law & Social Inquiry*, 15 (4) 633–663.

Marx, K. (1975) *Early Writings*, New York: International Publishers.

Marx, K. (1996) *Capital, Vol. 1*, Moscow: Progress Publishers.

Marx, K. and Engels, F. (1973) 'The Manifesto of the Communist Party', in *Karl Marx, Political Writings, Vol. 1: The Revolutions of 1848*, Harmondsworth: Verso.

Marx, K. and Engels, F. (1976) *The German Ideology*, Moscow: Progress Publishers.

Pashukanis E. B. (1951a) 'The Soviet State and the Revolution', in Babb, H. and Hazard, J. N. (eds) *Soviet Legal Philosophy*, Cambridge: Harvard University Press.

Pashukanis, E. B. (1951b) 'The General Theory of Law and Marxism', in Babb, H. and Hazard, J. N. (eds) *Soviet Legal Philosophy*, Cambridge: Harvard University Press.

Poulantzas, N. (2008) 'Marxist Examination of the Contemporary State and Law and the Question of the "Alternative"' in Martin, J. (ed.) *The Poulantzas Reader. Marxism, Law and the State*, London New York: Verso.

Quigley, J. (2007) *Soviet Legal Innovation and the Law of The Western World*, Cambridge: Cambridge University Press.

Sharlet, R. (1977) 'Stalinism and Soviet Legal Culture', in Tucker, R. (ed.) *Stalinism Essays in Historical Interpretation*, New York: W. W. Norton & Company.

Stuchka, P. I. (1951) 'The Revolutionary Part Played by Law and the State; a General Doctrine of Law', in Babb, H. and Hazard, J. N. (eds) *Soviet Legal Philosophy*, Cambridge: Harvard University Press.

Tosel, A. (2008) 'The Development of Marxism: From the End of Marxism-Leninism to a Thousand Marxisms: France-Italy, 1975–2005', in Bidet, J. and Kouvelakis, S. (eds) *Critical Companion to Contemporary Marxism*, Leiden Boston: Brill.

Vyshinsky, A. Y. (1951) 'The Fundamental Tasks of the Science of Soviet Socialist Law', in Babb, H. and Hazard, J. N. (eds) *Soviet Legal Philosophy*, Cambridge: Harvard University Press.

Waldron, J. (1990) *The Law*, London New York: Routledge.

Wetherly, P. (2005) *Marxism and the State*, London New York: Palgrave MacMillan.

Wood, A. (2004) *Karl Marx*, 2nd edition, New York and London: Routledge.

# Part III

# Practical processes

# 10 Petrifying, disregarding or reforming customs

## Can customary law be changed in a liberal way?

*Marc Goetzmann*

### Introduction

In most post-colonial states and other non-Western countries, the judicial as well as the legislative processes take place in a pluralistic context where formal state law might cohabitate with, and quite often conflicts with, diverse sources of social regulation, such as religious or customary law. *Customary law*, as a *normative* system, designates, in its most basic form, the kind of informal institutions whose process consists in "declaring" what the *custom* is, basing itself on an interpretation of what the practices of the community are.[1]

Confronting this fact, one encounters two non-exclusive attitudes: on the one hand, judges and legislators will base their decisions on what they *believe* the customary law of a community dictates them, in order to respect its core values and the community's opinion on what is good, and to avoid social disruption. This attitude can therefore be called *conservative* in a non-derogatory sense of the word. On the other hand, they might consider that some principles and/or rights, defended on rational grounds, supersede customary law and will issue decisions and legislations accordingly, which is a *reformative* attitude. In this way, judges and legislators are either utilitarian or principle-driven, or more likely a mix of the two: they see customary law as the boulder that slows down the improvement of the community's general welfare, or as an obstacle for the promotion of basic individual rights, such as human rights.[2]

Both conservative and reformative attitudes, respectively more *communitarian* and more *voluntarist*, have serious limitations: the customary-based method, especially in a common-law context, has an historical tendency to "petrify" custom while codifying it. Consequently, judges and legislators take

1 *Customary law* is here distinguished from *custom*. Consequently, customary law as understood here does not contain all the norms and practices that the word "custom" covers, sometimes quite loosely, from driving on the right to the steps of a wedding. Here, customary law designates only institutions, more or less informal, that exist parallel to a formal legal system. It emerges progressively, as disputes emerge, or when clarifications are needed in general. Therefore, it does not contain all the norms of one given society, only those that are made salient when dealing with conflicts.

2 One must remember how Bentham called custom a "tyrant" (Bentham, 1838–1843: 495).

a fluctuating and sometimes contradictory body of usages and turn it into a rather change-proof set of rules that are now unable to adapt to new circumstances. Meanwhile, the other method tends to take for granted the power of legislation, basing it only on its institutional legitimacy, guided by the desire to promote general welfare while defending some basic individual rights. Nevertheless, this second method will often disregard the normative authority of custom and will fail due to lack of constraining power on individuals. As a result, strict opposition of the conservative and reformative approaches is not desirable, especially as the conservative approach is mainly a matter of precaution to avoid social disruption. Its goal is also, eventually, a *natural* evolution of customary law, and the conservative approach places more weight on preservation of custom out of distrusting more active forms of reforming. This chapter intends to explain why these two approaches need to be reconciled and, if so, how the utilitarian and the rights-driven approach to social change *can* be reconciled.

A useful philosophical approach to this very practical problem is to get a comprehensive view of what is at stake by disentangling the various justifications behind both conservative and reformative approaches and overcoming their opposition. Any attempt at reforming customary law, to be both convincing and efficient, cannot disregard the *reasons* why customary law exists and deserves to be upheld. Conversely, in a world where the standards of the general welfare of a community and human rights are commonplace, the preservation of customary law that, at the local level, competes or conflicts with statutory law must answer to a *rational* explanation. This theoretical approach toward a pragmatic problem should allow us to avoid two extremes results: *either* the petrification of *or* the complete disregard of customary law, that both impede positive social change. "Positive" here is left open, but one could say that it consists, at least, in a change that goes in the direction of what the legislator would consider "good". Broadly conceived, this designates social improvement and economic development that both benefit individuals (hence the frequent reference to human rights) and the communities as a whole. The difficult balance between these two goals, which are roughly equivalent to the utilitarian and the rights-based approaches, is fully acknowledged in the chapter. Finally, the *process* is here more important than the *content* of that change: it needs to be harmonious and neither violent, nor ineffective.

An *effective* reformative approach would then be deeply rooted in the context it is striving to change, instead of considering abstractly the rationales behind the conservative and reformative perspective. This is why the pluralism of these situations cannot be forgotten: the judge and the legislator promote what they consider to be another legitimate norm than what is contained in customary law. Individuals are thus stuck in a dilemma where two (or more) normative horizons compete. Consequently, individuals are not just the distant beneficiaries of legal reforms: they are deciding, more or less consciously, to abide by one set of norms or the other, and their aggregated choices make any attempt at reforming customary law effective or not.

Therefore, the hypothesis of this chapter is the following: once the individual is considered the keystone of the success for any legal reform, the main rationales behind the voluntarist approach (utilitarian or rights-driven) can "mix-and-match" instead of contradicting each other, while the conservative and the reformative approach need no longer oppose each other. Any reformative attitude that promotes individual welfare by disregarding the individual's choice to live by the rules of his community is in full contradiction, for instance, with individual freedom as a right. The utilitarian approach (as it promotes an aggregated increase of welfare), when is it not qualified by some minimal considerations for individual rights, can lead one to ignore discrimination against vulnerable groups (like women and their rights) for the sake of the welfare of the community. Conversely, the idea of individual freedom as a right can be self-contradictory when it becomes an abstract principle *imposed* onto individuals as a standard. A conciliation of these different sets of allegedly contradictory perspectives should then set the bases for a *liberal* way to reform customary law, without petrifying or disregarding it. *Liberal* here means allowing change on a social scale while respecting individual freedom. This chapter will argue that this can be done by focusing on the context of the individual's choice in a competitive, normative environment.

The justifications for the preservation and institutionalization of customary law will be analyzed, along with their unexpected consequences, such as petrification. Since the mere upholding of customary law is not considered as an option, it is necessary to understand on which grounds a reform of customary law stands, before considering a pragmatic way of reforming it that avoids the negative results of the conservative perspective, using the concept of normative competition inside a "market for norms", to expand individuals' choice and bargaining power.

## 1 Legalizing custom: Between preservation and petrification

### *1.1 Why "legalizing" custom?*

The first approach when faced with the existence of customary law is to acknowledge and integrate it, in one way or another, into the fabric of law. This can take different forms (partial or full codification, constitutional recognition, judicial recognition as a source of law, etc.) that have different impacts on customary law which we cannot analyze in depth here. The concept of *legalization*, meaning the acknowledgement of custom as a source of law in a formal legal context, will then be used as a general term for these different degrees of recognition. From here, one needs to address the rational justifications of the legalization of customary law. It is first and foremost necessary to say that it cannot be defended on the tautological basis that it *simply is* custom, which would mean justifying tradition because it is a tradition, or just because it is "what people do". The problem is precisely that quite a few customs just seem to *happen* to be so, while *positive* norms tend to always be promulgated with a rationale backing them.

Quite often, the justification to uphold customs is just that it is good because it is what has always been. Defenses of the *legalization* of customary law, which cannot be mere defenses of customary law itself, thus rely on two main arguments, roughly divided into a *principle-oriented* approach on the one hand, and *pragmatic* approach on the other hand.

The main principle in defending customary law dictates that some customs embody the core values of a community, and that this is the first reason to respect them. It does not mean, however, that these values must be respected because they *simply are* the values of this community, in a purely relativistic point of view. Otherwise, one would fall back on the tautological justification rejected above. Similarly, the relativistic argument is not convincing: one could say that no conception of what is good for a community supersedes the other, but the major flaw in this argument is that it could be reversed at any moment. Indeed, why would one defend the way of life of some local community, making it an exception in a national or international context, if the conception of what is good that this community is defending cannot be defended on other grounds? Why would it be better than the national conception of what is good, or by international standards of what a good life is? Those questions need to be answered in order to defend customary law.

A stronger argument is that a political entity owes its very existence to a common definition of what is good, which implicitly *recognizes* local communities as political entities, even though they are theoretically included in a larger political order. As a consequence, the local community is to some extent a reference for its members, equal or even prior to the larger community the legislator refers to at a national level. Nonetheless, this sets strong limits to the reach of legislation that cannot avoid creating contradictions between normative orders.[3] A corollary to this argument is an objection to the utilitarian perspective of the legislator: even if one accepts the idea that the general welfare of a community needs to be improved through reforms, what is the target of these reforms once one accepts that some local communities are political units with their own normative order? Why would the members of local communities consider it legitimate that the legislator does not take into account their frame of reference?

To understand better how local communities can be considered as the main political horizons of their people, one can turn to another argument, more pragmatic and contextual: customs are deeply rooted social norms. This means that

3 For example, the Constitution of the State of Hawaii recognizes some autonomy to the customary law of the country, even in cases when it can contradict with US federal law or even constitutional principles such as individual property rights. Lately, Hawaiian courts have tended to uphold more systematically customary principles. The relevant passage in the Hawaiian constitution states: "The State reaffirms and shall protect all rights, customarily and traditionally exercised for subsistence, cultural and religious purposes and possessed by ahupua'a tenants who are descendants of native Hawaiians who inhabited the Hawaiian Islands prior to 1778, subject to the right of the State to regulate such rights" (Constitution of the State of Hawaii, 2018: Article XII Section VII).

customary laws and norms cannot be isolated from all the other norms and institutions of one community. Any promoter of reforms needs to be pragmatic and strategically take into account the fact that customs, as irrational as they may seem to him, are contained in a normative net. This is not, though, an argument strong enough to reject reforms aimed at changing or replacing customs, but is merely a call to be cautious in trying to do so, as disregarding the full normative context could prevent any reform from being effective.

However, the very contextual and localized nature of customary norms can lead to an argument that opposes change. From a functionalist perspective, the customs of one community in particular can actually be the most adequate kind of regulation for a specific way of life. The very basic role of norms, including customs and legal norms beyond them, is to stabilize expectations. Customs are thus nothing but a way of settling rules to organize life in common. For instance, communal property rights might be the best structure to ensure good management of resources by a community, even though it seems to contradict Western conceptions of property rights that tend to privilege individual and exclusive property rights (Ostrom and Hess, 2007). Disregarding this fact might lead to social disruption, since a community would be deprived of a normative order that would match its living conditions. This last argument has the great benefit of reuniting the idea that customary laws are contextual with the idea, mentioned above, that a community's norms rely on its definition of the common good.

A good defense for legalizing customary law is the following: customary law can legitimately be upheld by the legal system, on the main basis that communities living under customary law can be considered as political entities that deserve some degree of self-determination. As such, some of their customs embody their core values and conception of the common good, which is why refusing to take them into account can be a dangerous step for reformers. Other customs, even though they do not embody clear values, are connected to a social context, at least as mere parts of a thick normative network, but can also be part of norms correlated to a specific way of life, for instance the communal exploitation of resources. Not respecting such norms can create social disruption quite easily.

### *1.2 Petrification and codification*

The previous reflections lead to considering that the best option, in a pluralistic system, is to integrate customary law into the formal system by "legalizing" it. It is nevertheless necessary to tackle the issue of the "petrification" that this legalization can produce, especially when it takes the form of codification. Legalized petrification can indeed have two perverse consequences: on the one hand, it can contradict the nature of customary law itself, resulting in a formal system of law that would be customary only by name; on the other, it can obstruct any evolution of customary law, internal or external.

As previously noted, customs are nothing but a set of norms for the life of a specific community. An immediate consequence of this is that they can actually vary considerably by community, despite common characteristics and principles, and that, unlike what the association between customs and a fixed tradition tends to imply, customs are not rigid and can be rather flexible in order to adapt to new social, economic or environmental circumstances. Indeed, if many customs are, for instance, meant to make the common management of resources possible, variations in the availability of such resources will lead to an adjustment of customs to new practices (Acheson, 1975).

One thus needs to stress the substantial difference between custom and law that the term "customary law" tends to conceal. Due to their bottom-up nature and the role they are meant to play, customary norms are, as stressed already, tightly connected to actual practices and the inner equilibrium of the communities they regulate. Statutory laws are, rather, characterized by a top-down structure and are produced by institutions external to the lives they regulate. In this way, the legal system, especially in the shape it takes inside a fully developed modern state, produces regulations whose normative character is stronger. It is particularly visible in the way that authorities responsible to settle disputes in customary systems are seen as merely "declaring" what the custom is, rather than actually legislating or even adjudicating in the strong sense of the word (Sumner Maine, 1889/1871: 116, 26). Highlighting these differences makes the change in nature that customs undergo more salient when they actually become customary *law* in the process of legalization.

Nevertheless, there are obviously different degrees of customary law systems. Customary law appears, for instance, any time an *institution*, such as a village council, declares that the *custom dictates* this or that decision. The variability inherent to custom is still present in this decision because it is only valid for a very limited local area. Nevertheless, the gradual institutionalization of customary law, which expands it to higher levels, takes it further from what customs really are. For examples, the very criteria that British common-law applies to the recognition of customs as they were expressed by Blackstone in his *Commentaries* reveal the demanding constraints and the fictional nature of this process (Ørebech, 2016). Therefore, customs are nothing more than a *source* of law, not an autonomous set of norms, and they can be systematically rejected because of their inadequacy with constitutional norms in many legal systems. "Customary" is no longer the name of a specific system, but merely that type of law, now disconnected from actual practices and their evolutionary nature.

Consequently, varying and flexible customs are systematized through their integration in a formal system whose normative nature is deeply different, and this is the origin of what was described using such words as the crystallization, petrification or stiffening of custom, a process that is the most evident in cases of full codification of customs.[4] Not only customary law loses all its specificities, but it also becomes impervious to any sort of change, whether it comes from its

4 H. Sumner Maine (1889/1871: 44): "the native rules hardened, and contracted a rigidity which they never had in real native practice". For other examples with the words "crystallization" or "petrification", see Brett L. Shadle (1999: 5).

own adaptation to new circumstances by the emergence of new practices, or any cautious attempt at reform.

At the end of the 19th century, many colonial administrators advocated against any codification process (Sumner Maine, 1889/1871: 44; Shadle, 1999: 5). Indeed, what first was a conservative attempt to avoid social disruption (for instance, by introducing private property rights in contexts where those rights were mostly collective) was quickly seen as counterproductive: it prevented any natural changes from happening, and even made any further reform very difficult, because the principles of customary law were not backed by the full force of the law, just as they had never been before. Consequently, even though there are good arguments to preserve customary law, it must be in a way that avoids the consequences just mentioned, by ensuring that mechanisms are designed to preserve customary law as an autonomous set of norms capable of change, a characteristic without which it lacks legitimacy. Nonetheless, such an argument opens the door to a reflexive perspective on customary law that would bring it closer to the active capacity of reform that characterizes modern formal systems.

## 2 Discarding customary law?

### *2.1 The argument of human and minority rights*

With both strong objections against the "legalization" of customary law along with reasons to preserve it in mind, it, the reasons why it, perhaps, ***should*** be overcome need to be addressed. The most current justification is one of principle: customary law tends to deny individuals their rights, which refers to basic human rights, particularly the most vulnerable groups such as women or refugees. Those rights are specifically denied by customary laws, when the community faces changes in circumstances. The alleged flexibility of customary law, in these cases, turns against vulnerable groups: as the socio-economic context worsens, the rights of individuals belonging to these groups tend to be lessened. It is one natural characteristic of custom: while it is flexible on the one hand, it can become unable to change precisely because it is a rule set to live in common that individuals abide by because it is what the rest of the community does.[5]

On the contrary, formal law seems to offer rights more systematically and would then deserve priority over customary laws. More importantly, formal systems have a tendency to implement reform to get closer to the moral standards set by rights. One objection to this use of "rights", which Bentham expressed quite clearly, is that such a right, without the backing of any authority, is merely

5 A good example of a custom that people follow even though they suffer from it and even oppose it is infibulation, as studied by Gerry Mackie (1996). Mackie sees infibulation as a coordination problem: in the language of game theory, families and especially women still impose it on their daughters despite being even conscious of its uselessness, for the simple reason that others also do it, and that not being infibulated would damage their daughter's chances of marriage.

a matter of morals, and is nothing else than a *claim* (Bentham, 1816). Without going as far as Bentham on the topic and without requiring that the full force of the law should be any claim of this sort to make it a right, one must admit that human rights do have a constraining power when they are integrated in the constitution of countries, and generally when they are considered as binding in a way or another, even loosely. The problem here is precisely that these rights are no longer distant standards promoted only by non-governmental organizations (NGOs): they are embedded in the constitution of many African states, for instance,[6] and are thus backed by the force of the law, the issue being exactly the limited reach of the rule of law when it competes with customary orders. In a fair number of cases, resorting to the formal system is not even a possibility, so communities and individuals can be deprived of rights that the state grants them, but lacks the means of enforcement.[7] Does this mean that it is the duty of a state to be constantly able to enforce its laws? Of course, the rule of law does not get all its efficiency from an actual threat of enforcement: it also comes from the *interiorization* of norms. In the presence of customary rules, nonetheless, that are more present to their minds and immediately constraining, while formal law seems always distant and external to their communities, individuals just disregard formal law or simply have no knowledge of it. In such cases of legal pluralism, even the direct threat of law enforcement can be powerless. This would be the reason why, in order to enforce the actual rights that a state grants to its citizen, custom should be gradually replaced by formal law.

Nevertheless, one cannot overlook all the reasons why customary law should be respected that were stated before. Can one truly promote individual rights and freedoms by considering that communities are not free to live the lives they want, with rules adjusted to their condition? Any rights-based perspective needs to answer this question. First of all, it is a common statement that customary law tends to completely ignore the concept of individual rights, for the simple reason that it structures social relations by assigning obligations derived from a status to the members of a community (Simojoki, 2011: 45). Many members of such communities know important limitations to their freedom: those who do not belong to the ruling elite, those who are not male or who are men but submitted to the rule of an elder or a chief of the clan, or also those who are foreigners recently settled in a community. Heavy constraints are then imposed on individuals, but a key fact is that they are not born on all individuals *in the same way*. There is indeed a structural suppression of freedom inside the community

6 There are many examples of this, a clear one could be the article 36 of the Constitution of Mozambique, which explicitly refers to equality between men and women, while articles 82 and 83 "guarantee" the protection of rights and ownership and inheritance for women (Constitution of Mozambique, 2018).

7 One can refer to the words of Leah W. Kimathi "[h]igh usage of non-formal justice systems in rural areas does not automatically lead to the conclusion that those systems are the best; it could simply mean that they are the only one available" (Kimathi, 2005: 17).

that targets specific individual according to their statuses. As a consequence, one can argue that this breach of equal treatment undermines the argument that customary law deserves respect because communities get to define what they consider as a good way to live together.

Indeed, the previous account of customs systematically underestimated the potential of customs to be *inflexible* when regarding certain specific categories of norms: those that concern vulnerable individuals like women, children or outsiders. In these cases, the management of customary institutions by elite members is systematically biased against some populations. It has been showed, for example, that the limited flexibility customary law offers to women in terms of property and inheritance disappears quickly when customs need to adjust to changing circumstances (Kapur, 2011: 79). Therefore, the idea, developed above, that customary law needs to be capable of change cannot be limited to the preservation of its natural flexibility, but also needs to apply to the *weaknesses* of custom. This is where reforming custom, or more accurately, making it reform itself, becomes necessary. An essential feature of modern positive law can be introduced into customary institutions: a reflexivity that enables communities to challenge their norms, where they deny individuals' rights, and exist at the expanse of welfare of the community altogether.

The main point here is not that customary law disrespects an abstract right to be treated equally, but rather that some individuals are systematically excluded from the possibility of at least consenting to their conditions, which is the minimal degree of participation in a political community. Consequently, the argument according to which customary law is respectable because it is a form of self-determination lacks solid ground. This is the very reason why cautious programs aimed at reforming customary law systematically emphasize the need for more participation of women and other vulnerable groups in decision-making processes in order to challenge the dominant norms of such communities.

### 2.2 The "qualified" utilitarian argument

Another common argument is more utilitarian in nature:[8] a reform of customary law, complete or partial, that would increase general welfare through better economic development that increases opportunities and gives better life conditions to all. This argument is clearly not incompatible with one that promotes rights, at least in the common discourse of development. For instance, this discourse includes arguments like those that associate the enforcement of women's rights or the enforcement of clear and well-defined property rights with a better economic development for the whole community (Kapur, 2011: 77). As one can see here, these arguments tend to include both a larger set of rights for some

8 The word utilitarian is here accepted in its most general meaning. It describes a whole range of arguments that are consequentialist and point to the way general welfare will increase if customary law is reformed.

individuals as well as the development of their community. This utilitarian justification of the reform of customary law, according to which all would be better off if some individuals' rights are better protected, neutralizes by anticipation any objection against a purely utilitarian perspective.

Consequently, the classic rationale for reform made by governments, NGOs and other organizations is a qualification of the utilitarian rule. Indeed, it never implies that the utility of separate individuals can be simply aggregated in order to compare different social states or the efficiency of policies, nor that some individuals' utility can be sacrificed for the greater good. On the contrary, defenders of this argument consider that a minimal set of rights need to be protected, not only by principle, but because it maximizes general utility. It still remains to be determined whether this compatibility between the utilitarian argument and the principle of granting rights to individuals is anything else than accidental.[9] In any case, this rationale was then at the very basis of many legal or even constitutional reforms that promoted, for instance, equality between men and women in specific matters, such as inheritance, in stark contradiction with the rule of customary law, considered as a model to depart from.

## 3 Reforming custom in a liberal way: A *market* for norms

So far, this discussion has highlighted the delicate nature of customary law: if it deserves to be respected as a set of norms that embodies a way of life and some of the core values of a community, it cannot be petrified due to fear of social disruption or in order to preserve customs whose only defense comes from the fact that they are customs. The very nature of customary law makes it more fluid than any formal legal system, and its integration into formal law has unwanted circumstances as previously noted. A careful reform of custom seems to be the best way to promote rights and general welfare. However, this reforming enterprise can only proceed *incrementally* for two main reasons: from a *practical* point of view, the very limited scope of formal law when it is competing against customary law forces any serious reformer to take customary law into account and start from this point without trying to bypass it; second, when it comes to *principles*, an attempt at overthrowing customary law disrespects the autonomy and preferences of both communities and the individuals that compose them.

Consequently, such a perspective is neither effective, nor fully liberal. However, one cannot overlook the fact that this alleged autonomy is, in fact, very limited, and that customs are made laws not by reflexive adhesion, but rather by simple obedience to the "old ways". Both perspectives fail, as both disregarding and legalizing customary law through mechanisms like codification have one thing in

9 A consequentialist promotion of rights is, indeed, questionable, and one can wonder whether this perspective is not Rawlsian rather than simply utilitarian.

common: they are both an attempt at *dissolving* the normative tension between customary and formal law, either by reducing custom to law, or by crystalizing it. A potentially promising strategy is to rely on the autonomy of the communities living under the customary law, which is bolstered by participatory processes, yet this is unreliable for one reason: the community and its customs remain the only normative horizon, while a true pluralistic context would multiply the normative *fora*. The presence of an external norm makes less necessary to rely on the inner reforming potential of customary law.

A more comprehensive solution would be to turn the normative tension between customary and formal law into a real competition, where individuals would have an actual *choice* between different sets of norms. This solution is fully liberal in the way that it promotes freedom of choice in a non-abstract way; thanks to different mechanisms, resorting to an alternative, whether it is a formal system or customary law, becomes a real possibility, but only if the former is "affordable". In terms of standards of fairness and welfare, customary law also benefits from this process because, as it is compared with the formal systems, the heads of customary institutions now have an incentive to improve the service they provide to keep their community (and their authority) together. This competitive frame would provide the degree of reflexivity necessary for customary law to become closer to the standards of the formal law. Customary institutions, to sustain themselves, would need to remain open to potential change towards better standards of fairness and welfare.

Forcing communities and individuals living under customary law to change, even if to promote rights or general welfare, would indeed be a full denial of their autonomy and completely disregard their preferences. This is quite clear in the case of property rights, especially in Africa, where the implementation of individual and exclusive property rights without taking in consideration the customary claims that the community had on lands held in common, was for a time considered as an improvement for the general development of the states considered, and a positive promotion of individual rights. Nonetheless, different institutions now consider this paradigm as a thing of the past: faced with expropriation and destruction of communities and resources, what is favoured now is rather the empowerment of local communities through the recognition of their customary rights to own land in common, as a negotiation tool with governments and companies, under conditions of fair and sustainable development and of the protection and participation of vulnerable groups like displaced people, women or children. Community as well as individual *empowerment* are both keywords in the language of international institutions, NGOs and even state laws, but these do not come without the adoption of clear reflexive processes to manage resources in common. The situation is no longer the non-choice between the *status quo* and the destructive application of individual property rights imposed from the outside.

In the case of women's rights, customary institutions are not confronted directly; it is a matter of getting them to participate in the decision-making process through different mechanisms, which slowly but surely leads to questioning dominant and oppressive norms, by opening the normative horizons (Bhavani, 2009). Indeed, in most cases, the formal system and all its rights and benefits are not accessible to those who need them the most for physical or economic reasons, also because of extreme social pressures not to resort to it.[10] When the formal law is too distant, it is therefore necessary to make the best of the fluid nature of customary law. The process of *mediation* is one of the most promising elements already present in customary law, and its growth (development?) should be encouraged, provided that it helps resolve conflicts in a conciliatory way, without adversary adjudication, while promoting better rights for vulnerable groups. Actors in the field have noticed that mediation is an efficient way to reach compromises by appealing to moral reasons and that mediation processes are open to practical considerations and thus to change, rather than enforcing the discriminatory principles of customary law and their interpretation by dominant elites (Lankhorst and Veldman, 2011). Consistently, it has been observed that the promotion of individual rights was in some cases not incompatible with the very purpose of customary law institutions: preserving the harmony of the community (Johnstone, 2011: 25).

However, such measures tend to underestimate the degree of constraint that norms impose on individuals. Improving customary law by moving it closer towards more inclusive standards, still far from human rights and optimal living conditions, is not exactly equivalent to giving a real *choice* between customary law and the formal system.[11] One might also fear that there is only a little room for change in the scope of customary principles. Meanwhile, a situation of legal pluralism gives the opportunity to question norms by the existence of alternatives. The very nature of social norms goes against this pattern, since norms are mostly meant to be shared by the bulk of a certain group, whose members expect each other's compliance in order to cooperate. Consequently, norms, and especially customs, are not usually the result of a constant choice, and even less of a rational choice, such as computing the costs and benefits of abiding by another norm from outside one's own community. This is not to say that there is usually no

10 It is necessary to understand that any normative system is supposed to provide some security, even to vulnerable groups. For instance, women who were raped are often married to their aggressor in order to avoid both dishonour *and* the financial insecurity of being a single mother. In case one chooses not to resort to this "conciliatory" mechanism, the risk is that dishonour (which is actually never an isolated penalty) comes with severe consequences that can go as far as cutting off all links with the family group for the victim. Pressures also come from families and from local leaders, the latter relying on their customary duties to assert their power on the community.

11 On the importance of choice, see Harper, Wojkowska and Cunningham (2011: 178): "Genuine choice only exists when both options (formal and customary dispute resolution) are accessible, efficient, effective and viable . . . The capacity to make, and act on, free and informed choice is a fundamental characteristic of the legally empowered person. Further, access to recourse is important for legal empowerment as it represents another tool to challenge power imbalances and discrimination".

rationale behind norms, which is incorrect, but rather to point to the fact that situations of legal pluralism, if well exploited, can reveal the rationale behind norms that are often considered pure facts, challenge them or their interpretation, and make different rationales compete against each other. In cases where mothers do not see an escape from the current equilibrium, like the practice of infibulation, it is especially important that the efforts of organization should focus on bringing enough community members to change their behaviour simultaneously towards an "offer" that would make them all better-off (Mackie, 1996). Pushing the metaphor further, this would require putting in place an actual *market* for norms with *regulated* free competition, to question the normative monopoly of customary leaders.

It all boils down to giving individuals the possibility to compare the cost and benefits of the sets of norms available to them and increase their bargaining power. If one adopts the perspective of Aldashev et al., one could use the law as a "magnet" to custom, meaning that the existence of a moderate legislation, purposely not too distant from customary standards, could push traditional authorities to adopt more inclusive principles, just in order to avoid individuals leaving the community to resort to the formal system, thus undermining their authority (Aldashev et al., 2012).[12] Mechanisms to *nudge* customary institutions into evolving towards fairer and welfare maximizing standards in direct reference to the formal system, instead of ignoring it, could therefore complement other mechanisms designed to raise awareness of state norms, like the use of paralegals or counting on the expressive nature of norms to make state law the reference when there is a better one.[13] Nevertheless, they need to go hand in hand with policies that promote the reform of customary law from the inside, since it is the only normative horizon vulnerable groups have.

12 The point of the authors is that if law is inefficient, it is mainly due to the influence of customary law and how it captures individuals under its influence, who stay out of the reach of the formal legal system. To solve this problem, they propose to use an indirect approach: law should be a "reasonable" standard (that is not their term), close enough to customary law to make a deviation from it possible, but far enough to represent a model for positive change. Hence the metaphor of the magnet: a legal reform is not meant to rule individuals' behaviour directly, but rather to "attract" customary institutions into adopting reformed ways. The keystone of the process would be customary authorities; since they want to preserve their authority, when customary law is challenged by a credible competitor, a "reasonable" law issued from the formal system, they might have an incentive to make customary rules fairer towards vulnerable people like women.

13 The main job of paralegals is to be at the disposals of communities to help them with administrative processes, thus making the formal system more accessible, but first and foremost, their job is to raise awareness of the content of the law and of individuals' rights. This mechanism, as well as other recommendations from NGOs and authors on development, seems to rely on what Cass R. Sunstein (1996) would call the "expressive function of law", describing by that the way law contains "statements" on what should be done or not, and how it accounts for an essential part of the constraining power of law, which therefore cannot be reduced to the use of mere force.

## Conclusion

Situations of legal pluralism are extremely complicated for any administration that aims at legislating to improve the lives of its citizens. The solid justifications it can have in favour of change, both principles-driven and utilitarian, run against the legitimate autonomy of customary communities and the practical obstacles that make the rule of law inefficient on customary lands. Nonetheless, a progressive *integration* of customary law norms and institutions is possible, even though challenging, and it is desirable because it seems to be the best way to avoid social disruption, as well as benefit the community and all its members. It rules out any other form of extreme legalization that would resort into the petrification of customary law, always at the expense of vulnerable groups. Indeed, any reform of customary law is legitimate if it does not bypass its structures, provided that the rights and welfare of all, including members of vulnerable groups, are taken into account, which opens a path for reforms that neither petrify nor disregard customary law. The respect for the autonomy of communities living under customary law thus needs to be completed with a democratic perspective, which would allow all members of a community more participation in working toward the definition of values and priorities, a cost-efficient alternative that would rely on affordable and reachable institutions. However, this communitarian perspective, inspired from works on direct democracy, is not sufficient for the reasons mentioned above. This internal point of view needs to be complemented with an external one; even though customary and formal laws are said to *cohabitate*, along with other systems of regulations such as religious law, they actually tend to define *exclusive* and *enclosed* normative orders. Their simultaneous existing on the territory of the same state does not imply an actual *coexistence*, and it is often quite the opposite that happens. They are largely *monopolistic*, meaning that they are the only pole from which normative constraints originate. One could wonder whether, in pluralistic contexts, normative systems have a tendency to reinforce this inherent monopolistic nature, in order to preserve their dominion. As a result of this, the most interventionist and voluntarist state could see its reforms crushed by pure and simple disregard. Thus, when faced with a normative competitor, institutions like those that belong to customary law might devote part of their resources to remain hermetically sealed or *norm-tight*.

Such tendencies need to be countered by careful policies that enlarge the normative horizon for individuals, without compromising normative stability, by creating the conditions for a real *choice* between normative orders, within an open and competitive "market" for norms. Only a comprehensive approach could be effective in doing so: developing awareness of rights and state policies, providing local legal assistance, designing policies so that they can be viable alternatives to customary law, and more generally, tackling directly issues that make formal law inaccessible.

## References

Acheson, J. M. (1975) 'The Lobster Fiefs: Economic and Ecological Effects of Territoriality in the Maine Lobster Industry', *Human Ecology*, 3 (3), 183–207.

Aldashev, G., Chaara, I., Platteau, J.-P. and Wahhaj, Z. (2012) 'Using the Law to Change the Custom', *Journal of Development Economics*, 97, 182–200.

Aldashev, G., Chaara, I., Platteau, J.-P. and Wahhaj, Z. (2012) 'Formal Law as a Magnet to Reform Custom', *Economic Development and Cultural Change*, 60 (4), 795–828.

Bentham, J. (1816) 'Anarchical Fallacies; Being an examination of the Declaration of Rights Issued During the French Revolution'. http://oll.libertyfund.org/titles/bentham-the-works-of-jeremy-bentham-vol-2#lf0872-02_head_411 [accessed 01/02/2019].

Bentham, J. (1838–1843) *The Works of Jeremy Bentham*, published under the Superintendence of his Executor, John Bowring, William Tait, Edinburgh, 11 vols. Vol. X, https://oll.libertyfund.org/titles/2009 [accessed 20/04/2019].

Bhavani, R. R. (2009) 'Do Electoral Quotas Work after They Are Withdrawn? Evidence from a Natural Experiment in India', *American Political Science Review*, 103 (1), 23–35.

Constitution of Mozambique (2018) [adopted 2004, last amended 2007], www.constituteproject.org/constitution/Mozambique_2007?lang=en [accessed 02/02/19].

Constitution of the State of Hawaii (2018) [adopted 1949, last amended 1959], http://lrbhawaii.org/con/ [accessed 01/02/19].

Harper, E. (2011) *Working With Customary Justice Systems: Post-conflict and Fragile States*, International Development Law Organization, Rome.

Harper, E., Wojkowska, E., and Cunningham, J. (2011) 'Enhancing Legal Empowerment Through Engagement with Customary Justice Systems', in Harper, E. (ed.) *Working With Customary Justice Systems: Post-conflict and Fragile States*, International Development Law Organization, Rome, pp. 171–184.

Johnstone, N. (2011) 'Bush Justice in Bougainville: Mediating Change by Challenging the Custodianship of Custom', in Harper, E. (ed.) *Working With Customary Justice Systems: Post-conflict and Fragile States*, International Development Law Organization, Rome, pp. 15–32.

Kapur, A. (2011) 'Two Faces of Change: The Need for a Bi-directional Approach to Improve Women's Land Rights in Plural Legal Systems', in Harper, E. (ed.) *Working With Customary Justice Systems: Post-conflict and Fragile States*, International Development Law Organization, Rome, pp. 73–92.

Kimathi, L. (2005) 'Non-state Institutions as a Basis of State Reconstruction: The Case of Justice Systems in Africa'. Presented for the Codesria's 11th General Assembly, Maputo.

Lankhorst, M. and Veldman, M. (2011) 'Engaging with Customary Law to Create Scope for Realizing Women's Formally Protected Land Rights in Rwanda', in Harper, E. (ed.) *Working With Customary Justice Systems: Post-conflict and Fragile States*, International Development Law Organization, Rome, pp. 93–108.

Mackie, G. (1996) 'Ending Footbinding and Infibulation: A Convention Account', *American Sociological Review*, 61 (6), 999–1017.

Ørebech, P. (2016) 'Customary Law', in Nancy A. Naples (ed.) *The Wiley Blackwell Encyclopedia of Gender and Sexuality Studies*. John Wiley & Sons, Ltd, Chichester.

Ostrom, E. and Hess, C. (2007) 'Private and Common Property Rights'. Workshop paper in Political Theory and Political Analysis. Indiana University.

Shadle, B. L. (1999) 'Changing Traditions to Meet Current Altering Conditions: Customary Law, African Courts and the Rejection of Codification in Kenya, 1930–1960' *Journal of African History*, 40, 411–431.

Simojoki, M. V. (2011) 'Unlikely Allies: Working with Traditional Leaders to Reform Customary Law in Somalia', in Harper, E. (ed.) *Working With Customary Justice Systems: Post-conflict and Fragile States*, International Development Law Organization, Rome, pp. 33–50.

Sumner Maine, H. (1889/1871) *Village-Communities in the East and West*. Henry Holt and Company, New York.

Sunstein, C. R. (1996) 'On the Expressive Function of Law', *University of Pennsylvania Law Review*, 144, 2021–2053.

# 11 The "codification moment"

## An attempt to define factors of effective law reform illustrated with the example of the Swiss Civil Code of 10 December 1907[1]

*Maria Lewandowicz*

### Introduction

Research into the reasons, sources, and directions of changes that occur in legislation is particularly significant for contemporary considerations of law, as it enriches jurisprudence with a theoretical-methodological underpinning of the description of ongoing phenomena. This underpinning contributes to systemic stabilization of further evolution of the law. It must be remembered, however, that delimiting clear-cut boundaries in the development of law narrows the research perspective, thus impeding the proper identification of attitudes and beliefs shaped under the influence of centuries-long experience that guides contemporary societies and nations. History reveals to us a determined pattern of changes, which is a recurring one: similar reasons lead to similar consequences, thanks to which we can know the source of all events, shattering the conviction of the coincidental nature of certain phenomena. The effectiveness of future legal solutions, to a large extent depends on the understanding of the essence of the 'public reason', that is the way in which a given political society formulates its plans, prioritizes objectives, and undertakes actions to bring these objectives to fruition (Rawls 1998: 212).

In my work as a legal historian I focus on researching past events and institutions that may serve as a contribution to contemporary legal science. I attempt to seek reasons for the emergence of certain phenomena in the law and to explain the mechanism of actions taken by the legislator that brought about a positive change in the functioning of a society. Continuous change is an essential feature of society. Any society is composed of individuals, whose participation in that society is expressed through a concrete shaping of social relations between these individuals. These relations, in turn, are a derivative of values necessary for the satisfaction of interests shaped under the influence of specific life conditions of the individuals and of the society, such as: family relations, population density, and all other factors that affect the social order. Once a given order is consolidated,

1 This article was financed by the National Science Centre (Poland), under project no. 2017/26/D/HS5/00625.

societies tend to maintain it, even if the factors based on which the order emerged no longer exist. The need for social order usually overrides the need to adjust to the changing circumstances of life (Huber 1925: 87–91). Thus, societies are governed by two opposite desires: *stabilization* and *adjustment* to the evolving political, social, and economic conditions.

If we adopt the thesis of a cyclical process of social transformations, then the observation of modern-day legal evolution suggests that we are on the brink of changes. Soon, it will be necessary to answer this question about the future of private law: how the processes of European integration have pushed us in the direction of constant restriction of the role of national autonomy in shaping social relations (Milo, Lokin, & Smits 2014: 1). At the same time, a significant part of civil law relations in Europe is still governed by the provisions of the so-called Great Civil Codifications, which are works of the Enlightenment era and which bear the mark of national codifications responding to the needs of specific societies bound by culture and traditions (Varga 2001: 18–19). This gives rise to a number of questions concerning the design and the future of law. What concepts, values, and rules should be adopted as the key ones in building new normative solutions? Which institutions should act as carriers of these values? Should we employ the supranational regulatory mechanisms (Milo et al. 2014: 2), or, rather, leave the further integration processes to national legislators and judicatures?

More or less from the mid-18th century, national legislators asked themselves these very same questions, though on a national, rather than a supranational, scale. Enlightenment reformers sought regulatory methods that would represent a clean break with the existing state of legal uncertainty caused by the multiple particular, fragmentary, and mutually exclusive laws. The future, normative solutions were to guarantee certainty and stability of law as well as offer final settlements in all factual situations so as to prevent any room for arbitrary judgements, and thus to ensure individuals' protection from partiality and abuses from those in charge of justice (Sójka-Zielińska 2009: 30). The articulated need for a legal reform, proclaimed by representatives of the authorities and of the judiciaries, was only the seedling of a broader discussion that preceded actual codification works. In countries such as France or Austria, where codification and unification were processes initiated by strong central authorities, the reforms did not run into any significant political or social obstacles: they became one of the factors acting in favour of the strong authority of the ruler (Sójka Zielińska 1974: 149). Elsewhere, for example in Germany, and especially in Switzerland, where the state was based on a federal model and both society and its local authorities were attached to traditions of local sovereignty, unification through codification posed additional challenges before the legislator. Above all, it was necessary to prioritize the goals of the evolution of law and of the political system.

In the case of Switzerland, the main decision was whether to push for tightening confederate connections or to maintain the broad cantonal autonomy. Would the society be ready to support the change of the legal system, in the light of the previous political and legal experiences? Once an affirmative answer was given to building a confederate state, it became necessary to consider the tendencies according to which the unifying work would be conducted. Should the code be based on entirely new solutions, or perhaps it would suffice to redefine the traditional legal institutions in order to adjust them to the changed circumstances? What would be the influence of new code provisions on the existing detailed provisions at the supra-cantonal level? Should the code absorb them so that they would lose effect upon the implementation of the code, or should these acts be left as they are, or perhaps reviewed to make sure they match the new system? Finally, what would be the role of codes from individual cantons in the process of codification? Should – and to what extent does – the cantonal law serve as a source of inspiration for the designed, national code (Huber 2009: 35–41)? If yes, then what criteria should be employed in selecting the normative material?

Within this scope, it was important to evaluate the significance of customs and traditions in regulating social relations. Sometimes, improper identification of social attitudes toward regulatory instruments may render future code solutions ineffective. The history of codification of private law in Switzerland perfectly illustrates that it is possible, with a single legal act, to build a just and stable society of free and equal citizens, even if they are still deeply divided by reasonable religious, philosophical, and moral doctrines (Rawls 1998: 33), as well as by language and political traditions. The objective of this article is to show what political, social, and legal conditions must be met to enable an effective legal reform.

## 1 Swiss state and legal tradition

Looking at the history of the Swiss Confederacy, it is difficult to comprehend how the adoption of a uniform civil code was possible. Throughout its historical development, starting from 1291, Switzerland functioned as a union of free cantons which held full competences as regarding shaping of their internal relations. The federate competences also included such issues as foreign policy and administration of common goods. From its very inception, Switzerland was a heterogeneous entity. When a relative territorial stabilization of the country started in the 16th century, Switzerland was made up of regions that had one of the four statuses: 1) *eidgenössische Orte*, or federate regions bound with the agreement that established the Confederacy, 2) *zugewandte Orte*, that is associated regions, in alliance with the Confederacy, with rights and duties resulting from this alliance (*casus foederis*) unilaterally determined by the federate regions, 3) *gemeine Herrschaften*, that is loosely associated common bailliages under shared authority of two or more proper regions, and 4) *Sonderherrschaften*, as regions under the sole protectorate of associated regions.

In terms of the political systems, the Confederacy was a mosaic just as diverse. Three main forms of governance dominated. First, the Cantonal Assembly – Landsegemeinde (e.g. in Appenzel, Glarus), in which all adult males of a given canton participated, provided that they had public rights and were fit for military service (Lloyd 2006: 55). The competences of the Assembly covered matters of legislation and some chosen issues connected to jurisprudence, e.g. selection of judges (Wachholz 1936: 107–108). Second, there existed a guild system (e.g. Zurich), where all authority was in the hands of the city council, made up of a Great and Small Council, which only accepted representatives of various guilds (Branecki 2013: 97). Third, cantons such as Bern, Lucerne, and Friburg were governed by the patriciate, which meant that power was in the hands of rich aristocracy (Hangartner 1980: 11). Thus, the country was made up of regions with varying political positions and different systems of local governance.

Switzerland was also a country of great discrepancies in the social sphere, which began to be particularly clear starting from the 17th century. This was a time when tensions stemming from the mutual hostility between rich urban localities and poorer rural ones came to the fore, as well as an era of religious and political unrest. Since the times of Reformation, spread in Switzerland by John Calvin and Ulrich Zwingli, cantons had divided into Protestant and Catholic ones. This division turned out to be a lasting feature of Swiss tradition. In the era of restoration and regeneration (in the period between the fall of Napoleon and the adoption of the 1848 Constitution), Protestants supported the creation of a modern political system based on extension of civic rights and freedoms, and on a clear separation of the church from the state, while the more conservative Catholic cantons preferred to keep the political status quo (a union between the church and state, maintenance of feudal relations).

The conservative and liberal stances were also expressed in the visions of the Confederacy's future, whether the old tradition of a loose alliance of autonomous cantons were to be kept, or if the country's cohesion were to be furthered by extending the area of federal competences. The idea of the country's unity had been brought to Switzerland on the banners of the French Revolution. In 1789 Napoleon octroyed the constitution of the Helvetic Republic, pursuant to which all political and social differences were banned: each human had a natural and inalienable right to freedom, whose limits were marked only by the freedom of others and by the need to pursue the common good. As a result of the changes in the political system, as well as under the influence of Enlightenment and natural law ideas, private law was also to be reformed. This was stipulated primarily under Art. 48 of the Helvetic Constitution, based on which cantonal legislation and existing customs were to be gradually replaced with civil legislation (*gleichförmige bürgerliche Gesetze*) adopted by the legislative councils (Senate and the Great Council).

As per the revolutionary spirit, the new order was to be marked by freedom and equality (*Liberté, Égalité*) (Elsener 1975: 269), the first symptoms of which were clearly visible in the contents of Arts. 9 and 13 of the constitution, pursuant to which, respectively, no one could be deprived of personal liberty unless this was justified by public interest and without proper compensation, while real estate was to become a disposable good, without the possibility of encumbering them with perpetual easements of other burdens. These codification ideas, spreading across Enlightenment Europe, came to aid the reform tendencies. In Prussia, Allgemeines Landrecht was issued, the French were already working on their Code Civil, and the Austrians were busy drafting Allgemeines Bürgerliches Gesetzbuch, a part of which took effect already in 1787 as 'Josephinische Gesetzbuch'. In the wake of these transformations, a discussion on the need to create a uniform, as clear as possible, cohesive, and complete legal system in the form of a code also started in Switzerland (Staehelin 1931: 35). Although works were started on the unification of civil and penal law, the announced reforms were not ultimately implemented (Gruner 1991: 116).

Following the end of the Napoleonic era, Switzerland returned to its former constitutional order based upon broad cantonal autonomy. The Confederacy was made up of 22 cantons, which were guaranteed freedom, sovereignty, and security against the aggression of foreign powers, as well as peace and internal order. Internal politics were handled by the cantons themselves, including the establishment of their own financial systems, duties, weights and measures, as an effect of which the relations between cantons once again began to be frayed by tensions stemming from territorial particularisms. Frictions of religious and political nature (Catholic conservatists against liberal Protestants) led to the last civil war, the so-called Sonderbundskrieg, which ended after 26 days with the victory of the liberal faction.

Even before the beginning of the armed conflict, the Tagsatzung[2] (Federal Legislature) appointed a special commission which was to draft a revision of the 1815 Federal Treaty. The draft of the new constitution was approved by the Assembly on 27 July 1848 and submitted to individual cantons for deliberations. Cantons voted on the adoption of the constitution by way of a referendum or via the Landsgemeinde. On 12 September 1848, the Tagsatzung proclaimed the adoption of the constitution, known as the Federal Constitution, which transformed a loose union of canton-states (Staatenbund) into a federal state (Bundesstaat). In 1874 a new constitution took effect; it was a continuation of the 1848 constitution with some minor changes. The differences introduced by the 1874 constitution focused mainly on the strengthening of the federal authority within the scope of certain competences regarding the state economy, but above all they regarded the provision which gave the Confederacy the right to adopt provisions regarding economic transactions (*Verkehrsrecht*) (Gygi 1984: 9). This term encompassed "all legal matters regarding trading and trade goods" (Sójka-Zielińska 2012: 40).

This was part of an effort to unify private law, entailing laws of obligations, laws of bills of exchange, and commercial law on the federal level (Lewandowicz 2014: 95). As a result of success of the Law of Obligations (1881) and in the face of the need for further legal unification of the country, in 1898 an amendment of the Federal Constitution was passed, based on which the Assembly was entrusted with the task of unifying penal and civil law throughout the entire territory of the country, as well as other branches of private law. The provision gave the formal basis for commencement of works on a uniform Swiss civil code.

2 Tagsatzung – the Federal Diet of Switzerland was the legislative and executive council of the Swiss Confederacy which existed in various forms since the beginnings of the Swiss supra-cantonal cooperation until the formation of the Swiss federal state in 1848. It was responsible for regulating issues common to all members of the Confederacy. Since the 15th century its seat was located in Zurich.

## 2 Codification and unification

Before the need of unification of the law in the entire territory of the country was confirmed in the constitution, this issue was discussed by the Schweizerischer Juristenverein, a union of legal practitioners and theoreticians set up in 1861 with a view to developing and improving the law in Switzerland. Starting from the end of the 1860s, a discussion on the condition and future of the Confederacy's law was held on the pages of *Zeitchrift für Schweizerisches Recht*, published by the lawyers' union. In one of the works devoted to this issue entitled *Schweizervolk und sein Recht. Mahnruf zu größerer Rechtseinheit für Juristen und Nichtjuristen* (The Swiss Nation and its Law. An Appeal for Greater Unity of Law for Lawyers and Non-Lawyers), Urs Bigier (1896) emphatically described the reality of functioning in a country with excessive normative fragmentation.

Bigier wrote that when travelling across neighbouring France, one adheres to the rules and principles laid down in the Napoleonic Code. Having returned home, to Switzerland, one once again encountered the rules of the French Code in Geneva: after 45 minutes of travel to Waadt canton, one must remember to observe the rules of Waadtländische Zivilgesetzbuch. After another short trip, crossing the border of Neuenburg canton, one's actions will be judged from the perspective of another legal act, which applies to no more than 100 thousand permanent residents. The train may take one further, to Basil, and during this leg of the journey one crosses the border of Bern canton, where, again, with minor changes, the Napoleonic Code is in effect. From there one moves on to Solothurn canton, which had adopted its own code for its 70 thousand residents, and following yet another hour one reaches the old Bern canton, governed by two codes, one code for the old, and one code for the new part of the canton's territory. This way, between 10 a.m. and 1 p.m., one has been obliged to adhere to the rules of about 10 codes, of which each has at least 1000 paragraphs, which means that one should know the contents of 10 thousand paragraphs (Bigier 1869: 5–6).

Extensive overproduction and fragmentation of normative material gives rise to serious problems with the application of law, which translated into lower effectiveness of regulations. One of the main arguments in support of the need to unify law in 19th-century Switzerland was practical issues around the application of law. Territorial particularisms, with intensified migration of people and development of trade, could no longer be defended with attachment to local traditions. It was indispensable to take steps to do away with barriers in the development of trade and industry, as well as to enhance the certainty of law among the increasingly cosmopolitan nation of Switzerland.

The next important issues in the discussion on the need to unify law were political matters, which were emphasized by Johan Caflisch (1898) in his work entitled *Zur Rechtseinheit* (On the Issue of Uniformity of Law). He asserted that uniformity of law will translate not only into greater certainty of the law within the society, but will also strengthen the position of the country in the international arena. Fragmentation of the legal system into 25 different legislations, in a country with just over 3 million citizens, is a sign of its internal weakness, of its incapacity to work out a broad social consensus. An internally incoherent country, in turn, presents opportunities to imperial ambitions of neighbouring states.

Caflisch also broached another issue of importance to the Swiss, namely of cantonal sovereignty as the main source of anxiousness in relation to the unification of law. He wrote that legal unification of the country is not tantamount to the introduction of a unitarian state. It is possible to maintain the cultural and linguistic diversity, as well as the cantons' right to self-determination, according to the principle that what the cantons can do better or equally well as the Federation, should be left to the cantons, with a simultaneous building of cohesion of the Confederacy through the unification of law throughout its entire territory (Caflisch 1898). Thus, the second substantial reason supporting the undertaking of supra-cantonal codification works was the issue of maintaining internal and external political stabilization of the Confederacy. Having answered the questions 'why?' and 'on what basis?', we should now seek an answer to the question: 'how?'.

Works on the Swiss Civil Code (ZGB) were entrusted to Eugen Huber, a Bern professor of law, ideologically anchored in the teachings of the historical school of law. In his actions, Huber seemed to perfectly grasp the significance of the words by Friedrich Karl von Savigny, one of the creators of the historical school of law, that something which is not yet fully understood cannot be codified. As per his stance, the level of command of material that is appropriate for undertaking codification is not reached until the entirety of law binding on a given territory is understood. Each part of this law must be explored and researched. The point of departure for the commencement of works aiming at legal unification of a given territory is ensuring thorough access to the history of existing legal institutions. Only once this is accomplished, may one begin to combine the most fitting elements in the form of a code (Kelly 2006: 349). Savigny was also of the opinion that a code should incorporate old laws if their use in given socio-political and economic relations is possible; if not, new norms should be drafted, but with the application of old laws as a "guiding thought" (Kelly 2006: 349) of the entire codification.

When commencing his work on codification, Huber started from gathering and analyzing of the entire body of laws binding in Switzerland, starting from medieval law, all the way to contemporary institutions of private law. He systemized his work and published it in the form of a four-volume study under the title of *System und Geschichte des Schweizerischen Privatrecht* (Huber 1886–1889). Having prepared himself thoroughly, Huber began his codification, whose detailed plan he presented in his 1893 memorandum to the Department of Justice and Police. Therein we read that one of the chief aims of the unification was to create a system of national law, whose construction would account for progressive legal institutions loaned from foreign legislations, yet with great caution. The draft of ZGB was to primarily draw from Swiss traditions and norms built upon them, as they were the only ones that fully encompassed the spirit of nation, to which another outstanding Swiss lawyer and author of the Zurich Code of Private Law, Johann Caspar Bluntschli, had previously referred. Bluntschli wrote that:

> [An] act may only stand a chance of success if it manages to grasp the essence of the spirit of law that, even if unconscious, drives human strivings. An act may only stand a chance if it succeeds in reading the human soul and the needs and rights of the individual therein hidden, if it can express them clearly to the nation and win its approval.
>
> (Bluntschli cited in Bauhoffer 1927: 60–61)

It seems these same ideas guided Huber, who, although attached to the idea of faithfulness toward Swiss culture, was far from the orthodox legal historicism professed by Bluntschli.

The ZGB draft was to be shaped by two main tendencies: the progressive and the conservative one. The act as a whole was to efficiently regulate the contemporary and future legal relations based on adjusting these to requisite old Swiss norms and traditions. The area of issues that called for a fundamental reform, based on new institutions designed in the progressive spirit, were manifold. First, there were the issues of property and personal marriage relations, such as the right of wives to conduct a for-profit activity. Second, there were issues around the extension of the rights of testator to dispose of their assets towards persons to whom they were not related. Third, there were issues connected with the participation of the state in the system of succession where the testator had not appointed any heirs by way of will and where there was no way to establish statutory heirs. Fourth, were all matters in connection with the economic life of the nation, from rights and duties of persons participating in trade, through issues of the legal status of means used to run an economic activity, to issues related with the building of a strong and healthy national economy, including, in particular, countering the excessive fragmentation of agricultural land. Lastly, there were issues of credits and securing claims.

The conservative tendency in the code was expressed in one of the methods of implementing national cantonal norms in the Swiss legal system by adopting certain institutions directly, through their transformation or compilation. Until the commencement of codification for the entire territory of the Confederacy, some of the cantons managed to maintain the native Swiss law, while in many others, owing to the scarcity of regulations, the local authorities were forced to adopt foreign legal solutions. ZGB was to encompass the best and most typically Swiss norms, and to thus prevent the annihilation of the Swiss character of this act by well-established legislation of other states.

The completion of such a complex plan required broad cooperation of legal circles, who *collected* the legislative material binding in various cantons, *elaborated*, based on case law, issues that called for the attention of the legislator, and *actively collaborated* in works on individual parts of the code within expert groups. Thanks to the wide involvement of the Swiss academic circles, legal practitioners and the society itself, as well as owing to the extraordinary sense that Eugen

Huber had for discovering the 'Swiss soul' and for expressing the individual and collective needs in a clear language of the act, on 10 December 1907 it was possible to adopt the Swiss Civil Code, an act that consolidated the heretofore dispersed society into, as Rawls put it, a just and stable society of free and equal citizens, despite the divides that remained between them. How was this possible?

## Conclusion

Work on the Swiss Civil Code was undertaken with great dexterity and, most of all, at the "right moment". In 1848, a political transformation had taken place in Switzerland, as a result of which a union of states turned into a confederate state, with a change of the political system as needed as it was unexpected at the time. This took place right after the last armed conflict in 1847, which erupted between Catholic and Protestant cantons, and which stemmed from divergent views concerning the future of the Confederacy: liberal cantons strove to review the 1815 Federal Treaty with a view of broadening the civic freedoms and rights of Swiss citizens and of separating the church and the state, while the conservative cantons wanted to retain the order of the "Old Swiss Confederacy" (Aleksandrowicz 2009: 60). Following the Sonderbundskrieg (Wojtowicz 1976: 166–168) and a subsequent referendum, the Federal Assembly announced that 15 cantons and 1 semi-canton voted for the new constitution, and so the act could take effect. The 1848 constitution changed the political system of the Confederacy significantly and permanently. On 29 May 1874, the Federal Assembly introduced a new federal constitution, which in reality was a modified version of the 1848 constitution, but this time bases for the unification of a significant part of legal provisions were laid, especially concerning commercial and trade relations (Czeszejko-Sochacki 2002: 14). This was a pivotal change for unification of Swiss territories in terms of law, due to the fact that it provided formal foundations for codification, as well as elevating the idea of unification of law to the status of a principal constitutional value, defining the functional, axiological premises of the society and of the state.

The change of the system itself did not immediately transform social awareness, which would ultimately legitimize the reform, and finally allow for the implementation of the new law. As follows from the discussions held on the pages of *Zeitschrift für Schweizerisches Recht*, codification had as many supporters as opponents, with the latter concerned that the sovereignty of cantons, to which Switzerland had been attached since its very inception, would be abolished. With account for the differences, in a historically short period of a mere half century, there emerged a broad social consensus around the direction of political changes and their axiological anchoring. The adopted methods of works, historical and legal comparatives, introduced eclecticism into the system of values and principles expressed in the act, which in turn presented an opportunity for its supra-cantonal acceptance as a regulatory instrument.

The main objective of the codification works, expressed in the attempts at balancing the scientific features and taxonomy of the code with its folk character, was especially significant in this process. Eugen Huber wrote that there are two opposing forces in legislation: the need for adjusting current needs to the tried and tested customs of the past, and the need for progress, expressed in basing institutions of law upon new ideas and legislative techniques. Just as a legal act must satisfy the requirements of a scientific work, in order to be a stable cornerstone for reliable and just courts, it must also be imbued with a folk character, in order to regulate private law relationships in a simple and precise way that reflects human mentality (whether local or cosmopolitan) (Huber 1895: 3). Combining various worldviews under the umbrella of a single legal act was the greatest challenge ahead of the Legislature and yet it was of fundamental significance for the effectiveness of the future act. The act had to be 'popular' with the society; it had to serve each reasonable citizen in their striving to accomplish their goals, or else it would turn out to be "stillborn" (Munzinger 1865: 5). Thus, the only way to achieve unity of law while respecting the cultural diversity of individual cantons was to adopt the following main guiding principle: unification through freedom of shaping civil law relations in contracts. This way, freedom of contracts within the broad frameworks of a uniform law makes the act acceptable to all, regardless of how contradictory their expectations. In the words of the codification's architect: "*Die Rechtseinheit ist die Schwester der Rechtsfreiheit*" ("unity of law is sister to freedom in law") (Huber 1895: 7). This satisfied the second fundamental premise of an effective legal reform: social acceptance of upcoming changes.

Returning to the overarching goal, with special consideration toward identifying the 'codifying moment', the principal role is the issue of achieving the highest possible level of social agreement as to the directions of the introduced changes and the cultural, moral, and political justification. The second condition is to satisfy the procedural requirements in the form of an appropriate constitutional disposition, providing formal justification for codification works. Within the broad perspective of these considerations, several threats to Switzerland were the core factors that enabled the momentous transformation from the tradition of local particularism to unity of law. On the one hand, there was an internal threat: the ongoing political frictions between cantons, which gave rise to continued centrifugal forces. On the other hand, the position of Switzerland on the international arena was not yet stable, considering the threats of Austrian invasion, which also acted on behalf of Prussia, France, and Russia, and which articulated these threats during the course of work on the 1848 constitution.[3] From this perspective, legal unification of Switzerland consolidated the social and political unity of the country, contributing to the protection of Confederacy's further existence.

3 On 18 January 1848, Austria sent a diplomatic note, in which it warned the Confederacy that it would invade it in the event of unlawful attempts at changing the 1815 Treaty. This was prompted by the activities of the Commission, appointed on 16 August 1847 by the Tagsatzung to review the Federal Treaty (Aleksandrowicz 2009: 62).

We must, however, note that this threat was merely a motive for undertaking the effort of changing the political system and of going through with further unification of the country on the legal and social levels, a motive that placed the legal reform in a concrete historical moment. Yet, the condition that defined the level of codification readiness, which is the essence of the 'codification moment', was the satisfaction of formal requirements for the introduction of changes expressed in constitutional provisions, and reaching a broad social consensus as to the direction of the changes to be introduced. The 'codification moment', thus, is not a value that can be expressed on a timeline, but rather a breakthrough in social and state development.

## References


Aleksandrowicz, M. (2009) *System prawny Szwajcarii. Historia i współczesność [Legal System of Switzerland. History and present day].* Białystok, Wydawnictwo Temida 2.

Bauhoffer, A. (1927) *Entstehung und Bedeutung des zürcherischen privatrechtlichen Gesetzbuches von 1853–55.* Zurich, Helbing & Lichtenhahn.

Bigier, U. (1869) 'Schweizervolk und sein Recht. Mahnruf zu größerer Rechtseinheit für Juristen und Nichtjuristen', *Zeitschrift für Schweizerisches Recht,* Druck der Bepsel'schen Buchdruckerei, Solothurn, 1–55.

Branecki, T. (2013) 'Powstanie i rozwój Konfederacji Szwajcarskiego w latach 1291–1515' ['The Creation and Development of the Swiss Confederacy in the Years 1291–1515'], *Studia Iuridica Lublinensia,* 19, 83–99.

Caflisch, J. B. (1898) 'Zur Rechtseinheit', *Zeitschrift für Schweizerisches Recht,* Chur, Druch von Hermann Fiebig, 1–13.

Czeszejko-Sochacki, Z. (2002) *System konstytucyjny Szwajcarii. [Constitutional System of Switzerland].* Warsaw, Wydawnictwo Sejmowe.

Elsener, F. (1975) *Die Schweizer Rechtsschulen vom 16. bis zum 19. Jahrhundert unter besonderer Berücksichtigung des Privatrechts. Die kantonalen Kodifikationen bis zum Schweizerischen Zivilgesetzbuch.* Zurich, Schulthess.

Gruner, E. (1991) 'Die Schweizerische Eidgenossenschaft von der Französischen Revolution bis zur Reform der Verfassung (1789–1874)', in T. Schieder (ed.) *Geschichte der Schweiz- Handbuch der europäischen Geschichte.* Munich, Klett-Cotta Verlag.

Gygi, F. (1984) 'Die Verfassungsgrundlagen des Schweizerischen Obligationenrecht', in P. Caroni (ed.), *Das Obligationenrecht 1883–1983. Berner Ringvorlesung zur Jubiläum des schweizerischen Obligationenrecht.* Bern-Stuttgart, P. Haupt.

Hangartner, Y. (1980) *Grundzüge des schweizerischen Staatsrecht.* Zurich, Schulthess.

Huber, E. (1886–1889) System und Geschichte des Schweizerischen Privatrecht, 4 vols, Basel.

Huber, E. (1895) *Betrachtungen über die Vereinheitlichung des Schweizerischen Erbrechts.* Basel, Reich

Huber, E. (1925) *Recht und Rechtsverwirklichung Probleme der Gesetzgebung und der Rechtsphilosophie.* Basel, Gale, Making of Modern Law.

Huber, E. (2009) 'Confidentielle Mitteilung. Über die Art und Weise des Vorgehens bei der Ausarbeitung des Entwurfes eines einheitlichen schweizerischen Civilgesetzbuches', in Ch. Hurni, M. Reber, and Berner Kommntar (eds) *Kommentar zum schweizerischen Privatrecht. Materialien zum Zivilgesetzbuch,* Band 1, Stämpfli Verlag AG, Bern.

Kelly, J. M. (2006) *Historia zachodniej teorii prawa. [History of Western Theory of Law]*. Krakow, WAM.

Lewandowicz, M. (2014) 'Prawo handlowe w szwajcarskim Kodeksie zobowiązań' ['Commercial Law in the Swiss Code of Obligations'], *Czasopismo Prawno-Historyczne*, 2, 91–104.

Lloyd, H. D. (2006) *A Sovereign People: A Study of Swiss Democracy*. New York, Doubleday, Page & Company.

Milo, J., Lokin, J., and Smits, J. (2014) *Tradition, Codification and Unification. Comparative-Historical Essays on Developments in Civil Law*. Cambridge, Intersetia.

Munzinger, W. (1865) *Motive zu dem Entwurfe eines schweizerisches Handelsrechtes, im Auftrage des Tit. Schweiz. Justiz und Polizeidepartaments verfasst von dem Redaktor des Entwurfes*. Bern, Stämpflische Buchdruckerei.

Rawls, J. (1998) *Political Liberalism*. New York, Columbia University Press.

Sójka-Zielińska, K. (1974) 'Kodyfikacje wieku Oświecenia', in *Dzieje kodyfikacji prawa. Materiały na konferencję historyków prawa w Karpaczu*. ['Codification of the Enlightenment era', in *History of Codification of Law. Materials for the conference of legal historians in Karpacz]*. Karpacz, Polskie towarzystwo Historyczne.

Sójka-Zielińska, K. (2009) *Wielkie kodyfikacje cywilne. Historia i współczesność. [Great Civil Codifications. History and present day]*. Warsaw, Liber.

Sójka-Zielińska, K. (2012) 'Stulecie Kodeksu cywilnego szwajcarskiego' ['Century of the Swiss Civil Code'], *Czasopismo Prawno-Historyczne*, 2, 27–59.

Staehelin, H. (1931) *Die Civilgesetzgebung der Helvetik*. Bern, Stämpfli.

Varga, C. (2001) *Codification as socio-historical phenomenon*. Budapest, Szent Istvan Tarsulat.

Wachholz, Sz. (1936) 'Geneza i rozwój Związku Szwajcarskiego' ['Origin and Development of the Swiss Union'], *Czasopismo Prawnicze i Ekonomiczne*, XXX, 93–118.

Wojtowicz, J. (1976) *Historia Szwajcarii. [History of Switzerland]*. Wroclaw, Zakład Narodowy Imienia Ossolińskich.

# 12 Exogenous institutional change as coercion and the ideological neutrality litmus

## The case of Polish communism

*J. Patrick Higgins*

## Introduction

A common Polish national myth is that Stalin once remarked that forcing *communism* on the Poles would be like putting a *saddle on a cow*.[1] As Poland celebrates 100 years since its rebirth as a modern nation as well as 30 years since throwing off that hated saddle, it is only natural to reflect on the vibrant, intense search for both Polish freedom and identity, as well as the burden of historical interpretation of said struggle.[2] While such romantic feelings are important for political identity, there has now been significant historical distance to look at these events more objectively and for social scientists to ask: do these specific feelings present more general insights that can be systematized to contribute to general political theory?

Of course, for this argument to be coherent, a necessary step is to clarify what *communism* means, in a concrete sense. This provides a standard with which to compare other theories and systems of social change, so that more generalized insights will be possible. However, in keeping with the overall spirit of this volume as generally theoretical-historical, rather than empirical, this operationalization of communism inevitably remains close to a Weberian ideal type. The question: "what is communism?" is quite deep, with multiple possible dimensions. For example, it could mean: (1) any interpretation or implementation of Marxian historical materialism; (2) any theory or system that emerged as a critique of privatized economies,

1 Whether or not this was an actual remark by Stalin, or merely apocryphal, it has become symbolic of Polish communism's failure to build a successful political, economic, and social system. This phrase occurs frequently in the literature, often without source or further description. For a brief review of the literature, sufficient for a general intuition of how important this anecdote is for Polish identity, see: Hunter and Ryan (2008: 209, 2006: 151), Rzanna (2003: 193), Taras (2003: 15), Eberts (1998: 818), Piotrowski (1987: 262).

2 The burden of *history* is to reconcile its strands as both *science* and as *art*, that is when it is critiqued on being insufficient in terms of a positive conception of science, historians defend themselves as artists, but when critiqued as being too logical and systematic than artistic activity, historians defend themselves as scientists (White 1966). This broader theme of both trying to understand the particulars of the Polish case, as well as draw broader conclusions from those particulars, represents this difficult balancing act.

i.a. syndicalism, left-anarchism, or Marxism; (3) an extant world political order in the 20th century centered around Moscow; or (4) an ideology opposed to liberalism, democracy, capitalism, and anything "bourgeois". For my purposes here, "communism" is meant with a specifically *Stalinist* (or pretenders to Stalinism) idea, which is (4) combined with a ***deliberate, cynical political monism.*** As we shall see, Stalinism is not only opposed to traditionally "Western" ideas, values, and practices, but purposively overthrows natural social order while maximizing concentration of political power and cannot stand either internal or external dissent. In essence, I am arguing here that the imposition of communism in Poland by force created a kind of "Stalinism lite", which was ultimately unsustainable.[3]

If this institutional and ideological monism complement each other within Stalinism, then their conceptual and ethical opposite would be a cooperative framework of ***institutional pluralism and ideological neutrality***, such as one inspired from Rawls' work, i.e. ***that endogenous institutions are a natural pluralism that reinforces this neutrality.*** Rawlsian "philosophical neutrality" attempts to reconcile social contractarian with communitarian thought by creating a set of institutions[4] that is neutral and contextually determined per polity. They stress how this neutrality is possible via multicity of institutions, and that an ideological neutrality would be desirable for a modern system of law as it would also create the grounds for legitimacy: the overall rules of society would not favor specific groups or persons. This institutional-ideological neutrality ***via*** pluralism of endogenous institutions provides a theoretical tool to explain the failures of the Polish communist project: ***an ideological litmus test.***

While a complete test would have positive and negative components, it will only be introduced as a theoretical concept here. If the test is "passed" then the society meets the conditions of ideological neutrality, one minimum for a health polity; if the test is "failed" then there are structural problems: coercion, anomie, an unstable and/or illegitimate or repressive regime, etc. Naturally, Stalin's own admission, even if apocryphal, exemplifies extreme violation of these principles. However, this chapter will go beyond stating the obvious positive claim that totalitarianism is non-neutral, but rather make a normative claim that neutrality is a ***sufficient condition*** of a healthy society.

The argument will proceed as follows: first, a brief summary of necessary and sufficient political conditions in political theory; second, a theoretical claim from

3 Though Poland never adopted as powerful a version of Stalinism as other Soviet Republics, the structure of the Stalinist institutions, such as the 1952 Stalin Constitution remained powerful forces in Polish social and political life, though hated and considered illegitimate (Brzezinski 1991: 49–50, 86–94, 1993: 164–169).

For clarification of this point, the author thanks members of the de Tocqueville Center, particularly Prof. Zbigniew Rau and Dr Tobiasz Bocheński.

4 The definition of "institutions" here is from Douglas North: institutions are social phenomena in the form of social structures as processes, by also the guidelines for those same processes, i.e. as both game and "rules of the game". Of importance to the argument presented here is the idea of institutions as "equilibria". See: Hodgson (2006), Greif and Kingston (2011).

the Rawlsian/cooperative framework that ideological neutrality is a sufficient condition for a successful polity; third, clearly connecting this ideological neutrality with endogenous pluralism of institutions; finally, the application of this test as theoretical explanation of why Soviet-style communism failed in Poland.

## 1 Necessary and sufficient conditions in social and political theory

At its most simple, a *necessary* condition is something which *must occur* for an outcome, whereas a *sufficient* condition is one that *guarantees* an outcome.

As a simplified example:

(1) Eating is *necessary* to avoid starvation.
(2) Eating proper nutrients is *sufficient* to avoid starvation.
(3) Eating nutritious food is *necessary* and *sufficient* to avoid starvation.

Put another way, a necessary condition is a minimum, while *sufficiency* is the stronger relation. One must eat to not starve, but if a person eats only bread made with sawdust they will starve, whereas if one eats *sufficient* proper, nutritious food, *they cannot starve.* In the context of social and political theory, a *necessary* condition is one that allows for a healthy society to exist, but only a *sufficient condition guarantees* it. Political theorists have been interested in trying to conceptualize and measure these conditions since at least Aristotle.[5]

One element that is generally agreed upon is that the duty of the state is to establish social order through the monopoly of force.[6] To oversimplify, the debate revolves around whether the monopoly of violence is a necessary *and* sufficient measure of the state, or whether there is a set of sufficient conditions over and above it. A wide variety of traditions and cultures believe that these are two separate conditions, and variously view this sufficient principle as: securing the good life for the citizens, enacting the will of the people, provision of public goods, obedience to natural or theological law, etc. Some examples of adherents to this broad philosophical family would be Confucians, Hegelians, (neo-)Aristotelians, (neo-)Kantians, (some) natural rights theorists, (some) social contractarians, etc. What defines this group is that violence is only held in reserve to secure cooperation as a last resort. The cooperative framework clearly belongs into this category. This is an *optimistic* approach to constructive political philosophy.

The other category, in the widest sense, would be those *pessimistic* about constructive political philosophy, though the *degree* of this pessimism varies; it is

5 E.g. Irrera, on Aristotle's theory of friendship: "it will be sufficient to see that friendship is presented as the ground of political communities, rather than being introduced as an occasional, unnecessary partnership" (2005: 569); Cherry, on the Eleatic Stranger's claim that knowledge is necessary for ruling (2008: 4–5, 9).

6 The Hobbesian "First" political question (Williams 2005: 3).

| **Political cooperation possible?** | **Do sufficient conditions exist for the state?** | **Necessity of coercion for political order** | **Ideal political forms** |
|---|---|---|---|
| Possible | Yes | Necessary, not sufficient | Democracy, democratic socialism |
| Pessimistic | Possibly, but extremely limited | Necessary, likely sufficient | Libertarianism |
| Pessimistic | Do not exist | Necessary and Sufficient | Anarcho-capitalism |
| Cynical | Yes, must be* overcome | Necessary and sufficient | Totalitarianism |

*Figure 12.1* Sufficiency vs. necessity in ideal forms of political cooperation

* A defining feature of totalitarianism is not simply that it does not acknowledge that there are ways to build strong societies, it actually seeks them out to put them under the rule of force. This will be addressed in more depth later.

important to note how this only extends to *political organization* and cooperation; some theories, for example, may advocate for social or economic cooperation, whereas other approaches may be more cynical or nihilistic about human nature in general. The crux of the problem is whether coercion is both the necessary *and* sufficient condition for the state, perhaps formulated most clearly in the modern era by Weber.[7]

Whereas those in the first grouping agree on principle but disagree on what is the precise sufficient condition, those in the latter category all agree on the monopoly of coercion but disagree on whether the state is still justified, or whether this monopoly of coercion is ultimately a good thing. For example, Hobbes believed that the threat of returning to the state of nature was so

7 "A compulsory political organization with continuous operations (*politischer Anstaltsbetrieb*) will be called a 'state' insofar as its administrative staff successfully upholds the claim to the monopoly of the legitimate use of physical force in the enforcement of its order" (Weber 1978: 16).

constant and strong that the state would have to exert all its efforts to preserve society through force, hence the state was a ***necessary evil*** (Williams 2005: 3f), whereas Weber saw violence as part of the state and as ***malum in se***.[8] There are those who take Weber to his logical extreme and argue that no legitimacy or justification of the state is possible, simply because no sufficient political conditions exist.[9] Obviously, anarchists would fall into this extreme category.

This second group actually can be further subdivided, where others become so cynical that they embrace this coercion. To them, in essence, this prioritization of the necessity of coercion or violence is itself the supreme good, at the cost of other social, economic, or political considerations, such as the actual situation, or whether a reform is practical or possible, such as totalitarianism or religious fundamentalism. These categories may be briefly summarized as follows in Figure 12.1.

These divisions between accepting or rejecting the differentiation of necessary and sufficient conditions will be treated here as ***assumptions***: the task is not to systematically explore the merits of each position and to compare them, but rather to further investigate the cooperative model.

## 2 The cooperative model

Once necessary vs sufficient political conditions are differentiated, an important question emerges: how are these to be properly arranged? It may be possible for the right ***internal*** balance to be met for a prosperous and peaceful society, but the society may be weak to invasion. This would be a case where the necessary institutions are too weak. Another situation may be when these institutions are too strong and the coercive power in a society overcomes the cooperative power, e.g. a tyrant using his military might to plunder national treasure and undermine the good life.

This former situation is applicable to the case of Poland in the 18th century, where the ***liberum veto*** has been attributed to the weakening and eventual decline of the Polish-Lithuanian Commonwealth. The ***liberum veto*** was created in a time of relative peace and prosperity in the Polish-Lithuanian Commonwealth as one of the most powerful states of Europe: the nobles had the power to individually and unilaterally veto decrees of the national parliament. While this was highly effective in checking the power of the monarchy and other nobles, it also undermined the ability of the state to function and coordinate itself against its absolutist, militaristic

8 For this deeper comparison between Hobbes and Weber, see Goerner and Thompson (1996: 623f).

9 Presumably, those who hold the position that the state is defined by its necessary, coercive properties rather than those properties as constrained and evaluated by some greater, sufficient concept of the greater good, would theoretically not disagree with the general *logic* that sufficient conditions can justify necessary processes. They would simply believe, either consequentially or *a priori*, that are no *sufficient* conditions possible. This could be because they do not exist, are unknowable, or even the Hobbesian position that simply sees human nature as too flawed to be overcome by some principle other than force.

neighbors. After over a century of decline, warfare, and internal political squabbling, the Polish-Lithuanian Commonwealth was divided by its enemies and the nobles created a new Constitution in the 1790s with much weaker veto powers. These reforms were too late, and the nation was soon divided up by Russia, Prussia, and Austria, effectively being erased from the map of Europe for over 100 years. The Poles learned their lesson and have used weaker vetoes ever since.[10]

This second case inspired natural law theorists to create a "right to Revolution" where the people rebel to reclaim their rights, should the Sovereign ever overstep their bounds. This tension of both believing in a sufficient condition for a good society while also recognizing the need for a mechanism to ensure this in case it fails is exemplified in Locke's *Two Treatises* where the very first paragraph of the Preface is endorsing the Sovereign as protector of the people's natural rights, only to contend later in the treatise that if the Sovereign were to violate the natural rights of the citizens, those rights are "devolved" back to those citizens who retain a right to reclaim them, however necessary (Locke 1823: 202).[11]

This tension is continuously present throughout Rawls' works as well. Whereas in his earlier publications he was wrestling with how to explain sufficient and necessary conditions by way of the original position (Rawls 1963, 1975), by his later work his vision of liberalism as pluralism was attempting to politically construct "an overlapping" consensus (Rawls 1985: 246–247, 1987: 17). Ultimately, Rawls extends his principles of rights to a universalist "human" right, which lexically supersedes even this pluralistic overlapping consensus *within* a people, for a greater, higher order *among* peoples, noting that "They set a moral limit to pluralism 'among peoples'" (Rawls 1993: 39). Indeed, a valid way to interpret the entirety of Rawls' political project appears to be this attempt to reconcile sufficient with necessary conditions of justice in an agnostic, rationalist manner, rather than via natural law. However, we may go one step further in trying to systematize and then synthesize these insights with the benefits of both communitarianism and social contractarianism in an interplay between public reason and sociocultural context: how individual beliefs and behavior are both shapers of as well as shaped by their institutional environment.

It is necessary to turn, briefly, to an endogenous theory of institutions.

## 3 Law as an endogenous, coordinating institution

The very question of how law is created as a form of "public reasoning" and how that same public reasoning feeds back into society to facilitate successful social coordination – in previous terminology, *sufficient* conditions for a prosperous society – is asked by Hadfield and Weingast (2011). They stress the importance

10 For example, the 3 May 1791 Constitution explicitly banned the *liberum veto*, and the April 1997 Constitution does not even mention veto as a parliamentary apparatus.

11 For applications of these Lockean theories of rebellion to Poland under communism, see Rau (1991, 1998).

of law as "more than a mechanism of coercion by the state" that is "enforced by a wide variety of extra-legal mechanisms" (Hadfield and Weingast 2011: 3f). They specifically acknowledge that:

> Even though coercive state enforcement may play an essential role in fostering and making a particular legal system effective, as the efforts to generate legality in the former Soviet states demonstrate, the state's capacity to enforce compliance through sanction and threat is limited.
>
> (Hadfield and Weingast 2011: 4)

Law is a "process" that facilitates "decentralized" enforcement and must be *neutral and general* to provide legitimacy and stability. This in, turn, allows for individuals to have a shared understanding of right and wrong, how to interpret the laws, and rational expectations about daily life. By contrast, systems of arbitrariness or laws' applications that are driven by external ideologies, rather than moralities that have been internalized and contextualized by the citizenry do not possess a "rule of law" at all.

> Nonetheless, the participation constraint for individuals [to engage productively in society] requires that the law provide value for citizens, so the substance of the law cannot be arbitrary: it must be structured so as to make most citizens better off.
>
> (Hadfield and Weingast 2011: 23)

One of the key points in the Hadfield-Weingast thesis is that law as an endogenous institution serves to complement and minimize coercion: through the neutral and general legal system, individuals can coordinate their own beliefs and views with that of the legitimate public authorities. However, as law is a social process, it is also in a state of constant transition (coordination, in their language) that must be grounded in context of social reality, rather than arbitrariness. Laws, social and political institutions, and the public thus create a pluralistic system that works together and evolves with time. This perspective perfectly complements, and even has much to contribute, to theories of social cooperation.

*Neutrality* broadly follows along contemporary political economic (classical) liberalism, perhaps evidenced most clearly by the legal thought of Hayek: that the "neutrality" of an institution means that it is not specifically biased against a group or person, or, conversely, that everyone is subject to its consequences (both potentially positive or negative) (Harnish 2010: 192–193, Zywicki 2003: 4, 14–15, Caney 1991). It does not mean that the institutions are somehow passive or static, nor that society itself has taken no underlying ideological or philosophical positions, e.g. some kind of historical-cultural consensus. Under this consensus, it is obviously possible for coercion to exist, specifically for minorities that refute this consensus, i.e. religious or ethnic minorities. It is simply that, as the origin of the conflict is within society itself, it would take a different form than some externally induced sociopolitical problems.

*Pluralism* is used in the sense of a natural heterogeneity of institutions that can exist under any (non-totalitarian) system, at least theoretically (Kurczewska 1995, Dahl 1989). Pluralism, like neutrality, is a relative concept: in a society that is relatively geographically or culturally isolated, the diversity in society will be lower, whereas more open and metropolitan societies will be more diverse. This pluralism also means a mix of cooperation and competition on multiple levels simultaneously, and any combination is possible, e.g. political diversity but ethnic homogeneity. Neutrality and pluralism are thus complementary: a neutral environment will allow for this natural equilibrium to arise, as well as change, on its own, without interference, whereas pluralism, as diversity, will lead to natural competition among institutions to offset any person or group from arising that could challenge this neutrality.[12]

Of course, this natural set of institutions will dynamically change over time, both through natural social evolution and direct social agitation and socio-political movements.[13] The main point is that the primary mode of societal change is internal, though of course societies may actively seek out aid from other societies, attempt to borrow or copy alien institutions, societies may combine or divide, etc. As these processes of change are *internal* there is a natural minimization of coercion due to relatively high compatibility of political actors and their environment. Alternatively, external attempts to change a society are essentially built on a relationship of coercion, as the institutions that are implanted, as alien, are illegitimate as they are "unnatural" to the sociopolitical environment.

At this point, it is possible to create the broad outlines of the test itself. The logic is as follows: first, social systems each have their own context (with both an equilibrium of institution and institutions themselves as equilibria of social forces) that is both implicitly and explicitly constructed by human action. Second, this *endogeneity* of the system, as created by internal actors within the society, is also the source of legitimacy. Third, external attempts to artificially *force* changes in society clearly violate ideological neutrality, and some internal attempts at social change may violate this ideological neutrality as well. The operative word here is *force*: all societies are in a state of continuous change, and this change is not always gradual or peaceful, but historical examples such as civil rights movements, political revolutions, and other social movements are successful because they are authentic to their social, cultural, and political context and seek to actively change public will.

This is contrasted with authoritarian or oligarchic regimes who thrive off fragmenting society, often through pure (or implicit) violence and outside financial and military support; in the long-run they are simply unsustainable.

12 The idea that institutional pluralism may lead to ideological stability is not particularly new, either generally or in the specific context of Poland and other Eastern European post-socialist transformations (see Duffy, Sullivan, and Polakiewicz 1993).

13 It would be a mistake to consider that the analysis here is intended to be a purely structural one. See Storr (2011) for an attempt to develop North's "ideological entrepreneur".

| Ideological neutrality | Neutral | Non-neutral |
|---|---|---|
| Institutions | Pluralistic | Monistic |
| Sources of political change | Primarily endogenous, potentially exogenous | Exogenous |
| State coercion | Necessary but not sufficient | Necessary and sufficient |

*Figure 12.2* Ideological neutrality and sufficiency vs. necessity of political coercion

The final, necessary element for ideological neutrality via pluralism of social and political institutions is a public sphere protected by rule of law. Putting these elements together, we can now adjust our earlier table into a more complete version of the test to include endogeneity of institutions. This is given in Figure 12.2.

Institutions that are neutral are pluralistic and they change through a combination of endogenous and exogenous processes but are generally powered by internal processes of change. As there is some natural harmony within society, state coercion is held as a secondary, necessary mechanism should parties fail to cooperate peacefully. Alternatively, societies ruled by a very small set of, or even one, structure, rely on exogenous, external changes, at least initially. Any form of monarchy, empire, colony, etc. was originally established by one external group forcing changes upon another. Current monarchs, dictatorships, and one-party states often coordinate and send resources and military aid to each other, because often they can trust other dictators' interests more than those of their own people, and sometimes even their own ruling coalitions. As the pluralism in a society collapses, the reliance upon coercion necessarily increases, leading to a social equilibrium that is unstable and ultimately fails.

## 4 The historical robustness of Polish institutions

The Poles' hatred for, and continual resistance against, communism was a natural consequence of the nations' deep history. Since the medieval era, Poland has always been a crossroads and mixing ground of peoples and cultures in Eastern Europe. The old kingdoms of Poland and the later Polish-Lithuanian Commonwealth were unique for relative toleration of ethnic and religious diversity.[14] The Polish kings were weak by European standards and were often elected

14 While Europe was embroiled in religious warfare, the Act of the Warsaw Confederation of 1573 declared religious toleration and freedom of conscience nearly a century before these ideas became popularized by Locke and the Enlightenment.

by the nobility, who were granted equality before the law, the right of due process, and personal inviolability of property rights.

Further, the status of nobility was relatively fluid, where foreigners could be ennobled much easier than most other places on the continent. Academics were often elevated to positions of semi-nobility, and universities were allowed significant self-governance and independence,[15] rather than relying on the Crown or the Church. It has been estimated that as much of 10% of the whole population may have been nobles and able to participate in political life, certainly unique for a historic era dominated by absolutism (Rau, vel Grajewski, and Tracz-Tryniecki 2016: 133–143).

It has been argued that perhaps the local privileges of nobles were *too* strong and *too* decentralizing, leading to the collapse of the Polish-Lithuanian Commonwealth, but it is also clear that these institutions were robust enough to survive several centuries of partition. One example of this is the relative continuity between Polish constitutions from the reforms at the end of the 18th century through various brief attempts to restore Poland through the 19th century, and finally throughout the 20th century, despite the dictatorship of Józef Piłsudski, the National Socialists, and the communists forcing Poland away from its historical traditions. When the post-Soviet Polish constitution was written in 1997, it had clear references to this long, if complicated, tradition.[16]

Prażmowska succinctly describes a historic feeling felt by many Poles across the centuries:

> Independence was an aspiration nursed by all Poles and that objective continued to be the main and eventual aim of political activities. In spite of living areas which were ruled very differently, Poles everywhere were acutely aware that they had a language in common, and could refer to a recent past when there had a been a Polish kingdom. Frontiers between the empires were porous, and literature, newspapers, and politicians were able to travel between the three. Whereas political experiences divided Poles in the three occupation zones, a strong sense of national identity continued and indeed grew with time.
>
> (Prażmowska 2004: 156)

By the time the communists took power in Poland, they found they had to contend with both this historical feeling of Polish national identity and its institutional plurality. There remained elements of a capitalist economy, with many peasants retaining their own lands as well as "urban petty-entrepreneurs" (Zubek and Gentleman 1994: 336f) with some private craftsmanship acknowledged by communist leader Władysław Gomułka (Aslund 1984: 430f). Even the Stalinists

15 Rau et al. (2016: 16–19), see also: Leitgeber (1989).

16 For a deeper history of Polish constitutional debates and struggles, see: Wróbel (2010), Brzezinski (1991, 1997), Peck (2012: 50); Elster (1991), Grzybowski (1957).

did not dare directly challenge the Catholic Church, which not only kept much of its land, orchards, and gardens (Korbonski 1981: 2f), but also remained explicitly anti-communist and supported a pluralistic vision of civil society (Kurczewska 1995: 33f). Just after the Second World War there were attempts to marry communism with Poland's diverse civil society, including explicit attempts to create socialist democracy, which Stalinists quickly put down.[17]

In many ways, Poland was the absolute *worst* place for the Soviet project. A full five years before communism collapsed, Ash prophetically declared:

> But there was no society in eastern Europe *less* prepared voluntarily to accept *Soviet* socialism, imposed by Russian bayonets. Soviet socialism did not start from scratch in Poland; it started with a huge political and moral debit. Stalin himself said that introducing communism to Poland was like putting a saddle on a cow; the Poles thought it was like putting a yoke on a stallion. This fundamental, historic opposition and incompatibility is the most basic cause of the Polish revolt against "Yalta" and Soviet socialism in 1980. For thirty-five years Poland's communist rulers tried either to break the stallion to the yoke or to mould the saddle to the cow. It was always probably that they would fail.
>
> (Ash 1983[2002]: 6)

The regime tried to reform itself several times. Under Gomułka there was a miniature revival of "semi-sovereignty, semi-democracy, and semi-pluralism", both in the mid-1940s and later when he returned after 1956 and the Stalinist period ended (Wasilewski and Wnuk-Lipiński 1995: 671). Numerous experiments with market socialism were attempted, but political uprisings and strikes continued, as well as enforcement from Moscow. In 1976 there began a movement for a "surreal" interpretation of the constitution, in which the sovereignty, independence, and the democratic and rights-based dimensions of socialist constitutionalism were taken "seriously" rather than the "real" interpretation of Stalinism (Blokker 2015: 144). By 1985 the party set up a constitutional reform tribunal in a failing effort to increase its legitimacy.

The Jaruzelski regime saw the writing on the Wall after it fell: after a decade of battling with *Solidarity*, there began talks with its rival, the Catholic church, and other members of civil society about the transition to democracy. A rough agreement was struck where the communist parties would allow elections but rig the game to ultimately remain in power (Aslund 2002, Bernhard 2014). This ultimately

17 Grzybowski notes that the Manifesto of July 22, 1944 explicitly rejected Piłsudski's Constitution of 1935 and declared a return to the 1921 Constitution and parliamentary democracy (Grzybowski 1957: 55). Naturally, these ambitions did not survive long behind the Iron Curtain. Similarly, was the case of Jerzy Borejsza, a prominent communist minister and chief of the state press who in 1945 pronounced a "Gentle Revolution" where the communists would try to adapt to and absorb the historical plurality of Polish institutions, which would explicitly allow for dissent (Shore 2006: 269f). However, by 1947 more hardline communists were starting to take over the party, and by 1950 Borejsza lost his political position and influence before dying in 1952.

failed, as once Poles got a taste of democracy, revolutionary pressure only increased until there was a total transition to democracy.

After communism, the Polish political system has been characterized as "confrontational-pluralism", with a uniquely high level of political motivation of the citizenry (Seleny 1999). Though Poland has its own left vs right party rise and fall over the last 30 years, none has dared reassert the communism system. Interestingly, political commentators on the situation in Poland have claimed that there has been *too much* pluralism, with a fragmented and disorganized political system, akin to the *liberum veto*. From a repressive, single party regime to an *overly* active political environment within a generation – quite an accomplishment.

Now that a real-world situation, rather than a pure theory, has been presented, it is possible to complete the ideological litmus test, which essentially compares beliefs in necessity of coercion by Figure 12.3.

Passing the test requires a combination of respect for individual freedom, pluralism of institutions, and a *minimization of state coercion*. Note that endogeneity

| **Ideal types** | **Generalized political beliefs** | | | **Political practice** | | | **Ideological-institutional litmus test** |
|---|---|---|---|---|---|---|---|
| | **State coercion** | **Necessary conditions** | **Pluralism** | **Examples** | **Individual freedom** | | |
| Anarchism-deontological | Necessary and sufficient | Do not exist | Always | Anarcho-capitalism | Highest value | **Cleary passes test** | |
| Anarchism-consequentialist | Necessary, not sufficient | May exist | Almost always | Minarchism | Highest possible without violating rights of others | | |
| Cooperative political orders | Necessary, not sufficient | Yes | Generally pluralist | Democracy, democratic socialism | Freedom of opportunity under law | | |
| Hierarchy | Necessary, not sufficient | Yes | Limited diversity for elites | Aristocracy, enlightened-constitutional monarchism | Natural and some meritocratic elites enjoy freedom | **Clearly fails test** | |
| Totalitarian social orders | Necessary contra sufficiency | Yes – must be dominated | Must be destroyed | Fascism, hard communism | Only the ruler or party *may* be free* | | |

*Figure 12.3* The theoretical ideological-institutional litmus test

* An emphasis in a Foucaultian analysis of power would be that not even the rulers themselves are truly free, in that their freedom is illusorily, and they are bound by the very act of ruling itself. Thus, due to paranoia and the all-consuming nature of power itself, the ruler may be the least free person.

of institutions is not present in the general model, because this is a secondary product of pluralism and the proper balance of necessary vs sufficient political conditions. If a society has a plurality of institutions, most them must be endogenous and neutral, as multiple foreign exogenous institutions cannot co-exist, i.e. one cannot serve two masters. Further, most of them most be neutral, else a relatively small number of very powerful institutions would effectively "colonize" the public sphere into an oligopoly. Minimization of state coercion can either be *subject to a sufficient condition* (relative) or as an end unto itself (absolute): a successful democracy and a successful anarchy would both pass the ideological neutrality test. As remarked earlier, the choice of either some form of restricted state, e.g. a democracy, or (in the extreme) a stateless society depends on whether one believes there are sufficient conditions that constrain the necessity of state coercion, and/or whether or not one believes that anarchy is stable or possible.

This test has a strong Aristotelian flavor in that the middle categories (Minarchism, Democracy, and Aristocracy/Enlightened-Constitutional monarchy) are the "best" for creating a successful polity, as demonstrated by the majority of modern nations fitting into one or several of these categories. It should also be noted that "clearly fails" to "clearly passes" is a continuum, rather than fixed thresholds, and further that *the whole test is constructed with ideal types.* There is a trend moving away from complete rejection of these sufficient conditions to skepticism, to final acceptance of them, but a counter-trend of decreasing individual freedom and consequently declining pluralism.

Totalitarianism is the most unique type in that it accepts states as *necessarily violent*, as well as differentiates *necessity vs sufficiency.* As its name implies, its *totalizing* nature has inverted sufficiency constraining necessity of force, *to maximization of coercion to conquer and enslave these necessary conditions*, that is it actively seeks out to find and transform the totality of social, public, and private life to its will. However, the great strength of totalitarianism, its single-minded focus, is also the source of its greatest weakness: it remains an essentially alien and distant system, regardless of the context of its implementation as the only way to retain its monistic vision of society and political power. Thus, in the long run it is inherently unstable as it is not robust; it rejects the very mechanisms of change that it would need to adapt and to survive.

Hence, communism has only been successful in historic situations where societies were in chaos or transition where it is able to take advantage of the situation due to its superior organization and narrow, intense focus. Once societies become more diverse, wealthier, more educated, and/or more stable, the internal pressures of those societies slowly eat away at communism until it either collapses or transitions into something else; the case of China illustrates a country that is essentially communist in name only.

## Conclusion: Necessary contra sufficiency and failing the test

To put it plainly, communism in Poland failed specifically because it followed the Stalinist model, which explicitly sought to destroy the diversity of social, political, economic, cultural, and ideological life. Its explicit goal was to atomize society (Fitzpatrick 1986: 359) and establish an idealized concept of a necessarily superhuman being in the ruler (Casals and Daniels 1980/1981: 21). Centralized coercion explicitly replaced any potential differentiation (Campeanu 1990: 36–39, 45), and civil society was to be destroyed by absorption into the state. Prominent Marxist theorist Bukharin described Stalinism as a "military-feudal" dictatorship that led to social regression in service to forced industrialization, a modernism by pre-modern means (Reichman 1988: 63–67, Casals and Daniels 1980/1981).

Much like a person who has the least self-confidence talks a big game, it appears that almost from the very beginning, communism was a system of weak institutions. Even in Moscow, the heart of the Soviet Union, there remained institutional holdovers from the bourgeois era completely incompatible with the communist system simply because they were more natural and efficient. In his seminal work on the Soviet legal system Feifer notes how the cracks were even beginning to show in the 1960s, less than a decade after Stalin's own death:

> [T]he single central movement in legal practice since 1917 had been a steady development toward West European traditions. Soviet writers had always proclaimed their law to be something entirely new, better than, "higher" than, in every way diametrically opposed to, bourgeois law; but the laws themselves . . . were mostly repetitions of bourgeois laws, of the tsarist norms in fact, which borrowed from the German and French codes. In the end, the Party ended up with a system that operated much like Western ones . . .
>
> How Soviet jurists replaced talk of the "withering-away" of the law under socialism with arguments that its "greatest flowering" takes place only under socialism makes a fascinating story . . . From contempt of law – law in general, as well as bourgeois law specifically – Soviet writers had swung around to admiration. "Socialism alone develops the law fully and permits a genuine respect for legality".
>
> (Feifer 1964: 24)

A great "what if" of history is whether Poland could have transitioned to a multiparty democracy dominated by a communist party coalition, as the regime had clearly intended, had it been able to overcome the inertia of its Stalinist political legacy. Communist regimes could likely have survived in Eastern Europe, as they have done in China, Cuba, and other nations, and Poland may have as well, had it adapted to communism "with Polish characteristics". Instead, the ultimate cynicism of Stalinism and its descendants goes beyond simple reliance of force out of necessity, as with other imperial regimes, rather this necessary force is recognized, and then elevated over and above necessary conditions for a successful policy. Ironically, the very cause of Stalinism, its perpetuation by coercion, eventually seals its own doom by inflexible and illegitimate sociopolitical structures that cut off the very diversity that would allow them to adapt and to grow.

Among the Eastern bloc nations, Poland remained relatively pluralistic and tolerant, with its regime less repressive and less effective than others, but the diversity of the system did more to reinforce the status quo than allow for innovation (McHale 1995). This led to moderate groups and reformers becoming increasingly radicalized over time. *Solidarity* began as a moderate, reformist labor union, but after extensive repression of the regime, metamorphosed into a catch-all for anyone who was opposed to the system. Though the economic and sociopolitical problems both within and between Soviet bloc countries by the late 1970s made it increasingly unlikely that communism as a system would survive.

By the mid-1990s what had been attempted as a moderate reform effort had completely toppled the communist regime. A thriving, if unstable, democracy had been established. There were debates about rewriting the Constitution, wiping away the last formal vestiges of communist rule. In the 30 years since, Poland has remained one of the fastest growing economies in Europe, is a member of NATO, the European Union, and is now arguably the greatest economic and military power of the Central Eastern European nations.

It seems the cow really did wear out the saddle.

## References


Aristotle (2019) *The Politics*. https://classicalwisdom.com/greek_books/politics-by-aristotle-book-iii/7/ [Retrieved 21/1/2019].

Ash, T. G. (1983[2002]) *The Polish Revolution: Solidarity*. 3rd Edition. New Haven, Yale University Press.

Aslund, A. (1984) 'The Functioning of Private Enterprise in Poland', *Soviet Studies* 36/3, 427–444.

Aslund, A. (2002) *Building Capitalism: The Transformation of the Former Soviet Bloc*. Cambridge, Cambridge University Press.

Bernhard, M. (2014) *Institutions and the Fate of Democracy: Germany and Poland in the Twentieth Century*. Pittsburg, University of Pittsburgh Press.

Blokker, P. (2015) 'The (Re-)Emergence of Constitutionalism in East Central Europe', in M. Kopecek and P. Wcisli (eds) *Thinking Through Transition: Liberal Democracy, Authoritarian Pasts, and Intellectual History in East Central Europe After 1989*. Budapest, Central European University Press, 136–167.

Brzezinski, M. F. (1991) 'Constitutional Heritage and Renewal: The Case of Poland', *Virginia Law Review* 77/1, 49–112.

Brzezinski, M. F. (1993) 'The Emergence of Judicial Review in Eastern Europe: The Case of Poland', *The American Journal of Comparative Law* 41/2, 153–200.

Brzezinski, M. F. (1997) *The Struggle for Constitutionalism in Poland*. Berlin/Heidelberg, Springer.

Campeanu, P. (1990) 'Exit: Toward Post-Stalinism', *International Journal of Sociology* 20/1/2, i, iii, v–xiii,1, 3–155, 157–162.

Caney, S. (1991) 'Consequentialist Defenses of Liberal Neutrality', *The Philosophical Quarterly* 41, 165, 457–477.

Casals, F. G. and Daniels, G. (1980/1981) 'The Syncretic Society', *International Journal of Politics* 10/4, 1–90.

Cherry, K. M. (2008) 'Aristotle and the Eleatic Stranger on the Nature and Purpose of Political Life', *American Journal of Political Science* 52/1, 1–15.

Dahl, R. A. (1989) *Democracy and its Critics*. New Haven, Yale University Press.

Duffy, D. M., Sullivan, J., and Polakiewicz, L. A. (1993) 'Patriotic Perspectives in Contemporary Poland: Conflict or Consensus?', *The Polish Review* 38/3, 259–298.

Eberts, M. W. (1998) 'The Roman Catholic Church and Democracy in Poland', *Europe-Asia Studies* 50/5, 817–842.

Elster, J. (1991) 'Constitutionalism in Eastern Europe: An Introduction', *The University of Chicago Law Review* 58/2, 447–482.

Feifer, G. (1964) *Justice in Moscow*. New York: Simon and Schuster.

Fitzpatrick, S. (1986) 'New Perspectives on Stalinism', *The Russian Review* 45/4, 357–373.

Goerner, E. A. and Thompson, W. J. (1996) 'Politics and Coercion', *Political Theory* 24/4, 620–652.

Greif, A. and Kingston, C. (2011) 'Institutions: Rules or Equilibria?', in G. Caballero and N. Schofield (eds) *Political Economy of Institutions, Democracy, and Voting*. Springer-Verlag, Berlin, 13–44.

Grzybowski, K. (1957) 'Continuity of Law in Eastern Europe', *The American Journal of Comparative Law* 6/1, 44–78.

Hadfield, G. K. and Weingast, B. R. (2011) 'Endogenous Institutions: Law as a Coordinating Device', *University of Southern California Law School, Law and Economics Working Paper Series*, Paper 141.

Harnish, B. (2010) 'Alsadair MacIntyre and F.A. Hayek on the Abuse of Reason', *The Independent Review* 15/2, 179–199.

Hodgson, G. M. (2006) 'What are Institutions?', *Journal of Economic Issues* 40/1, 1–25.

Hunter Jr., R. J. and Ryan, L. (2006) 'A Retrospective Analysis and Future Perspective: 'Why was Poland's Transition so Difficult?', *The Polish Review* 51/2, 147–171.

Hunter Jr., R. J. and Ryan, L. (2008) 'The Ten Most Important Economic and Political Events since the Onset of the Transition in Post-Communist Poland', *The Polish Review* 53/2, 183–216.

Irrera, E. (2005) 'Between Advantage and Virtue: Artistotles' Theory of Political Friendship', *History of Political Thought* 26/4, 565–585.

Korbonski, A. (1981) 'The "Second Economy" in Poland', *Journal of International Affairs* 35/1, 1–13.

Kurczewska, J. (1995) 'Pluralism "Under Socialism": The Case of Poland', *Polish Sociological Review* 112, 325–339.

Leitgeber, B. (1989) 'Multi-Ethnic Glimpses of Old Poland', *The Slavonic and Eastern European Review* 67/3, 435–441.

Locke, J. (1823) 'Two Treatises of Government', in the *Works of John Locke. A New Edition, Correction*. 10 Vols. Prepared by Rod Hay for the McMaster University Archive of the History of Economic Thought. www.yorku.ca/comninel/courses/3025pdf/Locke.pdf [Retrieved 1/21/2019].

McHale, V. E. (1995) 'Democratic Transition and the Evolution of Mass Politics in Post-Communist Central and Eastern Europe', *Historical Social Research* 20/2, 74, 188–209.

Peck, A. (2012) 'The Polish Contribution to the Development of European Democracy: Interpretations in American Textbooks', *The Polish Review* 57/4, 47–61.

Piotrowski, H. (1987) 'The Soviet Union and the Renner Government of Austria, April-November 1945', *Central European History* 20/3/4, 246–279.

Prażmowska, A. (2004) *Civil War in Poland, 1942–1948*. London, Pallgrave MacMillan.

Rau, Z. (1998) *From Communism to Liberalism: Essays on the Individual and Civil Society*. Łódź, Łódź University Press.

Rau, Z. (1991) *Reemergence of Civil Society in Eastern Europe and the Soviet Union*. Boulder, Westview Press.

Rau, Z., Żurawski vel Grajewski, P., and Tracz-Tryniecki, M. (2016) *Magna Carta: A Central European Perspective of Our Common Heritage of Freedom*. Abingdon, Routledge.

Rawls, J. (1963) 'The Sense of Justice', *The Philosophical Review* 72/3, 281–305.

Rawls, J. (1975) 'Fairness to Goodness', *The Philosophical Review* 84/4, 536–554.

Rawls, J. (1985) 'Justice as Fairness: Political not Metaphysical', *Philosophy & Public Affairs* 14/3, 223–251.

Rawls, J. (1987) 'The Idea of Overlapping Consensus', *Oxford Journal of Legal Studies* 7/1, 1–25.

Rawls, J. (1993) 'The Law of Peoples', *Critical Inquiry* 20/1, 36–608.

Reichman, H. (1988) 'Reconsidering "Stalinism"', *Theory and Society* 17/1, 57–89.

Rzanna, E. (2003) 'The Democratic Re-Education in the Spirit of Cultural Determinism: A Comparison of West Germany and Poland in the Post War Period', *Polish Sociological Review* 142, 187–199.

Seleny, A. (1999) 'Old Political Rationalities and New Democracies: Compromise and Confrontation in Poland and Hungary', *World Politics* 51/4, 484–519.

Shore, M. (2006) 'Stalinism amidst Warsaw's Ruins', in *Caviar and Ashes: A Warsaw Generation's Life and Death in Marxism, 1918–1958*. New Haven, Yale University Press, 257–304.

Storr, V. H. (2011) 'North's Underdeveloped Ideological Entrepreneur', in E. Chamlee-Wright (ed.) *The Annual Proceedings of the Wealth and Well Being of Nations*. Beloit, Beloit College, 99–116.

Taras, R. (2003) 'Poland's Accession into the European Union: Parties, Policies, and Paradoxes', *The Polish Review* 48/1, 3–19.

Wasilewski, J. and Wnuk-Lipiński, E. (1995) 'Poland: Winding Road from the Communist to the Post-Solidarity Elite,' *Theory and Society* 24/5, 669–696.

Weber, M. (1978) *Economy and Society: an Outline of Interpretive Sociology*. G. Roth and C. Wittich (eds). The University of California Press, Berkeley and Los Angeles.

White, H. V. (1966) 'The Burden of History', *History and Theory* 5/2, 111–134.

Williams, B. (2005) *In the Beginning was the Deed: Realism and Moralism in Political Argument*. G. Hawthorn (ed.). Princeton, Princeton University Press.

Wróbel, P. J. (2010) 'The Rise and Fall of Parliamentary Democracy in Interwar Poland', in M. B. B. Biskupski, J. S. Pula, and P. J. Wróbel (eds) *The Origins of Modern Polish Democracy*. Ohio University Press, Athens, 110–164.

Zubek, V. and Gentleman, J. (1994) 'Economic Crisis and the Movement toward Pluralism in Poland and Mexico', *Political Science Quarterly* 109/2, 335–359.

Zywicki, T. J. (2003) 'The Rule of Law, Freedom, and Prosperity', *The Supreme Court Economic Review* 10, 1–26.

# 13 The coercive control offence

## A case study on overcriminalisation

*Melissa Hamilton*

### Introduction

The Parliament of the United Kingdom took an extraordinary step in 2015 by enacting a criminal statute to penalise coercive control in domestic relationships. The rationale is that abusers may use emotional, psychological, and financial control tactics (i.e., not just physical assaults) to dictate their victims' choices, activities, and associations. Coercive control can undermine a victim's autonomy and liberty. Humanitarians and advocates for the rights of women expect this new law to provide a significant tool for criminal justice officials in combating domestic violence, which has proven notoriously challenging to properly investigate, prosecute, and punish.

England is one of a few jurisdictions in the world to criminalise coercive control, though law reform commissions around the world have considered the same from time to time (Douglas 2015). This situation may mean that England is at the forefront of formally recognising the multiple harms that batterers perpetrate on their victims which do not necessarily involve physical violence. Or, it may signal that lawmakers have gone too far by treating as a criminal offence various behaviours that almost no other country finds rise to that level. We consider herein whether the new statute constitutes a form of excessive legislation in that coercive control may not appropriately be the subject of criminal law. It may be telling that the Australian Law Reform Commission not long ago rejected a proposal to create a coercive control statute (Australia Law Reform Commission 2010: Section 14), while Northern Island withdrew a coercive control bill in 2017 (Gallagher 2017).

This chapter addresses a type of excessive legislation called overcriminalisation by reviewing the main political philosophies that define which acts are eligible for criminalisation in the first place. These are the harm principle and legal moralism. We outline how overcriminalisation may occur in contemporary society and review the negative consequences thereof. It will be important to contextualise the meaning of the term coercive control in regards to domestic abuse. Then we analyse the new coercive control legislation by enquiring into whether it is an appropriate focus of criminal law, or if it represents a case study for overcriminalisation. Some of the more intriguing aspects of this particular case study are that the coercive control offence likely intrudes upon normative family dynamics and is invasive of private relationships.

## 1 Overcriminalisation

This chapter concerns the concept of excessive legislation. Alternative terms are legal inflation or legal creep. Yet because the subject matter herein concerns a criminal law – rather than civil legislation – perhaps the better term to use hereinafter is overcriminalisation. This is because there is something uniquely special about criminal law. Unlike other bodies of law or social control systems, criminal law imposes public condemnation and formal punishment upon offenders (Husak 2011). The particular penalty is a judgment about the degree of the offender's wrongfulness, harmfulness, and culpability (Luna 2005), ingredients that other forms of law do not necessarily require in order to regulate activity. As a result, there is a significant level of approbation associated with the label of "criminal" that is not present when a legal outcome designates a person as, say, a tortfeasor or a contract breacher (Luna 2005).

Overcriminalisation has been defined as "the misuse of the criminal sanction" (Campbell, Sahid, & Stang 1969: 551). That appears a simple enough concept, but it still begs the question. To understand a law as representing overcriminalisation (or not), insight is first needed into what conduct may be criminalised.

### *1.1 Philosophical theories of criminalisation*

Two competing philosophies, socio-legal and political in nature, are bandied about in criminal law literature to provide parameters around which acts are rightfully subject to criminalisation. They are (1) the harm principle and (2) legal moralism.

The classic version of the harm principle was laid out in John Stuart Mill's renowned book *On Liberty* (1859). Founded upon a libertarian ideal, the harm principal indicates that a democratic society ought not to interfere with the liberty of an individual unless doing so can prevent harm to others. Not any menial harm is enough, though. It must be a harm that prejudicially effects the individual rights of another person. Consequently, the "acts of an individual may be hurtful to others, or wanting in due consideration for their welfare, without going to the length of violating any of their constituted rights" (Mill 1859: 44). Citizens should be free of official constraint to commit acts which harm only one's own self-interests or the rights of another who consents (and is legally capable of consenting). In this last respect, Mill's theorisation of promoting individual liberty interests included the right of multiple people to regulate their interactions by mutual agreement without official interference, even if the consequences are injurious to themselves (Mill 1859: 44). According to an observer, the "right to consent to harm, either self-inflicted or at the hands of other participants, is grounded in the fundamental right to autonomy, liberty, and most importantly, human dignity" (Buchhandler-Rafael 2013: 301). One could also conjecture that a consenting participant cannot thereby be aggrieved (Scoccia 2013).

For proponents of the harm thesis, the identification of an act as harmful to another's interest is a necessary, but not a sufficient, condition to criminalise it (Feinberg 1984). More recently, harm philosophers, such as Douglas Husak and Andrew Simester, add a second element to the criminalisation equation of wrongfulness on the actor's part that is associated with the harm (von Hirsch 2014: 246). Harm philosophers denote another limitation in that criminal law be respectful of privacy interests. As Mill conjectured, "[f]ornication . . . must be tolerated," considering its characteristically intimate nature (Mill 1859: 58). There may be valid reasons to differentiate private versus public acts here. As an example, prostitution conducted in a private setting should not be criminalised, but public solicitation could be (Hart 1963).

Further, even when an act harms another's recognised interest, a weighing is necessary. The costs to society or the intrusiveness to privacy interests of investigating, prosecuting, and penalising a particular conduct may outweigh whatever benefits are likely to be achieved by criminalising it (Feinberg 1984: 15).

Nonetheless, a critic contends that in recent times the harm principle has been stretched so far that the identification of any nontrivial harm seems enough to trigger at least a debate about whether it can rightfully be criminalised (Harcourt 1999). This expansion is at odds with the original theme of the harm principle, which was to set stringent limits on society's right to punish individual behaviour (Buchhandler-Raphael 2013: 13).

The competing philosophy underlying criminalisation is legal moralism. An early prominent conservative to espouse this position was Sir James Fitzjames Stephen in his 1874 text titled *Liberty, Equality, Fraternity*. Under legal moralism, society may prohibit conduct that is immoral (Stephen 1874). Indeed, Sir Stephen considered that in a democracy the majority has the full right and authority to determine which behaviours it considers immoral, and to wage war on such through the state's instrumental power to punish.

Interestingly, legal moralists require some type of harm; they just envisage it differently than the classical harm theorists. Lord Patrick Devlin, a strong moralist advocate, considered immoral acts as wronging society because permitting widespread immorality threatens societal stability (Dworkin 1966). A newer version, known as positive legal moralism, posits that a society ought only to punish what are considered public wrongs (Duff 2014), though there remains debate among adherents as to the exact meaning of public wrongs and how much to rely upon politicians to determine it (Edward & Simester 2017).

For some legal moralism theorists, the conceptualisation of a behaviour as immoral does not necessary mean it should be criminalised. A few caveats have been recognised. One is an understanding that morals can change over time and by country (Stephen 1874: 22). Then, in any given time and locale, the law should punish only when the moral majority is "overwhelming" and the offence can be precisely defined and specifically proven (Stephen 1874: 159). Based as it is on the delimiting criterion of morality, the legislature should not seek to punish immoral behaviour when the intent is not about its immorality, but concerns some other goal, such as paternalism (Moore 2009).

Further, echoing harm theorists here, legislation "ought in all cases whatever scrupulously to respect privacy" (Stephen 1874: 160). For Sir Stephen, a primary example of this was with respect to the internal affairs of a family or with intimate relationships where the intrusion of the law, he opined, was likely to do more harm than good.

Michael Moore, another prominent legal moralistic, similarly thought that a sort of weighing is appropriate to determine if the costs of prohibition outweigh the benefits. Moore conceived that such a weighing would denounce prohibiting acts that are customarily done in private, that do not harm nonconsenting persons (i.e., victimless), and are strongly motivated in the sense that individuals are likely to engage in them despite the existence of a legal prohibition (Moore 2010). As for the latter, a reason not to prohibit an otherwise strongly motivated act is that the costs of enforcement will necessarily be much higher given the law's potentially weak deterrence value.

A major impediment to legal moralism is its orientation toward a societal consensus on what is immoral. There may well be widespread agreement on certain wrongful conduct, such as terrorism and murder. But Western countries tend to be pluralistic, without unity of judgment on many matters regarding morality (Campbell et al. 1969) Thus, political elites may well criminalise acts that otherwise are considered entirely legitimate and normalised in one or more subgroups, who may be offended by what they perceive as unfair labelling (Vuolo 2014).

The foregoing set forth a summary of the main philosophical perspectives on criminalisation. Assume for now that in contemporary times at least some degree of overcriminalisation exists in Western societies. This is not an overly pessimistic assumption considering the many prominent academics who have been weighing in on overcriminalisation crises as of late.[1] In any event, the next subsection considers some of the potential political and social reasons contributing to the overreach by systems of criminal law. We start with the blurring of the civil/criminal divide in terms of the criminalisation of social policies in contemporary times.

### *1.2 Socio-political issues*

From the 1980s onward, many Western countries have witnessed a significant growth of their penal states, which has often been a result of harsher criminal penalties in response to various social problems (Mehrota, Kimball, & Wahab 2016). A primary reason is the political embracing of tough-on-crime schemes meant to address social insecurities in general (Wacquant 2010: 213). While the growth in prison population was greatest in the United States, the leaders of such other countries as England, France, and Italy also ushered in law-and-order platforms (Wacuquant 2010: 213). For example, researchers indicate that the UK Parliament

1 Works of Larkin (2013) and Husak (2011) may serve as examples. This is not to suggest that overcriminalisation or the criminalisation of social policy (as discussed next) has only occurred in recent times. See generally Lacey (2009).

enacted at least 3,000 new criminal offences between 1997 and 2006 (Pantazis 2008) and another 1,760 in 2010–11 alone (McNamara & Quilter 2015).

There is a common method to this morphing of the government's providing civil services into meting out criminal punishments in tackling social problems. The criminalisation of social policy is accomplished by two key social mechanisms: boundary blurring, whereby the purposes of civil services versus criminal interventions are obscured, and displacement of goals, in which a social policy's previous reliance upon social welfare cedes to criminal justice ends (Rodger 2008). As a result, Western governments have become increasingly involved in regulating the minutiae of their citizens' private affairs, albeit through criminal justice initiatives (Pantazis 2008). The overall scheme of criminalising social policy has alternatively been referred to as the state "governing through crime" (Aharonson 2010: 301).

Laws are not passed in a vacuum. It is important to consider legislators as politicians and the role that interests group play. Legislators often have a focus on reelection such that enacting new forms of crime may be perceived as "politically pragmatic criminalisation" (Lacey 2009: 940). Seeking to make political hay, some legislator proposes a new law to make this or that a major felony or to raise the penalty or otherwise tighten the screws. Since other legislators know well that no one can lose voter popularity for seeming to be tough on crime, the legislation sails through in a breeze. That the chances of the legislation working to reduce crime are exceedingly low, and in some cases of it doing harm are very high, scarcely seems to be a relevant issue (Luna 2012: 789).

At times, it may be relevant interest groups who urge the enactment of new crimes to solve the social problem(s) for which the group advocates (Duminică 2014). Some see politicians acting on occasion as mere puppets of special interest groups in this regard (Duminică 2014). The trouble with overcriminalisation is not just a philosophical or political concern. Critics point to more functional consequences. A sense of overreaching with criminal sanctions can engender disrespect for the rule of law (Campbell et al. 1969). It distracts policing and prosecuting resources from pursuing more serious offences (Campbell et al. 1969). An excess of criminal laws additionally can render them unknowable to the public and therefore the underlying acts undeterrable (Duminică 2014). Hence, a criminal law system that is too uncertain cannot properly guide human behaviour and thereby reduces the effectiveness of criminal law as a rule (Stevenson & Harris 2008).

## 2 Coercive control

Criminal offences are typically based on an act that culminates in an identifiable, discrete injury (Youngs 2015). Consider murder and theft in this regard. The distinguishing nature of coercive control legislation is that it eschews this incident-based model. Instead, coercive control is conceptualised, at a high level of abstraction, as a *pattern* and *practice* of behaviours that cause a variety of direct and indirect harms.

### 2.1 *The theory of coercive control*

Coercive control is the term coined to describe an abuser's ongoing and systematic strategy to attain and maintain power and control in an intimate partner relationship (Velonis 2016). Tactics to establish domination may include such efforts as isolating the partner from family and friends (Stark 2012), depriving them of basic resources (e.g., money or transportation, see Dutton, Goodman, & Schmidt 2005), and/or regulating the minutiae of the partner's daily activities (Tanha et al. 2010). Coercive strategies may entail intimidation through violent and nonviolent means, degradation, and/or overt and covert surveillance of the partner's online and offline lives, to name a few (Stark 2012).

Domestic violence experts concede that episodic physical assaults occur in intimate relationships where coercive control does not exist. One attempt at differentiation is to envision threats and violent attacks not primarily for purposes to control as comprising situational violence, while the systemic abuser who uses violence as part of a domineering and controlling campaign represents intimate terrorism (Woodin, Sotskova, & O'Leary 2013).

Indeed, in the intimate terrorism version, violence may not be the main goal or even the principle tactic the abuser uses to maintain power (Dutton et al. 2005). In many cases an intimate terrorist may successfully attain great power so that, over time, violence (or the overt threat of violence) eventually may rarely be required to continue to dominate. The following is one possible scenario:

> The perpetrator may use a combination of physical and non-physical, criminal and non-criminal tactics amounting to a pattern of behaviour that regulates all aspects of the victim's life, with refusals to cooperate leading to punishment. As the victim seeks to avoid repercussions, the perpetrator's rules become internalised by the victim enabling the perpetrator to ensure compliance by use of less and less punishment behaviour. This can be achieved through a gesture or a look or words that have significance to the partners but not to the outside world.
>
> (Bettison 2016: 167–168)

There is, though, no one-size-fits-all model of coercive control, and accordingly no definitive list of tactics and techniques (Velonis 2016). Each abuser develops his own through trial-and-error based on his victim's personal vulnerabilities (Stark 2012). A distinguishing characteristic of coercive control is that the intimacy afforded in an interpersonal relationship furnishes the abuser access to exploit his partner's personal information to exercise power and control (Stark 2012).

Coercive control as a theory is decidedly gendered. This is because one's success in attaining power and control over a partner, at least for heterosexual couples, derives from both macro- and micro-level imbalances and hierarchies based on male–female dichotomies (Velonis 2016).

> The essence of coercive control is that its primarily male offenders exploit persistent sexual inequalities in the economy and in how roles and responsibilities are designated in the home and community to establish a formal regime of domination/subordination behind which they can protect and extend their privileged access to money, sex, leisure time, domestic service, and other benefits.
>
> (Stark 2012: 206)

Thereby, coercive control often entails men micromanaging female partners in their daily activities, "particularly those associated with women's default roles as mothers, homemakers, and sexual partners, and run the gamut from their access to money, food, and transport to how they dress, clean, cook, or perform sexually" (Stark 2012: 201).

The discussion in the next section refers specifically to the new English statute. It should be noted that this is not the first to officially target some forms of coercive control in its criminal law. The state of Tasmania in Australia, for instance, passed a law in 2004 to criminalise certain types of economic abuse (e.g., coercing the other to cede control over assets or withholding necessary financial support) and emotional abuse (a course of conduct "causing mental harm, apprehension or fear") regarding one's spouse or partner (Family Violence Act 2004, ss 8 and 9). As shall be seen next, the English statute is much broader.

### *2.2 Serious Crime Act 2015*

In August 2014, then-Home Secretary Theresa May launched an initiative to evaluate a proposal to criminalise coercive and controlling tactics (Home Office 2014a). Indeed, the doctrine of coercive control had already been incorporated into the government's policy statement on domestic abuse in 2013 (House of Commons 2016). With the proposal, the government issued a consultation – a procedure for seeking input from interested parties. Over 750 responses were received. Overall, 85% of respondents agreed that the law concerning domestic abuse generally should be strengthened, while 55% specifically favoured the proposed new criminal law (Home Office 2014b).

The coercive control offence was easily passed into law as Section 76 of the Serious Crime Act 2015 (House of Commons 2016). The law provides that, where A signifies a perpetrator and B is the victim, that person A commits an offence if (1) A "repeatedly or continuously engages in behaviour . . . that is controlling or coercive" towards person B, (2) to whom A is "personally connected," (3) the behaviour has a serious effect on B, and (4) A knows the behaviour will have a "serious effect" (Serious Crime Act 2015, s.76). The serious effect is further defined as "(a) the victim fearing a violent attack on at least two occasions, or (b) causing the victim 'serious alarm or distress which has a substantial adverse effect' on the victim's daily living. The maximum penalty is five years imprisonment" (Serious Crime Act 2015, s.76).

The Home Office has issued statutory guidance on the new offence, in which the agency confirms there is no exhaustive list of acts or behaviours that would qualify thereunder as coercion or control (Home Office 2015a). The guidance lists 17 bulleted examples, though. Some of these include physical violence that otherwise would be subject to pre-existing criminal laws, which is acknowledged. These include threats to kill, assault, rape, and criminal damage. Importantly, the list also covers non-assaultive acts, among them isolating the partner from family and friends, monitoring their time, controlling day-to-day activities, repeatedly putting them down, enforcing rules which humiliate, and preventing the other from working.

The statute provides a defence. To qualify, the defendant must show that when "engaging in the behaviour in question" he or she believed that they was acting in the other's best interests and the "behaviour was in all the circumstances reasonable" (Serious Crime Act, s.76). A Home Office fact sheet explains the defence attempts to avoid criminalising "ordinary power dynamics in relationships" (Home Office 2015b: 2).

## 3 Analysing the criminalisation of coercive control

We previously summarised the leading political philosophies which impart limiting standards regarding acts rightfully prohibited using the compulsory arm of criminal law. It is appropriate then to analyse coercive control legislation within those realms as the lens for this case study. As a relevant component of such, attention will be paid to whether this is a case of blurring the civil/criminal line in terms of criminalising social policy.

### *3.1 Applying the harm principle*

The classic harm principle requires the existence of an articulable harm infringing another person's right. The coercive control statute is unique in that it forthrightly fails to identify a close-ended list of discrete and clear harmful behaviours that qualify. In Parliamentary discussions on the bill, the solicitor-general declared that it was intended the law not contain an "over-prescriptive statutory definition" (House of Commons 2015: column 188).

Consistent with such an intent, the harm of coercive control is often conveyed in broad terms, such as a Parliamentary member's summary articulation in a house debate that coercive control practices produced "significant cumulative impact on the victim's everyday life, causing them fear, alarm or distress" (House of Commons 2015: column 176). The Home Office's statutory guidance expands upon various physical, psychological, emotional, and economic harms that an abuser can cause his partner to experience from his coercive and controlling actions (Dutton & Goodman 2005). Other commentators more directly assert that these harms impact on a victim's liberty (Stark 1995) and autonomy (Bettinson 2016), each of which represents an important interest which the harm thesis accredits.

Still, strict harm theorists could reasonably challenge these conceptualisations as extending the harm principle beyond reason. Harm theorists such as John Stuart Mill meant to provide a limiting standard, not a malleable one. It is not so certain that the statute addresses only important rights pursuant to the harm principle. Does one really have a *right* to be free from emotional suffering? From psychological distress? Does one enjoy a right not to feel economic pressure – even coercion – from a domestic partner? Realistically, intimate relationships are often fraught with emotional and psychological pain and with tension, even conflict, about the use and management of finances. The concern may be valid that the law criminalises "ordinary power dynamics in relationships," which the limited defence does little to obviate with its burden being placed on the defendant to show he reasonably acted on all charged occasions in his partner's best interests. If these are ordinary power dynamics, then it does not clearly qualify for the wrongdoing prong.

The idea of coercion is also problematic. Coercion is inherently subjective, both on the part of the actor and as perceived by the other (Kuennen 2013). Complicating matters is that personal relationships intrinsically involve components of power, persuasion, and influence (Dutton et al. 2005). Plus, these battles are not necessarily waged just within the dynamics of the partnership; they are also shaped and compelled by external influences, such as the expectations and norms invoked by family, neighbours, religion, and subcultures. Individuals make choices every day that to some degree are influenced by these internal and external pressures. As an illustration, one study found that women surveyed felt that pressures from social conventions on gendered obligations and commitments in a heteronormative marriage caused them to feel controlled in their daily lives (Crossman & Hardesty 2017).

Besides, victims often report feeling pressured and coerced by public officials about how to act, such as leaving their abusers and fully cooperating with authorities (Goodmark 2012). If coercion is so immoral, then why do government agencies do it so often with domestic violence victims? Then it is not as if coercion is necessarily dichotomous in nature – as in the victim was coerced or was not. Instead, coercion lies along a continuum (Kuennen 2013: 14).

The question of consent arises alongside these troubling issues. Oddly, neither the statute nor the statutory guidance addresses the concepts of consent or choice. The harm principle prohibits criminalising conduct against another person who has consented. An individual may not in all circumstances have the legal ability to consent to physical violence, but an adult surely may consent to allowing one's partner to control, in whole or in part, various aspects of their lives and relationship. For instance, one partner may permit the other to control their finances or to be the sole or primary decision maker about daily family activities or the discipline of children.

Likewise, one should have the right to consent to a partner's taking charge of daily activities, approving who the person has contact with, monitoring their time, and preventing them from working, all of which are listed in the Home Office's examples of qualifying behaviours. Consider the occurrence of some or all of these types of concessions which individuals regularly and lawfully make in other contexts. People surrender control over much about their day-to-day lives when they join the armed forces, enter institutional living (e.g. hospital, nursing home, a religious house of worship), enrol in a rehabilitative treatment program, or join a professional sports team. These individuals thereupon abdicate much personal authority for what they must believe is for their better good, despite the strict rules, limitations on movement, dictates on financial expenditures, and emotional baggage their commitments entail.

Entrenched in a libertarian ideal, harm theorists likely would agree that individuals should have the autonomy and liberty to enter into intimate relationships and to orchestrate their entwined lives without state interference (Hanna 2009). The exception would be when the state has a compelling interest to intrude, which is the case with physical violence, an act already outlawed in England.

Harm theorists would likely cringe at the idea of the criminal law so forcefully intruding into the intimate affairs of family life and mostly conducted within the privacy of their homes. Recall that the risk an act may cause harm by infringing upon an individual right is a necessary, but not sufficient, reason to criminally punish it. Under this philosophy a weighing of the costs and benefits is advisable. Such weighing will be considered after reviewing whether the coercive control law is justified under legal moralism as both theories promote this sort of balancing.

### *3.2 Applying legal moralism*

Various advocates for a coercive control offence justify it in legally moralistic terms. Theresa May, when publicly introducing the bill, stated that "it is wrong to put your partner or your family in fear" (Home Office 2014b: 3). In responding to the consultation regarding the advisability of the bill, a police official praised the idea to "recognise the social and personal unacceptability of subjecting someone within an interpersonal relationship to . . . harmful and abusive behaviours" (Home Office 2014b: 7). Other commentators assert that the matter is not as much about victim's rights as it is about protecting the public interest in that coercive control tactics violate a fundamental social value (Bettinson & Bishop 2015).

Nonetheless, it is not so clear that a coercive control crime is acceptable under the philosophy of legal moralism. There is little evidence provided that there is an "overwhelming" moral majority that regards non-physical, coercive or controlling tactics in intimate relationships as morally wrong. The moral majority likely understands, perhaps fosters, unequal power dynamics within relationships, particularly gendered ones. Indeed, almost half of the external responses to the UK's consultation approved the suggested coercive control law (Home Office 2014b), hardly evidence of "overwhelming" moral consensus.

Intimate partner relationships entail two persons navigating their individual and collective contributions, chores, decisions, and plans. Power sharing, or power delegation, is a part of that navigation. Around the world, cultures and subcultures continue to operate in gendered ways in terms of family dynamics. Macro- and micro-level advantages and disadvantages direct, structure, and modify family relations. This means that as far as the concept of coercive control has reached, aspects of it are more normative in some cultures (Candela 2016). At least a few respondents to the consultation were concerned with this aspect. One respondent expressed concern about criminalising traditional power dynamics within intimate relationships (Home Office 2014b: 6). As well, a law enforcement representative rather sardonically lamented that the "law cannot will the existence of good intimate relationships" (Home Office 2014b: 7).

The diffuse nature of the law's inclusion of non-physical acts is troubling from legal and fairness perspectives. Legal moralists require that criminal law be precisely defined and clearly proven. In contrast to these ideals, the coercive control law is open-ended, as is conceded by the Home Office. Also troubling is the Home Office's statutory guidance, which creates more ambiguity in its equivocating that the "types of behaviour associated with coercion or control may or may not constitute a criminal offence in their own right" (Home Office 2015a: 4). This is hardly precise and seems almost self-contradictory.

Violence and physical injuries are relatively easy enough to delimit. Emotional, psychological, and economic harms are far more formidable to define to any reasonable degree (Australia Law Reform Commission 2010). This means that the fine lines that the criminal law ought to make for legal moralists may not be possible here. With respect to economic abuse, as one commentator opined, we should not criminalise the "merely frugal or greedy" (Australia Law Reform Commission 2010: s.13.83). Concerning overcriminalisation generally, another writer muses that an individual may exhibit "mendacity, selfishness, treachery, greed, cruelty, hypocrisy, cowardice," all of which may well be villainous, but that does not mean they also ought to be made felonious (Katz 2002).

Other jurisdictions have confronted barriers to implementation because of issues of clarity. Concerns about the Tasmanian law's reasonable scope are ascribed as to why it took 12 years from the state's enacting offences regarding economic or emotional abuse to bring its first prosecution (Bevin 2016). The Australian Reform Commission declined to recommend a coercive control law, citing "substantial difficulties associated with conceptualising and defining effective and enforceable" offences (Australia Law Reform Commission 2010: s.13.83). Then Northern Ireland early in 2017 considered and then summarily rejected a bill that would criminalise coercive control in intimate relationships for the specific reason that its director of public prosecutions opined it was too abstract to delineate and to prosecute (Gallagher 2017).

Legal moralists, such as Sir James Fitzjames Stephen, would also likely denounce the law's intrusion into the intimate affairs of family life as invasive of privacy and likely to do more harm than good. For his part, Michael Moore counselled that the state should not seek to prohibit acts that are strongly motivated, private, and consensual (Moore 2010). Each of these criteria applies directly to intimate partner relationships. According to Moore, too, the right to liberty "immunize(s) a sphere of action from all state regulation save regulation justified by the most compelling of reasons" (Moore 2010: 763). Moore relates this right of liberty that trumps society's ability to criminalise, giving three examples which are relevant here: (1) individual decisions about one's own life; (2) free speech; and (3) being a parent. The coercive control law intrudes upon the individual decisions of each partner in intimate relationships even if that decision is to cede control. The coercive control law criminalises speech. The Home Office advice cites as representative acts such things as putting the other person down and threats to reveal private information, each of which implicates speech. With respect to the third example, Moore provides a hypothetical of immoral parenting, for which he asserts there is no basis for society to interfere:

> There are many kinds of parental abuse apart from physical and sexual abuse. Some parents make their favouritism between siblings apparent on a daily basis, making the less favoured develop feelings of worthlessness and despair. Some parents when they divorce poison their children against the other parent. Some parents make servants out of their children, others spoil them rotten. Some parents dominate their children's ambition, telling them exactly what they will be in all aspects of life. Some imbue them with religious beliefs that can only be described as deranged, and some simply ignore their children emotionally, leaving them to find what warmth they can in this life . . . [T]hese are deeply immoral behaviors, yet we tend to think that the state should not use the criminal law to punish such wrongs.
>
> (Moore 2010: 764)

Whilst the foregoing passage addresses the parent–child relationship, it is pertinent to intimate partner relationships.

The law is unjustified by legal moralism for another reason. This policy to regulate interpersonal behaviour between consenting adults because it goes against the legislators' judgment that intimate relationships ought to operate in more egalitarian terms basically constitutes paternalism. For legal moralists, paternalism is an insufficient basis to utilise criminal law (Moore 2010: 764).

In sum, the coercive control law appears to violate many of the standards underlying legal moralism. Still, it may be useful to consider other aspects. Both the harm principle and legal moralism are interested, even if an act causes harm or is immoral, respectively, in whether the law's benefits are outweighed by the costs.

### *3.3 Weighing*

Some of the important justifications offered for the new coercive control offence were to increase the number of domestic abuse arrests and to facilitate successful prosecutions in order to protect past and future victims (House of Commons 2015). Yet the net-widening that the new law is likely to cause can have some predictably negative consequences.

Years of experience with criminal justice interventions in domestic disputes should be a reminder that such intrusions yield significant negative consequences for victims. Police involvement in family matters may mean that the victims become the focus of official disapprobation. In many cases, governmental officials respond with scrutiny by judging the victims' competency as mothers and housekeepers, and on their sex and drug habits (Snider 2008: 39).

Expanding the scope of criminal victimisation by delineating greater and more extensive harms through the guise of coercive control may substantially increase victim blaming by police, prosecutors, and community if she failed to leave the controlling relationship (Bettinson & Bishop 2015). Victim blaming may be more likely even if the physical violence has diminished or ended, which might not have been the case before. At the same time, unless the couple is permanently separated, police involvement may mean further abuse is waged on the victim as it may render abusers "more bitter, resentful, misogynous, and significantly less employable" (Snider 2008: 39).

There is another lesson to recall from the earlier fight by feminist groups to pressure police responding to domestic violence calls into making more arrests. In the 1990s, many jurisdictions turned to mandatory or preferred arrest policies (Hester 2012). A common result was a substantial increase in dual arrests, meaning taking into custody both parties in the domestic dispute (Hamel 2011). Domestic violence advocates decried this unintended consequence as further harming victims (Laidler & Mann 2008).

The coercive control offence can only exacerbate this probability of arresting those who are actually victims. The statute itself is so broad and vague that there is a substantial risk that abusers will take to charging their victims with the offence (Department of Justice 2016: 13). Regrettably, actions that she takes in a self-protective mode could otherwise be regarded as coercive or controlling behaviours. Some examples here may be informative. Perhaps in response to her abuser's control of finances, the victim starts to secretly save money; this could in turn be conveyed as her controlling finances by hiding assets from him. Perhaps the abuser is negatively influenced by criminal family and associates causing his wife to discourage such interactions; this could be seen as her isolating him from family and friends.

As a further illustration, the Home Office statutory advice indicates that a type of controlling behaviour is monitoring the other person's activities. Many victims track the whereabouts of their abusers for security reasons. For instance, if she is able to confirm he is away from home, then perhaps it is then safe for her to return. Yet this could be construed under the statute as her monitoring his movements.

Indeed, coercive and controlling behaviours may not be as gendered as assumed by its main theorist. Some studies of samples in the general population indicate that women commonly engage in non-physical abuse against their partners, including psychological and emotionally controlling tactics.[2]

A further trouble regards the deterrence value. The vagueness of the law renders it basically unknowable. Accordingly, it will necessarily lack any strong deterrence value, and therefore likely to be rather ineffective at mitigating coercive control tactics in relationships. Further, the failure of the law to precisely demarcate the illegal acts it prohibits raises the spectre of leaving it to

2 See Hester et al. (2017), Hamberger & Larsen (2015), listing studies, and Tanha et al. (2010).

the arbitrary discretion of individual police officers, thus yielding potentially unequal and unfair enforcement (Doyle 2014).

Overcriminalisation also regards the potential overlap with preexisting statutes. Here, there are significant redundancies. In fact, the Home Office statutory guidance lists over 70 crimes that apply to domestic abuse situations, many of which are addressed again in its examples of coercive and controlling behaviours. The existence of civil law alternatives is relevant as well. At least a few of the agency respondents to the consultation preferred a non-criminal justice response (Home Office 2014b). Again, years of experience now with ramping up criminal justice responses to domestic disputes shows that arrest and punishment often fail to provide practical solutions to the daily realities of abusive relationships (Snider 2008).

In sum, it is eminently reasonable to conclude that weighing means that the costs produced by the coercive control law are greater than its benefits.

### *3.4 Criminalising family dynamics*

The final consideration is whether this coercive control law is an archetype for criminalising social policy. For over a decade now, there has been interest group involvement by feminist scholars and domestic violence advocates in promoting the centrality of coercive control in domestic abuse responses (Kuennen 2013), including in the UK (Bettinson 2016). Woman's Aid and other interest groups specifically campaigned for the coercive control bill (Bowcott 2015). Thus there was interest group involvement, and with their portraying the bill as designed to protect women and children, it may have been politically pragmatic for politicians across parties to assent thereto. This may explain why the politicians appear to have ignored the significant costs of the legislation and their unsupported assertions during Parliamentary debates that the law would deter coercive controllers.

There is also evidence in the UK that suggests a policy of focusing on correcting what is perceived as dysfunctional families in order to improve their economic stability and reduce overall governmental services otherwise assigned thereto (Cooper 2017). A commentator on UK policy provides further guidance:

> Underlying many recent developments in both social and criminal justice policy is a concern that the attenuation of the family as a foundational social institution must be addressed. Whether it is New Labour's focus on the failures of the family through its Children's Plan, or the Conservative focus on the "fractured family", the main site where the worlds of welfare and criminal justice converge is the relationship between the "dysfunctional family" and antisocial behaviour.
>
> (Rodger 2008: 19)

These tactics help explain more specifically the foray into criminalising domestic abuse, rather than the traditional treatment of it as a private affair, though deserving some focused social services. With respect to domestic violence as a threat to the traditional family, such an "agenda transformed the battered women's movement from a social change movement rooted in feminisms to services focused on individualized treatment and efficiency through criminalisation of [domestic violence]" (Mehrota et al. 2016: 154). This is exemplary of boundary blurring of civil/criminal spheres. Notice, too, that reforms such as these aimed to protect marginalised women feeds the focus of treating the social stratification of gender under criminal law, which alleviates responsibility therefor by broader social and economic structural disparities that play a role in domestic abuse (Aharonson 2010).

Perhaps for many of the reasons underlying the criticisms provided herein, the new coercive control law does not yet seem overly successful. A recent survey conducted by BBC Radio regarding the first 15 months the English coercive control statute was in force found just 202 persons charged under the coercive control statute, with 45 convictions (BBC Radio 2017). Of course, this could simply mean that police agencies need more time to train and incorporate new investigatory techniques. But it is at least equally as likely that police forces and prosecutors are themselves facing obstacles in articulating what behaviours and harms are justifiably entrenched in the new offence.

## 4 Conclusion

This chapter does not question that the proponents of England's coercive control law and the legislators who voted for it had a positive idealism for protecting victims from coercive intimate partners. Nor does it express doubt that the state should play a role in offering support and services to victims suffering from noxious partners. The question is whether the offence presents a case study of overcriminalisation, and the conclusion here is in the affirmative.

## References

Aharonson, E. (2010) '"Pro-Minority" Criminalization and the Transformation of Visions of Citizenship in Contemporary Liberal Democracies: A Critique', *New Criminal Law Review* 13(2), 286–308.

Australia Law Reform Commission (2010) *A National Legal Response*, ALRC Report 114) www.alrc.gov.au/publications/family-violence-national-legal-response-alrc-report-114 [accessed 02/02/2019].

BBC Radio (2017) 'Coercive Control', BBC Radio, 23 April www.bbc.co.uk/sounds/play/b08mv17j [accessed 02/02/2019].

Bettinson, V. (2016) 'Criminalising Coercive Control in Domestic Violence Cases: Should Scotland Follow the Path of England and Wales?', *Criminal Law Review* 3, 165–180.

Bettinson, V. and Bishop, C. (2015) 'Is the Creation of a Discrete Offence of Coercive Control Necessary to Combat Domestic Violence?', *Northern Ireland Law Quarterly* 66, 179–197.

Bevin, E. (2016) 'Tasmanian Man Accused of Preventing Wife from Making Decisions, Accessing Joint Accounts', *ABC News* www.abc.net.au/news/2016-08-01/tasmanian-man-prosecuted-for-alleged-economic-abuse/7679922 [accessed 02/02/2019].

Bowcott, O. (2015) 'Controlling or Coercive Domestic Abuse to Risk Five-Year Prison Term', *The Guardian*, 28 December www.theguardian.com/society/2015/dec/29/domestic-abuse-law-controlling-coercive-behaviour [accessed 02/02/2019].

Buchhandler-Raphael, M. (2013) 'Drugs, Dignity, and Danger: Human Dignity as a Constitutional Constraint to Limit Overcriminalization', *Tennessee Law Review* 80, 291–345.

Campbell, J.S., Sahid, J.R., and Stang, D.P. (1969) *Law and Order Reconsidered: A Report of the Task Force on Law and Law Enforcement*, Washington D.C., United States Government Printing Office.

Candela, K. (2016) 'Protecting the Invisible Victim: Incorporating Coercive Control in Domestic Violence Statutes', *Family Court Review* 54, 112–125.

Cooper, M. (2017) *Family Values: Between Neoliberalism and the New Social Conservatism*, Brooklyn, Zone Books.

Crossman, K.A. and Hardesty, J.L. (2017) 'Placing Coercive Control at the Center', *Psychology of Violence* 8, 196–206.

Department of Justice (2016) *Domestic Abuse Offence and Domestic Violence Disclosure Scheme – A Consultation: Summary of Responses*, www.justice-ni.gov.uk/sites/default/files/consultations/justice/domestic-abuse-offence-domestic-violence-disclosure-scheme-summary-of-responses.pdf [accessed 02/02/19].

Douglas, H. (2015) 'Do We Need a Specific Violence Offence?', *Melbourne University Law Review* 39(2), 434–371.

Doyle, J. (2014) 'Controlling Your Partner's Clothes and Friends Could be Made a Crime in Domestic Violence Shake-up', *Daily Mail* www.dailymail.co.uk/news/article-2574412/Call-make-controlling-behaviour-forcing-spouse-wear-certain-clothes-criminal-offence-domestic-violence-laws-shake-up.html [accessed 02/02/2019].

Duff, R.A. (2014) 'Towards a Modest Legal Moralism', *Criminal Law & Philosophy* 8(1), 217–235.

Duminică, R. (2014) 'Excessive Legislation: Cause of Legal Devaluation and Consequence of Ineffectiveness of Institutions Involved in the Legislative Process', *Law Annals Titu Maiorescu University* 2014, 66–84.

Dutton, M.A. and Goodman, L.A. (2005) 'Coercion in Intimate Partner Violence: Toward a New Conceptualization', *Sex Roles* 52, 743–756.

Dutton, M.A., Goodman, L., and Schmidt, R.J. (2005) *Development and Validation of a Coercive Control Measure for Intimate Partner Violence*, COSMOS Corporation www.ncjrs.gov/pdffiles1/nij/grants/214438.pdf [accessed 02/02/19].

Dworkin, R. (1966) 'Lord Devlin and the Enforcement of Morals', *Yale Law Journal* 75(6), 986–1005.

Edwards, J. and Simester, A. (2017) 'What's Public About Crime?', *Oxford Journal of Legal Studies* 37, 105–133.

Feinberg, J. (1984) *The Moral Limits of the Criminal Law: Harm to Others*, Vol. 1, Oxford, Oxford University Press.

Gallagher, C. (2017) 'Domestic Violence Bill Will Not Be Specific on Abuse of Partner', *Irish Times* www.irishtimes.com/news/social-affairs/domestic-violence-bill-will-not-be-specific-on-abuse-of-partner-1.3069039 [accessed 02/02/2019].

Goodmark, L. (2012) *A Troubled Marriage*, New York, New York University Press.

Hamberger, L.K. and Larsen, S.E. (2015) 'Men's and Women's Experience of Intimate Partner Violence', *Journal of Family Violence* 30, 699–717.

Hamel, J. (2011) 'In Dubious Battle: The Politics of Mandatory Arrest and Dominant Aggressor Laws', *Partner Abuse* 2, 224–245.

Hanna, C. (2009) 'The Paradox of Progress: Translating Evan Stark's Coercive Control into Legal Doctrine for Abused Women', *Violence Against Women* 15, 1458–1474.

Harcourt, B.E. (1999) 'Criminal Law: The Collapse of the Harm Principle', *Journal of Criminal Law & Criminology* 90, 109–194.

Hart, H.L.A. (1963) *Law, Liberty and Morality*, Stanford, Stanford University Press.

Hester, M. (2012) 'Portrayal of Women as Intimate Partner Domestic Violence Perpetrators', *Violence Against Women* 18, 1067–1082.

Hester, M., Jones, C., Williamson, E., Fahmy, E., and Feder, G. (2017) 'Coercive Controlling Violence? A Cross-Sectional Domestic Violence and Abuse Survey of Men Attending General Practice in England', *Psychological Violence* 3, 417–427.

Home Office (2014a) *Strengthening the Law on Domestic Abuse*, Home Office www.gov.uk/government/uploads/system/uploads/attachment_data/file/344674/Strengthening_the_law_on_Domestic_Abuse_-_A_Consultation_WEB.PDF [accessed 02/01/19].

Home Office (2014b) *Strengthening the Law on Domestic Abuse Consultation-Summary of Responses*, Home Office www.gov.uk/government/uploads/system/uploads/attachment_data/file/389002/StrengtheningLawDomesticAbuseResponses.pdf [accessed 02/02/2019].

Home Office (2015a) *Controlling or Coercive Behaviour in an Intimate or Family Relationship: Statutory Guidance Framework*, Home Office www.gov.uk/government/uploads/system/uploads/attachment_data/file/482528/Controlling_or_coercive_behaviour_-_statutory_guidance.pdf [accessed 02/01/2019].

Home Office (2015b) *Serious Crime Act 2015 Fact Sheet: Domestic Abuse Offence*, Home Office https://assets.publishing.service.gov.uk/government/uploads/system/uploads/attachment_data/file/416011/Fact_sheet_-_Domestic_Abuse_Offence_-_Act.pdf [accessed 04/21/2019].

House of Commons (2015) *Serious Crime Bill*, House of Commons Public Bill Committee January, www.publications.parliament.uk/pa/cm201415/cmpublic/seriouscrime/150120/pm/150120s01.pdf [accessed 02/02/2019].

House of Commons (2016) *Briefing Paper on Domestic Violence in England and Wales*, No. 6337, prepared by J. Woodhouse and N. Dempsey, Home of Commons https://southwestlincolnshireccg.nhs.uk/about-us/key-documents/safeguarding-1/domestic-abuse-1/domestic-abuse-documents/1311-house-of-commons-dv-briefing-paper/file [accessed 02/02/2019].

Husak, D. (2011) 'Reservations About Overcriminalization', *New Criminal Law Review* 14(1) 97–107.

Katz, L. (2002) 'Villainy and Felony: A Problem Concerning Criminalization', *Buffalo Criminal Law Review* 6, 451–482.

Kuennen, T.L. (2013) 'Analyzing the Impact of Coercion on Domestic Violence Victims: How Much is Too Much?', *Berkeley Journal on Gender, Law & Justice* 22, 2–30.

Lacey, N. (2009) 'Historicising Criminalisation: Conceptual and Empirical Issues', *The Modern Law Review* 72(6), 936–960.

Laidler, K.J. and Mann, R.M. (2008) 'Anti-Feminist Backlash and Gender-Relevant Crime Initiatives in the Global Context', *Feminist Criminology* 3, 79–81.

Larkin, P.J. (2013) 'Public Choice Theory and Overcriminalization', *Harvard Journal of Law & Public Policy* 36, 715–793.

Luna, E. (2005) 'The Overcriminalization Phenomena', *American University Law Review* 54(3), 703–743.

Luna, E. (2012) 'Prosecutorial Decriminalization', *Journal of Criminal Law & Criminology* 102(3), 785–820.

McNamara, J. and Quilter, J. (2015) 'Institutional Influences on the Parameters of Criminalisation: Parliamentary Scrutiny of Criminal Law Bills in New South Wales', *Current Issues in Criminal Justice* 27(1), 21–40.

Mehrota, G.R., Kimball, E., and Wahab, S. (2016) 'The Braid that Binds Us: The Impact of Neoliberalism, Criminalization, and Professionalization on Domestic Violence Work', *Affilia: Journal of Women & Social Work* 31, 153–163.

Mill, J.S. (1859) *On Liberty*, London, Longmans, Green & Co.

Moore, M.S. (2009) 'A Tale of Two Theories', *Criminal Justice Ethics* 28, 27–48.

Moore, M.S. (2010) *Placing Blame: A Theory of Criminal Law*, Oxford, Oxford University Press.

Pantazis, C. (2008) 'The Problem with Criminalisation', *Criminal Justice Matters* 74(1), 10–12.

Rodger, J.J. (2008) 'The Criminalisation of Social Policy', *Criminal Justice Matters* 74(1), 18–20.

Scoccia, D. (2013) 'In Defense of "Pure" Legal Moralism', *Criminal Law & Philosophy* 7(3): 513–530.

Snider, L. (2008) 'Criminalising Violence Against Women: Solution or Dead End?', *Criminal Justice Matters* 74, 38–39.

Stark, E. (1995) 'Re-Presenting Woman Battering: From Battered Woman Syndrome to Coercive Control', *Albany Law Review* 58, 973–1026.

Stark, E. (2012) 'Looking Beyond Domestic Violence: Policing Coercive Control', *Journal of Police Crisis Negotiations* 12, 199–217.

Stephen, J.F. (1874) *Liberty, Equality, Fraternity*, London, Smith, Elder & Co.

Stevenson, K. and Harris, C. (2008) 'Inaccessible and Unknowable: Accretion and Uncertainty in Modern Criminal Law', *Liverpool Law Review* 29, 247–267.

Tanha, M., Beck, C.J., Figuerendo, A.J., and Raghavan, C. (2010) 'Sex Differences in Intimate Partner Violence and the Use of Coercive Control as a Motivational Factor for Intimate Partner Violence', *Journal of Interpersonal Violence* 25(10), 1836–1854.

Velonis, A.J. (2016) '"He Never Did Anything You Typically Think of as Abuse": Experiences with Violence in Controlling and Non-Controlling Relationships in a Non-Agency Sample of Women', *Violence Against Women* 22(9), 1031–1054.

von Hirsch, A. (2014) 'Harm and Wrongdoing in Criminalisation Theory', *Criminal Law & Philosophy* 8(1), 245–256.

Vuolo, M. (2014) 'Incorporating Consensus and Conflict into the Legitimacy of Law', *Crime Law & Social Change* 62(2), 155–170.

Wacquant, L. (2010) 'Crafting the Neoliberal State: Workfare, Prisonfare, and Social Insecurity', *Sociological Forum* 25(2) 1970–2220.

Woodin, E.M., Sotskova, A., and O'Leary, K.D. (2013) 'Intimate Partner Violence Assessment in an Historical Context: Divergent Approaches and Opportunities for Progress', *Sex Roles: A Journal of Research* 69(3–4), 120–130.

Youngs, J. (2015) 'Domestic Violence and the Criminal Law: Reconceptualising Reform', *Journal of Criminal Law* 79(1), 55–70.

# 14 Individualism in times of crisis

## Theorising a shift away from classic liberal attitudes to human rights post 9/11

*Ian Turner*

### Introduction

If asked 'what are human rights?', rather than give an erudite, conceptual reply about the nature and significance of fundamental freedoms, a person is very likely to give examples of rights, drawing on the Universal Declaration of Human Rights (UDHR) for inspiration. The UDHR was proclaimed by the United Nations General Assembly in 1948 as 'a common standard of achievements for all peoples and all nations' (UNGA 1948). It consists of freedoms that people associate with the 'first generation'[1] of rights such as: the right to life, liberty and security of person, Article 3; no one shall be held in slavery and servitude, Article 4; and no one shall be subjected to torture or to cruel, inhuman or degrading treatment or punishment, Article 5. The UDHR also consists of rights that people associate with the 'second generation' such as: the right to work, to free choice of employment, to just and favourable conditions of work and to protection against unemployment, Article 23(1); everyone has the right to a standard of living adequate for the health and well-being of himself and of his family, Article 25(1); and everyone has the right to education, Article 26(1). The UDHR also consists of rights that people associate with the 'third generation' such as: everyone is entitled to a social and international order in which the rights and freedoms set forth in this Declaration can be fully realised, Article 28. Whilst some commentators have claimed that the UDHR is a source of customary international law (Steiner, Alston and Goodman 2007: 161), the majority of opinion, supported, by, for example, the ruling of the US Supreme Court in *Sosa v. Alvarez-Machain* 542 U.S. 692, 734 (2004), is that it is not (Posner 2014a). Thus, whilst the collection of rights contained in the UDHR is non-justiciable, specific rights located within the Declaration are in fact enforceable before the courts.

Using justiciability as an indicator of the primacy of a freedom within a catalogue of human rights, we can see that the first generation – 'civil and political rights' – clearly prevails. Although only a regional document, the European Convention on Human Rights (ECHR) is a classic source of justiciable, first generation rights, in that it permits individuals to make applications to the European Court of Human

1 The phrase 'generation of rights' is commonly attributed to the French jurist Karel Vasak (1977).

Rights (ECtHR) in Strasbourg, as per Article 34 of the ECHR. For example, over 93,000 applications by nationals alleging breaches of the Convention against their home countries were processed by the ECtHR in 2017 (Council of Europe 2018: 9). Indeed, when the United Kingdom, this author's country, wished to give a collection of human rights the force of law within the Human Rights Act 1998, it drew on the ECHR for encouragement, incorporating the rights directly into domestic law. 'Second generation' rights, that is, 'socio-economic rights', can be located in, for example, the International Covenant on Economic, Social and Cultural Rights (ICESCR). In addition to non-justiciability, the rights contained in ICESCR are not 'immediate', unlike freedoms from the first generation. According to Article 2(1) of the ICESCR, each state party only undertakes to take steps to achieve 'progressively' the full realisation of the rights recognised in the Covenant. The full realisation of second generation rights is also qualified in Article 2(1) by the phrase 'to the maximum of its available resources', further emphasising the supremacy of first generation rights over other generational ones. Thus, for the purposes of this chapter (at least for the time being), first generation freedoms are synonymous with the phrase 'human rights'.

Human rights are justiciable and immediate. Conceptually, they are 'negative' i.e. 'freedoms from' the state, such as 'freedom from' torture and 'freedom from' slavery. (Indeed, 'freedoms from', such as freedom from torture and slavery, are especially important justifying international conventions of their own: the UN Convention Against Torture (UNCAT) and the Slavery Convention respectively.) These 'negative' freedoms reflect traditional liberal fears that the state is a threat to the security of the individual.[2] Such fears are often attributed to the English philosopher, John Locke, and his *Second Treatise of Government* in particular (Locke 2011). Locke sought to effect a civil authority that maintained collective peace and order. Pre-the institution of civil authority, man lived in the 'state of nature' – 'a state of liberty' – which was a state of 'perfect freedom' and 'equality' (Locke 2011: Chapter II)[3] and 'peace, good will, mutual assistance, and preservation' (Locke 2011: Chapter III). Human rights for Locke, which he classified as 'life, liberty, and estate (property)', were very important. They were 'natural' and individual, conferred by God (Locke 2011: Chapter IX). But in the absence of security in the 'state of nature' to protect individuals' natural rights

2 In this chapter the author uses the term 'liberal' loosely. Here he positions John Locke as one of the founders of liberalism. But to be more precise, Locke would now be considered as a 'libertarian'. The following commentators epitomise modern libertarianism: Hayek (1960); Friedman (1962); and Nozick (1974). Libertarians support a minimal role for the state such as enforcing contracts, protecting private property from theft and keeping the peace. That is, in the name of human freedom, they oppose government regulation and favour unfettered markets. People should do whatever they want with their things as long as they respect other peoples' rights to do so – see, for example: Sandel (2010: 58–74).

3 Locke did qualify this, however: 'But though this be a state of liberty, yet is not a state of licence: though man in the state have an uncontrollable liberty to dispose of his person or his possessions . . . the state of nature has *a law of nature* . . . which obliges every one . . . that being all equal and independent, [not] to harm another in his life, health, liberty, or possessions' (Chapter II, my italics).

from those who sought to deny them, it was necessary for individuals to covenant – a 'social contract' – with a civil authority, a sovereign, to guarantee these rights.[4] With Locke reluctantly transitioning to a civil authority from the perfect freedom of the state of nature, it is unsurprising therefore that he approached the new sovereign with suspicion. So Locke advocated a minimal state whose power was limited to its preservation and could not be used 'to destroy, enslave, or designedly to impoverish the subjects' (Locke 2011: Chapter XI). Thus, in addition to emphasising the primacy of the individual, the classic liberal approach to the state as a guarantor of rights, but, perhaps more importantly, as a possible violator of rights, is a significant influence on the predominant idea of liberties as being 'freedoms from' the state. But since the 9/11 attacks, for example, in New York and Washington, by Al-Qaeda, and now the growing threat of Islamic State in Syria and Iraq, as well as Boko Haram in Nigeria, is the state still the principal threat to the security of the individual? Are human rights being violated much more by non-state actors such as suspected terrorists?

In 2017 the UK, for example, was the victim of several terror attacks from individuals with alleged links to Islamist groups: an atrocity committed on Westminster Bridge in London in March, where the attacker drove his car along the bridge deliberately killing 4 people and injuring a further 50; a similar incident occurred on London Bridge in June, where the attackers, having to abandon their van, ran at pedestrians at a nearby market, fatally stabbing 8 and injuring a further 40. And there was also a suicide bombing at an Ariana Grande concert in Manchester in May – the worst terror atrocity committed in the UK since '7/7' – killing 22 people and injuring a further 500. In addition, a bomb was left on a tube train at Parsons Green, west London, in September, but failed to fully explode. A further nine terrorist attacks, in 2017, were prevented (Johnston 2017). Recently, Andrew Parker, the director-general of MI5, the UK's Security Service, said that Britain was facing its most severe terrorist threat ever and fresh attacks in the country were 'inevitable' (Dodd 2017). The UK's terror threat level is currently at 'severe', meaning an attack is highly likely. Twice in 2017 it was raised to its maximum level, 'critical', meaning an attack was imminent, after the Manchester and Parsons Green attacks. The severe terror threat from non-state actors to the UK is real and set to continue.

The UK can expect further terror atrocities and further high profile arrests. Those that are detained will claim their human rights: the right to liberty, for example – the right to be either released or charged in a matter of days; and the right to a fair trial – the right to either challenge one's pre-charge detention, or, if one is charged, the right to be tried by an independent and impartial court or tribunal. But in the so-called 'War on Terror', many, particularly those in the media, see human rights as merely obstructions to countering terrorism. There are several headlines in the *Daily Mail*, for example, supporting this claim: 'Sorry,

4 The type of security provided by civil government was, for Locke, established laws, a body invested with the power of executing those laws and an independent arbiter to adjudicate on those laws.

human rights DO shield terrorists' (Daily Mail Comment 2017); 'PM vows to rip up human rights laws in war on terror' (Tapsfield 2017); and 'An insult to terror victims' (Bentley 2017), being just a few examples. Reviewing the comments section for one of these articles, one finds reader remarks such as: 'As usual, HIS "human rights" are considered to be MORE IMPORTANT than the lives of his potential victims'; 'Put British human rights ahead of those who are trying to murder us'; 'I really couldn't care less about his human rights, it's time we looked after this country's citizens' human rights, by weeding out these cockroaches'; and 'blow his human rights, what about ours?' (Bentley 2017). The common idea that freedoms are merely a vehicle to secure the 'undeserving' rights of terror suspects, for example, over the 'deserving' rights of victims has arguably contributed to a significant disengagement with the nature of rights. But even terror suspects are not best served by human rights either. According to the *Global Terrorism Index 2016*, significant factors causing terrorism, particularly in Europe, are socio-economic ones – inequality and youth unemployment – and drug crime (Institute for Economics and Peace 2016: 70). Indeed, other studies focusing on particular organisations or recruits from particular regions or cultures outside of Europe have found some common characteristics among individuals: exclusion and forms of discrimination (Institute for Economics and Peace 2016: 65). Similar findings were presented in the 2017 Index: 'Individuals whose expectations for social mobility and economic welfare have been frustrated are at a greater risk of radicalisation' (Institute for Economics and Peace 2017: 65). Moreover, in *Changes in Modus Operandi of Islamic State Revisited*, for Europol, the vast majority of terrorist attackers in Europe have been young men with a criminal past – not just a history of drug crime – who were not strict Muslims and only recently converted to Islam (Europol 2016: 8). Indeed, the *Global Terrorism Index 2017* states:

> Terrorist organisations have also recruited many fighters with extensive criminal backgrounds . . . A study across Europe found that 57% of individuals had been in jail prior to becoming radicalised while 31% of incarcerated individuals began the radicalisation process while in jail.
>
> (Institute for Economics and Peace 2017: 66)

The attacker responsible for the terror attack on Westminster Bridge in London in March 2017, for example, Khalid Masood, born Adrian Russell Ajao, was a Muslim convert, of African-Caribbean descent, with a history of violence spanning 20 years (Booth and Parveen 2017).

'Joe Public', or at least a typical reader of the *Daily Mail*, is contemptuous of human rights, especially in the so-called 'War on Terror'; the rights of a terror suspect apparently trump the rights of the general public. It will also be recalled that the classic liberal idea views human rights as protectors of the individual from the state. With an emphasis on the individual comes, for liberals, a natural corresponding scepticism towards increases in state power. Are human rights eschewing genuine efforts by the state to address drivers of terrorism, particularly in the West: discrimination, marginalisation and joblessness? Is there therefore a 'crisis' within human rights? On the one hand, there is a disengagement with rights since, in seemingly benefitting an undeserving minority, they are too individualistic and insufficiently majoritarian; and on the other hand, ironically, whilst suspected terrorists are accused (wrongly) of exploiting rights, freedoms are in fact too selfish and insufficiently inclusive, compromising security. Poor old human rights! It is time, therefore, for a 'rethink' about the nature and significance of human rights post 9/11, or at least move the discussion away from its traditional liberal, first generation foundations, which, for the purposes of this chapter, are insufficiently attentive to increases in state power pursuing legitimate collective goals. To that end, the next section of this piece will assess human rights (or at least those that rely on their enforceability by the courts) through the lens of critical legal theory, and critical legal studies in particular. Once legitimate criticisms have been raised about human rights as claims in law, this chapter will continue to assess human rights, theoretically, but from the perspective of communitarian ideals, since, in this author's opinion, critical legal theory can only take the debate so far – communitarianism is a natural, critical progression. Following communitarian critiques of liberal attitudes to rights, the African Charter on Human and Peoples' Rights (ACHPR) is examined. This positions human rights, it is believed, more appropriately within the clashes presented above.

## 1 Critical legal theory and its attitudes towards human rights

The most significant feature of critical legal theory is its rejection of what it is taken to be the natural order of things, be it the free market, patriarchy or the conception of race (Wacks 2014: 214). The myth of determinacy in the law is a significant component of the critical assault on law. Far from being a determinate, coherent body of rules and doctrine, the law is depicted as uncertain, ambiguous and unstable (Wacks 2014: 214). One critical legal theorist, however, Jack M. Balkin proposes an 'ambivalent' approach to the law, which recognises both the beneficial and harmful aspects of the law (Balkin 2009: 65). For Balkin, whilst powerful people have 'used law to subordinate others and secure their own interests' under the guise of promoting laudable goals like freedom, equality, liberty, consent, community and human dignity, he believes that, by choosing to speak in the language of law, powerful people and interests can sometimes be called to account, because they try to legitimate what they are doing in these terms (Balkin 2009: 68). In supporting an 'ambivalent' approach to the law, Balkin, perhaps unsurprisingly shows a fidelity to rights within his writings, particularly in times of crisis (Balkin 2008: 15–17).[5]

Within critical legal theory there is critical legal studies (CLS). For CLS, law is 'simply politics dressed in different garb' (Hutchinson and Monahan 1984: 206);

5 See also, for example: Balkin (1990, 1991).

it neither operates in a historical vacuum nor exists independently of ideological struggles in society (Hutchinson and Monahan 1984: 206). CLS also believes that legal doctrine not only does not, but also cannot, generate determinant results in concrete cases (Hutchinson and Monahan 1984: 206), meaning it can be 'manipulated' to justify an almost 'infinite spectrum of possible outcomes' (Hutchinson and Monahan 1984: 206).[6] Thus, in emphasising the manipulation of the law, Mark Tushnet, for example, rejects the idea of an autonomous and neutral mode of legal reasoning (Tushnet 1984a: 239).[7] Behind this veil of seeming neutrality, Tushnet believes that the law is merely synonymous with the principles of liberalism and the emphasis on the individual (Tushnet 1984a: 240). Liberal legalism, for CLS scholars, represents the status quo in society and it seeks to mask the injustice of the system (McCoubrey and White 1999: 216). With this apparent bias within the law, it is perhaps natural, therefore, for Tushnet and others to attack a 'darling' of liberalism: human rights (Tushnet 1984b).[8] It is within this CLS assessment of liberalism, and especially its critique of human rights, that this chapter begins to position a theoretical re-engagement with rights away from their classic liberal traditions and the related controversies presented hitherto.

Following CLS's criticisms with the law more generally, one finds many of these applicable to justiciable rights in particular. First, CLS scholars such as Mark Tushnet believe that the language of legal rights is open and indeterminate (Tushnet 1984b: 1371). Within a human rights claim, there is commonly a 'balancing' exercise – a trade-off between an individual's rights, such as free speech or freedom of assembly, and the legitimate interests of the state such as prevention of disorder and crime or national security (as per Articles 10 and 11 of the ECHR, for example). Tushnet believes for there to be an effective balancing exercise by the courts, competing interests must be reduced to some common measure of value, but in many instances this is simply not possible (Tushnet 1984b: 1371). Indeed, there is often a trade-off between rights which have a

6 Here one may wish to look further at the indeterminacy thesis. If one subscribes to the idea that laws have nothing to do with how cases are decided, that is, they are just window dressing that skilful lawyers and judges can manipulate to justify any decision they please, then this is indeed 'indeterminacy'. However, if a court is faced with a multifarious number of possible legal outcomes, meaning that a judge will simply have to decide for one party rather than another, then to be precise, this is 'underdeterminacy' rather than 'indeterminacy' – see, for example: Solum (2018). Solum states: 'The distinction between indeterminacy and underdeterminacy is rarely observed in the indeterminacy debate, but it is nonetheless important to assessing the debate. Claims that the law is radically indeterminate are implausible, but more modest claims about underdeterminacy may both be defensible and play a role in a radical critique of liberal legal theory'.

7 In its rejection of the neutrality in legal reasoning, there is maybe very little to distinguish CLS from the earlier 'American legal realism' of, for example, Karl Llewellyn and Jerome Frank. But, according to Tushnet, whilst the realists accepted the indeterminacy of legal reasoning, they remained firmly committed to liberalism. And whilst they wanted a better understanding of how the law worked, they wanted to make the existing processes work better – not reject them (1984a: 239). For other references to Tushnet's CLS 'credo', see, for example, Tushnet (1986, 1990).

8 But Tushnet does still believe citizens need protecting from the state, especially post 9/11 – see: Tushnet (2005).

similar level of constitutional protection. Which right does the court give greater priority (Tushnet 1984b: 1373)?

Drawing further on the indeterminacy argument within the law, Tushnet questions the 'utility of rights'. To say that rights are politically useful is to say that they do something, yet, for Tushnet, to say that rights are indeterminate is to say that one cannot know whether a claim of right will do anything (Tushnet 1984b: 1384). This suggests an indifference towards rights but in some circumstances Tushnet is much more explicit in his criticisms. In some situations, such as the emphasis on free speech in the First Amendment of the US Constitution, Tushnet believes that rights, rather than 'not doing much good', are positively 'harmful' (Tushnet 1984b: 1386). He believes:

> I have yet to run across a decent argument that access to sexually explicit material of the sort protected by the [Supreme Court's] obscenity decisions is itself a positive good. In the free press/fair trial controversy, the present balance between the interests of defendants and victims, on the one side, and the morbid curiosity of the press, on the other, is not obviously correct.
> (Tushnet 1984b: 1386)

In a separate article Tushnet further explores the criticisms of rights stated above. He claims that the discourse of rights reflects and produces a kind of isolated individualism (Tushnet 1993: 27). And on the indeterminacy thesis, and its corresponding rejection of neutrality, Tushnet claims that 'nothing whatever follows from a court's adoption of some legal rule . . . except the ideological dimension with which the critique of rights is concerned' (Tushnet 1993: 32).[9] Indeed, for Tushnet, legal victories can actually impede political goals. The victory may make those who won it complacent while galvanising their opponents to do all they can to minimise the effects of the ruling (Tushnet 1993: 30).

More recent critics of human rights law include Hurst Hannum (Hannum 2016), Dominique Clement and Eric Posner. Clement, for example, is concerned about conflating every grievance as a human right; illiteracy, poverty, lack of health care should be framed as violators of social justice rather than rights. The language of human rights, for Clement, means the law, which is an 'ineffective solution to a systematic social problem' (Clement 2018a: 160).[10] Moreover, the existence of a legal right must be premised on the ability of the state and society to guarantee such rights. Resources are limited, and any attempt to recognise all rights in an era of rights inflation forces people to prioritise some rights claims above others (Clement 2018a: 160). In contrast, Posner frames his criticism of rights at the international level in particular. For Posner the international legal effort to force countries to protect human

9 Tushnet uses the same words in another article, in attacking liberal legalism more generally – see: Tushnet (1981: 425).

10 See also Clement (2018b). To continue the debate about the so-called benefits of increasing human rights claims more broadly, see: Wellman (1998).

rights has failed; there is little evidence that countries that ratify human rights treaties improve their human rights performance (Posner 2014b).[11]

Thus far, addressing the apparent 'crisis' within human rights, especially post 9/11, the author maybe ought not to do so through the lens of critical legal theory: a preponderance of critical legal theory, and its criticism of human rights in particular, suggests a rejection of rights as a tool for remedying the challenges presented hitherto. However, Tushnet is not entirely dismissive of rights: he only says that a critique of rights must caution against an overestimation of the significance of legal victories and the contributions lawyers can make to social progress (Tushnet 1993: 25). Indeed, within his 'disutility' criticism of human rights, Tushnet attacks the predominance of 'negative' rights, suggesting an openness to other rights. He believes that people usually agree that the present balance between negative and 'positive' rights i.e. 'rights to', such as the 'right to work', is 'askew' and that positive rights should be created or strengthened. Yet it may be impossible to carry out that programme. In the US, for example, the language of negative rights supports a sharp distinction between the 'threatening public sphere' and the 'comforting private one'. Tushnet therefore opposes the 'contemporary rhetoric of rights' which speaks primarily to negative ones (Tushnet 1984b: 1392). Thus, employing a CLS approach, greater weight should be attached to other generations of rights, not only because of the first generation's strong association with the law and the courts, but also because of their traditional liberal foundations.

Furthermore, if we were to continue to defend addressing the challenges posed in this chapter from a critical legal perspective, there are many other arguments from that tradition that can be presented in support. For example, in addition to the 'ambivalent' approaches to the law already expressed by Balkin (2009),[12] there are also scholars of feminist jurisprudence and critical race theory, such as Elizabeth Schneider (1986) and Kimberle Crenshaw (1988), who believe that human rights claims are among the few resources that disempowered people have. Indeed, within the Marxist tradition, a philosophy well renowned for its rejection of liberalism, legal scholars such as Paul O'Connell defend rights, since, for O'Connell, social movements around the world 'continue to frame their struggles and demands, at least partly, through the language of human rights' (O'Connell 2018: 963).[13] Thus, this piece will continue to defend a re-engagement with freedoms from the perspective of human rights claims, acknowledging the legitimate concerns of CLS.

11 See also: Posner (2014c) and Hathaway (2001–2).

12 Within critical legal theory Balkin is not alone in having an ambivalent approach towards the law – see, for example: Hunt (1987). Hunt, who believes CLS is synonymous with critical legal theory (1987: 5), and therefore can be labelled as a CLS scholar, says: 'It is a travesty of the critical school to allege that their project is to show law in its worst light. A distinctive feature of critical scholarships is a deep perplexity about law. We perceive law as involving both negative and positive characteristics' (1987: 11). For a much more detailed discussion of Hunt's approach to CLS, see, for example: Hunt (1986).

13 There are scholars, such as Cass Sunstein (1999), who have deliberately sought to temper the CLS critical presentations of rights. Sunstein is not entirely dismissive of the CLS arguments: rather, their 'plausible' claims should be 'stated far more cautiously and narrowly' (1999: 729). First, Sunstein

Often critics of CLS claim the principle is too easy to criticise liberalism, and human rights in particular, but reluctant, within the terms of its own methodology, to propose a model of its own, as a basis for reform (McCoubrey and White 1999: 211).[14] In reply, the author views this, therefore, as an opportunity to move the rights debate forward, in bridging the valid CLS criticisms of liberalism, with that ideology's emphasis on the individual and antipathy towards increases in state power, which for this piece is particularly telling post 9/11, with other comparable theories more suited to addressing predictors of terrorism such as social exclusion and marginalisation. Communitarianism is arguably one such philosophy and is discussed in detail in the next section.[15]

## 2 Communitarianism and its emphasis on responsibilities

Communitarianism, such as that proposed by Alasdair MacIntyre (1981), Michael J. Sandel (1982), Charles Taylor (1989) and Michael Walzer (1983), began in the form of a critical reaction to John Rawls' *A Theory of Justice* (1971). In *A Theory of Justice*, for example, Rawls arrived at his conception of justice by considering what individuals in the 'original position' would choose as principles of justice for the basic structure of society. They would decide behind a 'veil of ignorance' which prevented them from knowing their place in society, their class position or social status, their fortune in the distribution of natural assets and abilities, their intelligence and their strength. This ensured that no one was advantaged or disadvantaged in the choice of principles (Rawls 1971: 136–142).[16]

agrees with CLS, for example, that rights are indeterminate, but only when they are in the abstract. For Sunstein, rights in fact become determinate – 'specified' – when they operate in law (1999: 742). It will also be recalled that Mark Tushnet was particularly dismissive of the US Supreme Court's interpretation of the First Amendment, the right to speech. Although not responding to Tushnet directly, Sunstein would question whether this is really an attack on a specific right, free speech, in particular, rather than an attack on rights in general? (1999: 743–744). Sunstein rejects the argument that rights as interests operate only negatively: 'The right to associational freedom is hardly individualistic. It is meant precisely to protect collective action and sociality' (1999: 745). Finally, Sunstein also states that many rights are best understood as a solution to a collective action problem, such as a lack of legal entitlements for specific groups within society such as prisoners (1999: 737).

14 In the defence of CLS, Hunt, for example says: 'Given the predominance of liberal legal theory, it is difficult to make the first steps in making out an alternative theory for each of us is deeply imbued with the influence of that tradition' (Hunt 1987: 13). That said, Hunt believes that is 'desirable and necessary' to advance a general theory of law (1987: 5), which he discusses and describes as a 'relational' theory of law (1987: 16–18).

15 Some commentators have sought to draw parallels with CLS and communitarianism much more closely – see, for example: Bauman (1988).

16 Individuals were not completely ignorant, however: they knew 'the general facts about society', for example (1971: 137). Rawls believed two principles of justice would be chosen in the 'original position'. The first of these, the 'liberty principle' was 'each person is to have an equal right to the most extensive of equal basic liberties compatible with a similar liberty for all' (1971: 302). That is, each person would have the maximum amount of liberty without interfering with the similar liberties of others, which even the general welfare could not override (1971: 61). These 'basic

There are many reasons for communitarianism's attack on *A Theory of Justice* but these are, sadly, beyond the limits of this piece.[17] For the purposes of this chapter, in rejecting Rawls's 'veil of ignorance' hypothetical exercise, communitarians did not believe that individuals were born free and unencumbered, wholly autonomous agents seemingly living isolated lives, strangers to one another (Walzer 1995: 53–54). MacIntyre, for example, believed that we all approached our own circumstances as bearers of a particular social identity:

> I am someone's son or daughter, someone's cousin or uncle; I am a citizen of this or that city, a member of this or that guild or profession; I belong to this clan, that tribe, this nation . . . I inherit from the past of my family, my city, my tribe, my nation, a variety of debts, inheritances, rightful expectations and obligations. These constitute the given of my life, my moral staring point.
>
> (MacIntyre 1981: 204–205)

Thus, for communitarians, liberalism, or at least Rawls' approach to liberalism, in representing an overly individualistic conception of 'the self', was insufficiently sensitive to the importance of community, traditions and lived experiences (Bell 1993: 4).

A more recent communitarian theorist is Amitai Etzioni,[18] who echoes the earlier communitarians in emphasising liberalism's apparent neglect of community. He believes that neither human existence nor individual liberty can be sustained for long outside the interdependence and overlapping communities to which we all belong. Nor can any community long survive unless its members dedicate some of their attention, energy and resources to shared projects (Etzioni 1995a: 11). But for Etzioni, another important communitarian principle, which is particularly relevant to this piece, is redressing the balance between liberalism's emphasis on personal autonomy and social responsibilities, otherwise society will continue to be 'self-centred and driven by self-interests' (Etzioni 1995b: 22).

liberties' were political freedoms, such as speech, assembly and conscience, freedom from arbitrary arrest and freedom of personal property (1971: 61). For Rawls, the first principle of justice, which is appropriate to this chapter, prevailed over the second one because, for example, this dealt with constitutional fundamentals (1971: 63). The second principle of justice, which had two limbs, 'the difference principle' and 'fair equality of opportunity' (1971: 159–161), dealt with merely the operation of these constitutional fundamentals (63).

17 For example, can we partake in Rawls' 'veil of ignorance' experiment from a neutral position? Sandel questions, for example, whether the principles of justice that govern the basic structure of society can be neutral with respect to the competing moral and religious convictions its citizens espouse? He believes that one way of linking justice with the conceptions of the good holds that principles of justice derive their moral force from values commonly espoused or widely shared in a particular community or tradition. This way of linking justice and the good is communitarian in the sense that the values of the community define what counts as just or unjust (Sandel 1982: ix–x). Thus, one of the main themes of communitarianism is that there are common formulations of the public good rather than leaving it to be determined by each individual; the state cannot remain neutral on the issue.

18 See for example: Etzioni (1996, 1998).

Rights talk, especially in the United States where Etzioni lives, is particularly silent on responsibilities. As an example, Etzioni refers to the opposition to seat belts and wearing motorcycle helmets. These people do not absorb the consequences of their acts. They are more likely to die and leave their children 'for society to attend to and pick up the pieces', as well as ignore the drain on public resources this will cause (Etzioni 1994: 6). Thus, for Etzioni, rights talk seemingly condones acceptance of the benefits of living in a social welfare state, without accepting the corresponding personal civic obligations. This is a view shared by Mary Ann Glendon. Glendon also believes that rights talk, particularly in America, captures a devotion to individualism and liberty, but omits America's traditions of hospitality and care for the community (Glendon 1991: xi–xii). But this is not to reject human rights completely: a right, which is less individualistic and more responsive to collective ideals, is, for Glendon, Article 29(1) of the UDHR. Article 29(1) states: 'Everyone has duties to the community in which alone the free and full development of his personality is possible' (Glendon 1991: 13).

## 3 The 'communitarian' African Charter on Human and Peoples' Rights

The recognition of duties and responsibilities within human rights law is particularly developed in the African region: the African Charter on Human and Peoples' Rights (ACHPR), for example. In relying on criticisms of liberalism, one can advance the ACHPR as a way of, not only a human rights re-engagement with the critical readership of the *Daily Mail*, but redressing, to some degree, indictors of terrorism such as inequality and unemployment.[19] The author has already noted that grounding his approach in rights via CLS, for example, and especially Mark Tushnet, may seem like an obvious contradiction. However, CLS criticisms of rights, and communitarian ones to a lesser degree, are founded on a hostility towards a liberal bias within the law, of which the natural, negative, 'freedoms' from the state are a principal target – the approach to rights adopted within the ACHPR is much less individualistic and much more progressive than classic models of rights.[20] The ACHPR includes a group of articles on socio-economic rights, as well as duties. The primary reason was that the founding states wished to put forward a distinctive conception of human rights in which civil and political rights were seen to be counterbalanced by duties of social solidarity (Rehman 2009: 311).

Before proceeding, however, a qualification: it is commonly accepted amongst human rights commentators that many of the rights contained within the ACHPR lack definition (Smith 2017: 141; Rehman 2009: 327). Indeed, one commentator

19 For more discussions about communitarianism and the ACHPR in general, see, for example: Metz (2014).

20 For criticisms of attaching too much weight to first generation rights in the African human rights debate, see, for example: Ake (1987) and Cobbah (1987).

goes as far as to say: 'The duties [for example] are of such breadth and so ambiguous in their connotations that a regime of serious enforcement without some degree of prior elaboration is difficult to imagine' (Alston and Goodman 2012: 520).[21] Thus, in the absence of a significant body of human rights law – other than the Charter itself – developed and refined by relevant institutions within the African region such as the African Commission on Human and Peoples' Rights and the African Court on Human and Peoples' Rights, the author of this chapter is free to propose an interpretation and application of the ACHPR of his own.

The ACHPR begins with 'negative' human rights from the liberal tradition: the right to life, Article 4; the prohibition of torture and cruel, inhuman and degrading treatment, Article 5; the right to personal liberty and protection from arbitrary arrest, Article 6; and the right to a fair trial, Article 7, for example. But it proceeds to socio-economic, 'positive', 'rights to', such as the right to work, Article 15; the right to health, Article 16; and the right to education, Article 17. More progressively, the ACHPR also includes rights more associated with 'communitarian' ideals, conferring rights on 'peoples', not just individuals: the right of all peoples to equality and rights, Article 19; the right of all peoples to economic, social and cultural development, Article 22; and the right of all peoples to national and international security and peace, Article 23 (Rehman 2009: 327).[22] Lastly, seemingly mirroring communitarian thinking towards responsibilities, there are 'duties' of the individual, rather than rights, which one human rights commentator has described as 'unprecedented in so far as human rights treaties are concerned' (Rehman 2009: 311): every individual shall have duties towards their family and society, the state and other legally recognised communities and the international community, Article 27; and every individual shall have the duty to respect and consider their fellow beings without discrimination, and to maintain relations aimed at promoting, safeguarding and reinforcing mutual respect and tolerance, Article 28. Indeed, Article 29 also states that each individual shall have the duty: not to compromise the security of the state whose national or resident they are; to preserve and strengthen social and national solidarity, particularly when the latter is threatened; and to preserve and strengthen positive African cultural values in their relations with other members of the society, in the spirit of tolerance, dialogue and consultation and, in general, to contribute to the promotion of the moral well-being of society.

In addressing the criticisms of human rights from, say, readers of the *Daily Mail*, the ACHPR does contain rights that some would naturally see as inhibiting the state's attempts to counter terrorism: the right to personal liberty and protection from arbitrary arrest, Article 6; and the right to a fair trial, Article 7. But the ACHPR does attach much less weight to the rights of the individual terror suspect, in conferring rights on 'peoples'. Article 23 of the ACHPR, the right of all

21 For further reading on the language of duties within the ACHPR, see, for example: Mutua (1995).

22 For a discussion of whether peoples' rights can actually legitimately claim to be human rights, since, for example, they are not rights of human beings, see: Jones (1999).

peoples to national and international security and peace, is one such right which could certainly divert significant attention away from the so-called undeserving terrorist towards those of the deserving victim. Moreover, there are also ACHPR rights that could inevitably address some of the indicators of terrorism outlined above, such as unemployment and poor educational opportunities: the right to work, Article 15; and the right to education, Article 17. The significance of the duties within the ACHPR, in preventing terrorism, for example, cannot be overstated either. Article 28, it will be recalled, imposes the obligation on individuals to maintain relations with their fellow human beings to promote, safeguard and reinforce mutual respect and tolerance. Of course terrorists could be in violation of this obligation but they would not be the only ones upon whom this duty was imposed: everybody could have a responsibility to look out for others in their community, particularly the young who are much more susceptible to exploitation, to avoid the perils of social isolation. Where there was a suspicion that a person had been radicalised, then Article 29 could be engaged, in imposing obligations on individuals not to compromise the security of the state. Again, terrorists could be in violation of this Article, but in this instance the individual, upon whom this duty could also be imposed, would not be the individual extremist, but could be someone else, perhaps a religious leader schooled in a counter jihadist narrative, or a community youth worker with an expertise in techniques of diversion.

## Conclusion

In the so-called 'War on Terror' many, particularly those in the media, see human rights merely as a vehicle to secure the 'undeserving' rights of terror suspects over the 'deserving' rights of victims. The idea that human rights protect the 'few' over the 'many' has arguably contributed to a disengagement with the topic of rights. But human rights are not the preserve of the classic liberal tradition, with its emphasis on protecting the individual from the state, as security is being compromised much more by non-state actors. Indeed, human rights law is more far reaching than liberalism suggests, as the rights of 'peoples' within the ACHPR signify. In particular, there is Article 23 of the ACHPR, the right of all peoples to national and international security and peace. A greater understanding of this right, for example, or a wider acceptance of it beyond the African region, should reassure a nervous populace, post 9/11, and redress the apparent bias within human rights towards an 'unworthy' minority. At the same time, the related liberal suspicions about increases in state power have seemingly ignored primary indicators of terrorism. Noting the nature of recent Islamist terrorists in the West – many are recent Muslim converts, with a criminal history – and the factors affecting their recruitment – inequality, marginalisation, unemployment etc. – perhaps, within current discussions of human rights, we should prioritise this apparent isolation and lack of educational opportunities and attach greater weight to collective ideals such as the positive, 'rights to' work and education? Such an approach is consistent with critical legal approaches to the law, and human rights in particular, since, for that tradition, the balance falls too much in favour of negative freedoms. However, a wider acceptance of rights, beyond the first and second generations, to those freedoms that are more socially inclusive, that foster a *communal* sense of duty and responsibility, along the lines of, say, Articles 28 and 29 of the ACHPR, are surely a significant, additional way forward in re-engaging with the topic of rights, particularly in times of crisis?

## References


Ake, C. (1987) 'The African Context of Human Rights', *Africa Today*, 34, 5–12.

Alston, P. and Goodman, R. (2012) *International Human Rights*. Oxford, Oxford University Press.

Balkin, J. M. (1990) 'The Rhetoric of Responsibility', *Virginia Law Review*, 76, 197–263.

Balkin, J. M. (1991) 'Ideology as Constraint', *Stanford Law Review*, 43, 1133–1178.

Balkin, J. M. (2008) 'The Constitution in the National Surveillance State', *Minnesota Law Review*, 93, 1–25.

Balkin, J. M. (2009) 'Critical Legal Theory Today', in Mootz, F. (ed.) *On Philosophy in American Law*. Cambridge, Cambridge University Press.

Bauman, R. (1988) 'The Communitarian Vision of Critical Legal Studies', *McGill Law Journal*, 33, 295–356.

Bell, D. (1993) *Communitarianism and its Critics*. Oxford, Oxford University Press.

Bentley, P. (2017) 'An insult to terror victims', *Daily Mail* 8 June www.dailymail.co.uk/news/article-4597508/Jihadi-fighting-stay-Britain-given-250k-legal-aid.html [accessed 02/02/2019].

Booth, R. and Parveen, N. (2017) 'Khalid Masood a violent criminal who was regularly on the move', *The Guardian* 24 March www.theguardian.com/uk-news/2017/mar/23/birmingham-neighbour-khalid-masood-winson-green [accessed 02/02/2019].

Clement, D. (2018a) 'Human Rights or Social Justice: The Problem of Rights Inflation', *The International Journal of Human Rights*, 22, 155–169.

Clement, D. (2018b) *Debating Rights Inflation in Canada: A Sociology of Human Rights*. Waterloo, Wilfrid Laurier University Press.

Cobbah, J. (1987) 'African Values and the Human Rights Debate: An African Perspective', *Human Rights Quarterly*, 9, 309–331.

Council of Europe (2018) 'European Court of Human Rights: Analysis of Statistics 2017', January www.echr.coe.int/Documents/Stats_analysis_2017_ENG.pdf [accessed 02/02/2019].

Crenshaw, K. W. (1988) 'Race, Reform, and Retrenchment: Transformation and Legitimation in Anti-Discrimination Law', *Harvard Law Review*, 101, 1331–1387.

Daily Mail Comment (2017) 'Sorry, human rights DO shield terrorists', *Daily Mail* 8 June www.dailymail.co.uk/debate/article-4583006/DAILY-MAIL-COMMENT-Human-rights-shield-terrorists.html [accessed 02/02/2019].

Dodd, V. (2017) 'UK facing most severe terror threat ever, warns MI5 chief', *The Guardian* 17 October www.theguardian.com/uk-news/2017/oct/17/uk-most-severe-terror-threat-ever-mi5-islamist [accessed 02/02/2019].

Etzioni, A. (1994) *The Spirit of Community: The Reinvention of American Society*. New York City, Touchstone.

Etzioni, A. (1995a) 'The Responsive Communitarian Platform: Rights and Responsibilities', in Etzioni, A. (ed.) *Rights and the Common Good: The Communitarian Perspective*. New York City, St Martin's Press.

Etzioni, A. (1995b) 'Old Chestnuts and New Spurs', in Etzioni, A. (ed.) *New Communitarian Thinking: Persons, Virtues, Institutions and Communities.* Charlottesville, University of Virginia Press.

Etzioni, A. (1996) *The New Golden Rule: Community and Morality in a Democratic Society.* New York City, Basic Books.

Etzioni, A. (1998) (ed.) *The Essential Communitarian Reader.* Lanham, Rowman and Littlefield Publishers.

Europol (2016) *Changes in Modus Operandi of Islamic State Revisited* www.europol.europa.eu/publications-documents/changes-in-modus-operandi-of-islamic-state-revisited [accessed 02/02/2019].

Friedman, M. (1962) *Capitalism and Freedom.* Chicago, University of Chicago Press.

Glendon, M. A. (1991) *Rights Talk: The Impoverishment of Political Discourse.* New York City, Free Press.

Hannum, H. (2016) 'Reinvigorating Human Rights for the Twenty-First Century', *Human Rights Law Review*, 16, 409–451.

Hathaway, O. (2001–02) 'Do Human Rights Treaties Make a Difference?', *Yale Law Journal*, 111, 1935–2034.

Hayek, F. A. (1960) *The Constitution of Liberty.* Chicago, University of Chicago Press.

Hunt, A. (1986) 'The Theory of Critical Legal Studies', *Oxford Journal of Legal Studies*, 6, 1–45.

Hunt, A. (1987) 'The Critique of Law: What is Critical About Critical Legal Theory', *Journal of Law and Society*, 14, 5–20.

Hutchinson, A. and Monahan, P. (1984) 'Law, Politics, and the Critical Legal Scholars: The Unfolding Drama of American Legal Thought', *Stanford Law Review*, 36, 199–245.

Institute for Economics and Peace (2016) *Global Terrorism Index 2016*, November http://economicsandpeace.org/wp-content/uploads/2016/11/Global-Terrorism-Index-2016.2.pdf [accessed 02/02/2019].

Institute for Economics and Peace (2017) *Global Terrorism Index 2017*, December http://visionofhumanity.org/app/uploads/2017/11/Global-Terrorism-Index-2017.pdf [accessed 02/02/2019].

Johnston, C. (2017) 'Two detained under Terrorism Act as UK arrests reach record high', *The Guardian* 29 November www.theguardian.com/uk-news/2017/nov/29/two-detained-under-terrorism-act-as-uk-arrests-reach-record-high [accessed 02/02/2019].

Jones, P. (1999) 'Human Rights, Group Rights, and Peoples' Rights', *Human Rights Quarterly*, 21, 80–107.

Locke, J. (2011) *Second Treatise of Government.* Ocean Shores, Watchmaker Publishing.

MacIntyre, A. (1981) *After Virtue: A Study in Moral Theory.* Notre Dame, University of Notre Dame Press.

McCoubrey, H. and White, N. (1999) *Textbook on Jurisprudence.* 3rd ed. London, Blackstone Press.

Metz, T. (2014) 'African Values, Human Rights and Group Rights: A Philosophical Foundation for the Banjul Charter', in Onazi, Oche (ed.) *African Legal Theory and Contemporary Problems: Critical Essays.* Dordrecht, Springer.

Mutua, M. (1995) 'The Banjul Charter and the African Cultural Fingerprint: An Evaluation of the Language of Duties', *Virginal Journal of International Law*, 35, 339–380.

Nozick, R. (1974) *Anarchy, State and Utopia.* New York, City Basic Books.

O'Connell, P. (2018) 'On the Human Rights Question', *Human Rights Quarterly*, 40, 968–988.

Posner, E. (2014a) 'The case against human rights', *The Guardian* 4 December www.theguardian.com/news/2014/dec/04/-sp-case-against-human-rights [accessed 02/02/2019].

Posner, E. (2014b) *The Twilight of Human Rights Law*. Open Global Rights 25 November www.openglobalrights.org/twilight-of-human-rights-law/ [accessed 02/02/2019].

Posner, E. (2014c) *The Twilight of Human Rights Law*. Oxford, Oxford University Press.

Rawls, J. (1971) *A Theory of Justice*. Cambridge, Harvard University Press.

Rehman, J. (2009) *International Human Rights Law*. 2nd ed. London, Pearson Education.

Sandel, M. J. (1982) *Liberalism and the Limits of Justice*. Cambridge, Cambridge University Press.

Sandel, M. J. (2010) *Justice: What's the Right Thing to Do?* London, Penguin Books.

Schneider, E. M. (1986) 'The Dialectic of Rights and Politics: Perspectives from the Women's Movement', *New York University Law Review*, 61, 589–653.

Smith, R. (2017) *International Human Rights Law*. 8th ed. Oxford, Oxford University Press.

Solum, L. (2018) 'Legal Theory Lexicon 036: Indeterminacy' http://lsolum.typepad.com/legal_theory_lexicon/2004/05/legal_theory_le_2.html accessed [02/02/2019].

Steiner, H., Alston, P. and Goodman, R. (2007) *International Human Rights in Context: Law, Politics, Morals*. 3rd ed. Oxford, Oxford University Press.

Sunstein, C. (1999) 'Rights and their Critics', *Notre Dame Law Review*, 71, 727–757.

Tapsfield, J. (2017) 'PM vows to rip up human rights laws in war on terror', *Daily Mail* 7 June www.dailymail.co.uk/news/article-4576146/PM-says-MI5-does-face-questions-London-Bridge-killer.html [accessed 02/02/2019].

Taylor, C. (1989) *Sources of the Self: The Making of Modern Identity*. Cambridge, Harvard University Press.

Tushnet, M. (1981) 'The Dilemmas of Liberal Constitutionalism', *Ohio State Law Journal*, 42, 411–426.

Tushnet, M. (1984a) 'Perspectives on Critical Legal Studies', *George Washington Law Review*, 52, 239–242.

Tushnet, M. (1984b) 'An Essay on Rights', *Texas Law Review*, 62, 1363–1403.

Tushnet, M. (1986) 'Critical Legal Studies: An Introduction to its Origins and Underpinnings', *Journal of Legal Education*, 36, 505–517.

Tushnet, M. (1990) 'A Critical Legal Studies Perspective', *Cleveland State Law Review*, 38, 137–151.

Tushnet, M. (1993) 'The Critique of Rights', *SMU Law Review*, 47, 23–34.

Tushnet, M. (2005) 'Controlling Executive Power in the War on Terror', *Harvard Law Review*, 118, 2673–2682.

UNGA (1948) 'Res 217', 10 December www.un-documents.net/a3r217a.htm [accessed 02/02/2019].

Vasak, K. (1977) 'A Thirty-Year Struggle: The Sustained Efforts to give Force of Law to the Universal Declaration of Human Rights', *UNESCO Courier*, 30, November, 29–32.

Wacks, R. (2014) *Philosophy of Law*. 2nd ed. Oxford, Oxford University Press.

Walzer, M. (1983) *Spheres of Justice: A Defense of Pluralism and Equality*. New York City, Basic Books.

Walzer, M. (1995) 'The Communitarian Critique of Liberalism', in Etzioni, A. (ed.) *New Communitarian Thinking: Persons, Virtues, Institutions and Communities*. Charlottesville, University of Virginia Press.

Wellman, C. (1998) *The Proliferation of Rights: Moral Progress or Empty Rhetoric?* London, Routledge.

# 15 Is the principle of legal certainty a human right?

## The legitimacy of the retroactive application of laws[1]

*Jan Tryzna*

### Introduction: The concept of legal certainty

This chapter deals with the principle of legal certainty and its role in legislative regulation of human conduct. It addresses the issue whether legal certainty can be considered as a human right. Human rights impose negative or positive obligations or duties on the state. The state is obliged not to interfere with these rights (e.g. right for life), to protect them against interference of other individuals (e.g. right to protection of property) or to adopt some measures insuring that such rights can be effectively exercised (e.g. right for social security).

We usually do not speak about the "right for legal certainty", but usually call it a "principle of legal certainty". As such, it may have some regulatory effect. The regulatory character of a legal principle probably differs from a regulatory character of most of human rights. Legal principles usually do not have a very exact meaning as regarding their legal consequences. Robert Alexy has called them "*orders for optimization*" (Alexy 1995: 204).[2] In my opinion, this is the case of the principle of legal certainty as well.

Therefore, legal certainty must be defined in order to indicate the direction of further considerations because, like many other legal principles, the principle of legal certainty is used in various meanings. It may be perceived as certainty that everyone will follow laws and that any illegal act will be punished. Another meaning might be the certainty that acquired rights will be protected and that their protection will be granted in case of their breach.

In the given context regarding the retroactivity of laws, the principle of legal certainty can be restricted to foreseeable human conduct based on knowledge of legal rules. Retroactive or retrospective laws govern situations or relationships that somehow have happened or were commenced in the past. It means that the predictability of the consequences of human conduct is curtailed because subsequent laws attach different consequences to previous conduct. Therefore, the principle of legal certainty can be understood as a principle of non-retroactivity.

1 The chapter was written with support of PROGRES Q04, a scientific program of Charles University (in Prague).

2 For various meanings of legal certainty see Avila (2016: vii).

## 1 Types of retroactivity of laws

Legal theory usually distinguishes between two basic kinds of retroactivity. The first one is called "*genuine retroactivity*". In common law countries, it is usually called "*primary retroactivity*" (Laitos 1999–2000: 1123, 1131).[3] It denotes situations in which a new law regulates the origins (establishment) of legal relationships due to facts that happened in the past. As a consequence, a new legal relationship is set up retroactively in the past and carries forward. Alternatively, legal relationships established in the past may have had different legal consequences from the very beginning. It means that parties of an existing relationship that has arisen in the past have different rights and duties from the very beginning than they had at the moment of creation of such legal relationship. The change of their rights and duties takes place from the commencement of the legal relationship.

The second type of retroactivity is called "*secondary retroactivity*"[4] in common law countries or "*non-genuine retroactivity*" in some of civil law countries. It means that a new law regulates existing relationships that have arisen in the past and continue from the moment when new law comes into force. The change in rights and obligations of parties occurs in the moment when the new law comes into force and applies for the future. It is apparent that there is no real retroactivity in these situations because the law does not regulate the past. Nevertheless, it is also apparent that legal certainty is touched in these situations because the legislator changes legal position (mutual rights and duties) of persons who are involved is some legal relationship.[5]

Retroactivity of legal regulation is usually considered as undesired even though arguments in favour of retroactive legislation are brought up.[6] The basic argument against retroactive laws is connected with the nature of legal regulation that requires certain type of human conduct while contradictory conduct is somehow sanctioned. Therefore, the only reasonable kind of human conduct is such that is known in advance.[7] On the contrary, in favour of retroactive legislation it is argued that it is often more effective because the legislator knows exactly the scope of legal relationships that are affected by retroactive regulation while effect

3 Other authors differentiate between "retroactivity" and "retrospectivity", the later denoting secondary retroactivity (see Juratowitch 2008: 6).

4 Terms "primary retroactivity" and "secondary retroactivity" will be used further in this chapter.

5 It should be noted that more detailed distinctions (varieties) can be drawn in cases of secondary retroactivity. These distinctions stem from the content of concrete rights and duties of the parties that are affected by new laws. These distinctions are irrelevant in the context of this topic.

6 American legal theory distinguishes a category of so-called *curative laws*. These laws provide for behaviour that was deemed appropriate even though it was not regulated by law. Therefore, it is considered as a correct solution if the law starts to regulate such behaviour retroactively. See Natelson (2002–2003: 505).

7 An objection can be raised that in common law countries a judicial precedent represents a similar kind of retroactive rule making. It is partly true but the topic is concerned with retroactive legislation. In addition, judges very often argue that they do not create new law. So-called declaratory theory was dominant in England until the 19th century. According to this theory, judges only find already existing legal rules that were perhaps unclear to parties of the dispute.

of non-retroactive regulation is sometimes hardly predictable. A question of justice is sometimes mentioned in favour of legitimating retroactive laws as well. The argument goes that the consequences of old laws that are considered unjust need to be remedied somehow and the retroactivity is the means to achieve it.

## 2 The significance of retroactivity

There are some situations in which retroactivity of legal regulation does not matter. The law operates with sanctions imposed when people's conduct is contrary to legal rules. Sanctions need not be punitive ones. For example, invalidating of a treaty is a sanction for breaching of legal rules governing the process of concluding treaties. If the new law does not impose any duties that were unexpected in the past, for example if the new law grants more rights than the old one although these rights are granted retroactively, there is probably no need to object to such a new law. The problem is that when the new law assigns more rights to one party of the legal relationship, the second party has more duties. Therefore, in many cases of retroactive legislation it is hard to assume that retroactivity does not matter since the position of at least of one party of the legal relationship is usually worsened.

Considering this perspective, it may be concluded that there is no principal difference between primary and secondary retroactivity when the principle of legal certainty is in question. Both kinds of retroactivity are undesirable only when the new regulation imposes duties, not rights. In my opinion, as long as legal certainty is at stake, it does not matter if the retroactive law worsens a legal status (rights and duties) of some person from the past (primary retroactivity) or if it begins operating since the effective date of the new legislation (secondary retroactivity). In both cases, legal certainty is violated. It is apparent that primary retroactivity of law violates legal certainty to some greater extent because of its inevitable consequences. Secondary retroactivity can be justified by a couple of arguments. First, it can be argued that it has no effect for the past but only for the future. Second, it is generally recognized that the legislator has power to interfere with existing relationships. As a result, a change of legislation is legitimate. Third, a principle of equality in rights requires that legal position of parties of a legal relationship set up according to new legislation would be the same as position of parties of already existing relationships.[8] However, it should be borne in mind that legal expectations of persons who are subject to legal regulation are undermined even in the case of secondary retroactivity. It may be concluded that while primary retroactivity of legal regulation that imposes only duties is strongly undesirable, secondary retroactivity of new legislation may be legitimate even if it imposes new duties.

8 It should be noted that this argument is not valid for all types of legal relationships. It is perhaps legitimate to provide for the same legal status of married couples notwithstanding the date of marriage. On the contrary, it need not to be legitimate to provide for the same legal status of parties of some type of contracts, one of them being concluded before the change of legislation and the second one afterwards.

## 3 Evolution of the principles of retroactivity and non-retroactivity

A general issue is whether there are some limits that the legislator must respect when adopting new laws. From a comparative point of view, it is very hard to find a unanimous approach to this issue. In my opinion, multiple sources of possible guidance can be identified. These sources differ based on the particular type of legal culture, region, state etc.

As a first source, some legal principles can be found that govern retroactivity in law. These principles, often unwritten, are considered as part of particular legal cultures. The problem is that these principles do not grant a great certainty as regarding their consequences for legal order as regarding retroactivity of laws. The second source is legislation, especially constitutions of particular states. Constitutions may contain special rules on this subject but very often they are incomplete in regard to different branches of legal regulation. Criminal law is among those that are usually explicitly regulated. The third source of such rules is the judiciary. This is typical for common law countries. Authors inquiring into this subject spend most of their efforts describing development in judicial decision making, changes, and prospective. Last but not least is the legal doctrine itself. The problem is that sometimes legal doctrine is not descriptive, but normative. It proposes "best" possible solutions for various legal concepts. If legal doctrine is considered to be one of sources of law (as it is in England), its influence is significant.

In my opinion, an issue of retroactivity (retrospectivity) of law belongs among legal issues that should be considered "neutral" in the sense that Jeremy Waldron (1990) describes the model of law. In the search for meaning of the concept "rule of law", Waldron describes two models of law (Waldron 1990: 11). The first one is called the ***partisan*** model of law. It describes law as an expression of the particular ideology or policies of a political party. The second model of law is the ***neutral*** theory as something that stands above party politics. We do not have to restrict our view of politics to some political party. Those who are active in law besides politicians, like judges, solicitors, theorists, teachers etc., do not have to show sympathies for a particular legal party but they may express their own views about the legal system. If we take into consideration that retroactivity directly influences the consequences that new laws have on legal relationships, and because the law is for the most part resultant of political decisions, it is apparent that the issue of the retroactivity of laws cannot be left untouched by politics. The problem is whether there are some limits that must be respected. In the following text, a short description of development and various aspects of the retroactivity of law will be given.

In Czech legal theory we often use a Latin phrase "*lex retro non agit*", meaning laws should not govern past situations. The Latin phrase indicates that the principle of non-retroactivity of laws comes from Roman law. On the one hand, this is true, but on the other hand it is not true: the Latin phrase was probably first used by Polish lawyer Stanislaw Wróblewski at the beginning of 20th century (Heikki 2006: 154). It seems that this phrase is used in Central and Eastern

European countries but, as far as I know, not in the countries of Western Europe. Roman lawyers were aware of the principle of non-retroactivity but it was not a leading principle of Roman law. An opposite principle, the principle of retroactivity, was used in criminal law and also in civil law (Skrejpek 2001: 617).

In Roman law, retroactivity had a different meaning than today. Basically, it denoted situations in which some later fact changed consequences of a previously created legal relationship (Berger 1949: 49). In Corpus Iuris Civilis, 25 rules were found in which clause "*ex post facto*" was used. This clause was not connected with later changes in legal rules as indicated, presumably, by the word "*facto*" meaning some fact, something that happened. Nevertheless, rules that resemble the contemporary meaning of retroactivity of law were known to Roman lawyers. Probably the most well known is the following rule: "*Leges et constitutiones futuris certum est dare formam negotiis, non ad facta praeterita revocari, nisi nominatim etiam de praeterito tempore adhuc pendentibus negotiis cautum sit*"[9] (Corpus Iuris Civilis, 1.14.7).

The clause "*ex post facto*" has undergone an inexplicable change in early Anglo-Saxon law. It was appended with the word "*law*", resulting in sentences dealing with "*ex post facto laws*". It was Henry de Bracton who used this phrase in his work *De Legibus Et Consuetudinibus Angliæ* (Smead 1935–1936: 775f). A few centuries later, Sir Edward Coke formulated a principle that laws should govern the future, not the past.[10] The phrase "*ex post facto* laws" was taken by the Founding Fathers who used it in the Constitution of United States of America. The American Constitution provides: "No . . . *ex post facto* Law shall be passed" (Constitution of the United States: Art. 9 s. 3).

While the connection between Roman law and common law as regards the concept of retroactivity is quite clear[11] and is very old, emergence of the principle of non-retroactivity in continental Europe is perhaps connected with modern codifications of law that were adopted at the turn of 18th and 19th centuries. Their predecessor is the French Declaration of Human and Civic Rights adopted by the French National Constituent Assembly in 1789. Its Article 8 stated: "The law should establish only penalties that are strictly and evidently necessary, and no one can be punished but under a law established and promulgated before the offense and legally applied" (Declaration of Human and Civic Rights, Art. 8). It is apparent that this rule governs criminal matters only. A more general rule is expressed in the French Civil Code: "Legislation provides only for the future; it has no retroactive effect" (French Civil Code 2017, Art. 2). This rule has a very broad meaning because it comprises both types of retroactivity – primary and secondary. The Civil Code is an ordinary statute. It means that it can be overruled by any other statute that may operate retroactively.

9 "It is sure that statutes and Emperor's constitution set rules for future contracts and cannot govern the past situations unless it is expressly stated that they rule the past and already stipulated contracts".

10 "*Nova constitutio futuris formam imponere debet, non praeteritis*" (Coke 1604: 87).

11 This may be surprising since a usual characteristic of common law is that it is not based on Roman law.

Similarly, in Austria, a General Civil Code was adopted in 1811. In its Preamble, section 5 states that the Civil Code will not affect any conduct preceding its entry into force. Similarly, in section 5 we read: "Laws have no effect for the past, they do not influence conduct done in the past and do not affect acquired rights" (Austrian General Civil Code: s.5). The meaning was slightly different in comparison with the French Civil Code. It clearly prohibits only primary retroactivity while secondary retroactivity is not forbidden so strictly. The French Civil Code "provides only for the future", meaning for any future conduct, but the Austrian Civil Code states that laws do not affect the past. It means that laws can regulate existing relationships since the day of effect because it is not "the past" anymore. It also protects "acquired rights", meaning the rights that had arisen in the past.

## 4 Contemporary rules regarding retroactivity and non-retroactivity of laws

Contemporary constitutions usually do not provide for admissible retroactivity or non-retroactivity of laws. If the constitutions prohibit retroactivity of laws it is usually retroactivity of criminal law only. First, they order the imposition of sentences according to the law that came into force before the commitment of some criminal act. Second, they order the use of a new law in a retroactive way if the new law is more favourable for the offender than the law that was in force at the moment of commitment of a criminal act. There are constitutions that can be interpreted as prohibiting retroactivity of any law. Article 9 section 3 of the Constitution of the United States was mentioned already. It can be interpreted so that retroactivity of law is forbidden as a whole. In fact, it is interpreted as regulating criminal affairs only.

It has been said that modern constitutions usually do not provide for prohibition of retroactive laws except for criminal law and sentencing. Therefore, the question arises of whether there is a general rule regulating admissible or inadmissible retroactivity of law. Such a rule, of course, need not be written down, but can be derived from legal principles or it can be formulated by the judiciary.

If we search through decisions of the European Court for Human Rights there seems to be no common approach to the issue of retroactivity of laws among the 47 member states of the Council of Europe. One may expect that questions of admissible or inadmissible retroactivity of laws would be raised at the Court, although the European Convention for the Protection of Human Rights and Fundamental Freedoms does not contain any general rule regarding retroactive laws, except for Article 7[12] that deals with criminal matters only. Despite this fact, complaints based on breach of human rights through national non-penal

12 "No one shall be held guilty of any criminal offence on account of any act or omission which did not constitute a criminal offence under national or international law at the time when it was committed. Nor shall a heavier penalty be imposed than the one that was applicable at the time the criminal offence was committed".

retroactive legislation were filed at the Court. Although the plaintiffs have complained about inadmissible retroactivity of national laws (usually a secondary type of retroactivity), in most cases the Court has not assessed the case on the basis of such argumentation and did not pay much attention to the alleged inadmissible retroactivity of the national law. One exception is the decision of the Court in case of Zielenski, Pradal, and Gonzalez, and others against France (ECtHR 8 June 2011). The Court in its decision declared that retroactive legislation in civil law is not prohibited as a principle.

The right for protection of peaceful enjoyment of property was in question[13] in many cases. It is private property (possessions) that is very often touched by retroactive legislation. The Court has not examined the retroactive character of the law itself but its compliance with guarantees contained in the Convention. For example, in the case of Maggio and others against Italy (ECtHR 31 May 2011) the Court reviewed provisions of Italian law retroactively curtailing an amount of pension for retired persons. It was an example of secondary retroactivity of law because already admitted pensions were reduced from some certain date. The Court did not consider it important that it was retroactive law. Instead, the Court deliberated the question of lawfulness of measures, impacts on the plaintiff (extent of loss of allowances), and the public interest on adopting such measures. Because all these conditions were met, the Court declared that national measures had been compatible with the Convention.

Another interesting case is the case of Baka against Hungary (ECtHR 23 June 2016). In Hungary, after the adoption of a new law, Baka, who was then president of the Supreme Court, had his term prematurely shortened under the normal six years, and subsequently lost his office. It is a typical case of secondary retroactivity. The president of the Supreme Court fought against the loss of his office, and the European Court decided in favour of the plaintiff. The judgment was not based on the fact that the term of office was retroactively curtailed, but on the fact that the plaintiff was not granted a judicial protection in relation to the loss of office (ECtHR 23 June 2016, sec. 121). Because the loss of office was automatic, since it was ordered by the particular law, the Court's requirement for judicial review was in fact pointless because there was nothing to review. Even so, the still Court ruled in favour of the plaintiff.

In light of this case, it can be assumed that there are some guarantees in the system of international protection of human rights in relation to retroactive laws. The European Court has emphasized the right for judicial protection in cases when retroactive law in form of secondary retroactivity were involved. The only thing the judicial review could consider would be admissibility of retroactive encroachment of the right for the exercise of public office.

13 Article 1 of the Protocol (no.1) to the Convention: "Every natural or legal person is entitled to the peaceful enjoyment of his possessions. No one shall be deprived of his possessions except in the public interest and subject to the conditions provided for by law and by the general principles of international law".

## 5 The approach to the retroactivity of laws in the Czech Republic

In the Czech Republic, as in other European countries, there is nothing approaching an explicit general rule on retroactivity of laws. The only constitutional rule is the one regulating criminal affairs, as was mentioned above. Despite this fact, a principle of legal non-retroactivity is recognized in the Czech legal order and, because it lacks clear constitutional support, it is derived from the principle of legal certainty, which is itself also unwritten and derived from the rule of law (legal state). The notion of "legal state" is unfortunately vague, i.e. the Constitution of the Czech Republic declares the nation a legal state. What *is* clear, however, is that this is an issue of constitutionality and, accordingly, the Czech Constitutional Court has taken several opportunities to rule upon this matter.

From the very beginning, the Constitutional Court has distinguished between primary and secondary retroactivity (US CR Pl ÚS 14/94). Without more detailed argumentation, the Constitutional Court declared that while primary retroactivity is basically unacceptable, secondary retroactivity is generally acceptable.[14] The Court has also given some examples of accepting primary retroactivity. Among them the Court has mentioned the retroactivity of rules that correspond to the general conviction of the citizens but that due to political reasons did not become a part of the legal order. This is questionable because it is hard to imagine that the prevailing will of citizens would not be reflected in statutes through their representation of elected members of Parliament. Perhaps the Constitutional Court meant totalitarian regimes in which the will of the citizens could not find its expression in laws. Such a situation is unimaginable in a standard democratic regime.

The Constitutional Court has applied this rule tacitly in a case (US CR Pl ÚS 19/93) when an indirect amendment[15] to the Penal Code adopted at the beginning of 1990s was subjected to constitutional review. Parliament declared that crimes committed during the old regime that were not prosecuted due to political reasons could be prosecuted even though time limitations for prosecution have expired. This can be considered as primary retroactivity because, according to the Czech theory of criminal law, legal conditions for prosecution of an offender form part of the criminal act. Nevertheless, the Constitutional Court described this situation as secondary retroactivity and declared the law was not contrary to the Constitution. The problem is that this example of retroactivity collides with explicit constitutional limitations regarding conditions of criminal prosecution. The issue had a strong political context because it was the intention of the legislator to allow criminal prosecution of those who were not punished for their crimes committed during the old regime due to political reasons.

14 This retroactivity is not explicitly provided for in constitutional law, and defines all branches of law except for criminal law and similar branches of law.

15 Law no 198/1993 Coll, on illegitimacy of the communist regime.

The problem was that such an intention was contrary to constitutional prohibition of retroactive criminal prosecution that was valid at the time the Parliament adopted the law. Strictly assessed, the Constitutional Court had to choose among the following alternatives. First, the amendment could be declared unconstitutional. That would mean that crimes of the past would not have been penalized. Second, the Constitutional Court could have admitted that the new regime can legitimately punish the old crimes and explained why the constitutional prohibition of retroactive punishment was not applicable in this case.[16] However, it failed to do so. The third option was to redefine the case as secondary retroactivity, which is not constitutionally prohibited, though this also did not happen. It cannot be doubted that the Court's decision was a political one. Constitutional courts are expected to oppose the political decisions of the legislator if these decisions are contrary to constitutional principles and restrictions. The Constitutional Court did not do so.[17]

Overtime, the Constitutional Court has developed criteria for assessing retroactivity in non-penal branches of law. The Constitutional Court rejects primary retroactivity if it means a disadvantage for private individuals. As for secondary retroactivity, the Constitutional Court rules that it is generally admissible even though it is to someone's disadvantage, meaning that the Parliament has the power to change existing relationships for the future. While the Constitutional Court usually argues that the Parliament must have a power to adjust the legal order to current social needs, the question is whether there are some implicit limitations on this power. There are still no clear constitutional rules on this subject.

Secondary retroactivity of laws is legitimated by the undisputed power of Parliament to adapt the legal order to social needs. Nonetheless, some competing interests may exist that deserve protection. So-called acquired rights belong to these interests. The Constitutional Court usually applies the test of proportionality[18] in cases in which such interests are touched by the new legislation. This includes deliberation about the necessity of such legal rules, about their suitability and, as a third step, proportionality in the narrow sense of requiring the weighing of competing interests or rights. The power of Parliament to change existing relationships generally allows for any change of existing rules, so there must be strong arguments against it, for example legitimate expectations about the legal consequences of particular legal rules. The Constitutional Court usually rules that there is nothing like an expectation that existing rules will not be changed. Regardless, there can be rules of such a kind that they establish the legitimate expectations that these rules will not be changed.

16 The problem is not similar, although it may seem so, to Lon Fuller's famous example of the grudge informer. See Fuller (1969: 245ff). The difference is that in Fuller's example the question was whether to punish for something that was morally wrong but not illegal. In the case described, the crimes that were newly allowed to be punishable were crimes according to laws valid at the time they were committed. They were not punished due to political reasons and the time limits had expired.

17 The decision raised a lot of criticism among legal scholars. See Pavlíček (1999: 127ff).

18 This test is inspired by the decision making praxis of the German Constitutional Court.

One of the famous cases of this kind dealt with state subsidies for photovoltaic energy. According to the particular statute, a purchase price for photovoltaic energy was guaranteed for a period of 15 years. The aim was to support production of so-called "green energy". The guaranteed price of photovoltaic energy was designed to compensate the considerable expenses of photovoltaic power plants. The legislator did not take into consideration that the prices of equipment for photovoltaic power plants would drop very quickly. Due to this reason, the guaranteed purchase price of photovoltaic energy became very advantageous, causing a rapid growth in the number of photovoltaic power plants. This was undesirable due to many reasons, creating rapid increase in the price of electricity, instability of electricity networks etc. Parliament adopted an amendment to the particular statute that significantly lowered the purchase price of photovoltaic energy. This happened in the fifth year of the 15-year period during which the price of electricity was guaranteed to be the same. The result was that the huge profit of photovoltaic power plant owners dropped. The constitutionality of the amendment was subjected to review, with the main argument being that the statute violated the right for the protection of peaceful enjoyment of property. The Constitutional Court ruled (US CR Pl ÚS 17/11) that the state had the power to regulate the price of energy even though the legislation had formerly granted the price for a strict period of time. The Court held that the decision of Parliament was supported with legitimate reasons, such as the lowering of prices of equipment for power plants. The Court ruled that the investment of particular owners of power plants would not be ruined by the amendment due to the fact that the costs of initial equipment of power plants had fallen so the investment should not be ruined.

There are other cases in which the legitimate expectations of individuals played a significant role. For example Parliament adopted the law changing a specific kind of right of usage of land into ownership of land,[19] with a one year transitional period and upon its expiry, the right of usage of land had to change into the ownership of land. At the very last moment, exactly one day before this happened, a new law came into force cancelling the existing rules about transformation of right of usage of land into property of land. The Constitutional Court held that such a change of decision of the legislator had breached legitimate expectations supported by the previous statute, and the amendment was found unconstitutional (US CR Pl ÚS 2/02) and was subsequently revoked. The Court held that adoption of the amendment had been unreasonable and thus had violated legitimate expectations as regarding the effect of the former law. This example, yet again, proves the significance of the principle of non-retroactivity.

There are some limits on the power of the legislator to change existing relationships by retroactive laws. Further, it is very difficult to find generally valid rules governing admissible and inadmissible retroactivity, and the outcome depends on many standards that must be taken into consideration. If we consider human rights

19 Law no 229/2001 Coll.

as standards that limit state authorities in exercising their powers, the principle of legal certainty can be regarded as a human right. If this limitation is unclear compared to other, "ordinary" human rights, some other arguments must be added.

Legal certainty was defined as foreseeability of human conduct derived from the knowledge of valid legal rules. Another aspect of legal certainty is the trust that there will not be a change in existing relationships due to change of legislation. As has been explained, the legislator is generally entitled to change legislation and thus *may* change existing legal relationships as well. Now, the question is whether there *must* be a clear intention on the part of the legislator to do so.

Earlier, we cited a Roman law maxim stating that statutes regulate for the future unless the emperor expressly states otherwise. In American constitutional theory, the Supreme Court of the United States has created a principle of strong presumption of non-retroactivity (Troy 1998: 39); it has been said that according to interpretation of the Constitution of the United States of America, retroactivity was forbidden only in criminal matters. Nevertheless, the principle of legal certainty played its role, such that if the Congress enacted rules that had to be applied retroactively, retroactive application was required to be ordered explicitly. However, the principle of non-retroactivity prevailed and new legislation was applied to newly established legal relationships only (*White v United States*, 191 U.S. 545 (1903)). The principle of "strong presumption against retroactivity" was abandoned later in favour of the principle of admissible retroactivity, meaning that new legislation had to be applied retroactively even though the legislator did not express it explicitly (*Thorpe v Housing Authority*, 393 U.S.268 (1969)). Later, there was a change in judicature again (*Landgraf v USI Film Products* 511 U.S. 244 (1994)) but the principle of strong presumption against retroactivity has never been restored in its former sense. A similar presumption seems to exist in the United Kingdom, and Ben Juratowitch has demonstrated that its importance is derived from the need for certainty to know what the law orders at the time when the law is being applied (Juratowitch 2008: 44).

Therefore, the question is if the new law should be applied according to the principles of secondary retroactivity if the legislator does not explicitly define it. If the principle of legal certainty is valid, the answer would be negative. While the principle of non-retroactivity derived from the principle of legal certainty is standard, retroactive regulation requires an explicit order of the legislator. At first glance, it appears that this is the correct way of legal interpretation and in some decisions of the Czech Constitutional Court, it had been adjudicated that if the legislator could have determined the applicability of new rules to already existing legal relationships (secondary retroactivity) and failed to do so, the new rule must be applied prospectively only (US CR Pl ÚS 38/06). Thus, the rule regulates newly established legal regulations only, and the Constitutional Court favoured acquired rights that had been touched by the new legislation without clear order by the legislator.

Unfortunately, legislative praxis is very negligent in the Czech Republic, so that the applicability of new rules on existing relationships, a question of great importance, is often neglected by Parliament, which fails to adopt necessary transitional legal rules. Sometimes this is quite intentional because it is a delicate political question. When the new rules should apply to existing relationships, parties of such relationships would consider the change as undesirable when it worsens their legal status. Such intended changes in legislation are often monitored very carefully by those who would be influenced by the change of legislation and Parliament is lobbied about the issue. While it is a sensitive problem, the legislator is sometimes unwilling to decide upon this matter clearly, and leaves the burden of deciding the matter to the courts. According to the prevailing jurisprudence of the Constitutional Court mentioned above, if the legislator does not expressly qualify otherwise, legal certainty should be preferred to diminish the encroachment on existing rights, and law should be applied in a non-retroactive way. This approach can be classified as *neutral.*

Although constitutional rules concerned with retroactivity are incomplete because they only expressly deal with criminal affairs, the approach of the Constitutional Court fills this gap in the Czech legal system by ordering how to assess doubtful cases in which the problem of potential retroactivity arises. This approach at least indirectly forces Parliament to decide explicitly on the transitional provisions of a new law, otherwise the law would apply prospectively only. This approach favours individuals as well because it largely gives certainty as regarding existing relationships.

Not very long ago, the Constitutional Court changed its approach and ruled otherwise on this issue in a case dealing with the legal consequences of a statutory amendment that was intended to change the content of existing agreements in the field of electronic communication (mobile phone services) (US CR IV ÚS 2989/16). The aim of the amendment was to improve the position of consumers as regarding their rights towards mobile operators. The amendment was intended to lower sanctions for premature termination of contracts, setting up some new duties of mobile operators etc. There were no clear transitional provisions dealing with the applicability of the new law regarding the exact time from which the existing contracts should change. The law ordered the mobile operators to change the contracts from a certain date, but it was unclear whether the new legal rules should apply from the effective day of the new law or from the moment the operators changed the contracts.

Due to unclear transitional provisions, mobile operators insisted that the new law should be applied in a non-retroactive way, at earliest, from the moment they would have changed general contractual terms, and refused to grant the consumers' rights according to the new law since its effective date. Some consumers tried to utilize newly granted rights from the effective date of the new law but mobile operators rejected their claims. The consumers complained in ordinary courts and sued mobile operators in order to seek remedy against them. The ordinary courts rejected the mobile operators' arguments that were based on the lack of clear transitional provisions. Courts stated that the amendment was intended to improve the legal position of consumers, and even though clear transitional provisions were missing the new law had to be applied according to the principle of secondary retroactivity.

Mobile operators finally brought the dispute to the Constitutional Court. Their argument remained the same: it was unfair that they had to bear the full cost and that the transitional provisions were unclear. This meant that the new legislation should not change the content of existing contracts since the effective date of the new law, but should apply to a certain future date moving forward. The Constitutional Court held that due to the fact that clear transitional provisions are missing, the new legislation should be applied so as to touch existing rights in the most moderate way.

The problem was that the statutory amendment was clearly in favour of one party in the agreements only (the consumers), while the mobile operators had to bear the whole burden of newly formulated conditions of existing contracts. Therefore, it was really unclear whose rights (or rather interests) should prevail in this matter. Some kind of balancing of rights was out of the question because only one party of the dispute could win. Should it be the interest of mobile operators who would otherwise suffer a loss of income or the interest of the consumers who would enjoy more favourable, newly formulated conditions of their agreements? The Constitutional Court did not explain whose interest should be preferred, so this question remained unanswered. The context of the rulings was clear, though. Consumers were considered to be weaker party of the contracts and the mobile operators were tacitly considered to be easily able to bear their loss. Notwithstanding the sympathies for consumers, the general problem is that the Constitutional Court changed the concept of dealing with retroactivity problems. The background of the decision can be considered political and the decision of the Constitutional Court "partisan" in the meaning explained above.

The Constitutional Court did not pay much attention to the argument of desirable legal certainty. The question is whether the principle of legal certainty could help to deliberate competing interests, but from the ruling of the Constitutional Court, it appears that the answer is negative. New legislation improves the legal position of one party over another because it receives additional rights, whilst the second party must bear more obligations, but the transitional provisions are often missing or are unclear. Whose position should be protected? Should it be the position of the obliged party based on the argument that due to missing transitional provisions legislation should only govern new relationships? Or, should it be the position of the entitled party based on the argument that the legislator *intended* to regulate not only newly established relationships but also the existing ones?

In my opinion, the solution based on accepting the validity of the principle of legal certainty falls within the concept of the neutral model of law. If the principle of legal certainty is the valid principle, it requires protecting existing relationships. It does not mean that the legislator could not provide for application of new legislation to already existing relationships, but if the legislator does not do so, the principle of legal certainty should prevail. The fundamental reasoning is that even if the legislator provides for application of new legislation to already existing relationships, the legislator must consider existing (acquired) rights and the change in the legal position of private individuals cannot be arbitrary,[20] as can be very clearly seen from the decisions of the European Court for

20 The Constitutional Court had said this expressly in its rulings file no. Pl ÚS 38/04.

Human Rights. The Court, when assessing national regulation that usually leads to asserted violation of rights guaranteed in the Human Rights Convention, had always tested if the national regulation was rational and legitimate. Similarly, the Czech Constitutional Court ruled that the choice of transitional provisions is not at the sheer will of the legislator.

The legislator must take into consideration competing interests and legal principles. Therefore, it may happen that the choice of the legislator will be found unconstitutional if the legislator fails to do so correctly. It should be noted that in all cases in which this problem was involved, the problem was the secondary retroactivity of law that was enacted, not the non-retroactivity of the particular law. If the explicit decision of the legislator regarding transitional provisions based on secondary retroactivity can be found unconstitutional, then there is no argument why the new legislation should be applied retroactively in the form of secondary retroactivity when there is no clear decision by the legislator.

There is one more argument in favour of non-retroactive application of the new legislation. This argument leads to the conclusion that a retroactive application of new laws is not automatic as one may think according to the statement of the Constitutional Court that "secondary retroactivity is generally admissible". It is well known that the legislature turns transitional provisions into statutes, and that these provisions provide for retroactive or non-retroactive application of the particular statute. The proper purpose of these provisions is to provide for retroactive application of laws, not for their non-retroactive application. This can be derived from the fact that in most cases these provisions order the retroactive application of the law. These transitional provisions would not be necessary if a retroactive application of the law would be obligatory as a general rule. On the contrary, only provisions regulating non-retroactive application would be necessary and would be enacted.

The principle of proportionality, which requires taking into consideration competing rights and interests and finding a fair balance between them, does not help very much when transitional provisions are missing, because the choice between retroactive application and non-retroactive application of some particular law is an arbitrary one. Only the legislator is entitled to make an appropriate decision because only then the choice is legitimate, yet if the legislator does not do so, the courts must decide. If the principle of legal certainty is a valid principle, non-retroactivity must prevail.

## Conclusion

Legal certainty is a very important value that is part of the neutral model of law. Human conduct is adapted to legal regulation. Change in legal regulation leads to changes in legal consequences of human conduct. The legislator is obliged to consider the impact of changes in law on the legal status of individuals. In some cases, the change of law can be found unconstitutional because it violates legitimate expectations, acquired rights, or any other legal values. This is the reason why primary retroactivity that disadvantages individuals is the least desirable.

As for secondary retroactivity, the legislator should take into consideration the principle of legal certainty. The legislator has power to order the application of new legislation retroactively on existing relationships but this decision cannot be arbitrary, but supported with rational and legitimate reasons. If the legislator does not explicitly express the reason for retroactive application, the law should be applied prospectively only. Thus the principle of legal certainty sets limits on the legislator, as other human rights do. An opposite approach can be assessed as partisan in the meaning of Jeremy Waldron because it does not reflect a principle that is generally recognized as an inevitable part of the law.

## References


Alexy, R. (1995) *Rechte und Prinzipien, in Recht, Vernunft, Diskurs Studien zur Rechtsphilosophie*, Frankfurt, Suhrkamp.

Avila, H. (2016) *Certainty in Law*, Switzerland, Springer International Publishing AG.

Berger, A. (1949) "Ex Post Facto in Roman Sources and Ex Post Facto Laws in Modern Juristic Terminology", *Seminar Jurist* 7, 49.

Coke, E. (1604) *The Second Part of the Institutes of the Laws of England*, https://openlibrary.org/works/OL109099W/Institutes_of_the_laws_of_England [accessed 03/02/2019].

Fuller, L. L. (1969) *The Morality of Law*, Revised Edition. New Haven, Yale University Press.

Heikki, M. (2006) *Comparative Legal Linguistics*, Aldershot, Ashgate.

Juratowitch, B. (2008) *Retroactivity and the Common Law*, Oxford and Portland, Hart Publishing.

Laitos, J. G. (1999–2000) 'The New Retroactivity Causation Standard', *Ala. L. Rev.* 51, 1123–1160.

Natelson, R. G. (2002–2003) 'Statutory Retroactivity: The Founders' View', *Idaho Law Review* 39, 489–529.

Pavlíček, V. (1999) "Some Remarks on Legal Principles in the Process of Transforming Constitutional Systems", in Boguszak, J. (ed.) *Legal Principles*, Pelhřimov, Vydavatelství.

Skrejpek, M. (2001) "Retroactivity and Roman Law", *The Lawyer* 6, 616–630.

Smead, E. E. (1935–1936) "The Rule Against Retroactive Legislation: A Basic Principle of Jurisprudence", *Minnesota Law Review* 20, 775–797.

Troy, D. E. (1998) *Retroactive Legislation*, Washington DC, AEI Press.

Waldron, J. (1990) *The Law: Theory and Practice in British Politics*, London and New York, Routledge.


## List of cases

### *European Court of Human Rights*

*Zielenski, Pradal, and Gonzalez and others v France* Apps no 24846/94, 34165/96, 34173/96 (ECtHR 8 June 2011)

*Maggio and others v Italy* Apps no 46286/09, 52851/08, 53727/08, 54486/08, 56001/08 (ECtHR 31 May 2011)

*Baka v Hungary* App no 20261/12 (ECtHR 23 June 2016)

### *Supreme Court of the United States of America*

*White v United States*, 191 U.S. 545 (1903)
*Thorpe v Housing Authority*, 393 U.S. 268 (1969)
*Landgraf v USI Film Products* 511 U.S. 244 (1994)

### *Constitutional Court of the Czech Republic (US CR)*

Rulings file no Pl ÚS 17/11
Rulings file no Pl ÚS 2/02
Rulings file no Pl ÚS 38/06
Rulings file no IV ÚS 2989/16
Rulings file no Pl ÚS 38/04
Rulings file no Pl ÚS 14/94
Rulings file no Pl ÚS 19/93

# Conclusion

## The philosophy of legal change as a research method

*Michał Rupniewski*

### 1 Interpreting law through political philosophy

As emphasized in the Acknowledgements, each contributor to this volume may have their own, separate views on the issues here examined, and therefore this concluding chapter is written on the editors' behalf. However, I believe that we can identify some important overlap, which I will demonstrate here. It seems that, regardless of the fact that the contributors may significantly differ regarding evaluating the processes or the directions of change, they share a general methodological orientation that can be summarized as *researching law through political philosophy*. Therefore, a particularly promising outcome of this book is a method of applying political philosophy to legal interpretation. The intent of Part III is to provide case studies illuminated by the politico-philosophical investigations made in the previous parts. This indirectly demonstrates that the categories used in politico-philosophical justification do have relevance for understanding the factual processes of legal change. As we believe, this book proves that issues such as codification, legalization of custom, changes in human rights law, excessive legislation, or systemic reform, cannot be properly examined without carefully decoding the underlying political philosophy. Political philosophy not only provides justification of these processes, but also shapes them in a significant way, at least in democratic societies characterized by civic participation and control. As a result of this, we might say that political philosophy is not just a tool for criticizing existing law (the law that is) by referring to the ideal law (the law that ought to be); rather, political philosophy might also serve as a heuristic tool, helping to understand and interpret the law that is.

The belief that the real impact that philosophy has on existing law can be systematically examined was inspired by the work Czesław Martyniak, a Polish legal philosopher from the early twentieth century. His goal (that could not be pursued due to his early death at the beginning of the World War II) was to develop a branch of legal research called 'the philosophy of positive law', a discipline aimed at decoding moral-philosophical ideas and the presuppositions underlying law posited and applied by authorities. Martyniak saw this research as focused on concrete, particular legal orders, to be examined with regards to their philosophical foundation.[1] This research was supposed to be axiologically *disengaged*: the intention was not to judge the truth or rightness of the philosophical background of legal institutions, but to make it explicit. Therefore, his concept was self-consciously designed to be *potentially comparative*: capable of examining how different ideas and principles are applied within and across different jurisdictions (Martyniak 2006: 507–527). The philosophy of positive law, so conceived, should be discerned from the application of the history of ideas in law. Whereas the latter is focused on the ideas present outside the law, the former is supposed to be legal all the way down, taking the legal material as its starting point. Its purpose is to examine the philosophical commitments that can be found in existing law, rather than merely examine how political culture influences the law. In developing the outline of the philosophy of legal change, we share these general commitments.

What considerably differentiates our way of thinking from that of Martyniak might be summarized in one slogan: law in action. Unlike Martyniak who focused on legal text (for instance, on the Napoleonic Code), we examine legal processes, particularly those of legal change that we consider the most important. To be sure, such orientation might include legal text (as in Chapter 13 by Hamilton, where she analyses a particular criminal statute), but we assume that the real meaning of the law is being shaped by the practice of its application. One might observe numerous examples in which the same legal provision is interpreted and applied differently as time passes (see Voight 1998). Therefore, we assume, a philosopher examining law must always work with a view to the changing social reality. Therefore, as explained in the Introduction by Chmieliński, the research methodology that has been applied in this volume constitutes a bridge between legal science proper and social sciences. We examine law as a 'living thing', constantly being influenced and re-shaped by the political-philosophical ideals found both in legal text and legal process.

At the first glance, such a project may seem to have a deconstructive, rather than instructive, purpose. Although we aim at the latter, we acknowledge that revealing political ideas behind the existing law may appear to result in putting the law into question rather than securing its proper understanding or application. The critical legal studies (CLS) movement is famous for having expressed the worry that the dynamics of power, also ideological agendas, influence legal processes to the extent that they cast the shadow of doubt even on well-established legal ideals such as the rule of law (Tushnet forthcoming). However, skepticism towards analyzing law as 'politically encumbered' is not limited to critical legal studies, and does not necessarily lead to law's authority being diminished or questioned.

1 The philosophy of positive law so conceived does not consist in philosophical reflection on law's positivity which is the case, for example, in the work of James Bernard Murphy (Murphy 2005). Our project follows Martyniak and strives for a philosophically informed interpretation of selected legal institutions.

For a legal positivist, the law's coordinating function largely consists in ending moral disagreement – not by virtue of finding the true moral principle, but by the commitment to "the community taking a position on an issue on which its members disagree" (Waldron 1999: 37). In this view, the disputes and debates in parliament, for example, are informed and driven by political-philosophical ideals or values, which is natural and welcome. But once the law is posited, there comes the cut: the law might and should be interpreted autonomously. Positivists do acknowledge that full independence from moral or political considerations is not possible in case of interpreting or applying law – it is not purely technical and morally neutral instrument. But as far as it can be, it should be interpreted in specifically legal terms, and according to specifically legal doctrines, in order to achieve neutral and authoritative, and thus not merely preferential, adjudication among competing claims and interests (Raz 1996: 330–340).

We do not intend to refute neither CLS nor legal positivism in their entirety. Our aim is the rejection of skepticism toward political-philosophical engagement as part of legal interpretation. First, such methodological orientation does not undermine the rule of law insofar as it takes the politico-philosophical moments within law as genuine public justification rather than ideology masking underlying interest. Of course, a full development of this thought (and thus a full response to doubts raised by CLS) would require a separate paper. For the purposes of this volume, however, suffice it to say that law certainly may reflect machinations of economic or political power, but this does not exhaust the role played by public justification. We take public justification seriously, as an important element of law's legitimacy and thus validity (similarly, Bankowski, MacCormick, & Summers 2016: 16–23). As I have attempted do show in Chapter 2, law lacking any justification whatsoever automatically loses legitimation, which raises natural doubts about law's authority and social efficacy. If so, a view of law's public justification should not be limited to the case of legislation. Rather, it should also be extended to the application of law in judicial processes, and that makes justification an intrinsic element of the law itself, at least in a democratic state. Such a way of thinking is more likely to be attributed to non-positivists or natural law theorists, seeking the ideal or moral dimension of law (Alexy 2017). However, in our view at least, the commitment to justification as essential to law should be acceptable also for the positivist. Indeed, justifiability seems to be a minimal requirement for the law, insofar as making and applying it is supposed to be different from herding sheep, to borrow a phrase from Waldron (Waldron 2011: 8). In other words: whichever theoretical position one adopts, one must acknowledge that law (if it is to be taken seriously) should provide genuine reasons for action, rather than mere incentives for behavior. Thus, both the lawmaker and the interpreter of the law are bound to engage in argumentation at least partly informed by the ideas and claims analyzed and interpreted by political philosophy, which makes the latter gain a content-related relevancy. The philosophy of positive law, or philosophy of legal change as its particular version, is supposed to explain political ideas and claims that are part of law's justification, and put them into the context of legal institutions functioning in a social reality.

To sum up: whereas legal science proper is *expository*, dealing with legal facts (determining the law that is), political philosophy proper is *critical*, that is, providing normative grounds for evaluation of assessment of existing law. The philosophy of legal change, as a special methodology of applying political philosophy in legal interpretation, is between those two. It plays an *explanatory* role – the underlying philosophical principles are interpreted as causes or reasons deeply explaining a law that exists. Thus, it can work together with social or political science to examine the mechanisms of institutions working in practice, as well as with legal dogmatics as an auxiliary discipline. This perspective assumes that the law is always 'encumbered' within a politico-philosophical framework, but not merely in the sense of an ideological agenda standing behind legal processes, but rather in the sense of law being addressed to people who are supposed to be capable of understanding, internalizing, and correctly applying the law. If the latter is the case, then whatever the mechanism of human decisions really is, each legal decision must be justified in a particular way, in order to make it justifiable for others. As the investigations in this volume hopefully have shown, such processes are never deprived of more general social context that includes first and foremost the philosophical ideas and claims that are observable in the societies' background culture and public reason. Thus, we believe that legal processes, the processes of legal change in particular, must be also researched with the use of political philosophy in a manner described above.

The above considerations have some relevance, as we believe, to judges and legislators. As far as the latter is concerned, the philosophy of legal change may help us understand the legislative process by examining its dynamics in terms of political philosophy focused on genuine, authoritative justification, and not merely in terms of political science focused on machinations of interest and power. Although in real life the latter plays an important role, the former is not completely deprived of relevance. As emphasized by Biernat in Chapter 1, legislative standards are to a large extent determined by normative considerations. Even if some legislation is heavily influenced by some partisan interest in the background, it must be proposed in a form that meets the minimal criteria of non-arbitrariness; and the transparent legislative process is to eliminate the most explicitly partisan elements. If that is true, then a proper understanding of the legislative process should identify the political-philosophical factors determining it. As I was trying to establish in Chapter 2, this does not undermine its legitimacy, insofar as this justification, even if based on reasons that we do not share with our fellow-citizens, provides non-arbitrariness of the regulation.

As far as the application of law is concerned, the philosophy of legal change may help illuminate what might be called the 'functional' dimension of legal interpretation. According to Jerzy Wróblewski, one might identify three basic context or dimensions of law when interpreting statues: the linguistic, the systemic, and the functional (Wróblewski 2016: 260). The linguistic context is the most obvious, as well as the most important: the interpreter is bound to stick to the legal language in which the interpreted provision is formulated, and should follow the ordinary meaning of the words used in the text, insofar as there is no specific definition in the fabric of law. Whatever decisions are made in the course of interpretation, the result should not, at least in principle, exceed the boundaries of the linguistic formulation of the legal text. Sometimes, however, the linguistic formulation alone is not sufficient to justify a decision, which is caused by factors such as the fuzziness of legal language or the multicentric nature of contemporary jurisdictions (for the latter see Zirk-Sadowski, Golecki, & Wojciechowski 2009). When that is the case, the interpreter should read a legal rule in the context of other rules: constitutional or international standards and principles, for example. This is the systemic context, which we do not need to examine here. However, as Wróblewski rightly notes, the law functions in an even broader, meta-legal context, composed of different factors such as moral norms, political values, the *ratio legis* or purposes of the statute, and the like (Wróblewski 2016: 265). As our investigations in this book reveal, the meta-legal context is to a significant degree composed of politico-philosophical elements. The philosophy of legal change, if pursued according to our program, might thus help to examine these elements, and therefore make the argumentation within the functional context better informed, systematized, and less arbitrary. Although this has only a limited application, as the linguistic context should be considered superior in terms of scope and priority, the role of functional interpretation is certainly growing, and this poses some threats to the law itself, as examined by Weiler in Chapter 3. Therefore, new tools should be developed, to enable its principled and self-limited exercise.

## 2 Sorting out the competing patterns of political justification

### *2.1 Recognizing normative pluralism*

Although it is Ronald Dworkin who is famous for having claimed that legal interpretation involves political and moral ideas, we see our methodological project as distinct from his view. Dworkin believed that political or moral ideas should be used to arrive at the *best* (in a very specific sense – the *true*) interpretation of legal rules and principles (Dworkin 2011: 123–156). We perceive our task differently, as examining and sorting out the pluralistic normative-axiological sphere in law, which we consider an important aspect of the law in action. As emphasized by Chmieliński in the Introduction, we perceive the law not only in a Dworkinian way, as an interpretative net of ideas, but also as part of social reality. Therefore, we look primarily at the law that is actually made and applied, and not at the law as it should be, at its best, which is the case in Dworkin's work. Although the normative sphere might be rightly associated with the ideal dimension of law, we believe that it plays a significant role also in the real processes, as part one demonstrates. Therefore, we adopt the notion of 'normative space', as applied by Biernat in Chapter 1. The normative space understood in this manner is part of social reality, and is persistently pluralistic. In different contexts and spheres of legal institutions, there is a multitude of competing political doctrines, and competing normative claims pertaining to law. Very often, a legal change consists in one doctrine (a set of normative claims) gaining greater social or political support, prevailing over another, and then being pursued via legislation. As in case of the above-mentioned project of Martyniak, we do not aim at judging who is right in these debates. It does not make us relativist, as we do not reject the idea that somebody actually *is* right. But for the limited purposes of this project, and this particular type of research, we aim at identifying the philosophical elements present in legal processes, and we abstain from moral judgment in the proper sense. Therefore, the philosophy of legal change aims at recognizing the normative pluralism that marks the contemporary legal, globalized world, and tries to provide tools to sort it out, or systematize.

Our attempt at systematization is reflected in the first two parts of this book. Part I established how the normative elements inevitably 'inhabit' the processes of legal change. Whatever the sphere or specific domain, be it legislation or adjudication, national or international institutions, pluralistic or state-centered processes, they can be depicted as an interplay between the normativity of public reason and that of background culture. This is what I have argued in Chapter 2. However, this dichotomy is not enough to map the substantive content of normative claims, whether they pertain to public reason or to background culture. Therefore, the purpose of Part II was to set forth the paradigmatic frameworks of substantive, politico-philosophical justification of legal change. As Chmieliński showed in Chapter 5, the point of reference common to all these frameworks is the dichotomy of individualism versus holism. Although those two categories are well established in political philosophy, rooted respectively in the contractarian and the Aristotelian traditions, they are very general and therefore might have a very broad, perhaps too broad, meaning. Therefore, some more specific categories were needed to serve as focal points in analysis of legal change. That is why Chmieliński proposes the following pair: legal creationism versus legal determinism. Whereas the latter is more individualist and interprets the law as a free creation of the human will, the former is committed to social holism and traces the extra-legal factors that determine legal processes.

Granted, the method we propose consists in identifying the focal points in political philosophy that serve as meta-categories providing ordering in the normative space. Those focal points, or meta-categories, are public reason/background culture and creationism/determinism. As we argue, the particular normative claims referring to liberty, rights, common good, or justice, are always formulated in the context of those meta-categories. Therefore, they provide an ordering of justification, and form the heuristic background for legal research focused on the politico-philosophical justification of change. We believe that combining those focal points in legal interpretation allows us to recognize normative pluralism, but at the same time avoids the normative space turning into chaos. Although we do not propose a quantitative research based on these categories, we claim that the interpretation of the practical processes using the focal points enables the researcher to identify the core normative elements and the deep structure of the interpreted law. New laws (or precedents or simply new judicial practices), as a product of legal change, might be better understood if we determine the creationist and deterministic elements, as well as trace the elements stemming from public reason and background culture.

### 2.2 Applying the meta-categories: An outline for a research program

As we believe, those two dichotomies – public reason/background culture, and creationism/determinism – should work together in a successful politico-philosophical interpretation of law. Whereas the creationism/determinism opposition considers the relation between the complex conditions of a legal community and institutions functioning within that community,[2] the former considers the public-universal and the cultural-particular aspects of legal institutions. In political philosophy pursued in a traditional manner (as a foundation of critique rather than explanation) these distinctions are perhaps not that important. For instance, when one intends to answer the question of what liberty really is, or what equality demands from public institutions, the question whether a particular account is more deterministic or creationist/voluntarist is of secondary importance; relevant, perhaps, for didactical purposes only. In our explanatory methodology, these questions become crucial: combining the meta-categories distinguished above yields a framework to map the political justification that guides the processes of legal change.

Of course, real life will always mix the ideal types. Nonetheless, the heuristic framework provided by them enables deep interpretation of those eclectic processes. Although the contributors to Part III of this book might have offered their own interpretations, we believe that those investigations might very well illustrate the use of our methodology. First of all, the case studies reveal the constant interplay between public reason and background culture that marks the processes of change, at least in democratic states. Justification is of a public reason type when it adopts a free-standing arguments, drawn from the inner logic of democratic institutions based on freedom, equality, citizenship, or public justice. Respectively, when a justification is focused on the history of a given society, its (political and non-political) culture, and social practices, it is of a background culture type.

This might be well illustrated, for instance, by Chapter 13, where Hamilton analyses an English criminal statute (Serious Crime Act 2015, Section 76) that penalizes coercive control, which is a form of domestic abuse not involving direct use of physical violence. The legislator penalizes such practices as abusive control of finances or excessive emotional control. The justification of that law, according to Hamilton, could be twofold: based either on the harm principle (an act of coercive control diminishing victim's rights) or legal moralism (coercive control being morally wrong). If we decided to apply only the harm principle, then the justification would be a clear-cut case of a public reason type. Legal moralism, although one might interpret that issue differently, belongs to background culture, insofar as the comprehensive morality and societal practices decide what kind of conduct is immoral. As the analysis of the legislative material shows, the real justification was eclectic, combining both public reason and background

2 The 'community' is here broadly understood, and can mean a local, state, or international community, depending of what kind of legal change is in question.

culture arguments. Besides that, Hamilton argues, there is another thing to be taken into account: the natural dynamics of family relations making the application of that law particularly problematic. Therefore, this chapter could be read as showing that each legislation, and application of law, should take into consideration the background culture and the natural dynamics of social practices that the changed law is supposed to effectively govern. However, making those normative elements and their different intellectual provenance explicit might be helpful in self-limited interpretation of this law. Any further legislative changes should also be informed by such an inquiry.

However, the opposition of public reason and background culture is not sufficient to fully interpret legal processes or laws themselves through political philosophy. Both public reason and background culture do have manifold substantive content that is changing over time and calls for systematization. To do this, we apply the second dichotomy, that of legal creationism and legal determinism. The first is a justification that is at bottom more individualist, and thus creationist in its character, when aiming at protecting individual rights or interest of separate individuals.[3] However, a deterministic justification evokes substantial (i.e. non-aggregative) common good, communitarian aspect of human legal life, or moral principles that tame the freedom of laws' creation and application. As Lewandowicz shows in Chapter 11 the codification of private law in Switzerland was an outcome of the Enlightenment, and therefore driven by individualist ideas and creationist justification. However, if the process was to be successful, the politicians and legislators had to take into consideration the extremely complex legal culture of the country. The codification process accommodated to these conditions, and in this sense respected the determinist part of the inner logic of legal institutions. As a result, the new civil code gained social legitimation. We believe that this study indicates that further and more detailed analysis of Swiss private law should be supported by the interpretation of the creationist and determinist moments inherent therein. Analogically, Higgins in Chapter 12 shows that the historical conditions of the Polish political society (freedom and pluralism) made the communist government an exogenous institution that could only be installed by force. By the same token, Higgins argues, the transition from communism to liberalism in Poland after 1989 has been relatively successful.

The above considerations enable us to formulate a research program, hopefully to be pursued in the future. A full interpretation of legal processes through the proposed categories would consist in the following steps: (1) identifying the public reasons backing the new law, (2) identifying the relevant elements of background culture, and (3) mapping the creationist and deterministic elements in the law. Such a procedure might help in large-scale analysis, like in the case of systemic transition, as well as a more detailed investigation, concentrated on a particular area of law or even a particular institution.

3 Individualism is also present in justification referring to general welfare, insofar as it means the aggregated welfare of separate individuals.

## 3 Prudential and moral concerns: Human rights, certainty of law, and stability

Although this concluding chapter is focused on the methodological aspects, it seems important to emphasize the most important moral-prudential conclusions and concerns that arise from this volume, and hopefully overlap among the contributors. Many examples show that the contemporary world has come to the point in which legal change is an obvious thing, being more frequent and deeper than it has, perhaps, ever been the case. This situation bears important consequences for many spheres of social life, but here I would like briefly to point out two: human rights and legal/social stability.

Human rights law, established in the contemporary form after the Universal Declaration of Human Rights (1948), is now in need of rethinking and reforming. As Riley shows in Chapter 4, the prospective reforms should take into consideration not only the empirical or even environmental conditions in which human societies function, but also the technological circumstances and the change of social relations following technology. On these rudiments, the political-moral values of cosmopolitan public reason should be pursued by judges and legislators. However, like other areas of law, human rights are influenced not only by the cosmopolitan elements, but also by the particulars of background conditions of a given society. This general desiderata are further exemplified by the analysis offered by Turner in Chapter 14, where he argues that, given the contemporary threats of terrorism in the first place, the individualistic human rights discourse should, which to certain extend is already happening, be shifted from individualism to some forms of collective or communal dimension of human rights law. The shape of human rights law will be, after all, decided by judges and regulators on different institutional levels, but certainly these decisions will have to be made with awareness and preference to more individualistic or holistic, more liberal-universalist or more communitarian-particularistic, commitments. Some new equilibrium will have to be reached, and we believe that legal interpretation in a manner presented here might contribute to reaching this equilibrium.

As far as stability and certainty of law is concerned, one must first observe that change is even more common in the spheres of law other than human rights, particularly, in every-day legislation in democratic states. The issues of legal inflation and excessive legislation are easily observable. In Chapter 15, Jan Tryzna expresses the worries connected with retroactivity of law, in the light of legal certainty which he formulates as a chief value of the legal system, and perhaps a human right. In the light of this, in this volume we have attempted to show how proper recognition of the background culture is a necessary condition of a good governance of the legislative activity in the democratic state, contributing to legal certainty. Important considerations in this regard are offered by Marc Goetzmann in Chapter 10. Analyzing different possible approaches to customary law in a pluralistic context of non-Western countries, he argues that the institutional legitimacy of the legislator is simply not enough if the legitimate legal reform of customary law is to be made. He does not undermine the legitimate authority at the state level; he argues only that the voluntarist (or creationist, in our terminology) component has to be reconciled with the deterministic-conservative moments. The more general conclusion that can be drawn from this chapter put in the context of the whole book would be as follows: although the universalistic claims stemming from public reason might be decisive in some cases, and basically all legal reforms are against the background culture in some respects, the latter constitutes important point of reference, both as a reservoir of meanings of the words used in a legal text, and as a natural social basis for the laws. In other words, actual people's concerns and commitments should be taken into account if the process of legal reform is to be effective and legitimate.

The fact that legal change is persistent, and growing, has been widely acknowledged. Undoubtedly, a principled and well-ordered discussion, enabling an awareness of what is really going on in our domestic and global institutions, is needed. What we see as our contribution to these discussions is revealing how deeply the practical processes of change have been influenced by politico-philosophical conceptions that determine their proper understanding.

## References


Alexy, R. (2017) 'The Ideal Dimension of Law', in G. Duke and R. P. George (eds) *The Cambridge Companion to Natural Law Jurisprudence*. Cambridge: Cambridge University Press, 314–341.

Bankowski, Z., MacCormick, D. N., and Summers, R. S. (2016) 'On Method and Methodology', in D. N. MacCormick and R. S. Summers (eds) *Interpreting Statues: A Comparative Study*. Abington and New York: Routledge, 9–27.

Dworkin, R. (2011) *Justice for Hedgehogs*. Cambridge, MA: The Belknap Press of Harvard University Press.

Martyniak, Cz. (2006) *Dzieła [Works]*. Lublin: Wydawnictwo KUL.

Murphy, J. B. (2005) *The Philosophy of Positive Law: Foundations of Jurisprudence*. New Haven and London: Yale University Press.

Raz, J. (1996) *Ethics in the Public Domain: Essays in the Morality of Law and Politics*. Oxford: Oxford University Press.

Tushnet, M. (forthcoming) 'Critical Legal Studies and the Rule of Law', in M. Loughlin and J. Meierhenrich (eds) *Cambridge Companion to the Rule of Law*, https://ssrn.com/abstract=3135903 [accessed 02/02/19].

Voight, S. (1998) *Implicit Constitutional Change: Changing the Meaning of the Constitution Without Changing the Text of the Document*. Max-Planck Institute, Institutional Economics Unit, Working Paper No. 12/98, http://dx.doi.org/10.2139/ssrn.131431 [accessed 02/02/19].

Waldron, J. (1999) *The Dignity of Legislation*. Cambridge: Cambridge University Press.

Waldron, J. (2011) *How Law Protects Dignity*. NYU School of Law, Public Law Research Paper No. 11-83 http://dx.doi.org/10.2139/ssrn.1973341 [accessed 02/02/19].

Wróblewski, J. (2016) 'Statutory Interpretation in Poland', in D. N. MacCormick and R. S. Summers (eds) *Interpreting Statues: A Comparative Study*. Abington and New York: Routledge, 257–309.

Zirk-Sadowski, M., Golecki, M., and Wojciechowski, B. (2009) *Multicentrism as an Emerging Paradigm in Legal Theory*. Frankfurt, Peter Lang.

# Centrum Myśli Polityczno-Prawnej im. Alexisa de Tocqueville'a

**Information on the Alexis de Tocqueville Center of Political and Legal Thought**

The Alexis de Tocqueville Center of Political and Legal Thought is a researched unit within the Faculty of Law and Administration at the University of Łódź.

The Center draws from the ideas and intellectual heritage of the author of *Democracy in America*. This heritage combines two traditions that dominate today, conservatism and liberalism, with the Christian vision of Western identity and the republican ethos of civic participation. It derives political, institutional and legal reflection from the analysis of actual social relations and avoids constructing any *a priori*, abstract and rationalist models of public life. It views the main values of today such as liberty, equality, democracy, the rule of law, efficiency of state authority, civil society and self government as being far from harmonious. It leaves room for axiological skepticism, inspires the dissemination of ideas and demands epistemological objectivism.

In all its endeavors the Center treats this heritage as important for both civic attitudes and research projects.

# Index

Locators containing 'n' refer to notes